TRADE,
TECHNOLOGY,
AND
SOVIET-AMERICAN
RELATIONS

CSIS PUBLICATION SERIES ON THE
SOVIET UNION IN THE 1980s

TRADE,

TECHNOLOGY,

AND

SOVIET-AMERICAN

RELATIONS

Edited by
Bruce Parrott

Published in association with the Center for Strategic
and International Studies, Georgetown University, Washington, D.C.

INDIANA UNIVERSITY PRESS • BLOOMINGTON

Library of Congress Cataloging in Publication Data
Main entry under title:

Trade, technology, and Soviet-American relations.

(CSIS publication series on the Soviet Union in the
1980s)
"Published in association with the Center for
Strategic and International Studies, Washington, D.C."
Includes bibliographies and index.
 1. East-West trade (1945–   )—Addresses, essays,
lectures.   2. Technology transfer—Soviet Union—Ad-
dresses, essays, lectures.   3. Soviet Union—Foreign
economic relations—United States—Addresses, essays,
lectures.   4. United States—Foreign economic relations—
Soviet Union—Addresses, essays, lectures.   I. Parrott,
Bruce, 1945–   . II. Georgetown University. Center
for Strategic and International Studies.   III. Series.
HF1411.T714   1985   337.47073   84-48549
ISBN 0-253-36025-0
ISBN 0-253-20351-1 (pbk.)

1 2 3 4 5   89 88 87 86 85

Contents

Part III: The United States and Western Trade with the USSR

FOREWORD

The present volume of essays deals with trends in East-West trade and technology transfer since the high point of detente in the mid-1970s. It contains the most thorough collection of expert studies yet assembled on this many-sided and controversial subject.

This book appears at an opportune time, as the United States and the Soviet Union seek to put recent tensions behind them and to find a more stable basis for their relations. Simultaneously, Washington continues its difficult search for a new Export Administration Act and for fresh understandings with its allies. If East-West relations now ease, then the atmosphere for dealing with East-West trade issues may improve as well. It is a good moment, then, for taking stock, and that is the task that the authors of this book have addressed.

After more than twenty years of study and debate, of attempted linkage, leverage, and denial, of carrots and sticks, what have we learned about East-West technology transfer and the implications for practical policy? This book develops five major themes.

The first is that just as there is no simple explanation for the pattern of strengths and weaknesses in Soviet technology, so also there is no simple answer to what the influence of imported technology is on domestic Soviet capabilities. In some cases the result is Soviet dependence on imports and atrophy of domestic technology; in others, imports are followed by vigorous and frequently original efforts to innovate at home. There is no substitute for careful examination sector by sector, and that is the approach used here.

The second theme is that where the assimilation and diffusion of foreign technology are concerned, the Soviets are their own worst enemies. The Soviets have denied themselves much of the benefit of foreign technology, both by limiting the volume of imports and by confining them to the least effective channels, i.e., purchases of goods instead of licenses, one-time deals instead of continuing relationships, limits on industrial cooperation, etc. Technology transfer is a "people-to-people" process, and by limiting movement of people the Soviets impose on themselves the strictest controls.

The third broad theme follows from the second: the Soviets remain fearful of long-term dependence on the world economy, and their imports are usually aimed at a specific and temporary purpose—to make a fast start in some new area of policy, and to fill in for shortfalls in the domestic economy. Cases in which the Soviets appear to accept long-term dependence—as in the chemical industry—are the exception and were probably unintended at the outset. Even the massive grain imports of the last decade are treated by the Soviet leaders as an expedient, until the modernization of Soviet agriculture—they hope—makes them unnecessary.

Soviet imports of militarily relevant technology are a special illustration of this point. Every wave of Soviet borrowing in military technology has been followed by intense and largely successful efforts to reproduce the equivalent or better at home. The latest generation of technology, however, presents the Soviet system with a special challenge. Microelectronics, modern composite materials, biotechnologies, and other new developments cannot be reverse-engineered. The essays in this collection explore the possibility that in these new specialties the traditional Soviet system of borrowing-plus-assimilation may no longer work as in the past.

The fourth broad theme of this book is that the impact of foreign technology on the Soviet Union is far greater on individual sectors than on the economy as a whole. It follows that our power to use economic instruments to alter Soviet policies or to shape their economy is limited. Since autonomy is so high on the Soviet leaders' list, they have shown that they are willing to endure whatever costs our trade policies impose on them.

What are the consequences for Western export policy in East-West trade? This is the book's final theme: it has become much more difficult than it was ten or twenty years ago to apply a systematic policy of economic leverage or denial. Our allies have different views of many aspects of East-West trade and will go along with us only on some, and then only part-way. Our farmers have understandably different views as well. But the real story of the last two decades is the broadening of the world economy and the spread of many technologies once considered American preserves to countries outside CoCom or OECD. It is painful but important to realize that in many areas of East-West trade the views of the United States have less and less weight.

The thrust of these five answers suggests a broad guideline for policy. It is this: changes in the flow of technology trade, as well as improvements in our understanding of how technology transfer operates and its comparative impact on the Soviet economy, suggest that we both can and should approach the difficult problems of East-West trade in a more business-like way than in the past. The sound course is to apply to East-West trade the tested principles of any public policy: to weigh benefits and costs, to pick one's targets carefully, and to be consistent. A careful concentration on the most militarily relevant dual-use technologies, a patient effort to produce agreement on these with our allies, a systematic vigorous program to limit their illicit transfer—these are the elements most likely to produce success in dealing with that part of East-West trade that truly matters most to Western security.

The findings in this volume are the result of a one-year study conducted by the Trade, Technology, and Soviet-American Relations Task Force of the CSIS Soviet Studies Program. This study was made possible by a generous grant from the Frederick Henry Prince Trusts. Bruce Parrott, Professor at Johns Hopkins School of Advanced International Studies and CSIS Adjunct Fellow, directed the task force, which consisted of some of the top experts from the United States and Great Britain.

> AMOS A. JORDAN
> President and
>   Chief Executive Officer
> Center for Strategic and
> International
> Studies/Georgetown University

Editor's Acknowledgments

Several people whose names do not appear in the Contents have made substantial contributions to this book. I am particularly grateful to John Hardt and Stephen Sternheimer, who generously agreed to serve as "outside experts" for the project and took the time to make detailed comments on two rounds of chapter drafts. Their suggestions have greatly strengthened the final work. Marina Marcoux and Lee Agree deserve special thanks for handling the logistics of meetings and communications with unfailing efficiency. I also wish to express my appreciation to James Allen, who served as rapporteur at a two-day conference of the contributors, and to Mark Ellyne, who compiled the statistical appendix.

Introduction

Bruce Parrott

ANYONE WHO glances back over the past fifteen years of U.S. foreign policy cannot fail to be struck by the sharp changes that have occurred in the prevailing American assumptions about how to deal with the Soviet Union. From the hopeful declarations during the heyday of detente, relations between the superpowers have passed into a phase of deep distrust and diplomatic strain. As part of this political sea change, Americans have revised their views on aspects of the Soviet-American relationship ranging from bilateral cultural relations to competition in the third world and nuclear strategy.

Trade and technology transfers have not been exempt from this painful reappraisal. Some of the sharpest controversies in the United States, and in the Western alliance, have focused on economic relations with the USSR. Since the end of 1979, when the Soviet Union invaded Afghanistan and the United States retaliated with economic sanctions, Western policy toward trade and technical contacts with the Soviet Union has been a subject of heated dispute. The debate has raised questions about the Soviet economic benefit derived from interchange with the West, the wisdom of Western efforts to link trade to Soviet political concessions, and the impact of East-West commerce on the national security of the Western democracies. The domestic American dispute over such issues has been reflected in the U.S. Congress's prolonged and frustrating attempt during 1984 to hammer out a new version of the Export Administration Act. In the West as a whole, the imbroglio over whether to help complete the pipeline designed to supply Western Europe with Soviet gas has highlighted the splits between the United States and its principal allies on these matters.

These striking developments call for new efforts to understand the process of trade and technology transfer between the Soviet Union and the West. That process has been shaped by a multitude of political and technical factors. Yet recent policy debates have encouraged both the proponents and opponents of East-West commerce to make exaggerated claims and oversimplify the complexities of the issue. The central purpose of this book is to improve the public understanding of the costs and benefits, the opportunities and constraints, that must be taken into account in formulating American policy toward economic interchange with the Soviet Union.

In weighing the choices facing the U.S., it is vital to understand the historical context of Soviet-Western commercial relations, because assumptions about the past contribution of Western technology to Soviet economic development play a central part in the debate over current American policy.[1] During the early 1930s the Soviet Union depended heavily on Western machinery and technical assistance to sustain Stalin's industrialization campaign, and most Western countries were eager to sell technology to the USSR. The Soviet regime managed to assimilate a large amount of foreign technology because it quickly built up a substantial native research and development establishment to facilitate this process, and because its draconian investment policies allowed the rapid construction of many factories based on Western designs. By the second half of the 1930s, however, the Stalinist authorities had greatly reduced the USSR's dependence on Western equipment and had sharply circumscribed the other channels through which Western know-how reached the country.[2] During World War II this pattern was altered somewhat by an infusion of American Lend-Lease technology, but after the war the inherent Stalinist tendency toward autarky again came to the fore.

This autarkic tendency was reinforced by a systematic Western attempt to control the postwar flow of technology to the USSR. The uneven impact of the war gravely damaged the Soviet economy and simultaneously elevated the United States to a position of political and economic dominance over the other capitalist powers. Under these conditions, the United States initially sought to use reconstruction assistance as a diplomatic tool to influence the conduct of the Soviet Union and its East European client-regimes. When this tactic failed, the United States embraced a comprehensive policy of economic denial. In 1949 it led in organizing CoCom, an informal committee of Western states, whose purpose was to restrict the flow of strategic goods to the socialist bloc. For more than a decade CoCom succeeded in preventing the eastward flow of a broad range of goods, many of them "strategic" only under an extremely loose interpretation of this word.[3] CoCom worked well partly because a mood of East-West confrontation prevailed in most Western countries during this period. Moreover, most members of the Western alliance, being dependent on the United States for both military protection and postwar economic assistance under the Marshall Plan, were reluctant to challenge American policies toward East-West trade.

By the end of the 1950s, however, new forces were impinging on efforts to control the flow of goods and technology to the socialist world. The rapid expansion of trade and technology transfers among the developed capitalist countries contributed to a dramatic spurt of Western economic growth during the decade and helped persuade Stalin's successors to try to purchase more Western technology. Meanwhile, the countries of Western Europe, increasingly reliant on trade as a source of prosperity, showed a heightened interest in commercial deals with the USSR. As these countries gradually recovered from the political and economic ravages of World War II, they became less willing to support the broad American policy of trade denial. Together with Soviet diplomatic efforts to undermine the trade restrictions, these intra-Western differences led to a narrowing of the range of exports prohibited under CoCom and to an expansion of Soviet trade with Western Europe in the 1960s.

By the end of the 1960s, the United States had also shifted from a policy of comprehensive trade denial to a policy recognizing the economic and diplomatic benefits of trade. The Export Administration Act of 1969, which provided for continued control of exports that might affect American national security or foreign-policy goals, also attached a new importance to nonstrategic trade with the East as a source of American economic well-being. The Nixon Administration was prepared to endorse wider trade with the USSR, not as an end in itself but as an inducement and reward in cases where the Soviet Union adopted cooperative foreign-policy positions. Although in the early 1970s this approach struck many observers as promising, the ensuing political frictions and accelerating military competition between the superpowers have since ignited a new round of controversy over the economic, diplomatic, and strategic consequences of Western commerce with the USSR.

In order to illuminate present U.S. policy options and choices, the contributors to this volume have examined recent trends from both the American and the Soviet standpoints. The first part of the book gives a political and economic overview of the Soviet approach to trade and technology transfers. Taking the postwar experience of Japan as an index of the economic results that can be obtained by using foreign technology, Josef Brada's chapter puts Soviet policies into a comparative perspective and balances the economic benefits gained by the USSR against the benefits it has foregone for political or institutional reasons. My own chapter examines the Soviet view of the relationship between diplomacy and East-West commerce, the domestic political influences on Soviet trade policy, and the impact of the worsening international atmosphere of the 1980s on the Soviet appetitite for Western products and know-how.

The second part of the book consists of case studies which examine in greater detail the way the Soviet system has made use of Western inputs and the benefits that it has derived from them. Some of the recurring issues in these chapters are the channels through which the Soviets obtain Western technology, the system's capacity to combine foreign inputs with domestic R&D, and its ability to diffuse Western know-how domestically. Philip Hanson's chapter examines the factors that affect Soviet assimilation of Western technology and pays special attention to the chemical industry, the Soviet sector most dependent on Western equipment. The chapter by George Holliday analyzes the Soviet assimilation of automotive technology and considers whether that branch's heavy draft on Western know-how has come to an end or is likely to recur. The chapter by S. E. Goodman traces Soviet progress in the computer industry and the degree to which the Soviets have succeeded in combining creative indigenous R&D with extensive utilization of Western technology. Robert Campbell's chapter explores Soviet needs for Western cooperation in extracting and refining energy. Campbell devotes considerable attention to the impact of the temporary American embargo of gas pipeline technology and assesses how well Soviet manufacturers compensated for the lack of American machinery and know-how.

Julian Cooper's chapter on the defense industry addresses one of the most controversial aspects of the current debate over technology transfers to the USSR. Relying on a close study of the historical record, Cooper weighs the available public evidence concerning the relative contributions of Western technology and Soviet domestic R&D to the USSR's military capacities. Anton Malish examines the role of agricultural imports in Soviet domestic policy and suggests that over the long term the regime will probably try to reduce imports of agricultural products but will have to increase imports of Western agricultural technology in order to do so.

The third part of the book looks at the dynamics of trade and technology transfer from the American side. Gary Bertsch considers the nature and causes of domestic American conflicts over economic interchange with the Soviet Union. Angela Stent examines the impact of this issue on American relations with Western Europe and Japan. James Millar analyzes the effect of U.S.-Soviet trade and trade denial on the American economy and explores the international economic factors that must be considered in any effort to promote concerted Western restrictions on the flow of nonmilitary goods to the USSR. The conclusion draws together the major themes discussed in the chapters and points out their implications for U.S. policy.

NOTES

1. For example, Antony Sutton's three-volume *Western Technology and Soviet Economic Development* (Stanford: Hoover Institution, 1968–1973) argues that Western technology was the decisive factor in the successes of the Soviet indus-

trialization drive. Relying on this conclusion, some observers have advocated much more stringent controls on current technology transfers to the USSR. See, for instance, Richard Pipes, "How to Cope with the Soviet Threat," *Commentary*, August 1984, pp. 26–30.

2. Bruce Parrott, *Politics and Technology in the Soviet Union* (Cambridge: MIT Press, 1983), Chapter 2.

3. Gunnar Adler-Karlsson, *Western Economic Warfare, 1947–1967* (Stockholm: Almqvist and Wiksell, 1968).

TRADE,
TECHNOLOGY,
AND
SOVIET-AMERICAN
RELATIONS

PART I
The Soviet Union and Trade with the West

Soviet-Western Trade and Technology Transfer: An Economic Overview

Josef C. Brada

Introduction

THE TRANSFER of western technology to the Soviet Union has absorbed the attention of both policymakers and scholars for decades. A perusal of three recently-published surveys of the literature on this topic reveals both strengths and weaknesses in our knowledge.[1] The strengths appear to be in our understanding of East-West technology transfer as a process sui generis. Since the bulk of the research has been carried out by specialists on the socialist economies and directed, explicitly or implicitly, at policymakers, such a tendency to focus on the unique and distinguishing characteristics of the flow of technology to the Soviet Union is not surprising. Nor has this work been unproductive. We have a large literature on the volume of technology being transferred, the means employed to transfer it and the systemic, economic, and political forces that promote or impede its transfer. The technical level of the Soviet economy and the effect of western technology on Soviet technical progress have also been extensively analyzed. While there are lacunae and disagreements among researchers over issues of both fact and interpretation, given the often intangible and unquantifiable nature of technology our knowledge of the facts regarding East-West technology transfer appears no worse than our knowledge regarding many other economic questions of interest to policymakers.

What does appear to be lacking in the literature is a broader perspective on the transfer of technology to the Soviet Union and the other planned economies. Such a perspective would view the Soviet experience as part of the international trade in technology and thus permit us to identify more clearly those aspects of the Soviet experience that are unique and those that the Soviet Union has in common with other coun-

I am indebted to John Hardt and Steve Sternheimer and to the other contributors to this volume for their help and advice. Needless to say, all shortcomings are entirely my responsibility.

3

tries. Unfortunately, in an essay of this length, I can undertake neither a systematic comparison of all issues commonly raised in connection with technology transfer nor a comparison with the experience of a large number of market economies. Thus what follows is not to be viewed as a full-blown exercise in the comparative economics of technology transfer, but rather as a selective and eclectic effort to place the Soviet experience with technology transfer in a broader perspective.

A Comparative Overview of Soviet Performance

By comparing the Soviet experience with technology imports to that of other countries it is possible to gain insights into important aspects of Soviet behavior that cannot be obtained by examining the Soviet experience in isolation. The Soviet leadership has expended a great deal of energy and resources on the development of the Soviet economy and on the raising of its technological level to that of the most advanced market economies. That this goal of achieving technological parity with the West has not as yet been met is evident. Through a comparison of Soviet achievements with those of other countries we can better understand to what extent the Soviets' failure to meet this goal is due to inadequate or misapplied effort, to the magnitude of the technological gap that was to be closed, or to western restrictions on technology exports.

Although in some instances I compare Soviet experiences to those of a number of western countries, the bulk of the comparisons is between the efforts and performance of the Soviet Union and those of Japan. I have chosen Japan for a number of reasons. The first is that there are some important macro-economic similarities between the two countries. As Table 1 shows, by the end of the 1970s, the two countries had almost the same level of GNP, ranking them second and third in the world in total output behind only the United States. This similarity in the level of GNP is important because it means that both countries have large economies, thus ensuring that the domestic market is sufficiently large to permit virtually all industries to operate at optimal plant size. Thus the economy of these countries is likely to encompass a full range of industrial products rather than being specialized in only one or several sub-sectors of industry. Consequently in both countries modernization and technological progress in industry, if it is to have any appreciable impact, must occur in many different sectors of industry and cannot be based on breakthroughs or expertise in one or several favored branches as might be the case in smaller economies. Although the populations of the two countries are less similar than their GNP, both may be considered to be large countries in terms of market size and diversity of market requirements.

There are also important historical and policy similarities between the

Table 1

Basic Economic Indicators for Japan and the U.S.S.R.

		JAPAN	U.S.S.R.
GNP	1950	72	278
(bill. 1979 $)	1979	1,030	1,375
Population	1950	83	179
(millions)	1979	116	262
Per Capita GNP	1950	867	1,553
($/person)	1979	8,880	7,682
$\frac{\text{Investment}}{\text{GNP}}$ (%)	1950	17	14
	1979	32	32

SOURCES: Kazushi Ohkawa and Henry Rosovsky, *Japanese Economic Growth: Trend Acceleration in the Twentieth Century* (Stanford: Stanford University Press, 1973). OECD, *Economic Survey, Japan* (Paris: OECD, 1980). Joint Economic Committee, U.S. Congress, *USSR: Measures of Economic Growth and Development, 1950–80* (Washington: USGPO, 1982). United Nations, *Population Yearbook* (Geneva: U.N., various years).

two countries.[2] Both attempted to industrialize in the late nineteenth century, Japan after the Meiji restoration and Russia somewhat later under the Vyshnegradski and Witte regimes. In both cases the government was heavily involved in promoting industrialization, and, as latecomers, both countries relied heavily on foreign technology. In neither case was this early effort at development remarkably successful. After World War II, economic policy converged again as both countries employed conscious and well-articulated strategies for development based on the rapid growth of industry supported by high levels of capital formation. In the case of the Soviet Union this represented a return to the policies of the first two Five-Year Plans; for Japan it was a somewhat more novel experience. The share of GNP devoted to capital formation was sharply increased in both countries. In the Soviet Union it grew steadily over the post-War period; in Japan it peaked at over 37 percent in 1972–73 and then declined so that, as Table 1 shows, at the end of the 1970s the proportion of output devoted to capital formation was the same in the two countries.

In both countries, the largest proportion of investment was devoted to industry, particularly to those sectors that were viewed as necessary for the further modernization and development of industrial production. Thus over the period 1951–65, the fastest growing sectors of the Soviet economy were ferrous and non-ferrous metallurgy (8.6 and 9.1 percent per year, respectively), electric power (12 percent), machinery (8.3 percent) and chemicals (11.4 percent).[3] The rapid growth of these sectors was duplicated in Japan, where for the period 1953–71 ferrous metallurgy grew at 14 percent per annum, machinery at 19.6 percent, chemicals at 14.8, petroleum and coal products at 17.9.[4]

Alongside these similarities in size, the level of development in 1950, and the post-War development strategy there are also some differences between the two countries. First, the economic systems differ, although the role of the state in shaping industrial policy is very important in Japan. Second, the Soviet Union is a country amply endowed with natural resources while Japan is dependent on imports of raw materials, food stuffs, and fuels. In part because of this difference in resource endowments the Soviet Union has been able to follow a development strategy geared to the needs of the domestic market while Japan has had to follow a development policy predicated on the need to export industrial products. On the other hand, Japan has not had to make the heavy investments in infrastructure needed by Soviet raw materials industries. Moreover, the "American umbrella" lifted the burden of defense expenditures from the Japanese economy, while the Soviet Union, in contrast, has matched United States defense expenditures despite its smaller economic potential, thus placing a heavy burden on its economy. As we shall see, these differences have had an important effect on these countries' experiences with technology imports.

The comparison with Japan is also valuable because it emphasizes a point that is often missed by students of the Soviet economy. As we shall see below, the Japanese experience demonstrates that a large and relatively backward economy, such as Japan's at the end of World War II, can catch up technologically with the most advanced countries in the world literally within a generation. Thus the question of technology and technology transfer is one of supreme importance both for the Soviet leadership and for western suppliers of technology. The Japanese experience amply demonstrates that technology imports do have the potential to produce rapid technological progress on a wide scale. On a somewhat less systematic basis, comparisons are also made between the Soviet experience and that of the smaller socialist countries of Eastern Europe. This is largely to aid in distinguishing between those aspects of Soviet technology import experience that have their root in Soviet policies and those that characterize all planned economies and are thus systemic in nature.

In making these comparisons it is not my aim to display Soviet weaknesses in the face of overwhelming, and singular, Japanese success. Certainly the Soviet Union has denied itself many opportunities for importing western technology and has been denied many such opportunities as well. Moreover, the Soviet economic system may be a serious barrier to large-scale imports of technology. Rather, the objective of the comparisons is to discover how much technology has been denied the

Soviet economy and to what extent Soviet policies and central planning have hindered or promoted the effective acquisition of western technology.

The Effectiveness of Technology Imports

Since the objective of technology imports is to speed technological progress and to close the technological gap between the importing country and those that are more advanced, we first need to examine the relative success of Japan and the Soviet Union in achieving these goals. We may assume that in 1952 the technological level of the Soviet Union was not likely to have been below that of Japan. As Table 1 shows, Soviet per capita output was twice that of Japan. Since the Soviet capital to labor ratio cannot have greatly exceeded that of Japan it appears safe to assume that Japan did not, in the early 1950s, have a significant technological lead over the Soviet Union.[5]

One way of measuring the level of technology is by estimating an aggregate production function that relates output to the available labor and capital inputs. Changes in output in excess of the growth of combined inputs (weighed at their marginal products) are attributed to improvements in the level of technology and possibly to other factors such as economies of scale and improvements in resource allocation.

In such a study of the technical level of the Japanese economy over the period 1952–74 Jorgenson and Nishimizu found that by the end of the period Japanese technology had reached the level of technology employed in the United States.[6] Since Japan started well behind the United States, with a technological level 75 percent below that of the United States in 1952, Japan clearly must have had a faster rate of technological progress. Jorgenson and Nishimizu found that, by the end of the 1950s, Japanese technology was 50 percent of the United States level and that in the 1960s, Japan's technological progress accelerated so as to close the gap with the United States by 1972–73. The remaining differences in per-capita output between the two countries were, they concluded, due not to differences in the level of technology but rather to differences in the availability of capital per worker.

A number of similar studies have been undertaken for the Soviet Union and although some controversy exists over the findings, the overall conclusion is that while the Soviet Union may have enjoyed somewhat faster technological growth than the United States, it still lags behind technologically.[7] For the post-war period ending in 1960 a number of studies of Soviet technological levels utilizing differing factor weights and pricing schemes placed Soviet technology between 33 and 98 percent of the United States level, with most of the findings at the lower end of the range. Studies of Soviet technological progress during the 1950s and early 1960s suggested that technological progress in the Soviet Union was somewhat faster than in the United States but slower than in the West European economies and Japan. Since then, studies based on Cobb-Douglas specifications of the production function show a sharp decline in the growth of technological progress. Bush, for example, computes the rate of growth of Soviet technological progress as 1.2 percent per year in 1951–60, 0.8 percent in 1961–70, and −0.6 percent in 1971–75.[8]

We may then assume that Soviet technology was roughly on a par with Japanese technology in 1960 based on the Jorgenson and Nishimizu estimates for Japan and an average of the estimates of the studies of Soviet technological levels. In this case, the Bush estimates indicate that the Soviet Union cannot have made any great headway in closing the technology gap between itself and the United States since 1960 and indeed may have fallen farther behind. It is worth noting that this view of Soviet technological progress has been challenged by Weitzman, who argues that the trend rate of technological progress in Soviet industry has held relatively constant but that growth of output has slowed due to a low elasticity of substitution between capital and labor.[9] However attractive such a finding may be from an econometric standpoint, it is worth noting that the ability to substitute capital for labor is, after all, a matter of technology and thus to appeal to a low elasticity of substitution as an explanation of the slow-down of Soviet growth is, in some sense, to fall back on a slow-down in the apparent pace of Soviet technological progress. Nevertheless, the residual between input and output growth may reflect a variety of forces at work other than technological progress. The greater need for long-gestation investments in infrastructure and raw materials production, the need to create a sophisticated urbanized labor force and the cumbersome system of planning may account for some of the failure of the Soviet residual to grow as rapidly as Japan's. Whether, given the time span over which the residual has been computed, some of these factors should have become less important or whether they can account for all of the difference between the apparent increases in technological levels in the two countries remains a matter for further research.

Another form of evidence of differences in the level of technology comes from sectoral studies. Such studies examine the level of technology in an individual sector in several countries and attempt to reach a conclusion on the relative level of technological advancement. Despite the fact that comparisons of technology, even at the level of the individual process or machine, can quickly become ambiguous, the results of such sectoral comparisons are in many ways the most palpable evidence that we have about the technology gap. Unfortunately the number of such studies is limited because of the difficulties involved. First, there are differences in technology that result from systemic influences; market and planned economies have differing goals in terms of quality, quantity, and diversity of products.[10] Second, it is often difficult to obtain reliable data on the performance and rate of diffusion of innovations. Finally, an inter-country comparison must establish criteria for evaluating the data that are neither ethno- nor geo-centric, but nevertheless yield a clear-cut decision if there is, indeed, a difference in technological level.

For Japan there are few such systematic studies encompassing a number of sectors. One useful study cited by Peck and Tamura reports on a survey of Japanese firms that imported foreign technology between 1950 and 1966.[11] At the time that the firms imported the technology 37.2 percent of them evaluated the technological level of their firm relative to those abroad as overwhelmingly backward; 46 percent as lagging considerably behind; and only 15.5 percent as roughly on the same level. By 1968 only 3.5 percent of the same respondents continued to rank themselves as overwhelmingly backward; 21.8 percent as lagging considerably behind; and 56.1 percent as roughly on the same level. Moreover, 18.6 percent of the respondents ranked themselves as "other," which could well mean advanced relative to foreign firms. Since much of Japan's technology was imported from the United States, this survey may be taken as the Japanese practitioners' view of the gap between Japanese and American technology. The results thus strongly corroborate the findings of Jorgenson and Nishimizu. Presumably, since then, whatever gap existed in 1968 has been at least closed.

Table 2 lists, by sector, the major western studies of the technology gap between the Soviet Union and the United States. Included are only those studies that explicitly set out to compare levels of technology and that explain the methodology and criteria employed in making such comparisons. Thus we exclude, for example, Sutton's case studies of technology transfer, Granick's study of the Soviet metal fabricating industry and OTA's study of the Soviet energy sector, although it is worth noting that these studies yield similar conclusions.[12]

The findings of the sectoral studies are roughly consistent with Soviet development priorities. The USSR leads or is at world standards in the high-voltage transmission of electricity, in machine tools, and in military technology. These sectors have traditionally received emphasis in development plans and in the allocation of resources. The lag in metallurgy is somewhat surprising since this has also been a priority sector. While the Soviets have made a number of advances in steelmaking the diffusion of these advances has been slow. Beyond these priority sectors it appears evident that the Soviet Union lags behind the West in the development and utilization of technology across a broad spectrum of economic activities.

In sum, then, the evidence indicates that it is possible for a large

Table 2

*Findings of Studies Comparing United States
and Soviet Technology by Sector*

Sector	Source and Year of Comparison	Conclusion
Agriculture	B-1962	Soviets behind U.S. by 32 years in mechanization, 17 years in use of fertilizers.
	W-1974	Soviets behind U.S. and advanced Western countries in both mechanization and use of fertilizers.
Automated Data Processing and Computers	B-1962	USSR well behind U.S. in use of computers.
	J-1970	USSR seriously behind U.S. in computer hardware, external and intermediate storage, and input-output devices. Software lag in 1968 was at least 10 years. U.S. has 50 times as many computers.
	W-1970	CMEA behind U.S. technology and use of computers by 10-16 years.
	ACD-1973	Soviets behind U.S. by 8-10 years in technology for central processors and peripherals. The Soviet lag grew in 1950s and early 1960s, stabilized, but appears to be increasing again in the 1970s. Computer lag hindering innovation in other industries.
Chemicals	ACD-1973	USSR is on a par with Western countries in basic chemicals and fertilizers; behind in heavy organic chemicals, petrochemicals, plastics, and synthetic materials. Soviet Union is dependent on the West for advanced chemicals and for chemical plants.

Generation and Transmission of Electricity	B-1962	USSR behind U.S. in generation, primarily because of emphasis on hydroelectric projects, but leads U.S. in high-voltage transmission of electricity.
	ACD-1973	USSR was among world leaders in use of high-voltage lines in 1960s, 1970s.
	W-1974	(Covers all sources of fuel and power.) Many lags in mining, oil exploration, power generation in CMEA.
Industrial Process Control	ACD-1973	Serious lags in technology; USSR is behind U.S., U.K., and West Germany. Progress hampered by lags in computers.
Machine Tools, Metal-working Machinery	B-1962	Metal-working in civilian sectors lags behind United States; insignificant lags and some possible leads in military sector.
	ACD-1973	Impossible to reach conclusion for such a broad sector. Study cites areas of Soviet inferiority, but no definite lead or lag can be established.
	W-1974	No conclusion; impossible to weigh leads and lags in various subsectors.
Machine Tools, Numerically Controlled	ACD-1973	USSR behind U.S. in 1960s, mainly because of lack of suitable computers. Now the Soviets are in a position to be in the forefront of technology in this sector.
Military Technology	ACD-1973	Impossible to judge in view of nonhomogeneous output. Gives some areas of superiority for U.S. and for USSR.
	W-1974	Same as ACD.
Rocketry	ACD-1973	Soviet Union has lost the lead it had over the U.S. in the 1960s.
Steelmaking	B-1962	USSR behind the U.S. substantially in the diffusion of new processes, although it does lead in some aspects of steelmaking.

	ACD-1973	USSR lagged in the diffusion of new technology in the 1960s vis à vis most industrialized countries, despite early leads in some technologies.
	W-1974	USSR is a world leader in some processes, but behind in mining and diffusion of new processes for steel production and specialty steels.
Transportation and Communications	B-1962	USSR behind the U.S. by 40 years in freight transportation but has progressed faster than the U.S. in passenger transportation. Behind the U.S. in communications.
	W-1974	USSR behind U.S. in many areas of transportation, by 20 years in communications.

SOURCES: Ronald Amann, Julian Cooper, and Richard W. Davies (eds.), *The Technological Level of Soviet Industry* (New Haven: Yale University Press, 1977), cited as ACD. Michael Boretsky, "Comparative Progress in Technology Productivity and Economic Efficiency," in Joint Economic Committee, U.S. Congress, *New Directions in the Soviet Economy* (Washington: USGPO, 1966), cited as B. Richard W. Judy, "The Case of Computer Technology," in Alexander Woroniak (ed.), *East-West Trade and the Technology Gap* (New York: Praeger, 1970), cited as J. Josef Wilczynski, *Technology in COMECON* (New York: Praeger, 1974), cited as W.

country such as Japan or the Soviet Union to raise its technological level to a standard equal to that of the most technologically advanced countries in a period of 20 to 30 years. The willingness to devote a large amount of current output to capital formation is evidently necessary for such an effort because much of the new technology requires new production processes or may be embodied in capital. Since both countries had high levels of capital formation while Japan was much more successful than the Soviet Union in closing the technology gap, we must look to the amount of technology that each country imported, the indigenous research and development effort undertaken, and the use to which imported and domestic technologies were put to understand the differences in outcomes.

The Volume of Technology Imports

One possible explanation for the difference between technological progress in Japan and that in the Soviet Union is the difference in the amount of technology imported by each country or in the mechanism employed by each country to transfer technology from abroad. In this section some quantitative and qualitative comparisons of various means of transferring technology are attempted in order to determine the extent to which the Soviet Union can be viewed as having denied itself or having been denied the opportunity to exploit fully the technology available in the West.

Cooperation and Exchanges in Science and Technology. A pervasive thread in the literature on technology transfer is that the international transfer of technology is a "people" process. That is to say, among the most effective mechanisms for the international transfer of technology are cooperation and exchanges among scientists and engineers from different countries.

Travel abroad to learn from foreigners has a long tradition in Japan, dating back to the Meiji restoration.[13] This tradition was continued in the modern era, not only for students but also for businessmen, engineers, journalists, and government officials both through public programs such as those of the Japanese Productivity Center and through private efforts.[14] Such visits by technical personnel resulted in the transfer of technical information. Those by businessmen, government officials, and journalists may not have resulted in the transfer of technical information but must have helped to make the Japanese aware of the urgency and magnitude of their effort to modernize their economy. Also important in facilitating the inflow of technology was the legendary scanning ability of Japanese trading companies. By placing thousands of their employees overseas these companies created a cadre of individuals who were able to seize on new technological developments around the globe and alert their company to the potential of this new technology.

There appears to be little in the Soviet experience to match the volume or quality of contact with foreign technology afforded to Japanese engineers, scientists, and businessmen. The Soviet Union does import and translate large amounts of western technical literature. It also engages in exchanges of scholars with western countries, and these are often criticized in the West for the high proportion of Soviet participants from engineering and the hard sciences.[15] No doubt the staff at Soviet embassies in developed countries also seeks to keep up with technical developments, but the broad range of developments they must cover and their lack of practitioners' insights renders them much less effective than their counterparts in Japanese trading companies. Overall in this category the transfer of technology to Japan is greater than that to the USSR although the difference does not lend itself to even crude quantification.

Licenses. The purchase of licenses from foreign firms is viewed as the most important mechanism for the transfer of technology to Japan. This is largely due to the fact that the Japanese government discouraged foreign direct investment. Thus foreign firms could serve the Japanese

Table 3

Payments and Receipts for Technology by Selected Industrialized Countries (million $)

	1961	1967	1971
Japan			
Payments	112	239	488
Receipts	3	27	60
Payments per $1000 GNP	0.795	1.054	1.138
France			
Payments	105	230	450
Receipts	56	195	264
Payments per $1000 GNP	0.676	1.114	1.563
United Kingdom			
Payments	NA	165	265
Receipts	NA	175	283
Payments per $1000 GNP	NA	0.947	1.324
United States			
Payments	80	171	218
Receipts	711	1,567	2,465
Payments per $1000 GNP	0.081	0.138	0.147
West Germany			
Payments	NA	192	405
Receipts	NA	90	149
Payments per $1000 GNP	NA	1.103	2.023

SOURCE: Adapted from Peck and Tamura, "Technology," Table 8-2.

market only by licensing Japanese firms or by exporting to Japan, with the latter a limited option at best.

Despite the attention focussed on Japanese purchases of licenses, Japanese licensing activity does not appear to be unusual by international standards. Table 3 shows that while Japan was the largest purchaser of foreign licenses, when adjusted for the relatively greater size of the Japanese economy these purchases were not unusual by international standards. Moreover, since 1971 Japanese expenditures on foreign technology have grown relatively slowly while in terms of new contracts signed Japan has been a net exporter of technology since 1972.[16]

The transfer of technology to the Soviet Union through licensing began in earnest in 1965 when the Soviet Union acceded to the Paris Convention for the protection of industrial property. Before this time neither western firms nor the Soviets had viewed licensing as a desirable means of transferring technology. Western firms were skeptical of the protection afforded their industrial secrets by Soviet industrial property legislation and, in the light of Soviet copying of western products, doubted that their patent rights could be effectively enforced in any communist country. By the mid-1960s, however, a change was evident on both sides. In the Soviet Union it was increasingly recognized that the unauthorized copying of western technology had significant drawbacks. First, it was time-consuming, not always altogether successful and diverted significant indigenous research and development resources from more advanced or original research projects. Second, copying implied the existence of a gap between Soviet and western technology since western products could be copied only after they had reached the market. Changes in the nature of technological progress also tended to reduce the usefulness of copying as a means of acquiring new technology. Machinery could be purchased, disassembled, analyzed and duplicated with some expectation that the duplicate would operate much like the original. In contrast computers, integrated circuits, plastics, new alloys, and the processes for their manufacture could not be "reverse engineered" as easily.[17] At the same time western firms began to show greater interest in obtaining additional returns on their proprietary technology by licensing Soviet enterprises, particularly in cases where exports of finished products to the Soviet Union were unlikely to materialize.

Despite the importance of East-West technology transfer, little useful data on the number and value of licenses sold to the Soviet Union is available, and what is available is quite contradictory.[18] The range of estimates suggests that by the mid-1970s the Soviet Union had purchased some 300–450 licenses from the West and was paying from 100 to 200 million dollars in royalties per year. A comparison of Soviet expenditures for licenses with those of the market economies reported in Table 3 reveals that the Soviet Union is much less active in the importation of technology through licenses than are most market economies. Indeed if the Soviet Union were to purchase licenses at the same relationship to GNP as the market economies (excluding the United States) then its expenditures on licenses in 1971 would have been between 850 and 1540 million dollars. Instead, Soviet license acquisitions most resemble those of the United States. The latter is, however, clearly an outlier among the industrialized market economies and, in any case, given the relative technological levels of the two countries, the relatively low licensing propensity of the United States hardly seems an appropriate model for the Soviet Union. In terms of the number of licensing agreements, the evidence is similar to that for payments. For example, in 1970 Japan had 1,157 licensing agreements in force for the importation of technology, two to three times the number signed by the Soviets by the mid-1970s.[19]

Not only are there quantitative differences between Soviet and western industrialized countries' licensing propensities, there is also evidence that in qualitative terms Soviet acquisition of foreign technology differs from that of Japan and possibly of other economies. In Japan, for example, licenses were purchased on the basis of agreements that ensured that the technology being purchased would be put to speedy and effective use. Thus licensing agreements provided for "patent rights; detailed drawings, operating instructions, and manuals; and interchange of personnel between the Japanese buyer and foreign seller."[20] In the case of sales of licenses to the Soviet Union relations between buyer and seller are less intimate and in many cases production based on foreign licenses has proven to be less successful than anticipated and required a much longer period between the purchase of the license and the startup of production than is common in the West.[21]

Another difference between Soviet and western, particularly Japanese, licensing strategy is that the Japanese government encouraged repeat purchases of technology. Thus one firm may have been given permission to purchase a foreign license for a given product. Since the firm granted the right to purchase the license would have a monopoly in Japan, competition for such permission was fierce, and firms made strong commitments to ensure that the imported technology was assimilated quickly and effectively. Then as the domestic market expanded other firms would be granted permission to import competitive technologies and allocated an appropriate share of the market.[22] Such sequential licensing put pressure on the firms that had purchased foreign technology earlier since they had to strive to update this technology lest they lose their competitive position to newcomers who purchased more recent technology abroad. In the case of the Soviet Union, sequential purchases of technology appear to be less frequent; often a license is purchased to meet current and anticipated market needs. Since there may be no follow-on purchases there is no incentive for the licensee to strive to update the technology through his own efforts. Instead the Soviets may wait until a new generation of technology appears in the West and then undertake a large-scale modernization of their production on the basis of this new technology. In those cases where sequential purchases of technology are made, there is no evidence that they have the same effect of creating technological and business competition for earlier recipients of technology that they do in Japan.

Japanese and probably other western firms as well also have a greater need to make effective use of the technology obtained through licenses because the output of the licensed technology is often exported and thus must meet the standards of the world market. For example, even as early as 1960, 50 percent of the exports of Japanese electrical machinery, 9 percent of nonelectrical machinery, 24 percent of chemicals, and 36 percent of steel were manufactured under license.[23] Since the share of licensed products in Japanese exports had been rising steadily in the 1950s, and since the proportion of the production of these industries' output devoted to export has also been increasing it is evident that Japanese utilization of licenses has been quite effective by world standards. While the Soviets have evinced some interest in exporting to western markets output produced under license, the actual quantities have been relatively small when compared to production. That the purchase of licenses is often seen primarily as a means of replacing imports rather than as a means of promoting exports is part of the problem. The chronic excess demand for intermediate and final goods no doubt also makes it difficult to divert supplies away from domestic claimants and toward foreign markets. Finally, the marketing of many of these goods abroad is hampered by the lack of an effective sales network.

The failure to export a larger number of goods produced under license is a much more serious shortcoming in the Soviet case than it would be in the case of Japan. One is invariably struck by the stress that Japanese businessmen place on the role of the domestic market in promoting the export competitiveness of Japanese goods. They regard the Japanese consumer as very quality-conscious and the domestic market as very competitive. Thus it is the domestic market that fosters quality and technical sophistication. In the Soviet case the reverse appears to be the case. The Soviet consumer is powerless to display much quality-consciousness and goods acceptable for the domestic market are likely to prove unacceptable to foreign buyers from quality or technical standpoints. Indeed, the Soviet attitude appears to be the exact opposite of the Japanese. The Soviet view is that production for export markets should make enterprises more aware of the need for quality and technical sophistication and thus transfer these characteristics to domestic production, rather than the other way around.

In comparison with Japan and with other developed market economies both quantitatively and qualitatively the Soviet Union appears to have greatly underutilized licensing as a means of improving the pace of its technological progress. The qualitative shortcomings appear to be largely systemic in nature. As for the quantitative difference, the major cause would appear to be Soviet policies. In some cases western controls over technology exports may hamper the purchases of licenses by the Soviet Union, but since Hungary, Czechoslovakia and Poland appear to have purchased foreign licenses in similar amounts despite much smaller economic potentials, there must have been potentially beneficial license purchases, not restricted by technology controls, that the Soviet Union declined to pursue. It is also not likely that the Soviets declined to pursue such purchases due to hard currency constraints, since the amounts of money involved in royalty payments for even a very aggressive program of technology acquisition through

Table 4

United States Foreign Direct Investment in Selected Countries
(billion $)

		FDI	FDI/GNP
Canada	1962	15.7	0.184
	1983	44.5	0.198
United	1962	5.4	0.027
Kingdom	1983	30.8	0.095
Federal Republic	1962	2.8	0.009
of Germany	1983	15.9	0.048
Other West	1962	8.7	0.007
Europe	1983	53.2	0.023
Japan	1962	.7	0.003
	1983	6.9	0.006

SOURCE: U.S. Department of Commerce, *Survey of Current Business* (Washington: U.S. Department of Commerce), various issues.

foreign licensing would not have been that large. Soviet reluctance to make greater use of licensing thus would seem to be a conscious decision reflecting Soviet difficulties in absorbing additional amounts of technology in this form, the lack of success in effectively exploiting some licenses, and a desire to rely on indigenous technology where possible.[24]

Foreign Direct Investment and Industrial Cooperation. Many specialists on the multinational corporation (MNC) believe that the MNC owes its existence to failures in the market for knowledge and technology. Because these failures prevent the efficient transfer of technology abroad, the MNC is able to establish itself in foreign countries by internalizing these transactions in technology. Thus transfers of technology between a parent firm and its affiliates occur more speedily, with lower resource costs, and with a greater chance of successful assimilation of the technology by the recipient than in the case of transfers of technology to other firms.

Despite this superiority of foreign direct investment as a means of transferring technology it was, by international standards, a method underutilized by the Japanese for reasons of policy and by the Soviet Union largely for systemic reasons. Table 4 provides an overview of the distribution of foreign direct investment by the United States. Since American firms are likely to be more interested in the Japanese market than are European firms, data on United States foreign direct investments are likely to overstate the overall foreign direct investment inflows to Japan relative to Western Europe. Nevertheless, despite a large increase over the 1962–83 period, American foreign direct investment in Japan is much less than it is in the Western European countries. This is particularly evident when we adjust the investments for country size by dividing by GNP. Neither the volume nor the rate of growth of foreign direct investment relative to GNP was as high in Japan as in Western Europe. Another way of putting the Japanese experience in perspective is to compare payments for technology in the form of licensing fees to profit remittances by affiliates of foreign firms. In Japan for 1968–71, license payments were about six times profit remittances, in the Federal Republic of Germany the two were roughly equal and in the United Kingdom profit remittances were approximately twice the value of license payments.[25]

The low level of foreign direct investment inflows into Japan was the result of government policies that virtually eliminated the possibility of foreign firms' establishing wholly owned affiliates in Japan and severely restricted their ability to establish minority joint-ventures with Japanese firms until 1967. Such restrictions of course facilitated the purchase of foreign technology since the large and rapidly growing Japanese market was attractive to western firms which viewed the sale of licenses as a second-best alternative to foreign direct investment.

In the case of the Soviet Union, no foreign direct investment is permitted, although some East European countries such as Hungary and Romania do permit minority foreign participation in joint ventures. To overcome the systemic barriers to foreign direct investment in socialist countries, a variety of non-equity relationships between western firms and socialist enterprises evolved as a substitute. Falling under the rubric of industrial cooperation (IC) such relationships substitute contractual rights for the property rights normally granted foreign investors and thus foster an intimate and potentially effective transfer of technology between the partners. In quantitative and qualitative terms the Soviet Union has been much less active than other socialist countries in fostering IC, especially in the more intimate forms of IC that can be viewed as viable substitutes for foreign direct investment.

Industrial cooperation evolved in the 1960s as a pragmatic solution to the perceived needs of both western sellers of technology and the socialist purchasers of such technology. Many western firms concluded that the market for their products in CMEA countries would be limited by the region's perennial shortage of hard currencies, by the import priorities established in national development plans, and by the stress on import substitution. Western purveyors of technology also recognized that they could obtain higher returns on their technology sales to the Soviet Union and Eastern Europe if they could maintain a continuing association with the exploitation of that technology in the CMEA market. Finally, some western firms perceived that planned economies could serve as a reliable, low-cost source of parts and components if provided with the requisite technology, equipment, and managerial expertise. To Soviet and East European leaders, IC appeared as a means of creating greater interest on the part of the transferrers of technology in ensuring that such transfers were as effective and successful as possible and that the technology received through IC agreements was updated on a timely basis. Moreover, IC was viewed as a means of obtaining not only western technology but also long-term access to western markets for the products of IC and a more competitive position within the CMEA market.

Among the less intensive forms of cooperation are:

Licensing and Product Payback. In licensing agreements, a western firm sells a license and provides technical documentation and possibly specialized equipment as well as continuing short-term technological updates and management assistance to a socialist firm. The payment for the technology and aid is in the form of the output of the process delivered to the western partner under a long-term delivery contract.

Turnkey Plants and Product Payback. The western firm supplies a complete plant or production process to the socialist country. Payment, total or partial, is made in the form of output of the plant.

Subcontracting. In a subcontracting arrangement the western firm provides technology, components or inputs, and possibly equipment to a socialist firm that undertakes to supply the western firm with components, parts, or even finished goods at a specified price. Subcontracting thus differs from the foregoing types of cooperation largely in the motivation of the western partner.

These three types of cooperation are of a relatively unintensive sort, in that the two partners have little impact on each other's operations and deal with each other on an arms-length basis. However, they have important advantages from the perspective of the socialist enterprise. First of all, because the western partner is bound to accept payment in the form of the output of the technology transferred to the socialist partner, there are stronger incentives for the western firm to facilitate a successful transfer of technology than would be the case in a simple sale of licenses or machinery. Second, the western firm is unlikely to sell obsolete technology because it will have to market the resulting output in the West. Moreover, the long-term dependence of the western firm on the output of its socialist partner suggests that innovations and improvements developed in the West will be transferred to the socialist partner more quickly than might otherwise be the case.

A more intimate form of cooperation between the western and socialist partners than the relations described above has also evolved. In some cases the two partners will specialize in the production of components for a product line and exchange the components so that each partner can assemble the finished product. Alternatively each partner

Table 5

Sectoral Distribution of Western Industrial Cooperation Agreements with East Europe and the Soviet Union

Sector	Western European* ICs with:		Sector	United States** ICs with:	
	All East Europe (%)	of which USSR (%)		All East Europe (%)	of which USSR (%)
Food, Beverages and Tobacco	4.7	2.6	Agriculture & Food	6.2	5.6
			Mining	3.4	6.1
Crude Materials excl. Oils & Fuels	2.6	27.3	Metals	5.0	6.1
Mineral Fuels	2.1	9.1	Textiles, Lumber and Paper	5.3	3.2
Chemicals	13.5	9.1	Chemicals	22.7	22.0
Transport Equipment	9.2	0.0	Non-elec. Mach'y	20.6	22.4
Machine Tools	7.2	18.2	Elec. Machinery	15.6	15.4
Mach'y Non-elec.	34.7	9.1	Trans. Equipment	5.5	3.7
Elec. Machinery	10.4	0.0	Trans. & Comm.	1.3	2.8
Other Man. Goods	13.5	18.5	Finance & Services	6.2	6.5
Other	2.1	9.1	Other	8.2	6.2
TOTAL	100%	100%	TOTAL	100%	100%
Number of Agreements	198	11	Number of Agreements	436	214

SOURCES: Paul Marer, John Holt, and Joseph Miller, *The U.S. Perspective on East-West Industrial Cooperation* (Bloomington: Indiana University for the U.S. Department of Commerce, 1976.) Carl H. Mcmillan, "Forms and Dimensions of East-West Inter-firm Cooperation," in C. T. Saunders (ed.), *East-West Cooperation in Business: Inter-firm Studies* (Vienna: Springer-Verlag, 1977.)

*As of early 1975
**As of January 1, 1976

can take responsibility for the complete production of some part of a line of products and the partners then exchange output so that each can market a complete line of products while reaping the benefits of longer production runs. Such arrangements are more intimate in that each participant's business success depends, in part, on the performance of the partner. Thus relations between cooperating firms tend to be long-term and to extend beyond cooperation in production to joint research, product development, and marketing.

Overall there are significant differences between the Soviet Union and the other East European countries in the extent to which they make use of industrial cooperation with the West and these differences reflect a greater reluctance on the part of the Soviet Union to participate in those forms of IC that most resemble foreign direct investment. In part this reflects a policy difference between the Soviet Union and other planned economies, with the latter viewing the ties resulting from IC much more positively. Moreover, the Soviet Union is under much less pressure to export manufactures to western markets and thus needs the intimate forms of IC much less. Table 5 shows that the Soviet Union does not participate very actively in IC with partners from West Europe, accounting for only 5 percent of such agreements. In contrast it accounts for about one-half of the IC agreements that involve partners from the United States. The compilation of cooperation agreements involving West European countries takes a relatively "narrow" conception of cooperation while the compilation of IC involving American partners uses a "looser" definition of cooperation and thus subsumes a larger number of arms-length arrangements. Thus we may conclude that the East European countries have been more active than the Soviet Union in establishing IC agreements that create long-term and intimate relations between the partners and thus most resemble foreign direct investment in their impact on technology transfer. In contrast, the Soviet Union has pursued those IC agreements that promote the transfer of technology without any great contact between participants and with minimum loss of control to the western partner.

Thus, as with licensing, the Soviet Union has, by international standards, been a modest user of industrial cooperation as a mechanism for the international transfer of technology. In part, this may be due to location. Subcontracting by Hungarian firms for Austrian or West German firms is facilitated by their proximity and supported on the socialist side by the overriding need to promote exports of manufactures to the West. Moreover, in the smaller East European countries, the domestic market is often unable to absorb production runs of an economical size and thus foreign markets must be sought out. In contrast the Soviet Union is both geographically and psychologically farther away from western cooperators and markets, is able to earn hard currencies through exports of raw materials and fuels, and has a large enough market to absorb any level of production dictated by the technology of the production process.

Imports of Machinery and Equipment. The international transfer of technology through commodity trade occurs in three ways. One is through the importation of machinery, equipment, and components that embody technology not available domestically. Such imports permit the receiving country to produce goods that could not otherwise be produced or to produce existing goods more cheaply. The increase in technological capability generated by such imports is proportional to the volume of such imports and to the gap between the technological level of foreign and domestic technology. A second form of technology transfer involves the importation of only a few units embodying new technology. These units are analyzed and, perhaps with some modifications to adapt them to local conditions, copied and put into production. Unlike the previous type of technology transfer, the volume of trade tells us little of the amount of technology transferred to the receiving country. More important is the ability to assimilate and disseminate the technology embodied in the imported samples. Finally, imports of technologically advanced goods may raise the level of technology in the receiving country because people in that country learn how to operate the new technology or to incorporate it in existing products. Thus for example, the ability to utilize computers can be raised through their importation without any increase in the importing country's ability to design or manufacture computers.

The importation of machinery to serve as models for domestic designs has been practiced by both the Soviet Union and Japan. Sutton provides extensive evidence of Soviet duplication of western machinery and equipment.[26] In some cases western machinery being employed in production was duplicated and subsequently manufactured on a large scale by the Soviets. In other instances small numbers of a variety of western models were imported, subjected to testing, and the model deemed most suitable for Soviet needs put into production. Despite his negative assessment of other aspects of Soviet scientific-technical achievements, Sutton argues that Soviet technicians were successful in choosing which western equipment to copy, in metricizing foreign equipment and in scaling-up designs to meet Soviet needs. Moreover, he argues that the Soviets were fairly effective in organizing the production of the copied equipment. Given the resistance of Soviet managers to innovation, one must wonder whether Sutton's case studies are exceptions to the Soviet pattern of slow diffusion of technology. Part of the seeming success in getting production started may have been due to the fact that for many products new factories were constructed, thus bypassing managerial resistance. A weakness of Soviet copying is that research and development efforts often stopped with the duplication of the western prototype. Little Soviet innovation and product improvement followed, and Sutton argues that Soviet efforts at improving on western designs were often unsuccessful. There is, of course, a tendency to overstate the amount of such copying since it has an illicit air about it and thus enables western researchers to stigmatize Soviet efforts. Consequently one should not overestimate the amount of technology transferred in this way.

The ability of Japanese, as well as other western firms, to duplicate foreign technology is constrained by patents. However, for many kinds of know-how and technologies, patent protection has lapsed or does not exist under the laws of the importing country, as in Japan, where process but not product patents exist. The image of Japan as a producer of cheap duplicates of western goods in the 1950s and 1960s suggests that

Table 6

Japanese and Soviet Imports of Machinery and Equipment

	Japan	USSR	
	SITC 7—Total Imports (bill. $)	SITC 7 Imports from OECD (bill. $)	Machinery Imports from CMEA (bill. rubles)
1961	0.606	0.361	1.198
1971	2.241	0.903	3.048
1975	3.824	4.576	5.616
1981	8.815	4.985	10.584*

SOURCES: Appendix Tables and OECD, *Directions of Trade-Series C* (Paris: OECD, various years.)
  *1980

this avenue for the transfer of technology must have been employed to some extent. Although there is no way of quantifying the amount of technology imported by either Japan or the Soviet Union in this way, there is evidence to suggest that the Japanese made better use of the technology obtained by these means. First, a large part of Japanese research and development efforts in the 1950s and 1960s were devoted to improving products and technologies obtained from more advanced countries; in the Soviet case there is little evidence of a comparable scale of effort. Second, there is evidence that in Japan a large proportion of investment outlays and of expenditures on engineering and plant layout and design were induced by imports of technology.[27] In this way the Japanese were able to make rapid and effective use of imported technology and to use it not merely as a means of catching up with more advanced countries but also as a springboard to further technological progress through indigenous efforts.

Table 6 provides summary data on Japanese and Soviet imports of machinery and equipment. Over the entire sample period the Soviet Union has placed greater reliance on imported machinery than has Japan. However, particularly before the 1970s, the bulk of Soviet machinery imports came from the CMEA countries. While machinery of East European origin may be technologically advanced over machinery of Soviet origin the margin is not likely to be great. Even if the East European countries have begun to increase their exports of machinery and equipment produced under license from western firms, such exports account for no more than 10 to 15 percent of the total machinery exports. Thus it is Soviet imports from OECD, the developed market economies of Japan and the West, that are the principal source of embodied technology exports to the Soviet Union. In the 1950s and 1960s,

Japanese imports of goods in SITC 7, machinery and equipment, were considerably greater than those of the Soviet Union. It is only for a few years following 1975, when Soviet imports doubled while Japanese imports declined slightly that the volume of Soviet imports exceeded that of Japan. However, as the tables in the Statistical Appendix show, Soviet imports of machinery and equipment from the West have held relatively steady since 1975 (especially in real terms) while Japanese imports have continued to grow.

In addition to differences in the volume of imports, there are differences in their origin. In Japan there has been a growing diversification away from the United States. In 1968–70, the United States supplied 61 percent of Japanese capital equipment imports while in 1976–77 the United States' share was 51.3 percent. Nevertheless, the United States has been and continues to be the principal source of Japanese capital equipment imports. The pattern of Soviet imports of machinery and equipment is much more erratic. With a few exceptions, in the 1960s the United States was a negligible source of such imports. During the early 1970s, the United States' share of OECD's SITC 7 exports increased to over 10 percent, but then declined in both absolute and percentage terms in the second half of the decade. The primary OECD sources of SITC 7 goods have been the Federal Republic of Germany and Japan, which between them have accounted for nearly one-half of OECD exports of SITC 7 to the Soviet Union. Although there are gaps in technology at the level of individual products between the United States and the other OECD countries there is no evidence to suggest that at the aggregate level the differences in the origin of Soviet and Japanese machinery imports are a significant factor in reducing the embodied technology imported by the Soviets in comparison to the technology available to Japan or to other market economies.

In any case, the amount of technology transferred to either country through machinery imports cannot be very large for several reasons. First, imports of machinery account for a very small percentage of total investment. From the data in Tables 1 and 6 it is clear that in the 1970s machinery imports accounted for about 2.5 percent of Japanese investment, and for the Soviet Union imports from the West thus accounted for a smaller percentage. Of course, not all investment is in machinery and equipment so in fact as a percentage of new machinery and equipment installed imports may account for two to three times their share in total investment. Against this, however, we must weigh the fact that not all foreign machinery and equipment embodies technology that is superior to that available indigenously; some items in SITC 7 are relatively unsophisticated.[28] A measure of the trade in technologically sophisticated goods is provided in Appendix Table 3. From this it is evident that a significant proportion of Soviet imports of machinery and equipment from the West consists of standard items that, while possibly superior to indigenous equipment, are not particularly technology-intensive. Indeed the proportion of technology-intensive goods in Soviet imports is not greater than that of most other countries of comparable level of development.

Although the transfer of technology through the importation of machinery and equipment is not the only means of transferring western technology to the Soviet Union, the magnitude of the effects of machinery and equipment imports on the Soviet economy has been the object of considerable study and controversy. Imports of machinery and equipment from the West have two effects on the Soviet economy. The first of these is to increase the proportion of resources devoted to capital formation. If Soviet domestic production of machinery plus that available from other CMEA countries does not in the aggregate or in assortment meet the investment needs of the USSR, then, unless equipment can be imported from the West, the volume of investment must be less than desired. In the case of the Soviet Union this effect is unlikely to be of great significance in the aggregate, though it may be of importance for individual industries, for several reasons. First, imports of western machinery and equipment are, as we have seen, a small percentage of total Soviet investment in machinery. Second, there is no evidence that producer goods have been in excess demand on the CMEA market. Indeed, with deflationary policies in force in most of the smaller CMEA member countries, machinery and equipment for export should have been in ready supply during the past decade. Even if imports from the West were to represent a net increase in capital formation, the effect of this additional capital on Soviet growth would be negligible according to Desai.[29] Desai estimated a CES production function for the Soviet economy and estimated the return to additional capital. Under reasonable assumptions she found the rate of return to range from 0.8 to 4.41 percent. Thus she concludes that imports of capital equipment from the West are of little value as supplements to domestic capital formation. Desai's estimates of the return to western capital are subject to challenge in two respects. First, as mentioned before, they depend upon a CES production function with very low elasticity of substitution, and it is unclear precisely why this elasticity should be so low. Second, an aggregate production function assumes that the distribution of capital among industries is optimal, and thus that the marginal product of capital is the same in each industry and equal to that calculated on the basis of the aggregate production function. Studies by Thornton and Desai and Martin have shown that the distribution of capital among industries is not optimal, and thus if imports are directed to sectors where the marginal product of capital is above average, returns will also be above Desai's estimate.[30] The extent to which this criticism bears on Desai's results depends, of course, on the distribution of western equipment among Soviet industries.

The examination of the impact of western capital at the industry level, unfortunately, has proven rather controversial. The first effort, by Green and Levine, estimated Cobb-Douglas production functions for Soviet industry and three of its sub-sectors: chemicals, petrochemicals, and petroleum products; machine building; and metal working.[31] With labor, indigenous capital, and western capital as separate inputs they claim that the marginal product of western capital is from 21 to 8 times that of Soviet capital. To give some impression of the impact of such highly productive capital imports on the Soviet economy they employ an econometric model of the Soviet Union to show that the growth of Soviet industrial output would have been 2.5 percentage points lower over the period 1968–73 in the absence of imports of western machinery and equipment.

The Green and Levine findings have been sharply challenged by Weitzman who argued on the basis of the same data that there is no evidence that western capital is more productive than that of indigenous origin and that the results obtained by Green and Levine stem from the restrictive nature of their production function.[32] Weitzman's methodology, though not his findings, was in turn criticized by Toda who purported to use a more general production function.[33] Two studies by Brada and Hoffman challenge both Weitzman's and Toda's methodology and findings.[34] They argue that the real impact of western capital should be in its ability to raise the productivity of the labor and indigenous capital employed with it. By using a specification of the production function that subsumes those employed in the previous studies they conclude that these were based on improper specifications of the production function and, more important, that western capital imports do tend to raise the productivity of cooperating resources.

As with other forms of technology transfer, the Soviet Union has, by international standards, underutilized machinery and equipment imports as a means of increasing the pace of its technological progress. Although the volume of such imports increased sharply in the early 1970s, they have not shown much growth since then. Thus, it may be that the upsurge in the 1970s is largely in response to the sharp improvement in Soviet terms of trade following the increase in oil prices and says little about changes in Soviet views regarding the desirability of acquiring western technology by these means.

The Indigenous Development of Technology

The promotion of technological progress through imports of technology is a particularly powerful technique because the purchaser has available the entire range of innovations developed throughout the world. However, any country that wishes to import technology must also undertake indigenous research and development efforts. In part this is due to the need to have the scientific and technical ability to select, use and improve upon imported technology. In addition, a country may wish to undertake research and development efforts beyond those needed to facilitate the acquisition of foreign technology. The desire to undertake indigenous research of this type stems from three sources. The first two are economic, the last political. A country may undertake research and development because the type of research and development being done abroad and thus available for importation does not meet the country's needs. Thus, the country may perceive high returns to indigenous research and development efforts because foreign suppliers have either not noted or not responded to such opportunities. This motivation for indigenous research efforts may play a role in explaining the relatively low reliance of the Soviet Union on imported technology. The Soviet Union differs from the developed market economies in a number of ways. First, its level of development, as measured by per capita income and by the technological level of production, is lower. This means that many technologies oriented toward high-income consumers will be irrelevant to the Soviet Union and that certain improvements in production processes will not be appropriate to Soviet needs. In this sense the Soviet economy faces the same problem of "appropriate technology" faced by developing countries which complain that the research undertaken in developed countries addresses neither the needs of low-income consumers nor the conditions of production and factor endowments found in developing countries. This lack of applicability of western technology may be exacerbated by systemic factors—innovations appropriate to the needs of firms in market economies are not particularly appropriate to the needs of enterprises in planned economies.

A second reason for undertaking indigenous research is that the country believes that the social returns to research outlays are sufficiently high relative to other uses of resources to warrant such outlays. In holding such a belief the leaders of the Soviet Union would not differ much from their colleagues in the developed countries of the West, as well as in some of the more advanced developing countries who believe that a mobilization of national scientific forces is necessary for economic progress if not for survival.

Finally countries may undertake research activities in order to be independent of foreign sources of technology. This independence is sought partly for purposes of economic control, that a nation have the technical wherewithal to shape its own economic destiny. Countries may also develop technology in order to have a certain degree of political autonomy, particularly but not exclusively in their ability to produce the

Table 7

Research and Development Personnel and Expenditures in Major Countries

*Scientists and Engineers Engaged in Research
and Development*

Country	TOTAL (thousands)		Per 10,000 Population	
	1965	1975	1965	1975
USSR	499.5	1115.0	21.6	43.8
JAPAN	118.0	250.0[a]	11.9	22.0[a]
US	494.1	540.5[a]	25.4	24.8[a]
FRG	57.0	103.0	9.7	16.7
FRANCE	42.8	60.0	8.8	11.0
UK	54.6	77.1[b]	10.1	18.8 [b]

*Research and Development Expenditures as a
Percentage of GNP*

Country	TOTAL R & D			DEFENSE R & D	
	1967	1975	1981	1967	1975
USSR	3.00	3.50	3.70	NA	NA
JAPAN	1.30	1.70	2.20	0.02	0.01
US	2.90	2.30	2.50	1.10	0.64
FRG	1.70	2.10	2.70	0.21	0.14
FRANCE	2.20	1.80	1.90	0.55	0.35
UK	2.30	2.10	2.10	0.61	0.62

SOURCES: National Science Board, *Science Indicators, 1976* (Washington, US Government Printing Office, 1977), Cols. 1–4. OECD, *Technical Change and Economic Policy* (Paris, OECD, 1980), Cols 5–8, except row 1, which is from Joint Economic Committee, U.S. Congress, *USSR: Measures of Economic Growth and Development* (Washington, USGPO, 1982).
[a]estimate
[b]1972

arms necessary for their defense. Clearly both in terms of the ability to carry out an economic policy that shapes the pattern of economic progress without external interference and to maintain a creditable defense industry the Soviets must desire a great deal of self-reliance in science and technology.

The facts of the matter are set out in Table 7. In terms of sheer numbers of scientists and engineers employed in research and development the Soviet Union far out-distances all other countries, including the United States. Indeed, the Soviets deploy a number of researchers that is roughly equal to that of all the OECD countries combined. Since Soviet science ought to be coordinated and should enjoy a greater potential for interaction among researchers due to a common language, it is reasonable to believe that it ought to outperform the sum of the researchers in the OECD countries who may serve competing rather than collaborative ends and who are separated by barriers of language. Moreover, the great number of researchers in the USSR is not simply a matter of country size. In terms of the proportion of human resources devoted to research the Soviet effort is double that of any market economy. Thus in terms of sheer manpower, there appears to be no reason why Soviet scientists should not be able to maintain a level of innovative activity comparable with that of the West.[35]

Table 7 also reveals that the material support for science, measured by the proportion of GNP devoted to research divided by the number of researchers, is much lower in the Soviet Union than elsewhere. Part of this is surely due to the differences in pricing of inputs for science in capitalist and socialist countries, but anecdotal evidence of shortages of equipment in Soviet laboratories suggests that material support for research activities lags behind that of the West. Second, the Soviet Union is required to keep technological parity in defense with the United States. If this requires, as a rough measure, an equal expenditure in dollar terms, then with a GNP roughly one-half that of the United States the Soviet Union may be expending between 1.2 and 2.2 percent of its GNP on defense-related research and development outlays.[36] This leaves Soviet outlays for civilian R&D as a percent of GNP at or below those of the market economies in our sample with the exception of the United States, which lags behind the other countries. Consequently one need not resort to the notion that Soviet science is somehow less effective than western science to explain the pace of technological progress in the USSR. If this pace, over the past twenty years, has been equal to that of western Europe and lagged only behind that of Japan, then, given the level of technology imports and the indigenous research devoted to non-military ends, Soviet science would appear to be performing at acceptable levels.

Concluding Remarks

The comparison of Japanese and Soviet experiences with technology imports reveals a number of differences. In general the Soviet Union has adopted a more self-reliant policy that seeks to reduce dependence on foreign technology to a level below that found among developed market economies. Although, as is evident in the case of Japan, the importation of foreign technology can have a great impact on growth and the technological level, it would be a mistake to conclude that a more liberal approach to technology imports would have correspondingly large benefits for the Soviet Union. First, the economic system itself may be a significant barrier to the effective assimilation of technology. In the case of Japan, systemic change was geared to the need to assimilate foreign technology; the Soviet system has other goals to meet that may inhibit system change in the direction needed to make better use of foreign technology. In our brief comparisons of Soviet and East European experiences with technology imports, it was evident that the smaller countries imported relatively more technology and employed mechanisms thought to promote the effective utilization of such technology. Yet there is no evidence that technical progress in East Europe has outstripped that of the Soviet Union and some experiences with technology imports, Poland being only the most obvious example, suggest that more imports of technology coupled with less control are hardly guarantees of faster technical progress. Second, the Soviet economy is more limited in the types of technology that it can acquire by the existence of western restrictions on technology exports. Although domestic research efforts have not made up the entire shortfall in technology imports, the costs of smaller technology imports have been borne rather willingly by the Soviet leadership. Although it is attractive to link changes in the volume of Soviet technology imports to internal struggles among competing groups within the Kremlin or to the state of United States-Soviet relations, a relatively strong case can be made that Soviet import policies reflect a relatively stable and consistent calculus of economic gains weighed against the opportunity costs of technology imports in terms of other imports and in terms of political costs that fluctuates much less than the vagaries of internal and external relations might lead one to believe.

There is also an important similarity between the Japanese and Soviet experiences that bears on our assessment of future developments in the Soviet Union. Both countries have financed technology imports with the export earnings of traditional sectors; labor-intensive industries in Japan, the raw-materials sector in the Soviet Union.

It seems possible, given the similarities in development strategy, that if the Soviets continue on this path, once the huge, long-gestation investment projects come on stream, the Soviet economy could experience the same sort of take-off in international competitiveness and technological level that Japan enjoyed in the 1960s and 1970s.

While there is some evidence of this, for example in Soviet efforts to export cars and other products based on foreign technology, export competitiveness in manufactures does not appear to be an important Soviet goal. So long as it remains unimportant neither the systemic changes required to bring Soviet goods to world standards nor the willingness to look beyond the large and ever-voracious domestic market will change, and without such changes a self-sustaining export orientation is unlikely. Rather, the Soviet Union will continue with its policy of self-restraint in technology imports and gear these to the needs of the domestic economy. Results will thus be modest, but so will the risks.

NOTES

1. Josef C. Brada, *Technology Transfer Between the United States and the Countries of the Soviet Bloc* (Trieste: ISDEE, 1981); Philip Hanson, *Trade and Technology in Soviet-Western Relations* (London: Macmillan, 1981); Eugene Zaleski and Helgart Wienert, *Technology Transfer Between East and West* (Paris: OECD, 1980).

2. These similarities have led to other comparisons of the two countries. In particular, see Angus Maddison, *Economic Growth in Japan and the USSR* (New York: Norton, 1969).

3. Joint Economic Committee, U.S. Congress, *USSR: Measures of Economic Growth and Development, 1950–80* (Washington: USGPO, 1982).

4. Edward Denison and William Chung in Hugh Patrick and Henry Rosovsky (eds.) *Asia's New Giant: How the Japanese Economy Works* (Washington: Brookings Institution, 1976), p. 74.

5. There are, of course, methodological problems in estimating the GNPs of the Soviet Union and of a war-disequilibrated Japanese economy in 1950. Nevertheless, the orders of magnitude in our comparison seem relatively robust in the face of even sizable errors.

6. Dale W. Jorgenson and Mieko Nishimizu, "U.S. and Japanese Economic Growth, 1952–1974: An International Comparison," *Economics Journal*, 88, no. 4 (1978), pp. 707–26.

7. A useful overview of many of these studies is provided in Ronald Amann, Julian Cooper, and Richard W. Davies (eds.), *The Technological Level of Soviet Industry* (New Haven: Yale University Press, 1977).

8. Keith Bush, "Soviet Economic Growth: Past, Present, and Projected," *Survey*, 23, no. 1 (1978), pp. 1–16.

9. Martin L. Weitzman, "Soviet Economic Growth and Capital-Labor Substitution," *American Economic Review*, 60, no. 4 (1970), pp. 676–92.

10. C. C. Gallagher, "The Influence of Economic Systems on Detailed Technology," *Soviet Studies*, 25, no. 4 (1974), pp. 346–52.

11. Merton Peck, with the assistance of Shuji Tamura, "Technology," in Patrick and Rosovsky, *Asia's New Giant*, p. 538.

12. Antony C. Sutton, *Western Technology and Soviet Economic Development*, 3 vols. (Stanford: Hoover Institution, 1968, 1971, 1973); David Granick, *Soviet Metal Fabricating and Economic Development*. (Madison: Wisconsin University Press, 1976); Office of Technology Assessment, *Technology and Soviet Energy Availability* (Boulder: Westview, 1982).

13. William W. Lockwood, *The Economic Development of Japan: Growth and Structural Change, 1868–1938* (Princeton: Princeton University Press, 1954), pp. 12, 510; Johannes Hirschmeier, *The Origins of Entrepreneurship in Meiji Japan* (Cambridge: Harvard University Press, 1964), p. 122.

14. Peck and Tamura, "Technology," pp. 536–37.

15. Allen H. Kassof, "Testimony," in *Hearings before the Commission on Security and Cooperation in Europe on Implementation of the Helsinki Accords* (Washington: USGPO, 1977).

16. Mary Saso and Stuart Kirby, *Japanese Industrial Competition to 1990* (Cam-

bridge: Abt Books, 1982), pp. 41–43. The judgment that Japanese license purchases are not unusual by international standards rests on the assumption of a linear relationship between GNP and expenditures on licenses. Clearly, little is known about this relationship; other factors as well as significant non-linearities may prevail, and Japan may thus be less normal than suggested here.

17. See, for example, the case study of technology transfer in computers in this volume.

18. Brada, *Technology Transfer Between the United States and Countries of the Soviet Bloc,* pp. 56–58; Zaleski and Wienert, *Technology Transfer Between East and West,* pp. 115–18. The figures cited here apparently do not include Soviet purchases of licenses in connection with purchases of production lines or complete plants.

19. Peck and Tamura, "Technology," p. 540.

20. Ibid., p. 537.

21. See United Nations Economic Commission for Europe, *Marketing of Licenses in the East: Case Study of Selling Canadian Licenses for Footwear to the U.S.S.R.* (Trade/Sem. 2/R. 12) (Geneva: United Nations, 1975), for a typical experience.

22. Terutomo Ozawa, "Technology Transfer and Japanese Economic Growth in the Postwar Period," in Robert G. Hawkins and A. J. Prasad (eds.), *Technology Transfer and Economic Development* (Greenwich: JAI Press, 1981), pp. 111–12.

23. Ibid., p. 109.

24. To the extent that the Soviet Union makes less use of licensing as a means of acquiring foreign technology because it has difficulties in absorbing such technology, its low licensing propensity is rational. Nevertheless, however optimal in this limited sense, the level is below that of the other countries examined and indicates a lower level of technology imports by means of licenses for the Soviet Union.

25. Peter G. Peterson, *The United States in the Changing World Economy,* vol. 2 (Washington: USGPO, 1971), Chart 71.

26. Antony C. Sutton, *Western Technology and Soviet Economic Development, 1945 to 1965* (Stanford: Hoover Institution Press, 1973), Ch. 19.

27. Terutomo Ozawa, *Japan's Technological Challenge to the West, 1950–1974: Motivation and Accomplishment* (Cambridge: MIT Press, 1974), p. 96.

28. They do, nevertheless, contribute to the growth of output.

29. Padma Desai, "The Productivity of Foreign Resource Inflow to the Soviet Economy," *American Economic Review,* 66, no. 2 (1979).

30. Judith Thornton, "Differential Capital Charges and Resource Allocation in Soviet Industry," *Journal of Political Economy,* 79, no. 3 (1971), pp. 545–561. Padma Desai and Ricardo Martin, "Efficiency Loss from Resource Misallocation in Soviet Industry," *Quarterly Journal of Economics,* 98, no. 3 (1983), pp. 441–56.

31. Donald W. Green and Herbert S. Levine, "Implications of Technology Transfers for the USSR," in NATO, *East-West Technological Cooperation* (Brussels: NATO Economic Directorate, 1976); Donald W. Green and Herbert S. Levine, "Soviet Machinery Imports," *Survey,* 23, no. 2 (1978), pp. 112–26.

32. Martin L. Weitzman, "Technology Transfer to the USSR: An Econometric Analysis," *Journal of Comparative Economics,* 3, no. 2 (1979), pp. 167–77.

33. Yasushi Toda, "Technology Transfer to the USSR: The Marginal-Productivity Differential and the Elasticity of Intra-Capital Substitution in Soviet Industry," *Journal of Comparative Economics,* 3, no. 2 (1979), pp. 181–94.

34. Josef C. Brada and Dennis L. Hoffman, "Technology Transfer to the

USSR and the Shape of the Production Function," *DeEconomist*, 130, no. 3 (1982), pp. 420–27; Josef C. Brada and Dennis L. Hoffman, "The Productivity Differential Between Soviet and Western Capital and the Benefits of Technology Imports to the Soviet Economy," *Quarterly Review of Economics and Business* (forthcoming).

35. Of course, Soviet science may not be as well-coordinated and Soviet scientists as free to exchange information as ought to be the case.

36. Converting R&D expenditures into dollar values for purposes of comparison is, of course, fraught with a number of conceptual problems, and thus our finding is an approximate one.

Soviet Foreign Policy, Internal Politics, and Trade with the West

Bruce Parrott

THIS CHAPTER examines the place of Western trade and technology transfer in recent Soviet foreign policy and domestic politics. Focusing on the late 1960s and 1970s, the first section analyzes the role of economic interchange in Soviet diplomacy toward the industrial democracies. It also explores the relationship between commerce with the West and Soviet internal policy, particularly policy toward economic reform. The second section discusses the political and bureaucratic groupings that favored the expansion of Soviet-Western economic cooperation during the detente period, as well as the groupings that were skeptical about the policy. Turning to the 1980s, the final section examines how Soviet decision makers have reacted to the tensions between the mounting Soviet need for Western agricultural and technological inputs, on the one hand, and the deterioration of Soviet-Western relations, on the other.

I. Policy in the 1960s and 1970s

The Brezhnev-Kosygin leadership's economic overtures to the West fitted into its broader foreign-policy calculations. In the late 1960s the USSR, engaged in a major arms buildup, was approaching strategic military parity with the United States. The American government's growing interest in nuclear arms control and its desire for Soviet assistance in facilitating a U.S. withdrawal from Vietnam offered the Soviet Union an opportunity to regulate the superpower military competition through arms negotiations. Failure to take advantage of this opportunity threatened to become especially costly once the Nixon Administration started to use improved U.S.-China relations to exert leverage on the USSR. Moreover, after the Soviet invasion of Czechoslovakia punctured West German hopes for an early loosening of Soviet influence in Eastern Europe, changes in the makeup of the West German governing coalition indicated that West Germany might accept the existence of the rival East

German regime as part of a broader diplomatic settlement in Central Europe, thereby satisfying one of the Soviet Union's principal postwar aims.

In these circumstances an economic opening to the West promised to serve Soviet foreign policy in several ways. Expanded trade, the Soviets believed, would create within the United States and the other industrial democracies a network of vested economic interests that would help ensure the permanence of detente. The influence of Western businessmen and workers with a material stake in East-West trade would help dampen any Western impulse to revert to hard-line foreign and military policies. No less important, wider commerce would buttress the Soviet client-states in Eastern Europe. Just as Western acceptance of East Germany and the East European status quo would enhance the international legitimacy of the Soviet order in the region, Western trade with Eastern Europe would yield greater domestic popularity for these regimes by contributing to a rise in their prosperity. It would also ease the mounting cost that the subsidization of the region was imposing on the Soviet economy.

The main purpose of the economic overtures, of course, was not to reinforce the USSR's diplomacy but to satisfy its domestic material needs. In the second half of the 1960s the Soviet leaders gradually recognized that their economy was experiencing a long-term slowdown attributable partially to the sluggish pace of technological advance in most nonmilitary sectors of industry. They also recognized that covert acquisition of Western technology, a policy that the USSR had long pursued in an effort to circumvent Western restrictions on Soviet access to a wide range of military and industrial goods, was insufficient to obtain the large infusion of advanced technology that might speed up the country's economic growth. Scarcely less significant were the needs of Soviet agriculture. Although Brezhnev and his associates committed an unprecedented share of total investment to the agricultural sector, the potentially disastrous agricultural shortfall of 1972 demonstrated the value of timely grain purchases from the West as a buffer against the sharp fluctuations in Soviet harvests. Such purchases, which became a regular feature of Soviet policy during the 1970s, were one means of fulfilling the Brezhnev Administration's commitment to steady increases in the Soviet consumer's standard of living—increases that were an important source of domestic political stability for the regime during the late 1960s and most of the 1970s.

As it emerged during the 1970s, the Soviet preference was for trade and detente with the industrial West as a whole. During 1969 and 1970 some Soviet leaders still advocated restricting the improvement of relations to Western Europe, in order to maximize the divisions within the NATO alliance.[1] But this approach had serious drawbacks. American cooperation was needed to resolve the status of West Berlin, which was a key to winning West German endorsement of a general European settlement and achieving a dramatic expansion of Soviet commerce with Western Europe.[2] Moreover, a policy of selective detente would hamper the negotiation of a strategic arms agreement with the United States and might accelerate the emerging American rapprochement with China. Thus the Soviet bid for detente, political and economic, was extended to the United States as well as to Western Europe and Japan. Although Soviet policy makers hoped that the process would exacerbate intra-Western differences, a deepening of such differences was not their main goal.

Most Soviet officials concluded that greater economic interchange with the West entailed political risks, but that these risks were acceptable. To begin with, Soviet national security had been substantially improved by the recent military buildup. Soviet analysts reasoned that the new Western interest in detente had been precipitated largely by the expansion of the USSR's military capabilities, and they assumed that further enlargement of those capabilities would continue to have a moderating effect on Western diplomacy. In addition, the architects of Soviet policy felt that the potential vulnerability of their system to external pressures was gradually diminishing. They pointed out that trade diversification would increase the USSR's ability to play off one Western country against another and that more trade would create Western, not just Soviet, dependence. They also suggested that the Soviet political system was strong enough domestically to withstand wider exposure to Western influences without suffering serious harm. Not least important, the Kremlin chiefs evidently felt that the invasion of Czechoslovakia had demonstrated their determination to maintain Soviet political hegemony in Eastern Europe and that this object lesson would help curb any tendency for expanded East European commerce with the West to erode the USSR's dominant position in the region.[3]

Although the Soviet leaders strongly resisted Western efforts to link expanded trade with Soviet political behavior, they tacitly accepted some linkages between trade and their domestic policies. While putting new pressures on the dissent movement, they allowed Soviet Germans to emigrate in exchange for widened trade with West Germany and they grudgingly permitted a dramatic increase in the emigration of Soviet Jews in return for the promise of expanded commerce with the United States.[4] The linkage of U.S. trade to Jewish emigration sparked disagreement within the party leadership and contributed to a veiled dispute over the relative importance of the USSR's domestic economic needs and its external political relations.[5] Nevertheless, Brezhnev and his allies implicitly accepted the connection between emigration and American trade. Only at the end of 1974, after it became clear that new legislation adopted by the U.S. Congress would impose a very low ceiling on American trade credits to the USSR, did they renounce this bargain.

While it is difficult to sort out the various factors shaping Soviet diplomacy during the early 1970s, the desire for Western trade and technology apparently exerted a moderating influence on some aspects of Soviet foreign policy as well. In his memoirs Henry Kissinger suggests that one motive for Soviet restraint in the Middle East during 1972 was the wish to purchase large quantities of American grain, and there is persuasive evidence that the Soviets made serious efforts to reduce the gap separating the U.S. and Soviet positions on how to settle the Mideast conflict. The Soviets did not abandon their search for influence in the area, but they did call for regional political and territorial accommodations that displeased their Arab allies and precipitated the expulsion of several thousand Soviet advisors from Egypt.[6] Economic motives were also among the factors that influenced Soviet policy toward the Vietnam war. After the U.S. stepped up military attacks on North Vietnam in May 1972, Brezhnev and his supporters overcame sharp internal Soviet opposition and met President Nixon to sign a package of agreements that included the SALT I treaty and accords covering bilateral economic and technological relations. The decision to receive Nixon in Moscow alarmed the North Vietnamese. Although it is uncertain whether the Soviets actually pressed them to make concessions in the Paris peace talks with the United States and South Vietnam, fragmentary evidence suggests that after the January 1973 signing of the Paris accords Soviet spokesmen counseled the North Vietnamese not to try for a quick military victory in the South. At about the same time the USSR, despite North Vietnamese requests, stopped supplying the North with weapons, making it necessary for the North Vietnamese leadership to postpone plans for a major new offensive against South Vietnam. In December 1974, when the prospects for a dramatic expansion of U.S.-Soviet trade were eliminated by Congressional enactment of the ceiling on American credits, the USSR resumed the weapons shipments, which permitted North Vietnam to proceed with the large-scale offensive that toppled the South Vietnamese regime.[7]

In such instances, Soviet willingness to accept implicit linkages between trade and Soviet political behavior depended on how the prospective economic benefits fitted into a larger balance of political opportunities and risks. Although the decision to allow Jewish emigration posed the neuralgic issue of allowing another country to judge and influence Soviet domestic policies, the decision promised to garner large economic gains and help improve other aspects of U.S.-Soviet relations as well. In the Middle East and Vietnam, the USSR gave diplomatic ground because the desire for American trade was buttressed both by the encouraging prospect of further U.S.-Soviet arms-control agreements and by the worrisome possibilities of a de facto Sino-American alliance and superpower confrontations in the Third World.

By 1975, however, the balance of benefits and costs had shifted. The initial Soviet hope for massive economic gains from commerce with the United States had been disappointed, while completion of the European diplomatic settlement had provided alternative Western partners who were reluctant to link trade to Soviet foreign policy. Moreover, President Ford, whose control over U.S. diplomacy had already been weakened by the Congressional reaction against the Vietnam and Watergate crises, was coming under fire from conservative Republicans determined to defeat him during the forthcoming Presidential primaries. These internal American developments clouded the prospects for completing a SALT II agreement, and they reassured previously fearful Soviet observers that there were definite limits on the ability of U.S. policy makers to sacrifice the interests of Taiwan and deepen the rapprochement with China.[8] Finally, the United States, though unable to mount effective resistance to Soviet involvement in Angola or to North Vietnam's renewed assault on the South, was engaged in Third World maneuvers of its own. Apart from helping bring down the Allende regime in Chile, the U.S. made an assiduous effort to exclude Soviet influence from the Middle East—an effort that achieved considerable success.[9] In these circumstances, the makers of Soviet foreign policy were not inclined to temper their diplomacy in exchange for Western trade and technology.

The Soviet pursuit of detente with the West created two potential connections between foreign economic relations and domestic economic policy. The first was between Soviet-Western trade and the economy's sectoral and regional structure. The greater the willingness of the regime to force the expansion of efficient economic sectors and cut back inefficient ones, the greater the gains from trade. Such changes would, however, require major alterations in the relative priority accorded to particular economic branches and regions—alterations about which the representatives of those parts of the economy would have strong feelings. There would, of course, be economic winners as well as losers, but such structural adjustments were still likely to be difficult. Moreover, real specialization in trade with the West would heighten Soviet vulnerability to politically motivated disruptions of trade, and this risk would be a source of concern for many members of the political elite.

The second possible connection between foreign economic relations and the domestic economy was between trade (including technology transfer) and domestic institutional change. It has become a commonplace to say that the political authorities attempted to make the economic opening to the West a substitute for internal economic reform. Although this proposition contains an element of truth, the real state of affairs is more complex and has changed over time. In the early years of the

Brezhnev-Kosygin administration, some top officials claimed that economic reform and expanded involvement in the world economy should go together, because reform was necessary to obtain a satisfactory economic yield from commerce with the West. For instance, Kosygin, who until the late 1960s was the most vigorous Politburo proponent of wider economic relations with the West, advocated decentralizing industry and relying more heavily on financial levers to guide the economy. In the mid-1960s Brezhnev, who was still skeptical of the wisdom of an economic opening to the West, opposed any devolution of authority to lower levels of the economic system.[10] Thus during much of the decade, major changes in foreign economic policy and domestic economic institutions tended to be regarded as complementary measures rather than alternatives. Khrushchev's successors took their first steps toward wider reliance on Western technology at the same time that they introduced limited reforms in the organization of industry and agriculture. These reforms occurred in 1965, when the regime was negotiating a pioneering deal to purchase a huge automobile plant from the Fiat Company and was beginning to conclude agreements for scientific and technical cooperation with Western governments. The internal pressure for further economic decentralization did not diminish significantly until near the end of the 1960s.

After 1968, as Brezhnev assumed a dominant role in the formation of domestic policy, the regime did move much closer to substituting Western commerce for the pursuit of major internal reforms. Brezhnev never ceased to urge that the economy's performance be improved through partial modifications of the administrative system, and he argued this point with enough force that he annoyed some other Politburo members.[11] But he shied away from proposing a significant decentralization of economic power that would expand the role of market forces. Instead he advocated improved central planning and the formation of large associations of enterprises as solutions to the economy's deficiencies. Many Soviet economists continued to doubt that this mix of internal administrative rationalization and expanded commerce with the West could stem the decline of the economy's dynamism. Nevertheless, during the 1970s official policy increasingly amounted to a wager on external economic ties and an abandonment of serious efforts at internal reform.

Although the regime anticipated large economic benefits from expanded interchange with the West, it also strove to limit the day-to-day interaction of Soviet society with Western organizations and specialists. Against the advice of some economists, it maintained the centralized apparatus for the administration of foreign trade, rather than restructure that apparatus to permit more direct contacts between Western suppliers and Soviet end-users of imports. While this arrangement ensured the government's ability to control the evolution of foreign economic relations and counter the Western manipulation of internal Soviet economic interests, it also perpetuated one of the most serious barriers to effective trade with the West.

Similarly, the political authorities allowed only slow growth in person-to-person exchanges, which constitute an important vehicle for the transmission of technical knowledge, out of a fear that such exchanges might undermine the loyalty of Soviet citizens. The party leaders were willing to accept the risk of a limited increase in human contacts with the West but were equally determined to keep the process from getting out of hand. Although Soviet society became more accessible to outsiders in the 1970s than previously, it remained a closed society by Western standards. Domestic Soviet barriers slowed the assimilation of Western scientific and technical literature and had an especially deleterious impact on the acquisition of Western know-how through personal communication. At the end of the decade, a systematic survey found that international scientific and technical meetings held in the USSR attracted less than one-fifth as many papers by foreigners as did comparable meetings in the United States. Even more striking, the number of Soviet researchers who were able to travel abroad to present papers and participate in international meetings was less than one-twentieth of the American number.[12] These figures indicate that the flow of technical information between Western and Soviet experts in many specialties continued to be seriously inhibited by inadequate communications and personal contact.

II. Decision Making and Policy Groups

This mix of policies, which emerged from vigorous internal discussions within the Soviet elite, was not the product of a thoroughgoing elite consensus. Inside the Soviet regime there have long been different schools of thought on the advisability of economic relations with the West. Some officials have regarded expanded commerce as a rational policy entailing minimal political risks and offering substantial advantages. Others have viewed wider interchange with the West as a political liability in the harsh military competition between the capitalist and socialist worlds.[13] The post-Khrushchev opening to the West represented a shift in the balance of elite opinion on this question. Some of those who had been skeptics became genuinely convinced of the wisdom of the new course, but others simply gave ground out of political necessity.

During the late 1960s and early 1970s differences over these points reached into the Politburo. Brezhnev, freshly convinced of the need for detente with Western Europe and the United States, had to overcome resistance from other Politburo members in order to inaugurate a major expansion of Soviet-Western commerce.[14] The picture of the top leaders' attitudes during the rest of the 1970s is less clear, because the leaders' statements have not been analyzed as closely for this period as for the earlier years. Western observers differ over whether interchange with the West continued to provoke disagreements at the apex of the political system.[15] In any case, if top-level differences did persist, they were much less public and less intense than those of the early 1970s.

Soviet policy toward interchange with the West has not been shaped solely by the members of the Politburo. The various political and economic bureaucracies, which gained increasing political weight under Brezhnev, have also had an impact. It should be said that the bureaucratic analysis of Soviet policy making poses analytical pitfalls that cannot be taken fully into account in a chapter of this length.[16] To cite only one difficulty, the officials of a particular bureaucracy may not agree with one another about which policy position follows logically from the organization's official responsibilities. But if we accept that majority and minority views may frequently coexist inside each bureaucracy, we can begin to identify the coalitions of officials, or policy groups, that have favored and opposed expanded interchange with the West.[17] Knowledge of the functional responsibilities of the various bureaucracies can help us discern the attitude that most, although not all, officials in each organization are likely to adopt.

According to Soviet accounts, most decisions about Western trade and technology transfer begin formally when the State Planning Commission (Gosplan) issues planning guidelines to the country's many economic agencies.[18] Although these guidelines are heavily influenced by the recommendations of central economic officials and science administrators, they undoubtedly incorporate the Politburo's judgments about the wider military, diplomatic, and political implications of alternative levels of Soviet-Western interchange. Officials of the Ministry of Foreign Affairs and the Ministry of Defense thus have a basis for influencing the guidelines because they can claim foreign-policy expertise and because both Ministers have been Politburo members since 1973. It is a fair guess that the KGB, the political police agency whose chief also belongs to the Politburo, expresses its views about the likely domestic political impact of proposed levels of contact with the West.

Several central planning organizations approach choices about Western economic relations in terms of narrower economic and technical criteria. These planning bodies include Gosplan itself, the State Committee on Science and Technology, the Academy of Sciences, the Ministry of Foreign Trade, and the Ministry of Finance. Also involved in the decision-making process are the numerous industrial and agricultural ministries that make recommendations on the acquisition of foreign goods and technology and actually apply Western know-how once it has been imported.[19]

In addition, regional officials, particularly republican and provincial party secretaries, have a bureaucratic stake in the level of economic interchange with the West. Soviet regions differ significantly in their relative dependence on exports and imports.[20] The local benefits or liabilities of East-West interchange are probably one determinant, although not necessarily the most important, of the views that regional officials adopt toward the trade targets proposed in draft economic plans. In individual cases such economic considerations have apparently affected these officials' attitudes toward broader foreign-policy issues as well.[21]

Each of these bureaucracies has official responsibilities and concerns that predispose it to look at Soviet-Western commerce in a particular light. The Ministry of Foreign Affairs is interested in diversifying its means of influencing foreign governments. Among the main foreign-policy agencies, the Ministry is probably the one that attaches greatest significance to using "reasonable" elements in Western states to neutralize "reactionary" groups hostile to the USSR. For this purpose, the promise of expanded economic interchange (or, occasionally, the threat of cutbacks) is a valuable tool. The lure of stepped-up commerce is a means of appealing both to Western business interests and to members of the general public concerned about reducing levels of unemployment in the West. Such economic themes have appeared regularly in the diplomatic pronouncements of the Minister of Foreign Affairs and his advisors.

The Soviet military, by contrast, has been unenthusiastic about expanded exchanges and commerce with the West. Western commentators have frequently suggested that the military establishment supported detente partly because it was eager to obtain advanced Western technology through commercial and academic channels. However, the available published evidence does not bear out this view. In the heyday of detente, some relatively junior officers did endorse wider trade with the West. But senior commanders kept silent on this subject even in circumstances where an endorsement would have been natural, and some military theorists warned against excessive dependence on Western sources of technology.[22] Evidently Soviet military leaders, like military officials in other powerful countries, feared that extensive economic relations with rival regimes would undermine their country's freedom of strategic maneuver. Moreover, they were determined to block the most ardent Soviet proponents of detente, who favored a curb on Soviet military expenditures as part of a comprehensive reduction of East-West tensions.[23] In cases where domestic R&D could not match the sophistication of Western weaponry, defense planners must have been happy to obtain valuable foreign military technology through covert channels. But there is little evidence that they wanted to enlarge Soviet reliance on commercial avenues of technology transfer. Perhaps they thought that even in an atmosphere of detente, the Western military technology they most desired could not be gotten past Western export controls and would still have to be sought through illegal means.

Some officials of the KGB have also expressed skepticism about larger commercial and cultural exchanges with the West. The covert acquisition of Western technology has long been one of the KGB's justifications for existence. Although members of the organization may have favored foreign business deals that gave special promise of concealing collateral thefts of Western technology, a substantial widening of overt interchanges with the West threatened to reduce the importance of the KGB both as a gatherer of foreign technology and as a mechanism of domestic political control. Much of the organization's bureaucratic power rests on its charter to maintain Soviet state secrets and defend the country against foreign subversion. KGB officials have frequently warned against the dangers entailed by extensive personal contacts between Soviet and Western specialists, and they have gone out of their way to rebut other officials—for example, spokesmen of the Academy of Sciences—who have downplayed this danger.[24] This suggests that most KGB representatives have tended to interpret economic detente narrowly and have made administrative decisions that inhibit the person-based transfer of Western technology through open channels.

Most of the central state agencies directly responsible for planning Western trade and technology transfers have favored such transactions—although they, too, have sought to protect their particular institutional prerogatives. Leaders of Gosplan have usually supported more interchange with the West because it is one means of reducing the overall resource demands on the planning system. During the 1970s the State Committee for Science and Technology and the Academy of Sciences both advocated wider Soviet-Western exchanges of specialists, but both strove to avoid the selective cutbacks in domestic R&D expenditures that would have been one of the gains from the utilization of Western technology. Moreover, although many of the Academy's social scientists were committed supporters of the economic opening to the West, at least one high Academy official warned against over-reliance on Western industrial equipment.[25] Not surprisingly, officials of the Ministry of Foreign Trade vigorously championed wider Western trade and argued that the political risks of such trade had declined. But out of institutional self-interest they also waged a determined battle, largely successful, to prevent any relaxation of the central controls that were hampering the effective use of equipment and know-how imported from the West.[26] Officials of the Ministry of Finance were evidently more cautious about the scale of Western equipment imports. The Ministry bore chief responsibility for protecting the Soviet balance-of-payments position, and the nature of the tax system gave the organization a preference for imported consumer goods, which contribute more to the state budget than imported producer goods.[27] Informed Western analysts believe that the Ministry's financial and banking officials were among those who argued successfully in 1976 that the growth of imports from the West should be slowed in order to correct a mounting balance-of-payment deficit in hard-currency transactions.[28]

The attitudes of the production ministries toward Western trade have been divided. The Ministry of Agriculture has probably welcomed imports of Western agricultural commodities as a buffer against bad harvests because these imports have not been accompanied by any reduction in the high investment priority attached to agriculture since the mid-1960s. A number of industrial ministries have been eager to import Western machinery to replace inferior machinery supplied by Soviet manufacturers. Probably the most prominent examples are the oil, gas, and chemical industries. But the machine-building ministries wear a second hat, as the producers of equipment for other ministries, and in this capacity they have sometimes resisted technological imports, which threaten the domestic seller's market that otherwise insulates them from competition. For example, a spokesman of the Ministry of Heavy, Power, and Transport Machine-building complained that his ministry's customers were allegedly biased in favor of Western imports and against the ministry's products.[29] Such resistance can be significant, because when ministries and republics apply to the planning agencies for machinery imports, they must present a certification "by the relevant machinery-building ministry that a comparable machine cannot be produced domestically in sufficient quantity." Knowledgeable Soviet specialists have stated that "the bureaucratic or political position of the importer is particularly important in this certification procedure."[30] No doubt officials of a top-priority sector can override resistance from domestic manufacturers. But potential importers lower in the political scale may not be able to do so.

The regional officials involved in economic planning also have divergent perspectives on the level of economic interchange with the West. Regions slated to be developed with the aid of large quantities of Western technology will receive new political prominence and an influx of the complementary domestic investment and manpower resources needed to build large installations. This may not automatically convince local officials that Western imports and technical assistance are desirable. They must also take into account factors such as the risk of political contamination through contacts with Westerners, which has obviously worried local party officials in metropolitan centers like Leningrad and Moscow.[31] But most party and state officials, who usually attach high value to economic growth, are likely to desire Western imports. Officials in regions that will be bypassed by such import plans, however, may oppose the plans—not just because of the loss of the imports but because of the diversion of the domestic resources needed to make use of them. Since 1972 the government has increasingly allocated resources among regions to meet national economic needs rather than foster regional equality and has taken fuller account of foreign-trade considerations in making such decisions.[32] This policy has produced some large material setbacks for parts of European Russia and for Central Asia, which have lost out to Siberia and the Far East in the bidding for new investment.[33] It has also added an element of interregional competition to national decisions about Soviet-Western trade and technology transfers, as we shall see below.

III. New Pressures in the 1980s

Events in the early 1980s put new pressures on Soviet policy toward Western trade and on the political coalition supporting the policy. The hardening American attitude toward the USSR, particularly after the Soviet invasion of Afghanistan at the end of 1979, produced an accelerated expansion of American military capabilities and a new American emphasis on the importance of military power in international affairs. At the same time, the invasion of Afghanistan provoked vigorous American steps to restrict the flow of grain and industrial technology to the USSR. By eroding the sense of enhanced Soviet national security that the party leadership had come to associate with detente, these American policies posed questions about the USSR's ability to keep tensions with the West at a manageable level that made rapid expansion of East-West commerce consistent with the dictates of prudence. Of course, Soviet policy makers could take consolation from the thought that American efforts to stiffen international opposition to the USSR might deepen the divisions in the West and facilitate a selective Soviet detente with Western Europe and Japan. The half-hearted initial Western response to the U.S. campaign for trade restrictions argued in favor of this line of action. However, the 1979 NATO decision to move toward European deployment of American intermediate-range nuclear rockets also raised the possibility that the Western allies might be more capable of coordinating their external policies than had previously been supposed—a possibility that called into doubt the wisdom of relying economically on almost any of the major capitalist countries. As in the formative period of detente from 1968 to 1972, decisions about foreign economic relations became closely intertwined with broader decisions about Soviet national security.

Events in Poland also had a powerful effect on Soviet thinking. The Polish crisis dramatically illustrated the cul-de-sac into which indiscriminate reliance on Western credits and imports could lead a socialist state. Whereas one aim of detente had been to gain tacit Western aid in the political and economic stabilization of Soviet control over Eastern Europe, the economic opening to the West now seemed a potential recipe for political disintegration and greater Western diplomatic leverage in the region. Although Poland was far more dependent on Western trade and credits than was the Soviet Union, the Polish crisis produced pressures to cut back the USSR's own economic dealings with the West.

There were, however, contrary internal pressures at work on Soviet policy. The lessons of the Polish crisis were ambiguous. If the crisis demonstrated the danger of dependence on the West, it also suggested that failure to sustain steady increases in consumption could contribute to political upheavals capable of destroying a communist regime. By the start of the 1980s the Soviet leadership was encountering increasing difficulty in maintaining the steady growth of consumption that had been a hallmark of the earlier Brezhnev years. Agriculture, in particular, was performing poorly, even though the regime continued to channel a very large share of total investment into the sector. In 1979–81 the country experienced three disappointing harvests in a row and could compensate for the losses only through large purchases of Western grain. Meanwhile, due to a continuing decline of the rate of innovation in the machine-building branches, the country's need for Western industrial technology had also increased. One logical answer to these internal needs was to widen Soviet reliance on Western imports and to expand Soviet energy exports to pay for the Western goods.

These new pressures did not all come into play simultaneously. Initially the Soviet leadership expected that the American campaign for Western economic retaliation against the invasion of Afghanistan would have little long-term effect. For almost two years Brezhnev persisted in the belief that East-West commerce, like East-West relations in general, could be restored essentially to the status quo ante. While adamantly refusing Western demands for the withdrawal of Soviet forces from Afghanistan, he predicted that divisions within the Western alliance and inside the United States would defeat the drive to cut back economic ties with the USSR. After the Polish crisis exploded in the summer of 1980, Brezhnev did note that it was necessary to follow "a balanced, realistic policy in foreign economic relations," but he plainly meant this as a lesson for Eastern Europe rather than the USSR. Emphasizing the domestic political importance of sustaining high levels of consumption,

Brezhnev acknowledged the Soviet regime's difficulties in supplying the population with food and indicated that both internal resources and foreign trade would be used to alleviate the problem. Nor did he attempt to chart a path away from large purchases of Western grain over the long term. Instead, he put very strong emphasis on the accelerated development of the gas industry, thereby shifting further from the relatively autarkic fuel policy pursued by the regime until the late 1970s, and remarked that the rapid development of the Siberian gas fields could supply both internal needs and exports, including exports to capitalist countries.[34] Although there were oblique hints of possible dissatisfaction within the Politburo over Brezhnev's plans for gas exports, no Politburo member publicly disputed his general prognosis for relations with the West.[35]

A number of economic bureaucrats and foreign-affairs specialists welcomed Brezhnev's reaffirmation of the Soviet commitment to Western trade and technology. The Chairman of Gosplan firmly backed the development of Siberian energy and raw-materials exports as a means of financing Western imports.[36] A top official of the Ministry of Foreign Trade praised the expansion of East-West commerce in the 1970s and asserted that it was "extremely important" to remember that the world trend toward greater technological exchange had "a long-term character."[37] Prominent industrial officials, while adopting a cautious stance in the light of the Western embargoes, obliquely signalled a continuing interest in Western inputs for their industries. The Minister of Gas Industry, for instance, expressed strong worry over the ability of the Soviet turbine and machine-building industries to meet the energy program's needs. Although he said nothing directly about East-West ties, this amounted to an indirect endorsement of reliance on Western suppliers for pipeline and other energy technology.[38] Economists and foreign-policy experts in the Academy of Sciences expressed the view that Western economic self-interest would ultimately defeat the embargoes, even in the United States, and they denied that acceptance of Western credits entailed any "special risk," since the credits fulfilled Western as well as Eastern economic needs.[39]

On the other hand, a few middle-level officials argued for less utilization of Western technology. Academy President Aleksandrov observed that "it is often simpler to order a purchase or two abroad, but the present situation shows that it is necessary for us to concentrate on making our country completely independent of any and all foreign deliveries." Although the USSR was "quite capable" of doing this, said Aleksandrov in an unusually clear reference to difficulties caused by the Western embargoes, "at times situations turn out to be quite dire."[40] Aleksandrov, who was closely involved in planning the future composition of Soviet energy production, had previously shown less enthusiasm for the expansion of gas than of coal and atomic power, and he may conceivably have harbored doubts about large-scale gas exports to the West as well as about Western imports.[41] Framing the issue more narrowly, the Minister of Energy Machine-building claimed that the Ministry of Gas Industry had obstructed tests of domestic compressors for gas pipelines and that Gosplan had shortchanged the development of domestic equipment while doling out hard currency for Western machinery.[42]

Despite such complaints, however, Brezhnev showed no inclination to revise the policies he had pursued during the 1970s. He told the Central Committee that foreign commerce would provide "a large reserve" for improving the economy's effectiveness, and he called for "all economic leaders to fulfill more responsibly the decisions adopted in this area" by the party and government. Offering an assurance that a recent "clarification" of West Siberian reserves had revealed plentiful supplies of gas and oil, Brezhnev indicated his opposition to any slowdown in the growth of energy production and pointedly named the several ministers who were responsible for meeting domestic fuel requirements and ensuring adequate exports to the Western market. He called the six gas pipelines under construction—specifically including the Urengoi-Uzhgorod export line—"the central construction projects of the five-year plan" and demanded that they be completed on schedule. He also urged the ministers of the oil, chemical, and mineral fertilizer industries to guarantee the timely commissioning of installations being constructed under compensation agreements with foreign partners.[43]

Rising international tensions, however, put new strains on Brezhnev's policies. The workability of Soviet-Western detente, including its economic component, depended on the maintenance of stable relations with the United States or on the willingness of other major Western countries to resist American policy. As the Reagan Administration launched an accelerated military buildup, worried Soviet military officers expressed reservations about the effectiveness of countering the buildup by playing off Western Europe against the United States and also hinted at doubts about the feasibility of gaining trade benefits by manipulating intra-Western disagreements. First Deputy Minister of Defense Ogarkov, in an article urging a large increase in defense spending, paid lip service to the party slogan of relaxing international tensions. However, he said nothing about developing mutually beneficial economic ties with the industrial capitalist states; he remarked only that the USSR was developing cooperative ties with the "majority of countries of the globe." Brezhnev and other spokesmen had expressed the belief that political opposition and intergovernmental differences in the West would undermine the economic sanctions, and they argued that the decision of the newly elected Reagan Administration to lift the U.S.

partial grain embargo validated this proposition. Ogarkov, on the other hand, insisted that the West's "various types of actions and diversions" against the socialist bloc had "a coordinated character" and were linked by a "single design" for subverting the socialist system.[44] While there were Western differences over trade with the East, said another officer, since World War II the main world contradiction had been between the socialist and capitalist camps. The Western powers were driven toward unity by their hostility toward socialism, and the greater the might of the USSR and its allies, the more pronounced such hostility would become.[45] This view, which conflicted with the notion of many foreign-affairs specialists that the fissures within the West were deepening, implied that an expansion of Soviet-Western commerce on the assumption that the capitalist states could not act in concert against the USSR would be a mistake. It was part of an emerging disagreement between officials who stressed the continuing utility of diplomatic maneuver and bargaining in East-West relations and others who believed that military power had now become the only reliable means of countering challenges from the capitalist world.[46]

The expression of such apprehensions about trade with the West evoked a sympathetic response from some party leaders. During April 1982 Iurii Andropov, in a comment that foreshadowed the strong interest in economic reform that he revealed after becoming head of the party, remarked that economic relations with the West were no substitute for domestic solutions to economic problems.[47] Under harsh pressure from imperialism, said Andropov, the building of socialism in the USSR "proceeds through the overcoming of internal difficulties. . . . As master of his country the Soviet person . . . [recognizes] that we can solve existing problems only with our own efforts. This concerns above all the overcoming of the lag of agriculture. . . ."[48] Other elements of Andropov's speech, particularly his accent on the manipulation of intra-Western disagreements to attain Soviet ends, make it doubtful that he was calling for a fundamental cutback in economic relations with the West. More probably he adopted this economic stance partly for tactical political reasons. By making an economic argument that appealed to Soviet conservatives on national-security grounds, he was apparently striving to gain the upper hand over Konstantin Chernenko, the ailing Brezhnev's preferred successor, who continued to advocate extensive economic ties between East and West.[49]

Whatever Andropov's motives, some elite members, deeply upset by the Polish crisis, opposed trade with the West for more than tactical reasons. About a month after the Reagan Administration countered the Polish declaration of martial law by curbing credits to Poland and embargoing exports of pipeline technology to the USSR, Kommunist ran an article by a Czechoslovak author who asserted that the West engaged in trade with the East for one of two reasons—either to destabilize the socialist regimes or to retard their economic development. There was no room in this picture for Western groups interested in trade for trade's sake; nor was there any differentiation among the aims of various Western countries. The enemies of socialism, remarked the author, were deeply dissatisfied with the position of the Czechoslovak politician Bilak, who had proclaimed that "to be indebted to the capitalist West would be the same as a Christian's selling his soul to the devil."[50] This claim, which went far beyond Brezhnev's recognition of the need for a balanced policy in East-West commerce, suggests that Soviet conservatives were striving to publicize their doubts about interchange with the capitalist world by airing the views of like-minded East Europeans.[51]

By 1982 the issue of the level of Soviet-Western economic interchange had become entangled not only with general foreign-policy questions but with the allocation of domestic resources. Energy and agriculture were Brezhnev's top priorities, and they threatened to absorb the lion's share of the investment pie at a time when other budgetary claimants were becoming increasingly assertive. As Brezhnev continued to push for the enactment of an expensive new Food Program, some planning officials began to argue that the country could not continue to invest in both energy and agriculture at current rates, and political controversy over the allocation of resources between Siberia and other regions intensified.[52] Shortly after the United States cut off shipments of energy technology to the USSR, the main party journal, following Brezhnev's lead, called for "heroic efforts" to ensure that enough energy was produced for export. Nonetheless, proponents of the gas program had to repeat their public justification of the "enormous expenditures" required for gas exploration and rebut the anonymous officials who "sometimes . . . say that we are handing over too much gas" to the West.[53] As for Brezhnev's proposed agricultural investments, military officials resisted them both before and after the announcement of the Food Program in May 1982.[54]

The disagreements over foreign policy and domestic resource allocation affected Brezhnev's public position on commerce with the capitalist world. In announcing the Food Program, Brezhnev sought to placate the critics by claiming that implementation of the program would help reduce food imports and would thereby protect the USSR against Western efforts to exert political leverage through trade.[55] Viewed as a reaction to Western restrictions on grain trade with the USSR, the statement was anachronistic. The Reagan Administration had lifted the U.S. partial grain embargo in April 1981 and had not reimposed it as part of the curb on American technology transfers adopted after the Polish declaration of martial law. Moreover, while the grain embargo had been in effect Brezhnev had never suggested that it required Soviet agriculture to become more self-sufficient. Brezhnev's statement did make sense, though, as a response to the continuing deterioration of the superpower relationship, exemplified by the American effort in the summer of 1982 to compel Western Europe to join the American embargo on transfers of pipeline technology to the USSR, and as a response to criticism from elements of the Soviet elite. In the fall, when Brezhnev met with a group of disgruntled Soviet officers to discuss possible increases in the defense budget, he told the audience that Soviet industry was "capable of creating everything necessary, depending almost entirely on its own native material and raw materials base," and that a great deal of work was being done to avoid purchases of grain from the West "in the long run."[56] Brezhnev's comment about industry may have been intended to counter the criticism that the country had made itself politically vulnerable by relying on Western assistance in developing its energy resources. His remark about agriculture was obviously meant to persuade the officers that high spending on agriculture served the country's foreign-policy requirements. In order to assuage the military's fears about national security and to justify his domestic programs, Brezhnev was taking a more autarkic line on East-West economic relations than he had taken since at least the mid-1960s.

After Andropov's selection to succeed Brezhnev as party leader, disagreements over diplomatic and economic strategy toward the West continued. Although the speeches of Andropov and most other Politburo members revealed no obvious discrepancies on this question, there were plainly strong private disagreements within the party leadership. Early in 1983 Marshal Ogarkov published a new appeal for stepped-up military spending and hinted that attempts to split the West by diplomatic means had little value in protecting the USSR from external military threats. Although Ogarkov mentioned the unprecedented scale of the contemporary antiwar movement in the West, he also contended that in the 1930s other countries had turned aside Soviet efforts to contain Nazi Germany, and he remarked that "in recent years, in a way similar to the 1930s, the world has become uneasy." In the USSR, just as in the West, analogies between Nazi Germany and contemporary states often play a role in foreign-policy debates, and Ogarkov probably meant to suggest that relying on some imperialists (such as the West Europeans) to restrain others (such as the Americans) was a dangerous tactic. Saying that the United States and its NATO partners were trying to turn back the wheel of history, he took no note of the existence of "realistic" Western political leaders or of differences between the NATO countries, and this accent on Western political solidarity spilled over into his comments on East-West economic relations. Avoiding any mention of the intra-Western economic tensions so often discussed by the proponents of commerce with the West, Ogarkov argued that the NATO countries were

pursuing "in essence a real economic . . . war" against the USSR. In view
of the Western military threat Ogarkov claimed to discern, it seems fair
to conclude that he meant this phrase to suggest that commercial dealings with the West increased the risks to Soviet national security.[57]

About a month later, Foreign Minister Gromyko published an article that took a very different line toward Soviet security requirements
and diplomatic strategy toward the West. The article was plainly intended to counter arguments from some persons for a more confrontational policy toward the NATO countries. Among its many striking
features were its unambiguous defense of the achievements of detente
during the 1970s, its lack of references to the recent worsening of East-
West relations, and its numerous allusions to misconceptions about the
Leninist approach to foreign policy. Gromyko hailed Lenin for saving
the country from hot-headed party members who had wanted to make
"accusatory speeches" and declarations about the inevitability of war at
international conferences. Lenin's observations on particular countries
were a valuable guide in developing a "differentiated policy" toward the
contemporary United States, West Germany, and other imperialist countries, and Lenin had waged an "uncompromising struggle" against party
radicals who wanted to risk Soviet security in the name of foreign revolution. If the USSR had not taken a Leninist approach to intra-Western
contradictions, said Gromyko, it would have been impossible to form the
Allied coalition against the Nazis—a coalition that, despite its internal
frictions, offered an example of cooperation between states from different social systems. The contrast with Ogarkov's view of intra-Western
relations and diplomacy during the 1930s was hard to miss.

In keeping with his belief in the utility of flexible diplomacy,
Gromyko emphasized the economic aspects of foreign policy and their
relation to domestic needs. Recalling Lenin's words that the USSR exerts
its main influence on the world revolutionary process through its economic policy, he effusively praised the skills of the Soviet diplomatic
corps but did not mention the military establishment or the importance
of military power. Lenin, said Gromyko, had attached large significance
to the use of economic levers in diplomacy because trade with the West
facilitated the fastest possible growth of the Soviet economy and gave the
West a material stake in good relations. Arguing forcefully that domestic
and foreign policy were integrally related, the Foreign Minister pointed
out that Lenin had repudiated the notion that foreign and domestic
policy were separable. Gromyko appeared to be suggesting that Soviet
foreign policy should take account of the country's domestic need for
detente, and that the regime could count on the domestic economic
needs of Western countries to temper their policies toward the USSR.[58]
Here, too, his views contrasted sharply with Ogarkov's belief that the
West was waging a "real economic war" against the Soviet Union.

Gromyko's article, which appeared shortly after the Soviet government failed to undermine NATO's scheduled intermediate-range missile deployments through political manipulation of the West German parliamentary elections, shows that the Soviet proponents of differentiated policies toward various NATO countries were on the defensive. They were still in control of Soviet policy. Gromyko was promoted to First Deputy Chairman of the Council of Ministers about the time his article was published, and in the summer of 1983 the USSR signed a new long-term grain agreement with the United States. Apart from its economic benefits, the agreement, which committed the U.S. not to impose a new embargo, must have appealed to leaders such as Gromyko because it would amplify the intra-Western strains caused by any further U.S. efforts to force cuts in West European and Japanese technology transfers to the USSR. Nevertheless, the tone of Gromyko's article shows that the Soviet advocates of a harder and less differentiated line toward the West were arguing their case vigorously in private.

Although individual Soviet scholars continued to advocate wider economic relations with the West, the elite's mounting concern about national-security issues had a marked impact on the analyses of the question that appeared in leading party and governmental publications. The fullest and probably most authoritative discussion appeared in two articles by O. Bogomolov. In an article on the future of CMEA published in the main party journal, Bogomolov stated that commerce with the capitalist world remained economically desirable and that the members of the bloc were striving to avoid a weakening of East-West economic ties. However, he said, the international situation was sliding back toward cold war, and under the pressure of events the bloc's approach to such ties might undergo "definite changes." The present international tensions made it essential to ensure "the necessary technical-economic independence from the capitalist market" for every CMEA country. "The risk of industrial cooperation with Western firms has been manifested with all obviousness," said Bogomolov, and "it is necessary to approach this cooperation more cautiously."[59] Echoing the rising sentiment among liberal Soviet economists for a substantial decentralization of the economy, Bogomolov added that the international situation required the socialist states to follow through on the "more radical" domestic economic reforms that were currently emerging.[60]

The basic thrust of Bogomolov's analysis was that commerce with capitalist countries should be channeled into forms involving less long-term dependence on Western imports and that CMEA members should step up their own cooperative research and production efforts. Future interchange with the West should entail fewer imports of products like pipe and grain and focus on obtaining the means to produce such products domestically.[61] Given the sanctions adopted by the Reagan Administration, the machine-building branches supplying equipment for large pipelines, agriculture, and other sectors should expand faster. In the same vein, Bogomolov counseled more caution in purchasing Western licenses. At one point, he held out the hope that the other socialist countries could help develop the large stock of Soviet basic scientific knowledge into operational technology. At another point, however, he suggested that Western Europe might aid the whole socialist bloc in developing and applying underutilized native technical ideas.[62] Perhaps this contradiction reflected the debate about whether the West was a cohesive political and economic entity that required a fairly uniform Soviet trade policy, or whether it was a collection of disparate countries to which sharply differentiated trade policies could successfully be applied. In any case, Bogomolov's gravitation toward a more conservative view of commerce with the West was a barometer of the changing mood inside the Soviet elite. Three years earlier, he had all but advocated establishing enterprises in the USSR with joint Soviet-Western ownership.[63]

IV. Conclusion

Although the experience of the last fifteen years has tempered the Soviet regime's initial optimism about the economic yield from expanded commerce with the West, its increasing wariness toward such interchange has less to do with economic than with political calculations. Heightened tensions with the United States and uncertainty about Soviet-West European relations have persuaded most members of the elite that they must be more cautious in economic dealings with the West. The dominant element within the leadership has clung to the hope that the Western countries can be played off against each other, thereby allowing a continuation of significant economic interchange with some parts of the capitalist world. Nevertheless, the wisdom and feasibility of counting on such intra-Western tensions have been challenged by officials concerned about Soviet national security, and the regime has proclaimed reduced dependence on agricultural imports as a long-term goal. While agriculture is evidently the sector in which the leadership feels most vulnerable, it has similar worries about other sectors. Despite what a Western observer might expect, the Reagan Administration's termination of the partial grain embargo and later abandonment of efforts to block the Soviet-West European gas pipeline have not allayed these fears.

In gauging how such fears will affect future Soviet policy toward commerce with the West, observers must consider the regime's internal circumstances as well as its foreign-policy concerns. A drastic change might be likely if the party authorities were willing to pay the domestic

political price for sacrificing access to Western agricultural and technological inputs. If the authorities were willing to accept a sharp decline
of popular consumption, they might terminate agricultural imports. But
the current leaders seem committed to further increases in popular
welfare, partly because they are apprehensive about the potential impact
of a decline of welfare on the stability of the political system. Although
some elite members evidently support a cutback in consumption as one
answer to the country's economic dilemmas, this view has not received
open support from any top leader. During his brief tenure as party chief,
Andropov, who was perceived in the West as the apostle of a harsh new
labor discipline, also spoke with unusual openness about the political
risks posed by the regime's internal social problems.[64] Andropov seemed
to favor a redistribution of consumer goods to spur labor productivity,
rather than a sharp reduction in the overall level of consumption. Since
1980, Chernenko, Andropov's successor, has been even more outspoken
about the danger posed by domestic popular dissatisfaction and has
vigorously defended the need for higher levels of consumption. It thus
seems unlikely that the regime will cut back heavily on the agricultural
imports needed to maintain or improve the diet of ordinary Soviet citizens.

Economic reforms that dramatically upgrade the efficiency of agriculture or the technological dynamism of industry could permit a decisive reduction in commerce with the West. During the last three years,
the regime's general economic problems, coupled with Western embargoes and diplomatic pressure, have emboldened the scholarly advocates
of reform to resume their public campaign for a far-reaching decentralization of economic authority. Some proponents of domestic reform, who
in the 1960s frequently saw it as a prerequisite for the effective use of
commercial ties with the West, now feel that the unreliability of these ties
has heightened the need for reform. For the time being, at least, they
seem to be arguing that major internal economic changes are necessary
in order to avoid excessive dependence on the West. Within the top
leadership, Andropov expressed this attitude most clearly.

But words are not action. In the USSR there is no powerful political
constituency that supports a market-oriented decentralization of the
economy, and thus far the changes of economic administration introduced by Brezhnev's successors have been quite cautious. In the
Soviet system such a reform would have to be imposed from the top. If it
ever occurs, it will happen only when a reform-minded leader has decisively defeated his political rivals and concentrated unusual bureaucratic
power in his hands—a prospect that seems especially unlikely under a
transitional leader like Chernenko. In the meantime, there is little likelihood that the regime will manage to scale back its economic need for
commerce with the West.

The leadership thus faces the difficult problem of reconciling contradictory goals. On the one hand, it is unwilling to allow the West to obtain political concessions through trade restrictions. It therefore wishes to minimize the USSR's vulnerability to economic pressure, as well as the vulnerability of Eastern Europe. On the other hand, the leadership feels compelled to meet the Soviet Union's own pressing domestic economic needs, for reasons not just of popular welfare but of political self-interest. Both of these are high-priority goals, and the dynamic tension between them is likely to prevent drastic alterations in Soviet policy toward commerce with the West. Instead the authorities, continuing the policy begun in the late 1970s, will probably aim for further modest growth of Soviet-Western trade and a more rapid growth of intrabloc commerce that will shift the overall balance back toward greater interchange with the country's socialist allies.

NOTES

1. Bruce Parrott, *Politics and Technology in the Soviet Union* (Cambridge: MIT Press, 1983), pp. 234–36; Kenneth Pridham, "The Soviet View of Current Disagreements Between the United States and Western Europe," *International Affairs* (London), 59 (Winter 1982/83), p. 20.

2. Pridham, "The Soviet View," p. 21.

3. William Griffith, "The Soviets and Western Europe: An Overview," in *Soviet Policy Toward Western Europe: Implications for the Western Alliance,* ed. Herbert J. Ellison (Seattle: University of Washington Press, 1983), p. 16.

4. Angela Stent, *From Embargo to Ostpolitik: The Political Economy of West German-Soviet Relations, 1955–1980* (New York: Cambridge University Press, 1981), pp. 189, 237.

5. Parrott, *Politics and Technology,* pp. 259–264.

6. Henry Kissinger, *Years of Upheaval* (Boston: Little, Brown, 1982), pp. 204–5; George W. Breslauer, "Soviet Policy in the Middle East, 1967–1972: Unalterable Antagonism or Collaborative Competition?," in *Managing U.S.-Soviet Rivalry,* ed. Alexander L. George (Boulder, Colo.: Westview Press, 1983), pp. 89–99.

7. Paul M. Kattenburg, "DRV External Relations in the New Revolutionary Phase," in *Communism in Indochina: New Perspectives,* ed. Joseph J. Zasloff and MacAlister Brown (Lexington, Mass.: Lexington Books, 1975), pp. 121–22; Kissinger, *Years of Upheaval,* pp. 317–18, 322. On the weapons shipments, see Stanley Karnow, *Vietnam: A History* (New York: Viking Press, 1983), pp. 639, 646, 660, 663–64. On North Vietnam's changing military plans, see Tran van Tra, *Ending the Thirty Years War* (Ho Chi Minh City: Literature Publishing House, 1982, in Vietnamese), pp. 157–60, 165–70, 180. I am indebted to Mr. Hung Nguyen for summaries of the relevant portions of this book.

8. Stanley Hoffman, "Detente," in *The Making of America's Soviet Policy* (New Haven: Yale University Press, 1983), p. 276; Kenneth G. Lieberthal, *Sino-Soviet Conflict in the 1970s: Its Evolution and Implications for the Strategic Triangle,* Report R-2342-NA (Santa Monica: Rand Corporation, 1978), pp. 44–45.

9. Hoffman, "Detente," pp. 246–47; George Breslauer, "Why Detente Failed: An Interpretation," in *Managing U.S.-Soviet Rivalry,* pp. 327–28.

10. Parrott, *Politics and Technology*, pp. 182–92, 212–217.

11. Ibid, pp. 239 ff.

12. Calculated from A. Schubert, S. Zsindely, and T. Braun, "Scientometric Analysis of Attendance at International Scientific Meetings," *Scientometrics*, 5, no. 3 (1983), pp. 177–87. For further analysis of this problem, see my *Information Transfer in Soviet Science and Engineering: A Study of Documentary Channels* (Santa Monica: Rand Corporation, 1981), pp. 23–35, and *The Diffusion of Information in Soviet R&D Through Informal Channels* (Santa Monica: Rand Corporation, forthcoming), Section III.

13. Erik P. Hoffmann and Robbin F. Laird, *The Politics of Economic Modernization in the Soviet Union* (Ithaca: Cornell University Press, 1982), p. 17 and passim; Parrott, *Politics and Technology*, passim.

14. Parrott, *Politics and Technology*, pp. 232–65.

15. Hoffmann and Laird, *The Politics*, p. 139; John P. Hardt and Kate S. Tomlinson, "Soviet Economic Policies in Western Europe," in *Soviet Policy Toward Western Europe*, p. 170.

16. See Hannes Adomeit, "Soviet Decision-Making and Western Europe," in *Soviet Strategy Toward Western Europe*, ed. Edwina Moreton and Gerald Segal (Boston: George Allen & Unwin, 1984), p. 53.

17. The term "policy group" was coined by Hoffmann and Laird, *The Politics*, pp. 82–83.

18. The Soviet decision-making procedure for purchasing foreign licenses without any associated equipment is somewhat different. For details, see the chapter by Philip Hanson in this volume.

19. For an informative discussion of the role of these planning and production organizations in trade planning, see H. Stephen Gardner, *Soviet Foreign Trade: The Decision Process* (Boston: Kluwer-Nijhoff Publishing, 1983).

20. For figures on the regional variations in relative dependence on exports (to all countries, not just capitalist ones), see *Razvitie mezhdunarodnogo razdeleniia truda i razmeshchenie promyshlennykh sil SSSR: teoriia, metody, praktika*, ed. N. N. Nekrasov (Moscow: Nauka, 1981), p. 54.

21. For details, see Peter Hauslohner, "Prefects as Senators: Soviet Regional Politicians Look to Foreign Policy," *World Politics*, 33 (January 1981), pp. 222–23. Between the 1960s and 1970s the attention given by regional party officials to foreign policy increased significantly, as did the frequency with which the Central Committee, on which these officials are heavily represented, discussed foreign-policy issues (Ibid., pp. 197, 204, 232).

22. Parrott, *Politics and Technology*, pp. 271–72; V. M. Bondarenko, *Sovremennaia nauka i razvitie voennogo dela: voenno-sotsiologicheskie aspekty problemy* (Moscow: Voenizdat, 1976), p. 64; Eric P. Hoffmann and Robbin F. Laird, *"The Scientific-Technological Revolution" and Soviet Foreign Policy* (New York: Pergamon Press, 1982), p. 112.

23. Parrott, *Politics and Technology*, pp. 252–53.

24. Ibid., pp. 267–68, 274–75.

25. Ibid., pp. 268–69.

26. Hoffmann and Laird, *"The Scientific-Technological Revolution,"* p. 77; Gardner, *Soviet Foreign Trade*, pp. 19–21, 69, 75.

27. Gardner, *Soviet Foreign Trade*, p. 49.

28. Personal communication from Dr. John Hardt.

29. Parrott, *Politics and Technology*, p. 270.

30. Gardner, *Soviet Foreign Trade*, p. 10 , summarizing personal interviews with Soviet specialists.

31. Hauslohner, "Prefects as Senators," pp. 222–23; Parrott, *Politics and Technology*, pp. 273–74.

32. I. F. Zaitsev, "Regional'nye problemy razvitiia vneshneekonomicheskikh sviazei SSSR," in *Metodologicheskie problemy sotsial'no-ekonomicheskogo razvitiia regionov SSSR* (Moscow: Nauka, 1979), pp. 183–84, 198–99.

33. David S. Kamerling, "The Soviet Geographical Chimera: The Contrasting Distributions of Natural Resources, New Supplies of Labor, and Developed Industrial Infrastructure," paper presented at the Fifteenth National Convention of the American Association for the Advancement of Slavic Studies, Kansas City, Missouri, 22–25 October 1983, pp. 4–9.

34. L. I. Brezhnev, *Leninskim kursom*, VIII (Moscow: Politizdat, 1981), pp. 247–50, 285, 364, 419; *XXVI s"ezd KPSS*, I (Moscow: Politizdat, 1981), pp. 26–27, 57, 61–63, 72.

35. Two Politburo members who may have had reservations about the gas program were Nikolai Tikhonov and V. Dolgikh. See Thane Gustafson, *The Soviet Gas Campaign: Politics and Policy in Soviet Decisionmaking* (Santa Monica: Rand Corporation, 1983), p. 34; George Breslauer, "Reformism, Conservatism, and Leadership Authority at the 26th Party Congress," in *Russia at the Crossroads: The 26th Congress of the CPSU*, ed. Seweryn Bialer and Thane Gustafson (New York: George Allen and Unwin, 1982), pp. 83–84; V. I. Dolgikh, "Povyshat' uroven' rukovodstva predpriiatiiami toplivno-energeticheskogo kompleksa," *Partiinaia zhizn'*, 1980, no. 1, pp. 16, 23.

36. Gustafson, *The Soviet Gas Campaign*, pp. 23, 35–36.

37. V. L. Mal'kevich, *Vostok-Zapad: Ekonomicheskoe sotrudnichestvo. Tekhnologicheskii obmen* (Moscow: Nauka, 1981), pp. 17–22, 29.

38. *XXVI s"ezd*, I, pp. 274–75, and II, pp. 53–55, 114–115.

39. O. Bogomolov, "Ekonomicheskie sviazi mezhdu sotsialisticheskimi i kapitalisticheskimi stranami," *Mirovaia ekonomika i mezhdunarodnye otnosheniia* (hereafter cited as *MEMO*), 1980, no. 3, p. 43.

40. Foreign Broadcast Information Service, *Daily Report: Soviet Union*, 21 April 1981, p. U1.

41. The evidence on his attitude toward gas exports is not conclusive. See *Izvestiia*, 11 April 1979, pp. 2–3; "Vystupitel'noe slovo prezidenta Akademii nauk SSSR akademika A. P. Aleksandrova," *Vestnik Akademii nauk SSSR*, 1980, no. 5, pp. 6, 11–12; and A. P. Aleksandrov, *Nauka—strane* (Moscow: Nauka, 1983), pp. 40–41, 64, 93, 130, 164, 199.

42. Gustafson, *The Soviet Gas Campaign*, pp. 94–95.

43. "Rech' tovarishcha L. I. Brezhneva na Plenume TsK KPSS 16 noiabria 1981 goda," *Kommunist*, 1981, no. 17, pp. 6–10.

44. N. Ogarkov, "Na strazhe mirnogo truda," *Kommunist*, 1981, no. 10, pp. 84–85; N. Ogarkov, *Vsegda v gotovnosti k zashchite Otechestva* (Moscow: Voenizdat, 1982), pp. 20–21, 24–30, 60.

45. N. Gusev, "Sovremennyi imperializm: agressivnost' vozrastaet," *Kommunist Vooruzhennykh Sil*, 1982, no. 11, p. 84.

46. Dan L. Strode and Rebecca V. Strode, "Diplomacy and Defense in Soviet National Security Policy," *International Security*, 8, no. 2 (Fall 1983), pp. 108–10.

47. For Andropov's later attitude toward reform, see Boris Rumer, "Structural Imbalance in the Soviet Economy," *Problems of Communism*, 33, no. 4 (July–August 1984), p. 25.

48. *Pravda*, 28 April 1982, p. 2.

49. K. U. Chernenko, "Avangardnaia rol' partii kommunistov: vazhnoe uslovie ee vozrastaniia," *Kommunist*, 1982, no. 6, p. 29.

50. Ia. Kashe, "Aktual'nye voprosy bor'by protiv sovremennogo antikommunizma i revizionizma," *Kommunist*, 1982, no. 5, pp. 72–73.

51. For similar incidents during the early years of detente, see Stent, *From*

Embargo to Ostpolitik, pp. 182–83, and Parrott, *Politics and Technology*, pp. 267–68.

52. "Rech' L. I. Brezhneva na torzhestvennom zasedanii v Tashkente, posviashchennom vrucheniiu Uzbekskoi SSR ordena Lenina, 24 marta 1982 goda," *Kommunist*, 1982, no. 6, p. 16; N. Tikhonov, "Edinyi narodnokhoziaistvennyi kompleks mnogonatsional'nogo Sovetskogo gosudarstva," *Kommunist*, no. 11, 1982, pp. 26–27.

53. "Luchshe rabotat'—luchshe zhit'," *Kommunist*, 1982, no. 2, pp. 8, 10; "Gazovaia promyshlennost': itogi i perspektivy," *Planovoe khoziaistvo*, 1982, no. 6, pp. 20–23.

54. *Krasnaia zvezda*, 7 May 1982, p. 2, and 29 May 1982, p. 1; *Pravda*, 1 July 1982, p. 2.

55. L. I. Brezhnev, "O prodovol'stvennoi programme SSSR na period do 1990 goda i merakh po ee realizatsii," *Kommunist*, 1982, no. 9, p. 10.

56. *Pravda*, 28 October 1982, p. 1.

57. *Krasnaia zvezda*, 23 February 1983, pp. 1–2.

58. A. Gromyko, "V. I. Lenin i vneshniaia politika Sovetskogo gosudarstva," *Kommunist*, 1983, no. 6, pp. 11–32.

59. O. Bogomolov, "SEV: ekonomicheskaia strategiia 80-kh godov," *Kommunist*, 1983, no. 7, pp. 77, 81, 84.

60. Ibid., p. 79. For an example of liberal economists' growing interest in decentralization, see "Aktual'nye voprosy metodologii i metodiki narodnokhoziaistvennogo planirovaniia," *Planovoe khoziaistvo*, 1982, no. 5, pp. 72, 75–76.

61. Bogomolov, "SEV," p. 76; *Planovoe khoziaistvo*, 1983, no. 4, p. 114.

62. Bogomolov, "SEV," p. 82; *Planovoe khoziaistvo*, 1983, no. 4, p. 113.

63. *MEMO*, 1980, no. 3, pp. 42–43, 48–50. In 1983, a few Soviet scholars still held views similar to this one. See, for example, L. A. Rodina, *Sotsialisticheskaia integratsiia i novye formy sotrudnichestva Vostok-Zapad* (Moscow: Nauka, 1983), pp. 42–43, 83–84, 116, 129.

64. Iu. Andropov, "Uchenie Karla Marksa i nekotorye voprosy sotsialisticheskogo stroitel'stva v SSSR," *Kommunist*, 1983, no. 3, p. 21.

PART II
Case Studies

Soviet Assimilation of Western Technology

Philip Hanson

THE AIM of this paper is to arrive at criteria for assessing Soviet performance in assimilating imported Western technology. Section A presents a working definition of assimilation. Section B describes Soviet procedures for choosing foreign technologies to acquire, and for assimilating them. Section C is a discussion of various measures of success in assimilation. Section D is a summary of previous studies of the assimilation of imported technology into the Soviet chemical industry: a major recipient of imported machinery and know-how, and an industry in which assimilation has been studied in detail. This leads in Section E to a listing and discussion of criteria for assessing performance in assimilation.

A. The Assimilation of Imported Technology

The word "technology," as used by economists, has been crisply defined as "useful knowledge pertaining to the art of production."[1] An improvement in process technology, from an economic standpoint, is any alteration of the method of production which leads, at given prices, to a higher ratio of output to inputs, excluding pure economies of scale. A product innovation is a less straightforward notion, but it also entails an increase in the productivity of inputs—this time through a given quantity of inputs being employed to produce a product which consumers value more highly than the nearest equivalent pre-existing product or products which could have been produced from the same inputs.

The word "assimilation" can be used, in the present context, in either a narrow or a broad sense. In the narrow sense, the Soviets would be said to have assimilated an imported license, machine, or complete plant when a production unit was operating at or close to its design capacity with the imported equipment or the licensed technology employed in it.

The broader sense, however, is the one that will be used here. In this sense "assimilation" is the whole process of acquiring, utilizing and deriving benefit from technology of foreign origin. This process is a continuous, long-standing, and almost ubiquitous element in the economic

63

growth of nations. It is not a peculiarity of the Soviet economy that it benefits from technology of foreign origin; all nations do, in some degree. Such benefits are a special case of the gains from trade and consist in an enhancement of the productivity of the recipient nation's resources, in comparison with what could be achieved with domestically available know-how. The size of the potential benefits depends on the gap between indigenous and foreign productivity levels insofar as that gap derives from differences in technology. This is not necessarily correlated with the research-intensity of the industry supplying the technology or the rate of change of the technology. The elements in the process of assimilation, on which the realization of these potential benefits depends, are the following.

First, there is the gathering and processing of information about the existence and broad characteristics of foreign technologies. (In the West a great deal of this is done in a decentralised fashion, by firms. Studies of the diffusion of new technologies among Western countries show that the diffusion of technological information is itself a process that takes time.)[2]

Second, there may be a process of acquisition of documents, informal know-how, product samples, licenses, batches of equipment, or complete plants from foreign sources. These acquired items will either convey in a disembodied form or embody in physical products the technologies in question or both. This element of the assimilation process may be omitted when the organization assimilating the foreign technology proceeds from information about the general characteristics of that technology directly to an attempted reproduction of it by research, development, and innovation (RDI) activities that are independent of the outside world in all respects save the initial information about the technology's existence and broad characteristics.

Third, there is initial utilization: "assimilation" in the narrow sense. This may or may not entail adaptation, i.e., modification of the characteristics of the foreign exemplar. Adaptation can range from the routine (e.g., altering measurements from nonmetric to metric) to the substantive (e.g., the cams added by the Chinese to keep the tracks more reliably in place on tanks). Even routine modification requires resources. A traditional Soviet practice has been "reverse engineering": the design and production of a domestic product on the basis of an analysis of an imported product. In the chapter on computers S. E. Goodman distinguishes between reverse engineering and close copying. The distinction cannot be drawn as precisely in some other industries as in computer development, but the general point is important: reverse engineering is by no means a merely passive or parasitic exercise. (Sometimes, a modification may be provided, to order, by the foreign supplier, as when a turnkey plant is designed for location in a particular climate and for utilization of particular qualities of raw materials.)

Fourth, there is the replication or domestic diffusion of the initial foreign-technology-based machine or production unit. This can involve further adaptation.

Fifth, and last, there is further technological development from the initial "acquisition" by means of domestic RDI. This shades into "adaptation," but may be thought of as a development capable of producing a new vintage of technology.

The observations that follow in this paper will be confined to Soviet assimilation of foreign technology that has been acquired from foreign sources at some significant cost. In other words, nothing will be said about Soviet assimilation via domestic RDI of ideas and information gleaned from foreign periodicals and similar open sources available at low cost.

"Acquisition from foreign sources at significant cost" includes illegal purchasing and espionage; insofar as these are activities over which Western governments may plausibly be supposed to be capable of exerting some influence, they ought to be considered in any policy-oriented analysis. There is in fact rather little in what follows which is specifically about technology acquired in these ways; but this is for lack of systematic information in open sources about the assimilation of such technology, not because it should be excluded from our discussion. Most of the discussion, therefore, is about the assimilation of technology acquired by commercial purchase without subterfuge. Commercial transfers are most readily measured by reference to the dollar value of transactions and physical quantities acquired. This is not entirely satisfactory, but it has to serve. The extent of human contact in the technology transfer process, for example, is certainly important to the success of assimilation, but it does not lend itself, as a rule, to measurement.

In general, close contact with the foreign source of an imported technology will ease assimilation. And the more complete a transfer is (e.g., a foreign supplier providing for design acquisition, installation, and commissioning of a new plant, along with transfer of know-how and staff training), the less the burden on domestic RDI.

B. Soviet Assimilation Procedures

A certain amount has been written on the methods of selection, acquisition, and assimilation of imported technology employed in the Soviet system. The difficulties in arriving at an accurate picture are, first, that practice differs from official guidelines and, second, that the management of the frequently clandestine acquisition and assimilation of militarily sensitive technology is not a topic on which the Soviets provide books and articles.

So far as non-sensitive technology is concerned, Soviet planning handbooks and monographs outline the prescribed procedures. Thus the branch ministry applying for the allocation to it of hard currency for a foreign machine or license is supposed to demonstrate to USSR Gosplan that domestic sources cannot provide the requisite amount and quality of the item in question. The demonstration of non-availability from domestic sources is supposed to take the form of statements to that effect from the relevant machine-building ministries. Relative costs are not mentioned as a criterion in the 1974 Gosplan official planning guidelines. How East European and Western imports are distinguished is not clear, but the former may be treated as equivalent to domestic inputs. As usual in Soviet planning procedures, the investment programs into which the imports are to be fitted, are exogenous: given "from above."[3] The application must also show that the installation and use of imported equipment have been fully planned for.

Procedures for pure license buying are less important, since the purchasing is on a smaller scale, but they have been more precisely spelt out.[4] Information on foreign technologies is supposed to be available in a systematic way from the All-Union Institute of Interbranch Information (VIMI), the State Committee for Inventions and Discoveries, the latter's Central Research Institute for Patent Information and Technical-Economic Research (TsNIIPI), and numerous branch information institutes. Enquiries to a potential foreign licensor have to be made through the specialist foreign trade organization, Litsenzintorg.

Actual applications to purchase foreign licenses are supposed to be vetted by the State Committee for Science and Technology (GKNT) and USSR Gosplan. The applicant must show that the investment based on the license will yield at least a 12 percent rate of return, with present value calculated using an 8 percent rate of time discount. (This was in line with the standard official criteria at the time the sources referred to here were published. The rather cumbersome use of two different discounting rates requires (1) that an investment has to yield a rate of return of at least 12 percent when the average annual flow of benefits is related to the capital value of the investment and (2) that a discount rate of 8 percent should be applied in converting variable flows of expected benefits in different time periods and/or investment costs spread over several time periods to single-period values. Soviet planners in evaluating projects are expected to treat the annual rate of the flow of output and the duration of the flow as given—by a higher-level plan.) More important, the applicant must also show that production cost on the basis of the license would be at least one-third less than on the basis of domestic R and D.

To judge from Soviet practice in activities like new-product pricing, these procedures will be followed with all the rigor and scruple that is devoted in the West to filling in tax returns and expenses claims. (Or perhaps less, because of the absence of a puritan tradition.) What is certain is that enterprises and branch ministries propose and request, and the central authorities—chiefly Gosplan—screen and ration.[5]

A recent *Pravda* article asserts: "There is no clear system of coordination of all the participants in the investment process with the foreign trade organization."[6] What this appears to mean is that a clear system exists on paper but not in practice. Two examples are quoted from the chemical industry of costly delays in installing and utilizing imported equipment.

In the example for which more detail is given, the sources of delay are described with some precision. The case concerns a production unit to manufacture 40 million aerosols a year, for which the contract was placed in 1973 or earlier but which is unlikely to come on stream before 1985. The delays in this case arose for the following reasons. First, the Ministry of the Chemical Industry placed the import order before it had decided where the new unit was to go. The unit was therefore not incorporated in the investment plan until 1977. This contravened the requirement that prior planning of implementation be arranged (and be shown to have been arranged). Second, the start of construction was delayed for a year because the ministry (the chemical ministry) had not prepared the site. This is routine for the general run of Soviet investment projects. Third, there was a further, two-year delay because the ministry's project-design organization failed to deliver technical documentation on time. (The designs were probably for ancillary and civil-engineering work.) This is normal. Fourth, the designated main contractor, a local trust of the Ministry of Industrial Construction, refused each year to undertake the volume of work requested by the customer (the Ministry of the Chemical Industry). It set itself instead an annual plan equivalent to a third to a half of that requested. This is not unusual. Fifth, the contractor failed to fulfill the plan. This is absolutely *de rigueur*.[7] The fulfillment percentage anticipated for 1983 was 4. At all events, the implementation process clearly does not always run according to plan. Indeed the article goes on to assert that such delays are common.

This article is not unusual. After the late-1970s deterioration in East-West relations, a number of articles detailing failures of technology imports from the West have appeared in the Soviet press. Sometimes the theme is that an indigenously developed product or process would have been better anyway, so that the initial resort to foreign technology was itself mistaken. In other writings the stress has been on indigenous bungling in implementation.[8] In addition, one Soviet economist has attributed the rising unit costs of new capacity in the Soviet economy in the late 1970s to the influence of increasingly costly imported machines.[9] There is clearly some reaction against technology imports, and weaknesses in assimilation are not infrequently referred to in this connection. In articles of this kind, worst cases are apt to be celebrated; on the other hand, the appearance of such "problem" articles requires that at least an influential section of the policymaking élite considers the problem in question to be a substantial one.

Procedures for acquiring and assimilating militarily sensitive technology are different, and are likely to be more closely followed in practice. An outline of what is claimed to be the institutional framework involved has been put forward by a senior French civil servant, Henri Regnard.[10] His account probably stems from information supplied by a Soviet defector in 1983.

Regnard's main points are the following. The Military-Industrial Commission (VPK) of the USSR Council of Ministers, operating under the guidance of the Party Central Committee and the Council of Ministers, is the main coordinating body. It is chaired by L. V. Smirnov and consists of the ministers of the nine military-related industries plus the ministers of the Chemical Industry, of Petroleum Refining and Petrochemicals, and of the Electrical Equipment Industry.

Tasks in the acquisition of militarily useful technology are set by the VPK for five organizations: KGB (Directorate T of the First Principal Directorate), military intelligence (the GRU), the State Committee for Science and Technology (GKNT), the Ministry of Foreign Trade, and the State Committee for External Economic Relations. The first two operate clandestinely or at least with some degree of subterfuge; the others work openly and for the most part legally. Funds for illegal acquisition are provided by the VPK, the GKNT, the KGB, and the Ministry of Defense.

The VPK distinguishes between "principal objectives," which are directly military, and "objectives," which are ancillary. It oversees acquisitions and can arrange cooperation between the organizations working to it. In the implementation stage, the GKNT assists in coordinating the work of the branch ministries and their R and D institutes. VIMI monitors and records the interbranch information flows.

This description is consistent with the *Penkovsky Papers* of 1965 in identifying a substantial KGB presence in the foreign activities of the GKNT.[11] It is also consistent with what can be gleaned from Soviet published sources, as Julian Cooper notes in his chapter.

Any formal organization can look impressive on paper, and there is nothing in Regnard's account to demonstrate that acquisition and assimilation of militarily sensitive technology are more efficient than acquisition and assimilation of civilian technology. But the system Regnard describes does have the flexibility of alternative institutional channels; it will certainly be given high priority; and it may well be better coordinated than the strictly civilian arrangements. Certainly Cooper's chapter provides evidence that much past Soviet assimilation of militarily-directly-useful imported technology has been more successful than the assimilation of most "civilian" technology.

C. Assessing Success in Assimilation

The strongest evidence, as a rule, of successful use of an imported technology is the successful development of exports based on that technology to competitive markets. If the volume of exports is large enough—given what is known about production for the home market—it may indicate that there has been successful domestic diffusion, as well as initial use. If a strong export performance is sustained through successive vintages of a technology without further recourse to technology imports, this will be evidence of successful independent further development from the vintage of technology initially acquired.

Such evidence is readily available—both in case studies and in more aggregated, statistical forms—for Japan[12] and for the small group of newly industrializing countries which emerged in the 1970s.[13]

There are instances that can be pointed to as evidence of at least some degree of success, by this test, in Soviet assimilation. Gas exports to the West have required the successful installation and operation of compressor stations and the successful assembly of trunk gas pipelines from Western large-diameter pipe. At the same time, this particular instance shows very little Soviet success in developing indigenous production of large-diameter pipe and efficient 25 MW turbines for compressor stations—until, perhaps, very recent times.[14]

The Soviet export of Lada cars on the basis of technology acquired through Fiat presents a somewhat similar picture: cars have been successfully made and sold to the West, but diffusion or upgrading of the initial car-plant technology has been limited, as Holliday's chapter shows. On the one hand, the Soviets have developed some variants of the original Lada (Zhiguli) car at the Volga Automobile Works (VAZ). On the other hand, the next major car-plant development, a modernization of the Moskvich plant to produce a new model, has required a further resort to Western know-how: a contract with Renault for the design of both the new car and the new plant, after which new machinery orders from the West are expected.[15]

Assimilation performance in an aggregate sense, as demonstrated in foreign trade, might be measured by identifying imports of technology (machinery imports being the proxy indicator) by branch user, and exports to Western markets by branch of origin, and testing for statistically significant relations between them. It may be hypothesized, for example, that

$$\frac{XW_{it}}{XW_{it-\ell}} = f\!\left(\frac{MKW_{it-\ell}}{I_{it-\ell+1}}\right)$$

where XW_{it} denotes exports to the West of the ith good in year $t;$

$\quad\ell$ denotes the lead-time for introduction of imported technology and the start-up of production utilizing it;

MKW_i denotes imports of Western machinery for use in the branch producing good i, and XW and MKW are in constant prices unless it is hypothesized that plans incorporated expectations of changes in world prices.

$\quad I_i$ denotes equipment investment to produce product i.

A rank correlation test for 7–9 industrial branches in the USSR, Hungary, and Poland between 1970 and 1977 found no significant relationship (at the 5 percent level) for any of the three countries or for the branches concerned between export growth and the import-intensity of investment, as defined above.[16] It is true that the limitations of such a test are severe: the most detailed (unpublished) commodity categories of the Standard International Trade Classification (SITC) have to be regrouped in order to relate branch-user machinery imports to branch exports, and this is a process with room for errors of identification;[17] the specification of a lead-time is a matter of judgment—again possibly erroneous—from case-study information; the indirect effects of imports of technology into branches supplying the "exporting" branch are not allowed for and market restriction clauses in license contracts may be sufficiently extensive to preclude a strong correlation. But at least where the planners have stated that technology imports are intended to be self-financing through the subsequent generation of hard-currency exports, the test is an appropriate one.

The trouble is that it has not so far been appropriate for the USSR. The Soviet balance-of-payments equilibrium has been maintained by windfall gains from export-price rises for oil, gas, gold, and the like. Soviet planners have not needed (ex post) to make technology imports self-financing in this sense. Nor have they generally and clearly said that this (ex ante) was their intention. It could however be an appropriate test in the future if further windfall terms-of-trade gains are not expected.[18]

Insofar as the test is appropriate, it would be useful to make it a comparative test and apply it to newly industrializing or South European countries, as well as to communist countries. At present the re-grouping of data to allow such a test for non-CMEA countries has not been carried out. It can however be shown that the Soviet and East European market shares in total OECD imports of manufactures have fallen since the mid-1960s, while those of the newly industrializing countries (NICs) and

Table 1

Percentage Distribution of Western Imports of Manufactures, 1965 and 1981

	1965	1981
Intra-Western (excluding S. Europe)	88.78	82.54
Southern Europe[a]	0.84	2.10
NICs[b]	2.74	6.95
East European Six + Albania[c]	1.56	1.46
USSR	0.82	0.51
Rest of the World	5.26	6.95

SOURCE: UN ECE, *Economic Bulletin for Europe*, vol. 35 (1983), p. 3.18
[a]Greece, Portugal, Spain and Turkey
[b]Mexico, Brazil, Argentina, Venezuela, Taiwan, S. Korea, PRC, Hong Kong, Philippines, Singapore, India, Morocco, Tunisia, Egypt
[c]Including FRG-GDR trade

Southern Europe have risen. The Soviet fall is proportionally large. In an absolute sense it is less, however, than the fall in the West's share of its own markets.

The UN ECE study investigated market shares at the 2- and 3-digit levels of the SITC, as well as in more aggregated terms. This did not give scope for identifying technological factors. To pick up differences in level of technological sophistication within a product group it is usually necessary to disaggregate to 4- or 5-digit levels. At this level of disaggregation, however, data for Soviet investment are largely lacking, and the allocation of machinery import categories is more problematic, so that the import-intensity of investment cannot, as a general rule, be calculated. The link between export performance and technology imports can therefore be investigated only through case-studies.

One such study, by Poznański, is impressionistic but based on a wide range of material, and quite persuasive.[19] He takes a number of industries and reviews evidence about East European export performance in them in comparison with that of NICs. What he concludes about the East European Six will tend in general to apply even more strongly to the USSR (see Table 1). He finds, for example, that several NICs have moved ahead of Eastern Europe in the sophistication of their ship-building and steel-industry exports; Brazilian car and car-component exports by 1980 exceeded those of the East European Six; more sophisticated types of machine-tools are being exported by the NICs than by Eastern Europe; and so on.

Studies of this sort may well be telling us that openness to international investment—i.e., to multinational companies (MNCs)—is a major advantage for a country engaged in "catching up." For some NICs this has probably been important. But MNCs are not welcomed throughout this group. The most successful NIC of an earlier era, Japan, has, with a few exceptions, prohibited direct foreign investment.[20] Japan's success in technological catching up can be ascribed above all to indigenous cultural characteristics and institutional arrangements, including close government-industry cooperation in the screening and selection of foreign technologies for importation by means of licensing.[21]

There is no political or legal reason—at least of a formal kind—why the USSR should not allocate far more resources to the acquisition of foreign licenses than it does.[22] A relatively large expenditure on license imports can be compatible with, and probably contributes to, rapid technological progress and rapid growth of exports of manufactures. South Korea in 1977 was allocating 1.2 percent of GNP to license imports and 0.8 percent to indigenous R and D.[23] Yet pure license imports are relatively little used by the USSR—probably for the good reason that such imports by themselves do not solve the key problem of implementation; it is in implementation that the USSR is particularly weak.

Other tests of success in assimilating imported technology concern the domestic economy alone. Again, there are severe limits to studies of an aggregated kind. In this category I would include not only economy-wide and sectoral studies, but analysis at the industry-branch level. Once more (and partly because of gaps in Soviet data) the case-study approach is more promising. Before the discussion of criteria for use in case studies, however, it is necessary to say something briefly about more aggregative analysis.

If technology of whatever origin is successfully assimilated into production, output per unit of capital and labor will, other things equal, increase. An obvious test of performance in assimilation of imported technology, therefore, would be a measurement of the relationship between technology imports and total factor productivity (TFP): for example, between changes in the western-import-intensity of the capital stock and changes in TFP.

There are several reasons, however, why this approach has so far been inconclusive. First, the specification of production functions so as to obtain a reliable measure of changes in TFP is problematic. Second, factors other than "technological progress proper" (Bergson's term for the introduction and diffusion of new products and processes) will affect TFP. Bergson has tried to separate technological progress proper (TPP) for the USSR in 1950–75 from other elements in TFP change, the latter being derived from a fixed-weight Cobb-Douglas production function calculation for Soviet material-sector GNP.[24] Among the elements in TFP apart from TPP, Bergson posits such influences as natural resource exhaustion, farm-industry labor transfers, labor quality change due to educational advance, and changes in average weather. This exercise is valuable for identifying and roughly quantifying at least some sources of growth and decline, but there is scope for differences over the order of magnitude of some of these influences and also for adding further likely influences not considered by Bergson.[25] Estimated TPP, being a residual, can be greatly altered by such alternative calculations—even if the Cobb-Douglas approach itself is accepted. Finally, data problems (notably valuation) make measures of the import-intensity of the capital stock somewhat unreliable as well.

These problems are well-known as a result of some controversial estimates and counterestimates for the Soviet industrial sector and certain branches of industry.[26] Once more, the alternative of case studies is more promising. It does not, in this field, preclude quantification and testing of general relationships: within a single branch or sub-branch of industry it may be possible to compile a substantial number of observations relating to individual projects and products.[27] It was possible to adopt this approach in studies of assimilation of imported technology in the Soviet chemical industry.

D. The Case of the Soviet Chemical Industry

A summary of the findings of studies of assimilation in the Soviet chemical industry will illustrate the sort of picture that can emerge from work of this sort.[28]

The chemical industry has accounted over the past decade or so for only 3–3½ percent of Soviet investment.[29] Nonetheless since the late 1950s it has received about a quarter of Soviet imports of Western machinery. At least a quarter of the industry's equipment investment in that period has consisted of Western machinery. This injection of Western technology has transformed the industry, forming the basis of major new sub-branches which scarcely existed before. Large proportions of the output of polyethylene, polyester fiber, ammonia, and several other important chemical products are produced on imported plant.

A 1978 survey of British and West German chemical plant contractors found that the average lead-time[30] for acquiring, installing, and commissioning imported chemical plant was nearly seven years. This was twice as long as would be needed, on average, for comparable projects in Western Europe. There was a weak positive relationship between lead-time and contract size, and no significant relationship between lead-time and date of contract (and hence no evidence of improvement over time in transfer performance) over 15–20 years. Output levels on completed plants were on average slightly below, and manning levels significantly above, comparable West European figures, so that labor productivity averaged about two-thirds that on comparable Western plant. There was very little evidence of successful replication (diffusion) or of subsequent indigenous adaptation or further development. The lead-times for implementing these technology imports, however, appeared to be well below those for indigenous RDI in chemicals, which are, on average for the branch, longer than in most other areas of Soviet technology.[31]

A separate study was made of the mineral fertilizer sub-branch. From published sources (including transcripts of Soviet broadcasts) it was possible to build up a picture of the contribution of Western equipment imports to Soviet production and supply. It was found that the contribution of these imports was chiefly to the expansion of nitrogenous and complex fertilizer supply, with potash and phosphate nutrient supply depending more heavily on indigenous inputs. Even within the nitrogen sub-branch, however, there was a blending of indigenous, East European and Western equipment, which suggested a careful selection process aimed at cost-effective spending of limited hard-currency allocations.

An attempt was made to estimate the rate of return (in world prices) on this hard-currency "investment" by identifying the effect, both direct and indirect, of these imports, net of the contribution of cooperating indigenous inputs, on Soviet agricultural output in the mid-1970s. The outcome was less than conclusive: estimated annual rates of return ranged from 15 to 60 percent, depending on the precise assumptions employed in the calculation. The upper part of this range, however, was somewhat more persuasive than the lower. In general, it was hard to resist the conclusion that Soviet investment and technology choice, and the utilization of the imported technology, were in this case quite efficient. Even here, however, there was little evidence of successful diffusion and further development.

Whether the allocation of so much hard currency for so long to the chemicals branch as a whole has been a wise choice, is more doubtful. It is likely to have been the outcome of a series of short- or medium-term decisions rather than a deliberately chosen long-run strategy. After the initial Khrushchev chemicalization drive of 1959–65,[32] the force of bureaucratic inertia may have operated in favor of the chemical industry. Mr. Leonid Kostandov, the minister directly responsible for a large part of the industry for more than two decades (he now has wider responsibilities, as a deputy premier) is a forceful character, and he had created a well-trodden path between the Foreign Trade Bank and the Ministry of the Chemical Industry. If, as Regnard says, Kostandov's Ministry and the Ministry of Petroleum Refining and Petrochemicals are two of only three "non-military" branch ministries represented in the VPK, that may be another factor perpetuating large hard-currency allocations to the chemicals branch. But there are also good economic reasons for a continued high priority: the particularly large technology gap in chemicals, in conjunction with the potential contribution of the industry to Soviet food production[33]—latterly an extremely high priority. The question is whether such reasons are sufficiently strong to justify the especially large and prolonged allocation of hard currency to the chemical industry.

This example of chemicals suggests that success in Soviet assimilation is somewhat circumscribed even in an area where special efforts have been made.

E. Case Study Methods, and Differences Among Industries

Many of the methods used in studying the Soviet chemical industry should be applicable to other branches of production in the USSR. Certain obvious limitations apply, however, to the scope of application of the sort of approach used for the chemical industry.

First, Soviet military production will be a special case. Acquisition of Western machinery and know-how for direct application to the production of military devices is subject to Western strategic export controls; moreover, the Soviets would not wish to be dependent on Western suppliers for this purpose. Acquisition will tend both to be clandestine and to be as far as possible unpublicized even after the event by the Soviets. Documentation of successful past acquisition of militarily useful technologies is sometimes possible, as Cooper's chapter shows. But Cooper also shows that reconstruction of past acquisition and assimilation of Western technology simply from information about weapons and other military devices subsequently fielded by the Warsaw Pact may not always be as conclusive as some writers claim.[34]

Second, agriculture presents some special problems because useful agricultural know-how can often be either of a "disembodied" kind—cropping systems and the like—or embodied in rather special ways, as for example in breeding cattle, or even not transferable across national boundaries, as in the case of plants bred for specific climatic and soil conditions. It is therefore not surprising that the approach of Anton Malish's chapter is somewhat different from those of the other case studies.

With these *caveats*, the following check-list of points on which assimilation case-studies require information is offered:

1. What are the scale and level of sophistication of domestic R and D? (R and D manpower data, and patents registered abroad would be among the possible indicators; Western leads may in some cases be measurable by reference to dates of first pilot-plant or other experimental production.)
2. How successful is implementation of domestic R and D? (Implementation lead-times may be deducible from the journal *Vnedrennye izobreteniya*).[35]

3. Where there are failures in implementing domestic R and D, what are the crucial barriers? Weaknesses in project management; in maintaining quality and precision in manufacture? Are Soviet licenses sold abroad for products and processes not implemented in the USSR?

4. What is the evidence of imported Western technology being treated as a substitute for, rather than a complement to, domestic RDI? (Policy discussion; published Soviet criticisms of particular projects; evidence of a pattern of specialization, with Western elements being blended with indigenous elements—e.g., foreign program controls with domestic machine tools.)

5. What role have machinery and know-how imported from Eastern Europe played in the industry? Do they substitute for or complement imports from the West? Are they a channel for indirect acquisition of Western know-how?

6. What evidence is there of domestic R and D being weakened by reliance on imported Western technology? (Closure or non-development of R and D activities in fields marked by extensive Western imports, for example).

7. Which channels of transfer are utilized, and what factors determine the choice? (Where the technologies involved are not rapidly changing, and where Soviet-Western gaps at the R and D stage seem small, it may be that the utility of the imports resides chiefly in the Western production quality and project management that come with them.)

8. How does the particular technology's level of sophistication (roughly corresponding to the R and D: sales ratio of the industry supplying the technology) affect the transfer and assimilation processes?

9. How does the rate of advance of the technology in the West affect the transfer and assimilation processes?[36]

10. What role is played in the assimilation process by the transfer of personal skills? (This could include Soviet design engineers learning by cooperation in design, as well as training of technicians, etc.)

11. Is the activity for which the technology is imported given a high priority ranking? Is the priority stable over time? How large are the complementary domestic inputs assigned to implementing the imported technology?

12. Have imports of Western technology been continuous or lumpy? How has this affected assimilation? Is there evidence of improvement over time in assimilation?

13. What organizational changes affecting assimilation can be observed?

14. Which specific interests and individual advocates (as Leonid Kostandov in the case of chemicals) can be discerned behind the technology imports in question?

In practice, these questions will not all be answered satisfactorily. But they are all worth posing, and trying to answer.

When it comes to the basic question of how well a particular Soviet activity has managed to assimilate technology imports, experience in studying the chemical industry suggests a number of specific kinds of information which are relevant and which may be obtainable.

For "non-military" industrial technology it will often be possible (though laborious) to match up Western contract and supply information and Soviet information on plant commissioning, etc., for branch and product-group case studies. To assess assimilation performance, then, (as distinct from analyzing the factors affecting that performance), it is necessary to assemble as much of the following information as possible.

1. Value, location of use, production profile, and design capacity of imported machinery; licenses, know-how, and training supplied.
2. Domestic construction and other inputs to enable the imported machinery to be used.
3. Start-up date and subsequent output and manning levels for the imported machinery.
4. Domestic replication of the imported machinery.
5. Domestic modification and adaptation of the imported machinery.
6. Substantial further development of the technology embodied in the imports, by means of indigenous RDI.
7. Any Soviet recourse, over and above the original contract, to additional Western assistance to implement the imported technology.[37]
8. Evidence of any subsequent Soviet return to Western suppliers for new "injections" of imported technology following the development in the West of a new vintage of the technology in question.
9. Subsequent Soviet license sales and patent registrations in the West which indicate that Soviet RDI has "built on" the initial technology purchase.[38]

This is not the place to draw general conclusions from the analysis in this book and elsewhere of Soviet assimilation of imported technology. What is worth stressing, however, is the differences that seem to obtain between industries. It is a general characteristic of empirical studies of the economics of the innovation process that they often lead to conclusions that hold for particular kinds of technology rather than across the whole range of technologies.

The Soviet experience of assimilating foreign technology is one which brings in yet further distinctions—between high and low domestic priorities and between clandestine and open acquisition. The general sluggishness of the Soviet economic system with respect to technological change shows up in the limited success in assimilating imported chemical technology. But there are areas where systemic impediments may be worse (agriculture? computers?). And there is defense production, where success has on the whole been greater because domestic priorities have been consistently high and indigenous RDI activities more effective.

In general, the largest potential economic gains exist in branches where the technological lag behind the West is greatest. But domestic capacity to assimilate what is imported probably tends to be greater where the gap is smaller, and domestic RDI processes more effective. This trade-off cannot be easy for Soviet planners to judge.

At the same time, the Soviet planners must also allocate technology imports in the light of the strength of their desire for "independence." There are perhaps two main styles of technology importing. The first is open, large-scale, long-run, and tending to substitute for domestic R and D, which is followed above all in consumer-oriented branches where "dependence" gives the West little leverage. The second is clandestine, episodic, opportunist, and intended only to supplement a domestic RDI process which is meant to be an independent source of national strength: the obvious instance is military technology. It is likely that the greater part of Soviet commercial acquisition of Western technology has been in the first category.[39]

NOTES

1. J. Jewkes, R. Sawers, and R. Stilleman, *The Sources of Invention* (London: Macmillan, 1969).

2. L. Nabseth and G. F. Ray (eds.), *The Diffusion of New Industrial Processes* (London: Cambridge University Press, 1974).

3. *Metodicheskie ukazaniya k razrabotke gosudarstvennykh planov razvitiya narodnogo khozyaistva SSSR* (Moscow: Ekonomika, 1974), p. 595.

4. *Metodicheskie*, pp. 9–20, and E. Ya Volynets-Russet, *Planirovanie i raschet effektivnosti priobreteniya litsenzii* (Moscow: Ekonomika, 1973), pp. 55–135.

5. These topics are discussed at greater length in P. Hanson, *Trade and Technology in Soviet-Western Relations* (New York: Columbia University Press, 1981), chapters 6 and 7.

6. "Mnogolikaya bezotvetstvennost'," *Pravda*, 21 December 1983, p. 2, dis-

cussed in Hanson, "More Problems with Imported Technology," *Radio Liberty Research*, RL 26/84 (13 January 1984).

7. For a systematic description of normality in Soviet investment, see David A. Dyker, *The Process of Investment in the Soviet Union* (Cambridge: Cambridge University Press, 1983).

8. For a discussion of this material see Hanson, "Changes in Soviet Policy in Technology Imports," *Osteuropa-Wirtschaft*, June 1982, pp. 128–34.

9. V. K. Fal'tsman, "Zakaz na novuyu tekhniku," *Ekonomika i organizatsiya promyshlennogo proizvodstva*, no. 7, 1983, pp. 3–20; also conversation with Professor Fal'tsman in Moscow on 7 September 1983, in which he made it clear that he had chiefly Western imports in mind.

10. Henri Regnard, "The USSR and Scientific, Technological, and Technical Intelligence," *Défense Nationale*, December 1983, pp. 107–21. An English translation, rather than the original, has been available to me.

11. Oleg Penkovsky, *The Penkovsky Papers* (London: Collins, 1965). This book is based on the testimony of a Soviet double agent. The testimony has presumably been doctored.

12. T. Ozawa, *Japan's Technological Challenge to the West* (Cambridge: MIT Press, 1974).

13. K. Poznański, "New Dimensions in International Trade: East-South Competition in the West," mimeo 1982.

14. See Robert W. Campbell, *Soviet Technology Imports: the Gas Pipeline Case* (Santa Monica: California Seminar on International Security and Foreign Policy, Discussion Paper no. 91, 1981) and Campbell's chapter in the present volume.

15. *Ecotass*, 26 November 1983, and *Economist*, 3 December 1983. For details and assessment, see the chapter by George Holliday.

16. Philip Hanson, "The End of Import-Led Growth? Some Observations on Soviet, Polish and Hungarian Experience in the 1970s," *Journal of Comparative Economics*, vol. 6, no. 2 (June 1982), pp. 130–147.

17. Zdenek Drabek and John Slater have re-grouped SITC data for OECD.

18. From a balance-of-payments point of view, successful assimilation could be equally well represented by import-substitution by branches with earlier import-intensive investment. Because of the weaker quality standards of the domestic economy, however, this test will not generally be so persuasive. But it may well be appropriate for Soviet agriculture, for example—where recent indications are that Soviet policies are shifting in favor of imported agricultural and food-processing technology. See Economist Intelligence Unit, *Quarterly Economic Review of the USSR*, 1984, no. 1.

19. Poznański.

20. M. Y. Yoshino, "Japan as Host to the International Corporation" in C. P. Kindleberger (ed.), *The International Corporation* (Cambridge: MIT Press, 1970) pp. 345–70.

21. T. Ozawa, *Japan's Technological Challenge to the West* (Cambridge: MIT Press, 1976). See also Ozawa, "Government Control over Technology Acquisition and Firms' Entry into New Sectors: The Experience of Japan's Synthetic Fibre Industry," *Cambridge Journal of Economics*, vol. 4, no. 2 (June 1980), pp. 133–46; G. C. Allen, "Industrial Policy and Innovation in Japan," in C. Carter (ed.), *Industrial Policy and Innovation* (London: Heinemann Educational Books, 1981), pp. 68–88.

22. On the small scale of Soviet license purchases, see Hanson, *Trade and Technology in Soviet-Western Relations* (New York: Columbia University Press, 1981) pp. 132–133.

23. Colin Merrett, "Technical Progress," *Barclays Review,* February 1981, pp. 10–15.

24. Abram Bergson, "Technological Progress," in Abram S. Bergson and Herbert S. Levine (eds.) *The Soviet Economy: Toward the Year 2000* (Winchester: Allen and Unwin, 1983), pp. 34–79.

25. For instance, a case can be made for "natural resources exhaustion" reducing GNP by about 0.6 percent per annum in 1967–82, against Bergson's 0.1 percent for 1950–75; and changes in labor morale and effort and in the severity of supply bottlenecks are plausible additional candidates. See Hanson, "Brezhnev's Economic Legacy," paper presented at the NATO Economics Directorate Colloquium, Brussels, April 1984.

26. In particular by Donald Green and Herbert Levine, and Martin Weitzmann. For a review, together with an alternative estimate for the Soviet chemical industry, see Hanson, *Trade and Technology,* chapter 9.

27. I have tried to do this in studies of the assimilation of imported technology in the Soviet chemical industry and the sub-branch of mineral fertilizer production (Hanson, *Trade and Technology,* chapters 10 and 11).

28. What follows is based on Hanson, *Trade and Technology,* chapters 10 and 11, and *Strategies and Policy Implementation;* and on CIA, *Soviet Chemical Equipment Purchases from the West: Impact on Production and Trade* (Washington, D.C., 1978), ER 78-10554.

29. *Narodnoe khozyaistvo SSSR v 1982 g,* pp. 339 and 341.

30. Starting from what respondents judged to be the first serious contact relating to a subsequent specific import order.

31. Soviet evidence on domestic RDI lead-times came mainly from J. A. Martens and J. P. Young, "Soviet Implementation of Domestic Inventions: First Results," in U.S. Congress Joint Economic Committee, *Soviet Economy in a Time of Change,* part 2 (Washington: USGPO, 1979). A recent *Pravda* article by a professor of chemistry refers to at least 8–10 years' being needed to implement most Soviet chemicals inventions, of which 4–5 are needed for pilot-plant testing and evaluation. The writer is particularly critical of procedural bottlenecks delaying the construction of pilot plants. S. Karpacheva, "A vremya ukhodit . . . ," *Pravda,* 25 December 1983, p. 2.

32. The definitive account of this in English, so far as domestic policies are concerned, is R. Amann, "The Chemicalization drive and the problem of innovation," in R. Amann and J. M. Cooper (eds.) *Industrial Innovation in the Soviet Union* (New Haven: Yale University Press, 1982), pp. 127–209.

33. See Hanson, "The Soviet chemical industry's response to agriculture's needs," *Outlook on Agriculture,* vol. 12, no. 4 (1983), pp. 197–201.

34. On the gap between evidence of transfers and evidence from completed weapons systems, see also David Holloway, "Western Technology and Soviet Military Power," paper prepared for the Millennium Conference on Technology Transfer and East-West Relations in the 80s, London, May 1983.

35. See Martens and Young, "Soviet Implementation," pp. 472–510.

36. For evidence on this within the non-communist world, see David Teece, *The Multinational Corporation and the Resource Cost of Technology Transfer* (New York: Ballinger, 1976).

37. Some examples of this are given in *Trade and Technology,* chapter 11. A striking recent example is Soviet recruitment in the UK of computer programmers and systems analysts familiar with advanced IBM and Digital Equipment Corporation (VAX) computers. The Soviets were reportedly offering short-term contracts at £1,000 per week plus expenses, which was said to be a higher rate than for similar work in the more disagreeable Middle Eastern

countries. Over 50 programmers were said to be on their way (*Guardian*, February 3, 1984, p. 17). (How many thousands applied was not reported.) Another recent example is initial Soviet failure to make use of sophisticated positioning equipment for controlling imported deepwater offshore drilling ships in Barents Sea oil development. Here assistance was obtained from the original Norwegian supplier of the equipment—a state-owned ammunition works. Reuters report from Stavanger by Richard Wallis, 2 November 1983.

38. Citations of Western patents in Soviet patents registered in the West are a possible source of useful information, to which Mr. Alan Couchman has drawn my attention. See Keith Pavitt, "Patent Statistics as Indicators of Innovative Activities: Possibilities and Problems," revised version of a paper given at the 1983 annual meeting of the American Association for the Advancement of Science (Sussex University, Science Policy Research Unit, mimeo 1983).

39. This, at least, has been my impression from inspection of the array of published chemical final products in the USSR. The branch obviously provides *some* inputs into defense end-uses, but so do all branches. The reported relationship to the VPK, however, raises a question about this.

Western Technology Transfer to The Soviet Automotive Industry

George D. Holliday

Introduction

INCREASING POLITICAL tensions between the Soviet Union and the United States, accompanied by criticisms of technology transfer policies in both countries, have raised questions about the future prospects for East-West economic and technological ties. This case study examines the contribution of Western technology to the Soviet automotive industry since the 1960s and explores Soviet attitudes toward further technological interaction with the West in the industry. It discusses the likelihood that political, economic, and technological factors will lead Soviet economic planners to reduce the automotive industry's reliance on imported Western technology. Are Soviet planners and industry officials generally satisfied, or are they disappointed with the results of importing Western automotive technology? Are they likely to promote further technological ties with Western industry, or do they intend to rely more heavily on domestic resources for technological progress?

The Soviet automotive industry has been one of the primary beneficiaries of Western technology transfer to the Soviet Union. During the 1960s and early 1970s, when Soviet imports of Western machinery, equipment, and know-how grew rapidly, the automotive industry accounted for a large share of total Soviet imports. Like most other industries, however, the automotive industry's imports of Western technology have declined in the late 1970s and early 1980s. The decline coincides with more prominent criticism in the Soviet press of past decisions to import technology and of the ways some Soviet enterprises use imported technology. The critics have complained of squandering hard currency on imported technologies that are no better than domestic technologies. They have also pointed out instances of delays in installation and inefficient use of imported machinery and equipment. Soviet publication of such criticisms, combined with a decline in the monetary value of imported technology, suggests to some observers a possible disenchantment on the part of Soviet leaders with past technology import policies.

The answers to several questions may help in determining whether Soviet leaders and industry officials are changing their approach to Western technology. Have problems in assimilating Western technology persuaded Soviet planners that they are spending too much on imports? Is Soviet automotive technology now at a sufficient level to allow Soviet planners to rely on their own resources to insure further technological progress? To what extent has a shortage of hard currency constrained Soviet imports of Western automotive technology? Has the deterioration of East-West political relations discouraged Soviet leaders from becoming more dependent on Western technology? Are variations in the level of imports largely explained by patterns of domestic investments?

In looking for evidence of a change in attitudes and policies in the Soviet automotive industry, this chapter begins with a discussion of the original rationale for large-scale imports of Western automotive technology. It describes trends in production, investment, technological change, and imports in the industry and assesses the industry's needs for the 1980s. It then attempts to answer the question of whether past technology import policies are relevant to the industry's present and future needs.

Expansion and Modernization of the Soviet Automotive Industry, 1966–75

In the past two decades, Soviet economic planners have given the automotive industry high priority as a recipient of imported technology: the industry has accounted for a significant share of total Soviet imports of machinery, equipment and technical assistance from the West. The Soviet Union began a major effort to expand and modernize its automotive industry in the mid-1960s. At that time the industry was characterized by a production capacity that was considered by Soviet planners to be insufficient for the needs of the Soviet economy, by a level of production technology that was far behind that of the West, and by products that were widely considered to be inferior.

The poor condition of the Soviet automotive industry was the result of many years' neglect from Soviet planners and relative isolation from technological developments of the Western automotive industry.[1] In the late 1950s and early 1960s, Soviet planners had made half-hearted attempts to expand and modernize both passenger car and truck production. Such efforts had been thwarted, however, by inadequate investment and an inability, because of hard currency constraints and Western export controls, to import new Western technologies.[2] Truck production began to stagnate, and efforts to expand production of a new passenger car faltered.

The political leadership that assumed power in 1964 recognized the poor state of affairs in the automotive industry. In a 1965 speech to the State Planning Committee, Premier Alexei Kosygin bluntly criticized the previous leadership for stubbornly adhering to the idea that the Soviet Union did not need to develop production of passenger cars on a large scale. He suggested that the new leadership would assign significantly more resources to this goal. Kosygin also criticized the automotive industry for manufacturing trucks that did not meet the needs of the Soviet economy, claiming that Western manufacturers had long ago ceased production of some types of trucks still being produced in the Soviet Union. He was openly pessimistic about the Soviet automotive industry's ability to improve the situation: "We are reconstructing ZIL and GAZ for output of vehicles with greater capacity, but I am not certain that everything has been done properly."[3]

Kosygin's 1965 speech thus suggested the rationale for a major change in the direction of the Soviet automotive industry. Soviet planners would rapidly expand and modernize the industry in an effort to satisfy consumer demand for passenger automobiles and the transportation needs of the economy. This effort would require a huge increase in domestic investment in the industry. Although Kosygin did not refer explicitly to technology imports, his invidious comparisons of Soviet manufacturers with their Western counterparts foreshadowed significant imports of the latest Western production technologies and product designs.

Soviet planners introduced a new 15-year plan for transportation (1966–80) that called for large-scale production of a wide variety of trucks, buses, and passenger cars.[4] The first phase of the plan emphasized a massive growth of passenger car production, from a mere 201,000 a year in 1965 to 1.2 million by 1975. The planned increase in passenger car production was part of a general effort to expand production of consumer goods in order to provide incentives to improve labor productivity. The second phase of the plan emphasized a large increase in truck production in order to provide a more balanced freight transport system for the Soviet economy. To implement the planned expansion, the Soviet Government allocated a 220 percent increase in investments for the automotive industry during the Eighth Five-Year Plan (1966–70).[5]

Modernization and Expansion of Passenger Car Production

The most important project during the Eighth Five-Year Plan was the construction of a huge new passenger car plant, the Volga Automobile Plant (VAZ). The value of Soviet purchases of Western machinery and equipment for VAZ exceeded $550 million.

Because passenger car production had been a low priority for the Soviet automotive industry, industry officials were keenly interested in the latest Western developments in both production technologies and product designs. The Soviet machine tool industry had insufficient capacity to produce special machines and automatic lines for mass production, and the automotive industry was unable to design and put into production passenger cars that met contemporary world performance standards.[6] Perhaps most important, the industry lacked experience in managing production of automobiles on the scale envisioned in the long-term transportation plan.

Soviet officials, after considerable study and long negotiations with a number of Western firms, selected the Italian automobile manufacturer Fiat to provide technical assistance to VAZ. Fiat's involvement began in 1965 with the signing of a protocol for scientific and technical cooperation with the Soviet State Committee for Science and Technology. The protocol provided a framework for discussions between Fiat and Soviet automotive officials which led to the signing of a contract on August 15, 1966. The contract provided for Fiat assistance in designing a passenger car and in building a production facility with an annual capacity of 660,000 vehicles. Fiat agreed to serve as a general consultant for the project: it provided designs for the production process, specified which machinery and equipment should be purchased in the West and who the Western manufacturers were, and trained Soviet specialists in the operation of the machinery and equipment. Fiat also sold the manufacturing rights for the Fiat-124, a contemporary car that was the prototype for the vehicles produced at VAZ, and agreed to assist in adapting the vehicle to Soviet operating conditions. Finally, Fiat supervised the assembly and installation of all imported equipment and assured its successful operation.[7]

Soviet importers assigned to Fiat a role that was much more active than usual in Soviet acquisitions of Western technology. Fiat was involved in every phase of the technology transfer process, from initial planning of the project to startup. Its active participation is illustrated by the enormous (by Soviet standards) exchange of personnel between Fiat and the Soviet automotive industry. About 2500 Western specialists, including 1500 from Fiat and others from subcontractors, traveled to VAZ. At the same time, about 2500 Soviet technicians and managers went to Italy to be trained at Fiat production facilities.[8] Perhaps the most important contribution of Fiat was extensive training of top management of VAZ in the organization and management of mass production of passenger cars. Almost all of the managers of the functional administrations of the general board of directors of VAZ were sent to Fiat headquarters in Turin to work on the organization of production, automatic information processing systems and production management.[9]

While VAZ was the major recipient of Western automotive technology during the Eighth Five-Year Plan, other Soviet automotive firms also benefited. Particularly noteworthy was the assistance of the French firm Renault in modernization and expansion of the Moscow Lenin Komsomol Passenger Car Plant (AZLK), which produces the Moskvich, and in the conversion of the Izhevsk Machinebuilding Plant to production of the Moskvich. Renault signed an agreement in 1966 to assist in production engineering and selection of foreign equipment for the Moskvich plants. The value of equipment supplied to the plants was about 700 million francs ($142 million at the 1966 exchange rate).[10] The car produced at the modernized plants was designed primarily by Soviet specialists.

To support VAZ and other automotive plants, the Soviet Union also imported Western technology to construct new, or modernize existing vendor plants supplying the automotive industry. Among the new vendor plants built in the early 1970s with Western assistance were: a rubber fittings plant at Balakovo, built with the assistance of Pirelli of Italy; plants for making oil and air filters and upholstery materials, purchased from Japanese firms; a plant for car seats purchased from West Germany; a plant for oil seals at Kursk; and an anti-friction bearing plant at Vologda.[11]

Modernization and Expansion of Truck Production

During the Ninth Five-Year Plan (1971–75), Soviet planners concentrated new investment on truck production. The automotive industry's technology for truck production was relatively more advanced than it had been for automobile production. Truck production, however, also suffered from lack of innovation and insufficient capacity. As Premier Kosygin had observed, new designs were put into production too slowly, and the resulting products and production technologies still lagged behind world standards. Soviet truck plants lacked the capacity needed to expand production fast enough to meet the needs of a growing transport sector. A major deficiency was the shortage of heavy-duty trucks with large-load capacities that could be operated on poor Soviet roads.

To expand and modernize truck factories, Soviet planners invested large amounts in retooling existing plants, such as the Moscow Likhachev Plant (ZIL) and the plants in Gor'kiy (GAZ), Ul'anovsk and Minsk, and in building a major new truck-manufacturing facility, the Kama River Truck Plant (KamAZ). (ZIL and GAZ were then responsible for the bulk of Soviet truck production, producing a wide variety of multi-purpose trucks. Other Soviet truck plants were much smaller, with a more specialized output.) Western technology aided the modernization efforts at a number of Soviet plants.

KamAZ, however, took the lion's share of both domestic resources and foreign technology. KamAZ alone required an investment of over five billion rubles. It was designed to produce 150,000 diesel trucks of 8-ton capacity and an additional 100,000 diesel engines for trucks and buses produced in other Soviet plants. When completed, KamAZ will produce a major share of Soviet truck transport capacity: the carrying capacity of its annual output is expected to equal one-half the carrying capacity of all trucks produced in the Soviet Union in 1975.[12]

When Soviet officials first began construction of KamAZ in 1969, they began to search for a Western firm to undertake the role of general consultant—a role similar to the one that Fiat played at VAZ. They discussed the project with a number of Western firms, but, for various reasons, all rejected the offer. Ford Motor Company and Mack Trucks backed out of the project after they encountered problems with U.S. export control authorities. Other firms were concerned about the risks of taking on such a large project or about the possibility of assisting a potential competitor on world markets.[13]

In the end, Soviet officials had to forego the type of Western assistance that had been provided by Fiat at VAZ and to coordinate themselves purchases from a number of Western firms. Soviet industry also undertook to supply a major share of the equipment for the plant: whereas they had originally considered buying all of the necessary equipment from the West, they later tried to limit foreign procurement to the first stage of the plant's development.[14]

Nevertheless, the contribution of Western firms to KamAZ was enormous. The value of Soviet purchases of Western machinery and equipment, including contracts with dozens of Western firms, is estimated to exceed $1 billion. Among the largest contracts were: an agreement with Swindell-Dressler (U.S.) for design and equipment of the foundry; a contract with Renault, for design and equipment of the engine plant; and a contract with Liebherr Verzahnungstechnik, Gmbh (Federal Republic of Germany), for design and equipment of the transmission plant.[15] The trucks produced at KamAZ are basically of Soviet design. Soviet officials did, however, enlist the help of Renault to make improvements in the diesel engines, because the Soviet-designed engines were not up to world standards.[16]

An important, but often overlooked, element of Western technology transfer to KamAZ, was the effort of KamAZ specialists to assimilate Western management techniques. Although KamAZ managers did not benefit from a long-term, close working relationship with a Western firm in the pattern of VAZ-Fiat cooperation, Soviet management specialists have acknowledged the influence of Western management science at KamAZ. B. Z. Mil'ner, a researcher at the Institute for the Study of the U.S.A. and Canada in Moscow and one of the top Soviet management specialists, stated that KamAZ's managers would use "the leading domestic and foreign experience in organizing the management of the big production complex."[17] Mil'ner and his fellow researchers at the Institute worked with specialists from KamAZ and other enterprises to apply Western management techniques, particularly systems analysis, mathematical modeling, and computer science, to Soviet industry.

Trends in Production, Investment, Technological Progress, and Imports During 1976–85

Assimilation problems delayed startup and attainment of capacity production for both VAZ and KamAZ. The contract signed with Fiat projected production of the first cars at VAZ in 1969 and attainment of full capacity in 1972. Actual serial production began in August 1970, and the plant attained capacity production in 1975. VAZ currently produces over one-half of the total Soviet output of passenger cars.

Construction and installation delays at KamAZ have been much more serious. A Communist Party decree in January 1971 originally projected production of the first trucks at KamAZ by the end of 1974. Soviet planners expected the plant to reach full capacity (150,000 trucks and 100,000 diesel engines for other Soviet truck plants) by 1978.[18] In fact, the plant has progressed much more slowly. The Soviet press claimed the first vehicles were produced in February 1976 and that the first stage of KamAZ (that is, the capacity to produce 75,000 trucks and 40,000 engines) began operating at the end of 1976.[19] Even Soviet claims about the delayed startup for the first stage of KamAZ, however, mask considerable problems in achieving capacity output, a goal that was apparently reached only in 1981. (KamAZ produced 70,000 trucks in 1980 and 85,000 in 1981).[20]

The delays in the second and final stage of KamAZ have been equally bad. Once the Soviet automotive industry's top priority for the Tenth Five-Year Plan, the second stage subsequently became the top priority for the Eleventh Five-Year Plan. The Soviet press reported at the beginning of the 26th Party Congress (in February 1981) that the first vehicles had been produced in the second stage, but the plant was far from reaching capacity production. The production of KamAZ diesel engines for other Soviet truck plants also appears far behind schedule. In August 1982, a Soviet automotive specialist noted that attainment of capacity at the KamAZ diesel plant and the supply of diesel engines to other truck plants remained an important goal of the Eleventh Five-Year Plan.[21]

Despite the slow achievement of capacity at VAZ and KamAZ, the output of the Soviet automotive industry expanded dramatically in the late 1960s and early 1970s. Production of passenger cars increased by six and one-half times and truck production doubled between 1965 and 1978. Since 1978, however, Soviet production has stagnated (see Table

Table 1

Soviet Production of Automobiles

Year	Total	Trucks vehicles	Trucks total carrying capacity, tons	Passenger cars	Buses
1965	616,300	379,600	1,377,000	201,200	35,500
1970	916,100	524,500	2,266,000	344,200	47,400
1971	1,142,600	564,300	2,429,000	529,000	49,300
1972	1,378,800	596,800	2,551,000	730,100	51,900
1973	1,602,200	629,500	2,639,000	916,700	56,000
1974	1,846,000	666,000	2,751,000	1,119,000	61,000
1975	1,964,000	696,000	2,900,000	1,201,000	67,000
1976	2,025,000	716,000	3,056,000	1,239,000	70,100
1977	2,088,000	734,000	3,320,000	1,280,000	74,600
1978	2,151,000	762,000	3,429,000	1,312,000	77,400
1979	2,173,000	780,000	3,878,000	1,314,000	79,200
1980	2,199,000	787,000	4,001,000	1,327,000	85,300
1981	2,198,000	787,000	4,129,000	1,324,000	86,900
1982	2,173,000	780,000	NA	1,307,000	85,700

SOURCES: SSSR, Tsentral'noe statisticheskoe upravlenie, *Narodnoe khoziaistvo SSSR, 1922–1982* (Moscow: Finansy i statistika, 1982), p. 196. *Narodnoe khoziaistvo v 1982* gives data only for bus production. *Foreign Economic Trends and Their Implications for the United States: USSR* (U.S. Department of Commerce, Washington, D.C., December 1983) gives 1982 data for cars and a combined figure for trucks and buses.

1). The automotive industry met its goal for passenger car production for the Tenth Five-Year Plan (1976–80), but fell considerably short of its goal for truck production. Industry officials had planned to expand production of trucks to 800,000–825,000 and to increase the average carrying capacity of Soviet trucks to 6.4 tons. Actual 1980 output was 787,000 trucks with an average capacity of 5.1 tons. Moreover, production of both trucks and passenger cars has declined since 1980. Production of passenger cars peaked at 1,327,000 in 1980 before declining in 1981 and 1982. Truck production peaked at 787,000 in 1980–81, but declined in 1982.

The decline in Soviet production of automobiles is somewhat mysterious, in light of the expansion of capacity at a number of truck and passenger car plants. A number of problems both within the industry and in other industries charged with supplying materials and equipment to automotive plants largely explain the apparent paradox. A 1979 survey of the automotive industry in the Soviet weekly *Ekonomicheskaia gazeta,* for example, placed major blame for the shortcomings of the automotive industry on other ministries. It blamed the Ministry of Con-

struction for delaying construction of the Roslavl Brake Plant, the Ministry of Heavy Industry for delaying the Vologda Ball Bearing Plant, and
the Ministry of Industrial Construction for delaying construction of a
new forge and press shop at Kuibyshev. The survey claimed that many
new and reconstructed plants were slow to achieve full capacity and that
many were not achieving their planned output. It emphasized the need
to "force" the construction of KamAZ and its supplier plants and the
attainment of capacity at the Yaroslav Diesel Plant, the Krasnoyarsk
Truck Trailer Plant, and others.[22]

KamAZ is a major victim of the industry's faulty supply system.
Inadequate supplies from other ministries are at least partially responsible for the delays in the second stage of KamAZ. Soviet machine-tool
makers, for example, have not met their goals for supplying equipment
to the plant. Although KamAZ officials planned to use only Soviet machinery and equipment for the second stage, they are using some imports from the West. Orders for Western machinery for the second stage
continued at least through 1979, when Soviet importers signed a number of contracts with West European and U.S. firms, with deliveries
scheduled for 1980–81. (U.S. export controls may have also contributed
to the delays at KamAZ. See page 106 below.) Failure to reach capacity
production at KamAZ, in turn, has created supply problems for other
parts of the automotive industry. Since the KamAZ diesel plant is to
supply diesel engines to other truck plants, its delayed attainment of
capacity is undoubtedly adversely affecting production at those plants.

Official Soviet trade statistics provide an indication of the severity of
the supply problems. Soviet imports for the automotive industry from
Western countries are not limited to high-technology machinery and
equipment. The automotive industry is also spending significant
amounts of hard currency for imports of parts and components for
trucks and cars and for such material inputs as rubber and sheet metal.
In 1982, for example, the Soviet Union imported parts and components
for trucks and garage equipment from the Federal Republic of Germany
valued at over 40 million rubles.[23] Given Soviet hard currency constraints, it is likely that such imports are unplanned, stopgap measures to
cover shortfalls in output at domestic factories supplying Soviet automotive plants.

Another major factor contributing to the stagnation of Soviet automobile production may be the ongoing modernization efforts at several
automobile plants. Retooling for model changes may be causing shut-
downs of assembly lines and reduced output. Workers at VAZ, for example, are now replacing large amounts of equipment that was installed at
VAZ in 1969–72. Investment strategy for the industry has shifted from
the past emphasis on construction of new plants to an emphasis on
completion of ongoing construction and modernization of existing

plants. In this regard, investment in the industry is consistent with the overall strategy for Soviet industry of devoting a larger share of investment to new machinery and equipment and less to buildings and other structures.[24] Thus, new investment is aimed more at improving the efficiency of production processes and the quality of products than at expanding output.

Soviet passenger car producers may also be confronting reduced demand for their products. While the industry's output is far from satisfying consumer demand for cars in the Soviet Union, officials may have decided that the Soviet infrastructure—roads, fuel, service facilities, and spare parts—is inadequate to sustain further large increases in production. In addition, a reduction in foreign demand for Soviet exports may be a factor in reduced production (see Table 5).

There is, however, no reduction in demand for Soviet trucks. On the contrary, shortfalls in truck production are causing serious problems for other sectors of the economy. Perhaps the greatest problem exists in agriculture, which is reportedly experiencing a shortage of trucks and other specialized vehicles. According to official Soviet statistics, the supply of trucks to agriculture actually declined from 228,500 vehicles in 1975 to 216,500 in 1981.[25] (Data for 1982 were not published.) The problem has been serious enough to attract the attention of the Central Committee of the Communist Party, which in 1978 severely criticized the automotive industry for not supplying enough vehicles adapted to the needs of agriculture.[26] The criticism was probably aimed largely at KamAZ, since much of its production is designed for use in agriculture.

The Relationship between Domestic Investment Trends and Imports of Technology

After a rapid increase in the Eighth and Ninth Five-Year Plans, Soviet investment in the automotive industry appears to have decreased significantly. Unfortunately, published Soviet statistics do not give detailed data on investment in the automotive industry. The trend in Soviet investment in the industry is reflected, however, in Table 2, which provides data on the commissioning of new automobile manufacturing capacity through the construction of new plants and the expansion and reconstruction of existing plants. (Commissioning of new capacity naturally lags behind actual investments.) The data clearly reflect the startup and expansion of production at VAZ between 1970 and 1972 and the commissioning of part of KamAZ in 1976. The slower increase in new manufacturing capacity after 1972 reflects the inevitable slowdown after the attainment of capacity at VAZ and the delay in commissioning new capacity at KamAZ. The size of the VAZ and KamAZ projects relative to the industry as a whole has produced a lumpy pattern in Soviet investment and commissioning of new capacity in the industry.

Table 2

Commissioning of New Automobile Manufacturing Capacity And Imports of Equipment for Factories Producing Automobiles

		Imports of Equipment[2]		
		(a)	(b)	(c)
	Total New Capacity[1]	Value in	Value in 1000	Value in 1000
	(1000 vehicles)	1000 rubles	current dollars	constant dollars
Year				(1975 = 100)
1961–65 (average)	31.3	*	—	—
1966	66.7	*	—	—
1967	57.8	*	—	—
1968	43.4	*	—	—
1969	73.1	263,561	292,553	NA
1970	177.7	199,162	221,070	320,391
1971	504.3	62,962	69,888	104,310
1972	288.7	59,999	72,999	102,815
1973	33.8	128,792	175,157	216,243
1974	75.7	337,645	445,691	495,212
1975	71.4	287,521	399,654	399,654
1976	92.4	224,082	298,029	289,349
1977	47.3	194,860	261,112	233,136
1978	40.8	118,055	172,360	133,612
1979	40.3	144,768	220,047	158,307
1980	23.9	139,767	215,241	143,494
1981	42.9	132,514	184,194	124,455
1982	NA	164,881	227,536	153,741

[1]SOURCE: *Narodnoe khoziaistvo SSSR.* New capacity measures the commissioning of new automobile manufacturing capacity through the construction of new plants and the expansion and reconstruction of existing plants.

[2]SOURCES: Ruble values in column (a) are from *Vneshniaia torgovlia SSSR.* In column (b), rubles are converted to current dollars at the official exchange rates. In column (c), dollars are deflated using the "Export Price Index of Machinery and Transport Equipment for Selected Countries," United Nations, *Monthly Bulletin of Statistics,* February 1984 and earlier issues.

*Soviet official data report only small or insignificant imports of equipment before 1969.

Table 2 also includes official Soviet data that provide a measure of technology imports for the Soviet automotive industry—specifically, imports of equipment by automobile-manufacturing plants. Soviet foreign trade data are particularly useful as an indicator of the sectoral distribution of technology imports because they indicate the end use of imported machinery and equipment. It should be emphasized that, while imports of machinery and equipment are an important mechanism for acquisition of Western technology, they are not the only one. The Soviet automotive industry extensively uses other means of acquiring Western technology, such as purchases of licenses, technical data, books and periodicals, participation in foreign conferences and seminars, visits to the production facilities in other countries, and scientific and technical cooperation agreements with Western firms, that are not fully measured in foreign trade statistics. Imports of equipment do, however, provide a useful indicator of the trends in technology imports. They are often associated with other forms of technology transfer, such as licensing agreements, training, and assistance in installation, and startup of plants.

Table 2 juxtaposes the trend in commissioning of new automobile-manufacturing capacity and the trend in imports of equipment for producing automobiles. The rapid increase in commissioning of new capacity during the early and mid-1970s (reflecting the construction of VAZ, part of KamAZ and the modernization of other plants) was accompanied by a rapid increase in imports of equipment. The completion of VAZ in the early 1970s and the slowing of equipment purchases for KamAZ by the late 1970s, on the other hand, are accompanied by declines in imports.

In crude terms, Table 2 suggests that the decline in imports of equipment for automotive plants may be due largely to domestic investment trends. That is, the lower level of imports in the late 1970s is associated with a winding down of construction of new plants. A corollary suggestion is that other factors, such as assimilation problems, concern about overdependence on Western technology, political tensions, and hard currency constraints, may have been relatively less important factors. Indeed, given the apparently lower level of investment in the automotive industry, imports of technology have remained surprisingly high by historical standards. The data suggest that, while Soviet planners may be placing lower priority on expansion of capacity in the automotive industry, they are continuing to rely heavily on Western technology for the modernization that is still taking place.

The Relationship Between Domestic Technological Progress and Imports of Technology

Since the large-scale transfer of Western technology to VAZ, KamAZ, and other Soviet automotive plants in the late 1960s and early 1970s, the pace of technological change in the Western automotive industry has been exceedingly rapid. There have been major developments in both product technologies and production processes. In response to government regulation and a rapid escalation in oil prices, Western manufacturers have introduced features to improve safety, emission control, and fuel efficiency in passenger cars and trucks. Of particular interest to Soviet automotive industry officials are new technologies to improve fuel efficiency—increased compression ratios and improved combustion processes for gasoline engines; quieter and smoother diesel engines; improved transmission systems through more widespread use of front-wheel drive and transversely mounted engines; weight reduction through substitution of lighter steels and plastics; and improved aerodynamics. Soviet officials are also interested in Western innovations to reduce production costs, particularly the use of labor-saving flexible manufacturing systems and industrial robots, metallurgical processes that permit manufacture of longer-lasting parts, computer-aided design and manufacturing processes, and lasers.

Accordingly, key goals set for the automotive industry for the Eleventh Five-Year Plan included lowering the weight of Soviet vehicles, improved aerodynamics, improvements in gasoline engines, wider use of diesels, improvements in metallurgy, replacement of steel with plastics and alloys, and improvements in automation. With regard to specific products, Soviet officials have called for expanded production of diesel engines, specialized freight transport vehicles and trailers—goals which the completion of KamAZ will help attain—and development of new trucks for inter-city and international transport, off-road uses, and other tasks. The key goal in passenger car production is the development of a new generation of lower-weight, front-wheel drive vehicles at VAZ, the Moskvich plants in Moscow and Izhevsk, and Zaporozh'e.[27]

The Soviet decision to modernize passenger car production is the primary stimulus to technology imports during the Eleventh Five-Year Plan. While technology imports are unlikely to equal the volumes attained during the peaks of construction and installation activity at VAZ and KamAZ, modernization of Soviet passenger car production is likely to require a substantial increase in imports. The upturn in imports during 1982 (see Table 2) may foreshadow several years of growth in imports of machinery and equipment. A major modernization of VAZ has already begun to stimulate imports of Western machinery and equipment. Soviet officials have also announced plans to use Western technical assistance to modernize the Moskvich plants in Moscow and Izhevsk. Although no specific plans have been announced for the heretofore neglected Zaporozh'e Automobile Plant, the design and mass production of a new Zaporozhets may require Western technical assistance. Major new developments for Soviet truck plants probably await attainment of capacity at KamAZ. Some modernization, however, continues, accompanied by imports of truck-manufacturing technology from the West.

Developments at Soviet production facilities for producing the VAZ and Moskvich passenger cars illustrate both successes and failures in the industry's attempt to stimulate technological progress. VAZ is generally considered to be the technological leader, with regard to both product and process technology, among Soviet passenger car producers. It is also the largest, producing over one-half of all Soviet cars. AZLK, which, with its sister plant in Izhevsk, produces approximately 420,000 Moskviches, is the other major producer. (The Zaporozh'e Automobile Plant produces about 150,000 Zaporozhets' and the Gorkiy Automobile Plant, a smaller number of larger, more expensive cars.[28]) Although VAZ and the Moskvich plants have made some progress toward introducing new process and product technologies, Soviet specialists acknowledge dissatisfaction with the pace of technological innovation. Their dissatisfaction is reflected in decisions to rely heavily on Western firms in retooling for production of new models.

VAZ's first products were three adaptations of Fiat models produced in the mid-1960s—a standard sedan, the VAZ 2101, and a station wagon, the VAZ 2102, based on the Fiat-124; and a luxury sedan, the VAZ 2103, based on the Fiat-125. (The VAZ car is named Zhiguli in the Soviet Union and Lada for export.) VAZ's manager originally planned frequent modifications of the Zhiguli, with continual improvements and a new basic model every five years. The plant's engineers and designers have introduced numerous improvements, such as quieter, cleaner and more efficient motors, improved upholstery, new safety devices, and new exterior body designs in the VAZ 2105 and 2107.[29]

In 1977, VAZ also introduced a completely new car, the Niva (VAZ 2121). Annual production of Nivas was initially about 15,000 and, during the Eleventh Five-Year Plan, is expected to increase to 75,000.[30] The Niva is a small, all-wheel drive passenger car with an engine about the size of the Zhiguli's. It is slower and uses considerably more fuel than the newer Zhigulis. It is not a replacement for the Zhiguli, but a specialized vehicle designed specifically for rural areas with rough terrain. It appears to have been developed with little foreign assistance and is assembled on equipment that is mostly of domestic origin.[31]

VAZ has not followed its original plan of replacing its basic model every five years. A Soviet observer noted in 1981 that the first model produced at VAZ, the VAZ 2101, was still in production, even though it was obsolete. It was gradually being replaced by the modernized VAZ 2105 and 2107.[32] The first basic model change now appears likely to occur in the mid-1980s with the introduction of the VAZ 2108 and 2109. The model changeover requires a major modernization of VAZ's production processes.[33] Such a modernization of VAZ had been proposed as early as 1975 by the Soviet economist E. B. Golland, who suggested then that it was already time to formulate a complete program for reconstruction and modernization of VAZ. Golland noted that the world level of automobile-manufacturing technology was progressing rapidly and that VAZ's machinery and equipment were becoming obsolete and worn out. He suggested modernizing the plant both by creating a domestic industry capable of producing modern automobile-manufacturing machinery and equipment and by purchasing foreign equipment and licenses.[34]

While VAZ's managers have introduced selective improvements in

Table 3

Selected List of Machinery Orders for Modernization of VAZ, 1981–83

Technology	*Western Supplier*
Joint development of new passenger car	Porsche (F.R.G.)
Robot-operated line for body-welding	C. Itoh and Kawasaki (Japan)
Stamping line for manufacturing side body panels	C. Itoh (Japan)
Licenses and equipment for producing aluminum radiators	Sofica (France)
Casting equipment	Press & Shear Machinery (U.K.)
Automatic line for mechanical processing of cams	Huller-Heller (F.R.G.)
Machinery and equipment for production of front-wheel drive subassemblies	Jung-Schleifmaschinen (F.R.G.)
Lathes for production of front-wheel drive vehicles	Maschinenfabrik Heid (Austria)
Automated line for mechanical forming and finishing of connecting rods	Nabenfabrik Alfing Kessler (F.R.G.)
License and automated equipment for manufacturing aluminum cooling units	Valeo (France)
License for production of Wankel engines	Audi-NSU (F.R.G.)
Welding and machining equipment for plastics and light alloys	Triulzi (Italy)
Automatic test benches	AVL Gesellschaft für Veerbrennungskraftmaschinen und Messtechnik (Austria)
License for production of clutches	Valeo (France)
Plant to manufacture piston rings	Riken (Japan)
Equipment for producing car seat covers and rugs	DOA/Dr Otto Angleitner and Chemiefaser Lenzing (Austria)
Robot soldering line	Comau (Italy)
Engine test equipment	Froude Engineering (U.K.)
Computer-controlled production line for welding car doors	FATA European Group (Italy)
Plant for manufacturing oil filters	Savara (Italy)
Equipment for cleaning carburetor parts	Ultrasons-Annemasse (France)

SOURCE: *Business Eastern Europe*, 1981–83.

the production processes, including small-scale imports of Western technology, the major modernization effort prescribed by Golland apparently began only during the Eleventh Five-Year Plan. The design of the new VAZ models and the modernization of the production processes is being aided with another large-scale infusion of Western technology. VAZ has enlisted the West German firm Porsche to help develop the new VAZ 2108 and 2109 models. The new vehicles will be the first front-wheel drive cars to be put in serial production in the Soviet Union. They will have new, improved engines, possibly including Wankel engines for which Western licenses have been purchased. They will include improved safety and emission control devices and, judging from Soviet machinery orders, will make greater use of plastics and light alloys (see Table 3). VAZ is purchasing a variety of computer-controlled equipment, robot-operated lines, and other machinery from Western firms. VAZ ordered the machinery and equipment listed in Table 3 during 1981–83, with most deliveries planned for 1983–84. It plans to produce the first new models in late 1984.[35]

Like VAZ, the Moskvich plants benefited greatly from imports of Western technology during the late 1960s, when they began production of the Moskvich 412. The Moskvich plants also have enjoyed a significant advantage over most civilian enterprises in the Soviet Union, in that they receive considerable assistance from the Ministry of Defense Industry. For example, all engines for the Moskvich are made at the Ufa Aero-Engine Building Association, and gearboxes for the car are made at the Omsk Aero-Engine Works.[36] The Izhevsk Plant was formerly a part of the Ministry of Defense Industry. Thus, the Moskvich appears to be the product of both significant Western technological inputs and the best domestic technological resources.

The Moskvich 412, which was basically a Soviet-designed vehicle, was considered by Soviet specialists to be on a technological par with equivalent Western models during the early 1970s. It also received fair marks from Western specialists. Tests of the Moskvich in the United Kingdom in 1973 found that the car performed adequately, compared with Western cars in its price range. They detected significant shortcomings, however, in safety, body finish, ventilation, and heating.[37]

Since the introduction of the Moskvich 412, AZLK and Izhevsk have made numerous improvements in their products, but no changes in their basic model. In 1976, they introduced their current models, the Moskvich 2138 and 2140, which are modernized versions of the older Moskvich 412. In 1981, the Moskvich plants introduced a more comfortable 2140-SL luxury model, with new, improved transmission boxes, fuel injection systems, carburetors, distributors (produced under license from the West German firm Bosch), and radial tires. The 1981 cars were also the first Soviet cars to use bumpers, hubcaps, and exterior trim made entirely of plastic. AZLK planned to produce about 40,000 of the new cars, primarily for export.[38]

Despite such changes in their products, the Moskvich plants have not kept pace with the rapid improvements in product and process technologies introduced in the West. Like VAZ, they are producing modernized versions of automobiles designed in the 1960s. Also like VAZ, they will receive considerable Western assistance in modernizing their production processes and designing a new model, the Moskvich 2141. Renault signed a protocol agreement with the Soviet Union in 1983 to help develop the new car. Renault is to help improve the Soviet prototype version, carry out tests on roadholding, bodywork, aerodynamics, and weight reduction. The new model will be a five-door hatchback with a new, 80-horsepower transverse engine. It will make extensive use of plastics and other lightweight materials. Lighter weight and improved aerodynamics are expected to result in a major improvement in the Moskvich's fuel efficiency. Renault is also to supply technical and engineering studies for tooling equipment, a pressing shop, an assembly line, and a paint shop. The new Moskvich production lines are to incorporate a flexible production system with adjustable flowlines and programmable industrial robots. Soviet importers are to spend about FFr 300 million ($36 million) on the Renault contract and a total of FFr 1 billion ($121.5 million) on machinery and equipment from France. Production of the new Moskvich model is planned for 1986.[39]

The experiences of VAZ, AZLK, and other Soviet automotive enterprises suggest several barriers to technological innovation which have encouraged reliance on imports of Western technology. Among the most important are shortcomings in the work of domestic R&D institutes, inadequate capabilities of other branches supplying the automotive industry with modern, specialized equipment and new materials, and slow diffusion of new technologies from innovating enterprises to others in the industry.

Although the Soviet automotive industry has developed a large R&D base, Soviet automotive specialists complain that the industry is not getting enough output from its investment in R&D.[40] Soviet designers and engineers have worked on many of the new technologies that have been developed in the West, but have not kept pace with their Western counterparts in introducing such technologies into the production process.

One of the reasons for poor R&D performance, according to Soviet automotive specialists, is the tradition of separating R&D facilities from the production process. This separation leads sometimes to R&D work that is irrelevant to the needs of the enterprise while more important tasks are left undone. A specialist at ZIL, for example, complained about the failure of designers at the Leningrad Polytechnical Institute, which had been appointed the head institute for robot technology, to develop a reliable robot for ZIL. The institute, he said, had been attracted to work on the development of a talking robot, and ignored the production needs of the industry.[41] VAZ officials have also complained that the automotive ministry's central research institutes are inadequate to meet their needs.[42]

Soviet automotive enterprises have responded to such problems by attempting to perform more R&D at the production facilities and by improving their contractual ties to R&D institutes. VAZ, for example, was built with R&D facilities that were better equipped than other Soviet automotive plants. One Soviet observer complained in 1976, however, that the facilities were understaffed. He proposed that the ministry establish a complex scientific-research and design center at VAZ.[43] There is no evidence, however, that his proposal has been accepted. ZIL has attempted to improve R&D performance by developing longer-term contractual relations with the research institutes, making specialists at the institutes more responsible for their recommendations up to the point of industrial application. Changes in the relationship between ZIL and the research institutes and organizational changes at the enterprise, according to one ZIL specialist, have resulted in faster introduction of innovations.[44]

Despite efforts to improve R&D performance, the Soviet automotive industry lags behind Western firms in introducing important new technologies. Among the major shortcomings of the automotive R&D institutes, according to Soviet observers, are inadequate improvements in fuel efficiency of engines, servicing life of trucks and cars, labor-saving automation in automobile manufacturing, and waste-reduction (especially metal-saving) techniques. The plans to import Western technology for VAZ and AZLK suggest that officials in the Soviet automotive industry have decided to continue to rely heavily on imports to compensate for such shortcomings.

Automotive firms depend heavily on sources outside of the industry to supply materials, machinery and equipment. In the Soviet Union, the inability of other branches to supply the automotive industry with inputs embodying new technological developments has impeded the industry's efforts to introduce new products. In 1975, for example, VAZ's general manager A. A. Zhitkov complained of the tendency of Soviet suppliers to "lower the technical level of equipment offered to us." He claimed that VAZ's ability to make improvements in its products depended on improving the quality of machinery and materials supplied to the plant.[45] Similarly, in 1982, ZIL engineers complained of their inability to obtain new materials, such as metallic powders, and new, specialized machine tools from other branches.[46]

A common solution to this problem in the automotive industry has been the establishment by each enterprise of a production base for manufacturing many of its own inputs. A ZIL specialist, for example, noted that of 350 automated lines in operation at the enterprise, 110 were designed and manufactured at the ZIL plant, even though it was not economically advantageous to do so.[47] An alternative solution, one that is probably more attractive to Soviet automobile manufacturers, is to import the equipment from Western firms.

Soviet plans for cooperation with Western firms in development of a new Moskvich and modernization of Moskvich production facilities bear a close similarity to the ongoing modernization of VAZ. The apparent similarity of technology transfers for the two projects, with both VAZ and AZLK purchasing the same types of product and process technologies from Western firms, suggests substantial barriers to the diffusion of new technologies in the Soviet automotive industry. John Young, in a study of Soviet purchases of Western automotive technology in the 1970s, noted a tendency of Soviet importers to go back to the same Western suppliers to buy similar technologies for different Soviet projects.[48] The recent purchases of similar Western technologies for modernization of VAZ and Moskvich production suggests that the pattern described by Young has persisted.

A. I. Buzhinskiy, Deputy General Director for Economics at ZIL, has explained one important reason why there is inadequate diffusion of new technologies in the Soviet automotive industry. He complained that there is no incentive to the innovating firm to transfer its technology to another firm. Such transfers involve costs which must be borne by the transferor firm, but there is no adequate compensation for the transferor firm's efforts.[49]

The slow diffusion of new technologies among Soviet automotive enterprises appears to have created a technological hierarchy in the industry, with VAZ and KamAZ—the primary beneficiaries of imported technology and domestic investment funds—the technological leaders. The Moscow-based enterprises, ZIL and AZLK, are examples of secondary beneficiaries of imports and domestic resources, and some plants, such as Zaporozh'e, are relatively deprived. One Soviet specialist, for example, suggests that KamAZ and VAZ have set the standard in the Soviet automotive industry for automation of metal-working processes.[50] He urges that the technological level of new metal-working machinery to be introduced during the Eleventh Five-Year Plan should, at a minimum, correspond to the level of machinery already introduced at KamAZ. His statement is typical of many official exhortations to Soviet automotive enterprises to learn from KamAZ or VAZ. Soviet automotive officials appear dissatisfied, however, with the extent of the borrowing and the pace at which other firms are borrowing technology from the leaders of the industry.

The inability to diffuse rapidly imported technologies from the immediate recipient to other plants increases the industry's total demand for imports. If Soviet planners have decided to update continually the technological level of all plants, there is a potential for considerable increases in imports of technology. The planned modernization of the Zaporozh'e Automobile Plant for production of a new model, for example, may require additional Western technology transfers to the Soviet passenger car industry in the near future.

Soviet Attitudes toward Imports of Western Technology

Most Soviet assessments of the costs and benefits of importing Western technology for VAZ, KamAZ, and other automotive plants during the Eighth and Ninth Five-Year Plans are positive. Few Soviet automotive specialists appear to be overly concerned about becoming too dependent on technology imports. Indeed, the importation of foreign technology is seen by some Soviet specialists as a healthy development in the industry. In explaining the Soviet decision to rely on foreign technology for the construction of VAZ, for example, one Soviet specialist observed that the most developed automotive industries in the world are not closed in their own national markets. "Large highly automated mass production," he maintained, "is now impossible without the accumulated advances of worldwide science and technology."[51] A Soviet foreign trade official noted the positive experience of purchasing 380 foreign licenses for VAZ. He used the VAZ experience, as well as the Japanese experience in purchasing foreign licenses, to show that Soviet enterprises raise the technical level of domestic products by importing more technology. Soviet enterprises, he maintained, buy absolutely too few foreign licenses.[52]

Such views probably typify specialists in the automotive industry and the foreign trade bureaucracy—officials who have a vested interest in promoting technological ties to the West. They may diverge from some Soviet officials who do not share such a vested interest. For example, officials in ministries charged with supplying machinery and equipment to the automotive industry, specialists in the automotive industry's central research institutes, and central planners with responsibility for the country's hard currency reserves may tend to think that the industry is spending too much on imported technology. The automotive industry, however, has not been a primary target in published criticisms of past technology import policies.

Soviet specialists appear virtually unanimous in judging the construction of VAZ and KamAZ as major leaps forward for the Soviet automotive industry. Soviet specialists claim that productivity at VAZ is much higher than at other Soviet passenger car plants.[53] VAZ cars and

KamAZ trucks are said to be significant improvements over similar Soviet vehicles. There is also a generally favorable assessment among Soviet automotive specialists and foreign trade specialists of the mechanisms used to import technology. VAZ, in particular, seems to be considered by some Soviet specialists a model for technological cooperation with Western firms.[54]

While the overall assessment of Soviet automotive specialists of importing technology for VAZ and KamAZ has been positive, they frequently described shortcomings in efforts to assimilate Western technology at VAZ and KamAZ. They noted serious problems at both projects in meeting schedules for construction, installation and startup that Soviet planners had set. The Soviet press criticized domestic suppliers to the two construction projects for failure to meet delivery schedules, faulted construction organizations that were unable to attract sufficient skilled workers, and criticized bad working conditions that contributed to poor worker morale and high labor turnover. Soviet observers also criticized the poor coordination of machinery and equipment deliveries and installation at KamAZ. After startup at both plants, suppliers were criticized for delivering materials, parts, and components that did not meet the high standards set for the modern production processes.[55] Such criticisms appeared to be efforts to improve the assimilation process rather than a questioning of the underlying rationale for importing Western technology.

While Soviet automotive specialists rarely question the strategy of importing technology, they do sometimes downplay the contribution of Western technology to the automotive industry. Some Soviet assessments, for example, tend to emphasize the contribution of Soviet specialists to the building of VAZ and KamAZ. While they acknowledge that Western firms played a role in equipping the plants, they portray the two projects as primarily Soviet achievements. Some Soviet commentaries emphasize, for example, that Soviet specialists and workers were responsible for construction of buildings and infrastructure, active participation in the design of production facilities, and adaptation of foreign designs to Soviet conditions. The emphasis of Soviet observers on the achievements of Soviet industry is largely justified. Many of the material and technological inputs involved in the creation of VAZ and KamAZ came from domestic sources.[56] Moreover, the mastery of new technologies, whether of foreign or domestic origin, on such a scale is truly an impressive achievement.

To some extent, however, many Soviet observers, looking retrospectively at the creation of VAZ and KamAZ, appear to flavor their assessments with a heavy dose of technological chauvinism. Such observers tend to underrate the contribution of Western technology, to overlook the shortcomings in Soviet automotive technology that made the large-scale import of Western technology necessary, and to ignore the considerable problems encountered in assimilating Western technology and achieving capacity output at the projects.

Such chauvinist attitudes may have been stimulated by U.S. economic sanctions, directed partially at the Soviet automotive industry (see page 106 below) and by increasing U.S.-Soviet tensions in general. Changing Soviet attitudes do not appear to have led to a decision to stop or curtail sharply imports of Western automotive technology. They may, however, have influenced the selection of Western suppliers to the Soviet automotive industry. Specifically, changing Soviet attitudes may have contributed to a tendency of Soviet importers to rely less on U.S. firms and more on European and Japanese firms to supply machinery and equipment for the automotive industry.

Selection of Trade Partners

Various factors have influenced Soviet choices of trade partners in the automotive sector. Most Soviet statements on this subject emphasize the preference of Soviet importers for the latest available technologies. Soviet importers evidently believe that most of the advanced automotive technologies that they need to import are available only in the West. They have shown by past import decisions that they do not consider the East European countries to be on a technological par with Western firms. In choosing among Western firms, Soviet importers undoubtedly consider other factors that commonly influence foreign trade decisions— price of products, reputation of firms, ability to meet delivery schedules, and experience in transferring technology. In addition, varying trade policies of Western governments appear to have strongly influenced Soviet import decisions. Soviet imports of automotive technology have come primarily from firms whose governments have actively promoted economic ties with the Soviet Union and reduced the burden of export controls.

Sources of Soviet Imports of Automotive Equipment
According to official Soviet foreign trade statistics, Western Europe has been the primary source of automotive technology since the late 1960s (see Table 4). Throughout, firms in the Federal Republic of Germany, Italy, and France have been the largest suppliers, selling equipment to VAZ, KamAZ, and other Soviet plants. At least four firms in those countries—Fiat, Renault, Daimler-Benz, and Citroen—have signed long-term agreements on scientific and technological cooperation in the automotive industry. U.S. firms were significant suppliers to VAZ from 1969 to 1970 and major suppliers to KamAZ from 1973 to 1977, but have played a relatively minor role in later years. Japanese firms

Table 4

Major Foreign Suppliers of Equipment for Soviet Automotive Factories
(Value in 1000 rubles)

Year	Total Imports	Major Western Suppliers*							Major Eastern Suppliers	
		F.R.G.	Italy	France	Japan	Switz.	U.S.	U.K.	Cz.	Hung.
1969	263,561	66,431	100,425	52,084	—	4,604	22,589	12,646	—	—
1970	199,162	39,980	86,680	46,981	—	2,099	9,755	11,259	—	—
1971	62,962	10,761	29,679	10,028	1,148	509	1,638	5,359	—	5,359
1972	59,999	13,738	9,552	14,798	1,597	4,755	1,238	7,433	—	7,433
1973	128,792	38,417	17,334	11,941	7,149	7,640	16,412	3,327	13,091	—
1974	337,645	138,796	39,502	51,453	18,138	16,793	25,999	3,199	14,815	—
1975	287,521	105,699	40,729	46,537	3,790	7,416	34,801	5,530	17,321	—
1976	224,082	92,567	22,284	14,956	7,016	16,339	32,589	5,747	14,135	—
1977	194,860	72,071	20,472	4,679	37,498	7,411	17,079	4,739	9,237	5,395
1978	118,055	23,832	9,825	7,926	25,103	5,234	6,500	747	5,917	16,129
1979	144,768	70,441	10,944	16,411	17,222	5,754	4,019	1,567	1,265	2,358
1980	139,767	58,246	24,115	8,949	15,534	13,408	3,428	5,572	1,714	270
1981	132,514	50,472	29,885	7,453	18,038	7,387	2,215	3,877	1,941	—
1982	164,881	72,636	27,992	13,963	19,140	9,628	3,824	4,743	3,579	—

SOURCE: Ministerstvo Vneshnei Torgovli, *Vneshniaia torgovlia SSSR*, various years.
*Austria, Belgium and Sweden have supplied smaller amounts of equipment to the Soviet automotive industry.

have become important suppliers since the mid-1970s. Firms in the United Kingdom and Switzerland have also been significant suppliers.

Of the East European countries, only Czechoslovakia and Hungary have supplied significant amounts of equipment to the Soviet automotive industry. Compared to the major Western suppliers, they have played a small and declining role in equipping Soviet automotive plants. Czechoslovakia sold significant amounts of equipment to the Soviet Union in the mid-1970s, probably for KamAZ. According to a 1971 agreement in the Council for Mutual Economic Assistance (CMEA), the Soviet Union and Czechoslovakia were to specialize in production of heavy-duty trucks.[57] Hungary is a technological leader among CMEA countries in bus production and may have provided assistance to Soviet plants producing buses.

Western Trade Policies

Major differences in the trade policies of Western governments have also influenced Soviet import decisions. For example, the availability of financing, especially official export credits, was an important factor in the Soviet choice of Western suppliers for VAZ and KamAZ. Official Italian export credits, extended at favorable terms, helped Fiat to win many of the orders at VAZ, and U.S. Export-Import Bank credits similarly helped U.S. exporters compete for contracts at KamAZ. Conversely, the fact that the U.S. Government has not extended official credits to the Soviet Union since 1974, while other Western governments continue to do so, has put U.S. suppliers of automotive technology at a competitive disadvantage.

Differences in Western export control policies have probably had a greater effect on Soviet import decisions. Until the early 1960s most Western governments restricted the export of many specialized machine tools and other production technologies that might otherwise have been useful to the Soviet automotive industry. West European governments, however, began to implement less restrictive export control policies during the early 1960s, while most U.S. controls remained in place. Thus, when the Soviet automotive industry began to expand and modernize, West European firms were clearly more attractive trade partners. One Soviet observer stated, for example, that U.S. export control policy had been an important consideration in the Soviet choice of Fiat over U.S. competitors as the primary partner in the construction of VAZ.[58] (The U.S. Government did, however, permit some U.S. firms to participate indirectly as subcontractors to Fiat.)

Important changes in U.S. export control policy later encouraged Soviet importers to trade with U.S. firms. Enactment of the Export Administration Act of 1969 called for a significant redirection of U.S. policy. While retaining the President's authority to impose export controls for national security, foreign policy or domestic economic reasons, the Act called for removal of controls on goods and technologies that were available to communist countries from non-U.S. sources. It also limited export controls to those items that would "significantly increase the potential military capability" of a potential adversary. Such statutory changes facilitated the Nixon Administration's efforts to expand trade with the Soviet Union in conjunction with its policy of detente.[59]

The Nixon Administration's trade promotion efforts coincided with an upsurge in Soviet orders for Western automotive technology to be used in the construction of KamAZ and modernization of other plants. U.S. exporters received a number of export licenses to supply important machinery and equipment, some of which were of advanced design and previously unavailable to the Soviet Union from any Western source.

In January 1980, when U.S. intelligence agencies reported the use of KamAZ trucks in the Soviet invasion of Afghanistan, many observers in the United States began to question the earlier decisions to license exports to Soviet truck plants which were producing trucks for military as well as civilian purposes. (While no precise numbers are available, it appears likely that only a small part of KamAZ's output is supplied to the military.) Among the economic sanctions imposed by President Carter in response to the invasion of Afghanistan were measures that effectively prohibited the export of spare computer parts or truck engine assembly lines to KamAZ. The sanctions revoked licenses that the Department of Commerce had already granted for computer parts and required the Department to deny a pending application for export of an engine assembly line for the second stage of KamAZ.[60] In March 1982, President Reagan extended the prohibition to include any technical data or equipment for the manufacture of trucks at KamAZ or ZIL. He included exports to ZIL on the grounds that ZIL also produces trucks for the Soviet military.

Both the Carter and Reagan Administrations maintained that the sanctions were effective in delaying the expansion of KamAZ and in forcing the Soviet Union to forego the planned production of a substantial number of trucks.[61] Their assessments appear credible in light of the substantial delays in startup of the second stage of KamAZ. Other factors, however, also contributed to the delays. Both administrations also acknowledged that, in time, the Soviet Union would be able to obtain the machinery and equipment denied by U.S. sanctions, either by manufacturing it domestically or buying it from other foreign sources.

The controversy over exports to KamAZ and ZIL illustrates the dilemma faced by export control authorities in making decisions on so-called "dual-use" technologies. Trucks, like many other products, can be used for both civilian and military purposes. More significant, much of the sophisticated equipment used in automobile production, such as numerically controlled machine tools, robots, lasers, and computer systems, can be diverted to production of other military equipment. In deciding whether to grant licenses for such exports, authorities must consider the likelihood of diversion and the potential contribution that such exports, if diverted, could make to the Soviet military effort. In the past, U.S. export control authorities have taken steps to insure that sophisticated automobile-manufacturing equipment is not diverted. (For example, the Soviet Government was required to give written assurances that a computer system sold by a U.S. firm for the KamAZ foundry would not be diverted.) On the other hand, exports of automotive technology have not been considered a "significant" contribution to Soviet military capabilities merely because they help the Soviet Union to expand and modernize truck-manufacturing capacity. Since 1969, the U.S. Government has not denied licenses for such exports for national security reasons. The sanctions against KamAZ and ZIL are consistent with the interpretation that automotive technology is not militarily sensitive: they were imposed for foreign policy, not national security reasons. In other words, the U.S. Government imposed sanctions to signal its disapproval of Soviet behavior and not to constrain Soviet military power.

While the immediate effects of foreign policy and national security controls on U.S. exports to KamAZ and ZIL are the same, the distinction between the two types of controls is important as an indicator of future U.S. and other Western export control policies. Since U.S. export control authorities have not (since 1969) considered expansion of the Soviet automotive industry a significant national security threat, a change in political relations could easily foster a normalization of U.S.-Soviet trade in automotive equipment. Moreover, since governments in Europe and Japan tend to reject the use of export controls for foreign policy purposes, exporters of automobile-manufacturing technology in those countries are unlikely to be encumbered by export controls.

One effect of U.S. trade policy in the 1980s is almost certainly to discourage Soviet importers from buying machinery and equipment for the automotive industry from U.S. firms. At the same time, the failure of governments in Western Europe and Japan to support the U.S. prohibition on exports of automotive technology has probably reassured Soviet importers of the reliability of suppliers in those countries. It is likely that differences in Western export control policies are a major factor in the decline in the U.S. share of the Soviet market for automotive machinery and equipment and the corresponding increases in European and Japanese shares (see Table 4).

Soviet Exports of Passenger Cars

Soviet automotive officials have made a major effort to promote exports of passenger cars, especially to Western countries. Exports of

Table 5

Soviet Production and Exports of Passenger Automobiles
(Number of vehicles)

Year	Total Production	Total Exports	Exports to the Industrial West
1965	201,200	48,600	10,086
1966	230,300	66,500	13,495
1967	251,400	68,900	9,026
1968	280,300	82,300	9,092
1969	293,600	73,800	7,980
1970	344,200	83,800	8,250
1971	529,000	149,700	9,894
1972	730,100	194,900	26,903
1973	916,700	237,500	45,088
1974	1,119,000	287,326	42,373
1975	1,201,000	295,616	62,546
1976	1,239,000	344,743	92,987
1977	1,280,000	361,993	87,405
1978	1,312,000	387,806	94,315
1979	1,314,000	378,825	116,577
1980	1,327,000	328,782	80,948
1981	1,324,000	253,041	111,222
1982	1,307,000	252,415	118,633

SOURCES: *Narodnoe khoziaistvo SSSR* and *Vneshniaia torgovlia SSSR,* various years.

cars grew rapidly during the 1970s, keeping pace with the rapid expansion of total production. During the 1970s, the overwhelming majority of Soviet exports went to other socialist countries and developing countries; a small, but steadily increasing share went to the West. In the early 1980s, the trend changed. Overall exports of cars declined by more than one-third from their peak in 1978, primarily as a result of a reduction of exports to CMEA countries. Exports to the West, on the other hand, have stabilized at their highest level. In 1982, the Soviet Union exported 118,633 passenger cars to Western, primarily West European, countries, about 47 percent of total Soviet exports (see Table 5).

Soviet officials appear to believe that exports of passenger cars to the West are a potentially important source of hard currency earnings. (The Soviet Union has exported few trucks to the West and has made little effort to promote such sales.) Earnings in 1979 were estimated at $269 million, making automobiles the largest earner of hard currency among Soviet exports of finished manufactures.[62] Earnings from exports of cars to the West have been small relative to the Soviet Union's major hard currency earner, petroleum products. Soviet planners, however, are probably concerned about the possible constraints on their ability to continue large-scale exports of oil. They would like to expand exports of manufactured goods to compensate for stagnation or a decline in earnings from traditional exports to the West. Thus, in the "Guidelines for the Economic and Social Development of the USSR for 1981–1985 and the Period Ending in 1990," issued at the 26th CPSU Congress, the leadership proclaimed the need to "improve the structure of exports, above all through increasing the production and deliveries of engineering and other finished products."[63]

Generally, the Soviet Union has had little success in exporting finished manufactured goods to the West. Most Soviet enterprises suffer from a lack of experience in marketing goods in highly competitive markets. Soviet producers of machinery and equipment have a reputation for poor maintenance, inadequate after-sales servicing, and lack of responsiveness to special needs of customers in Western markets. Most important, with regard to automobiles and other machinery, the products of Soviet enterprises tend to be of poor quality and technologically obsolescent in comparison with the products of Western competitors. Nikolai Smeliakov, Deputy Minister of Foreign Trade, has argued that such shortcomings are responsible for the low level of Soviet machinery exports to the West.[64]

Soviet exports of passenger cars, while not a spectacular success, do represent a modest exception to the general performance of Soviet machinery exports. Several factors have contributed to the limited success of Soviet automobile exporters. Avtoeksport, the foreign trade enterprise that is responsible for exports of Soviet automobiles, has pursued an aggressive (by Soviet standards) marketing strategy. It has invested in foreign-based joint stock companies, mostly in Western Europe, which provide the advertising and after-sales servicing that are necessary to promote sales in Western markets. Another important factor has been low prices. Soviet exporters compensate for technological obsolescence by charging prices significantly lower than their competitors. Ladas, which make up two-thirds of Soviet exports to the West, cost about 75 percent as much as similar Western models.[65] In 1984, in response to declining sales in the United Kingdom, Avtoeksport reduced the prices charged for Ladas.[66]

Another contributing factor to the success of Soviet automobiles on foreign markets has been continuing efforts by Soviet automotive plants to improve their products. The attempt to penetrate and remain competitive in Western markets has provided a major incentive to technological innovation in the industry. A. A. Zhitkov, general director of VAZ, described the relationship between VAZ's export orientation and introduction of the modernized VAZ 2105 and 2107. The improvements in the Zhiguli, according to Zhitkov, were necessary to "solve the problem of maintaining competitiveness" in the late 1970s and early 1980s.[67] Since Zhitkov does not have to worry about the Zhiguli's competitiveness on the domestic market, he was obviously reflecting his concern about the vehicle's international competitiveness. Similarly, AZLK incorporated improvements in the Moskvich 2140-SL designed specifically to appeal to Western consumer preferences for safety, appearance, and comfort.

Because the success of Soviet exporters is dependent on the ability of Soviet automotive plants to innovate, the export effort generates an increased demand for technology imports from the West. The import of Western technology for the new VAZ and Moskvich models is motivated in part by Soviet efforts to maintain or improve their competitive position. During the initial negotiations between Soviet importers and Western automotive firms over technical assistance in building a new Soviet passenger car, Soviet negotiators proposed substantial buy-back obligations by the Western partner. Western firms, however, were reportedly unwilling to agree to accept Soviet cars in payment for their assistance.[68] Nevertheless, a major portion of the new models seems destined for Western markets. According to a Soviet source, 100,000 of the new Moskviches will be sold on foreign markets.[69]

Competing successfully in Western markets in the future will be no mean feat for Soviet exporters of automobiles. The Western automobile market is highly competitive and is likely to become more so. Soviet exporters will have to compete not only with the advanced automotive industries of the industrial West, but increasingly with exports from emerging industries in the newly industrialized countries and from the Soviet Union's East European allies. Several of the newly industrializing and East European countries are expanding their capacities to manufacture modern compact cars. Soviet exporters must also compete against the new international marketing strategies of the major Western firms, which are increasingly locating plants in or near foreign markets and engaging in joint R&D, joint production, and joint marketing with their foreign competitors.

There are two likely strategies that Soviet exporters might pursue to compete in Western markets in the future. They might either attempt to export passenger cars that are distinguished by their high quality and technological level, or they might attempt to capture certain specialized segments of the Western market. In the 1970s and early 1980s, they followed the latter strategy. They exported Ladas and Moskviches that were somewhat obsolescent, but sturdy and inexpensive. Such cars found a limited market among customers who did not need the most modern automotive technologies and who were attracted by low prices. Similarly, the Soviets have exported the Niva to a limited, specialized Western market, composed of customers who are attracted to its performance in rough terrain and its low price. The development of "a new generation" of Ladas and Moskviches, however, may signal a Soviet intention to penetrate a wider market, composed of customers who need the latest improvements in fuel efficiency, comfort, safety, and emission controls. Competition in the wider Western market challenges Soviet automobile manufacturers to implement rapidly the latest developments in automotive technology.

Conclusions

Despite assimilation problems, hard currency constraints, and East-West political tensions, Soviet policy makers appear generally satisfied with the results of large-scale imports of Western technology for the automotive industry and are likely to continue to promote technological ties to the West. While such impediments to technology imports may have somewhat influenced Soviet import decisions during the 1970s, they do not appear to have undermined the basic Soviet rationale for relying heavily on Western technology.

Variations in Soviet imports of automotive technology appear to be explained largely by domestic investment trends. The Soviet automotive industry has imported large amounts of Western technology during periods when it was building new plants and modernizing and expanding existing plants. In particular, the construction of two massive projects, VAZ and KamAZ, during the late 1960s and mid-1970s explains the lumpy pattern of Soviet imports of Western automotive machinery and equipment. Western deliveries to VAZ and KamAZ resulted in upsurges of overall Soviet imports of automotive equipment, and completion of those deliveries resulted in declines in Soviet imports. Despite the completion of the major purchases for construction of VAZ and KamAZ, imports of machinery and equipment for the industry have continued at a rather high rate and may increase significantly in the 1980s.

Several factors appear to be contributing to continued Soviet demand for Western automotive technology. First, some of the factors that may have led to a retrenchment in Soviet import plans for other industries appear to have had only mixed effects on imports for the automotive industry. Assimilation problems, for example, may have slowed purchases of machinery and equipment for some projects, but stimulated additional purchases for others. On the one hand, it is likely that slower than planned startups of VAZ and KamAZ delayed further acquisitions for other parts of the industry. Since the demands of these massive projects on domestic suppliers were not being satisfied, Soviet planners may have decided to delay other modernization and expansion requiring inputs of foreign technology. On the other hand, barriers to diffusion of new technologies from VAZ and KamAZ may have increased the demand for foreign technology. The automotive industry has imported technologies for other plants that were similar to those already imported for VAZ and KamAZ. In addition, the failure of some domestic suppliers to meet their obligations to new projects may have forced Soviet importers to turn to Western suppliers for unplanned purchases. Imports for the second stage of KamAZ are an example of relying on additional imported technology to compensate for domestic assimilation problems.

Similarly, while a chronic shortage of hard currency may have constrained Soviet purchases of technology for other industries, it may have stimulated purchases for the automotive industry. Soviet planners appear to see the automotive industry as a part of the solution to their long-term hard currency problems. They are making a major effort to increase exports of passenger cars to Western markets. Their desire to produce a competitive product is a powerful incentive to stay abreast of new technological developments in the industry, both through domestic R&D efforts and imports of new Western technologies.

Although East-West political tensions may have affected Soviet decisions on importing automotive technology, their primary effect appears to have been on the choice of Western partners rather than the overall level of imports. In the late 1970s and early 1980s, as U.S.-Soviet relations deteriorated, Soviet importers have shown a growing preference for Western European and Japanese firms as suppliers of automotive technology. One consideration in choosing foreign trade partners has probably been the international political environment and differences in the trade policies of various Western governments.

More fundamentally, the Soviet automotive industry has continued to rely heavily on imports of Western technology because it has not been able to meet the technological needs of the industry through purely indigenous efforts. Soviet automotive managers have compelling reasons to introduce the latest product and process technologies developed in the West. They are under pressure to expand production while improving labor productivity, reducing consumption of energy and other materials and producing an internationally competitive product. In this regard, the basic Soviet rationale for importing Western automotive technology has not changed since the mid-1960s. What has changed is that the pace of technological progress in the world industry has quickened. The Soviet industry has to do more to merely maintain its relative standing among the world's producers.

Soviet reliance on imported automotive technology is not unusual; no national automotive industry has developed or is developing solely through its own technological efforts. The automotive industry in the West has become an international one, in which capital and technology flow quickly across national borders. What is remarkable about the

Soviet experience is the relatively slow and sporadic nature of Soviet assimilation of the latest technological developments in the industry. Its performance in this regard is a significant improvement over the past because Soviet planners are giving more emphasis and allocating more resources to technological progress. To develop and maintain an internationally competitive industry, however, will probably require continued reliance on imported technology and an improvement in the mechanisms for introducing new technologies.

NOTES

1. George D. Holliday, *Technology Transfer to the USSR, 1928–1937 and 1966–1975: The Role of Western Technology in Soviet Economic Development* (Boulder, Colorado: Westview Press, 1979), pp. 137–41.

2. Central Intelligence Agency, *USSR: Role of Foreign Technology in the Development of the Motor Vehicle Industry*, Washington, D.C., October 1979, pp. 6–7 (hereafter cited as CIA).

3. A. N. Kosygin, "Povyshenie nauchnoi obosnovannosti planov—vazhneishaia zadacha planovykh organov," *Planovoe khoziaistvo*, April 1965, pp. 6, 9–10. ZIL is the Moscow Likhachev Automobile Plant and GAZ, the Gorkiy Automobile Plant.

4. CIA, p. 7.

5. S. Matveev, "Perspektivy razvitiia avtomobil'noi promyshlennosti v novom piatiletii, " *Planovoe khoziaistvo*, July 1966, p. 28.

6. CIA, pp. 6–7.

7. Details of the agreement are discussed in Holliday, pp. 141–54, and Boris Katsman, *Ekonomika i organizatsiia promyshlennogo proizvodstva*, no. 1 (1982), pp. 154–70; no. 2 (1982), pp. 157–72; no. 3 (1982), pp. 195–210; and no. 4 (1982), pp. 145–58. The articles by Boris Katsman are translated in Joint Publications Research Service, 81438, 3 August 1982, pp. 1–43.

8. V. Buffa, "Economic and Commercial Cooperation Between East and West," draft of a speech delivered on 3 November 1973. (Buffa was in charge of Fiat's operations at VAZ.)

9. Katsman, *Ekonomika i organizatsiia promyshlennogo proizvodstva*, no. 1, 1982.

10. Chase World Information Corporation, *KamAZ, the Billion Dollar Beginning* (New York: 1974), p. 16.

11. Imogene U. Edwards, "Automotive Trends in the USSR," U.S. Congress, Joint Economic Committee, *Soviet Economic Prospects for the Seventies* (Washington: US GPO, 1973), p. 296.

12. CIA, p. 8.

13. Holliday, pp. 155–56.

14. CIA, p. 8.

15. For details of these and other KamAZ contracts, see Chase World Information Corporation, pp. 7–21.

16. Edwards, p. 309.

17. B. Mil'ner, "On the Organization of Management," *Kommunist*, no. 3,

(February 1975). (Translated in Joint Publications Research Service, 64452, 1 April 1975, p. 50.)

18. Chase World Information Corporation, p. 55.

19. G. M. Alekseev, "V sem'e edinoi. Avtomobilestroenie k 60-letiiu obrazovaniia SSSR," *Avtomobil'naia promyshlennost'*, no. 12 (December 1982), p. 3.

20. G. Mikhailov, "Vstrechnyi 'KamAZa'," *Ekonomicheskaia gazeta*, no. 4 (January 1982), p. 3.

21. A. I. Titkov, "Avtomobil'naia tekhnika v XI piatiletke," *Avtomobil'naia promyshlennost'*, no. 8 (August 1982), p. 4.

22. "Razvitie avtomobil'noi promyshlennosti," *Ekonomicheskaia gazeta*, no. 9 (February 1979), p. 2.

23. *Vneshniaia torgovlia v 1982 g.*, p. 170.

24. For a discussion of the change in Soviet investment strategy, see Robert Leggett, "Soviet Investment Policy in the 11th Five-Year Plan," in U.S. Congress, Joint Economic Committee, *Soviet Economy in the 1980s: Problems and Prospects*, Part 1, 31 December 1982, pp. 129–46.

25. Tsentral'noe statisticheskoe upravlenie SSSR, *Narodnoe khoziaistvo SSSR, 1922–1982* (Moscow: 1982), p. 240.

26. "Razvitie avtomobil'noi promyshlennosti," p. 2.

27. For discussions of the automotive industry's goals for the Eleventh Five-Year Plan, see Titkov, pp. 1–5; A. I. Titkov and E. A. Ustinov, "Resheniia XXVI S"ezda KPSS—v zhizn'," *Avtomobil'naia promyshlennost'*, no. 3 (March 1981), pp. 1–3; and "Razvitie avtomobil'noi promyshlennosti," *Ekonomicheskaia gazeta*, no. 23 (June 1981), p. 2.

28. M. J. Berry and M. R. Hill, "Technological level and quality: machine tools and passenger cars," in Ronald Amann, Julian Cooper and R. W. Davies, eds., *The Technological Level of Soviet Industry* (New Haven and London: Yale University Press, 1977), pp. 550–51.

29. A. A. Zhitkov, "Nekotorye deiatel'nosti i perspektivy razvitiia Volzhkogo obyedineniia 'Avtovaz'," in *"Avtovaz"—Sovremennoe proizvodstvennoe Obyedinenie (Znanie*, no. 11, 1977), p. 13.

30. V. Kolomnikov, "Shagi sozidaniia," *Za rulem*, no. 1 (1981), p. 3.

31. CIA, p. 14.

32. *Ekonomicheskaia gazeta*, no. 23 (June 1981), p. 2.

33. Zhitkov, p. 13.

34. E. B. Golland, "Tekhnicheskaia osnova vysokoi proizvoditel'nosti truda," *Ekonomika i organizatsiia promyshlennogo proizvodstva*, no. 1 (1976), pp. 85–86.

35. *Financial Times*, 30 August 1983.

36. I am indebted to Julian Cooper for information about the contribution of the Ministry of Defense Industry to production of the Moskvich.

37. Berry and Hill, pp. 553–55.

38. A. I. Titkov and E. A. Ustinov, pp. 2–3, and V. Iakovlev, "V ispolnenii 'Liuks'," *Za rulem*, no. 1 (1981), p. 8.

39. Details of the Renault-Moskvich contract are provided in *The Economist*, 3 December 1983, p. 79; *The Financial Times*, 26 April 1983 and 28 November 1983; and *Business Eastern Europe*, 14 October 1983, p. 326.

40. Official Soviet sources provide little data on R&D spending for the automotive industry. One Soviet observer states that the industry's annual spending on R&D is 40 million rubles (*Ekonomicheskaia gazeta*, no. 9 [February 1979], p. 2); another that the R&D workforce includes over 20,000 scientific workers (G. M. Alekseev, p. 3).

41. M. M. Fishkis, "Use of Lasers, Robots in Automating ZIL Production Discussed," *Ekonomika i organizatsiia promyshlennogo proizvodstva*, no. 10 (October 1981). Translated in Joint Publications Research Service (JPRS), 82943, 24 February 1983, p. 32.

42. "Organizatsiia nauchno-issledovatel'skikh razrabotok na VAZe," *Ekonomika i organizatsiia promyshlennogo proizvodstva*, no. 1 (1976), pp. 159–61.

43. Golland, pp. 85–86.

44. S. V. Gorikhin, "ZIL Scientists Bridge Research, Development Gap," *Ekonomika i organizatsiia promyshlennogo proizvodstva*, no. 10 (October 1981). JPRS 82943, pp. 15–21.

45. *Pravda*, 28 August 1975, p. 2.

46. V. D. Kal'ner, "Ways to Reduce Use of Metal at ZIL Explored," p. 26, and Interview with Aleksandr Ivanovich Buzhinskiy, "Problems of Introducing New Technology Contrasted with ZIL's Success," pp. 36–37, *Ekonomika i organizatsiia promyshlennogo proizvodstva*, no. 10 (October 1981), JPRS 82943.

47. Interview with Buzhinskiy, p. 37.

48. John P. Young, "Impact of Soviet Ministry Management Practices on the Assimilation of Imported Process Technology." Paper presented at the joint annual meeting of the Southwestern and Rocky Mountain Associations of Slavic Studies, Houston, Texas, April 13, 1978.

49. Interview with Buzhinskiy, pp. 40–41.

50. V. F. Rzhevskii, "Sovremennoe oborudovanie—baza nauchno-tekhnicheskogo progressa," *Avtomobil'naia promyshlennost'*, no. 6 (June 1982), p. 21.

51. Katsman, *Ekonomika i organizatsiia promyshlennogo proizvodstva*, no. 1 (1982).

52. N. Smeliakov, "I Spros zavisit ot predlozheniia," *Trud*, 24 July 1981.

53. Katsman, *Ekonomika i organizatsiia promyshlennogo proizvodstva*, no. 2 (1982).

54. V. N. Sushkov, "Sotrudnichestvo s firmoi 'Fiat' rasshiriaetsia," interview in *Vneshniaia torgovlia*, no. 8 (1966), p. 44.

55. For additional discussion of assimilation problems at VAZ and KamAZ, see Holliday, pp. 137–65.

56. For a Western assessment of the contribution of Soviet organizations and specialists at VAZ and KamAZ, see CIA, pp. 13–15.

57. L. Gavrilov, "Avtomobil' i integratsiia," *Za rulem*, no. 11 (November 1980), p. 8.

58. Boris Katsman, *Ekonomika i organizatsiia promyshlennogo proizvodstva*, no. 1 (1982).

59. See Gary Bertsch's chapter in this volume for further discussion of the change in U.S. East-West trade policy.

60. U.S. Department of Commerce, *Export Administration Annual Report, FY 1980* (Washington, D.C.: 1981), p. 35.

61. See the reports to the Congress on extending and amending foreign policy export controls, *Export Administration Annual Report, FY 1980*, p. 149; *FY 1981*, p. 161; and *FY 1982*, p. 152.

62. Hedija H. Kravalis, "USSR: An Assessment of U.S. and Western Trade Potential with the Soviet Union Through 1985," in U.S. Congress, Joint Economic Committee, *East-West Trade: The Prospects to 1985* (Washington: USGPO, 18 August 1982), p. 33.

63. *The 26th Congress of the Communist Party of the Soviet Union. Documents and Resolutions* (Moscow: Novosti Press Agency Publishing House, 1981), p. 236.

Cited in Vyacheslav Seltsovsky, "Quantitative Assessment of Foreign Trade's Effect on Soviet Economy," *Foreign Trade,* no. 2 (February 1984), JPRS-UIE-84-007, 22 March 1984, p. 16.

64. Smeliakov, *Trud,* 24 July 1981.

65. Kravalis, p. 33.

66. *The Financial Times,* 31 December 1983.

67. Zhitkov, p. 13.

68. *The Economist,* 9 December 1978, p. 89.

69. "Citroen Delegation: Talks on Reconstruction of Motor Car Works," *Ecotass, Economic and Commercial News Weekly,* no. 25, 2 July 1979, pp. 9–10, cited in "East-West Co-operation in the Automotive Sector and Reciprocal Trading Arrangements," *Economic Bulletin for Europe,* vol. 34, no. 2 (1982), pp. 251–82.

Technology Transfer and the Development of the Soviet Computer Industry

S. E. Goodman

I. Scope

THIS CHAPTER considers the transfer and assimilation of Western general-purpose, digital computer technology by the USSR.[1] Our primary concerns are with the Soviet computer industry, rather than with the computer using community, and with technology transfer, rather than with trade.[2]

We define technology as the know-how to specify, design, build, maintain, and use a product. The sale of a product is a technology transfer only to the extent that it reveals this know-how. Normal trade in computer products may often be a weak form of technology transfer.

Computing technology is a spectrum of widely differing subtechnologies. These range from the know-how for reducing line width on very high-density integrated circuit chips, to the know-how needed to manage the efforts of a large group of applications programmers, to general ideas for national development programs. The Soviets have pursued transfers across the entire spectrum. We shall consider a broad sample of transfers, but length constraints make it impossible and inappropriate to cover any subtechnology in detail.[3]

Section II presents a set of complementary overviews of the development of Soviet computing. It contains a broad historical perspective and brief updates of activities over the last half dozen years. Section III is concerned with the forms and effectiveness of the transfer mechanisms used by the Soviets. With this background, we are in a position to provide an assessment of the contemporary Soviet computer industry. This is done in Section IV. The concluding section considers Soviet progress and problems within the context of a discussion of the dynamics of computing, and computer-related technology transfers, in a rapidly evolving international technological and business environment.

II. Selected Overviews

Interest in electronic, digital computers and Western work in this technology date back to the 1940s, and it is important to explicitly consider technology transfer and the development of Soviet computing within the context of several interwoven long-term overviews. These cover:

1. Soviet perceptions of the importance of computing.
2. The level and relative importance of domestic technological innovation.
3. Interest in, and the pursuit of, Western technology.
4. The ability of the Soviet computer industry to absorb acquired foreign technology.
5. The role of Eastern Europe.
6. Soviet progress relative to those countries from which they acquire computer technology.

1. Soviet perceptions of the importance of computing

Some of the first, and most important, applications of electronic digital computers were for military uses, including ballistics, nuclear weapons design, and air defense systems. Given the intense Soviet concern over such things during the decade after World War II, the practical development of computer technology quickly found a home in the military-industrial-academy establishment, notwithstanding some Soviet ideological denunciations of cybernetics. Although the Soviet electronics and electromechanical industries were not up to their U.S. counterparts in the development of advanced systems, by 1953–54 Soviet computer specialists had a number of substantial accomplishments to their credit.

Interest in computer technology continued to rise in some military-industrial-academic circles. Evidence of this includes the steady appearance of new computer models, expanded production facilities and rates, etc. This continued into the early-1960s.

By the mid-1960s, the Soviets were having to contend with some increasingly serious problems: slowing growth rates, decreasing productivity, more sophisticated technological requirements for military and space applications, problems managing the economic planning process, and difficulties operating very large systems like the railroad network. As a result, a broader set of interested groups started to consider a broader range of computing needs. There are actually two points of change here: one reflecting an increased priority with an effort to meet it through primarily domestic efforts; the other indicating a major policy shift and reorientation towards Western technology (see overviews 2 and 3).

Soviet interest in computing continued to rise sharply, with a gradual decrease in the rate of increase by the late 1970s. This change reflects a kind of "settling in of reality"; enough practical experience was gained to produce more realistic expectations. But interest continued to grow at a respectable rate. A serious commitment remains into the 1980s, partly because of the enormous investments, partly because there has been fulfillment of some nontrivial expectations, and partly because there are no acceptable and better alternatives.

2. *The level and relative importance of domestic technological innovation*

As noted under Overview 1, during the early 1950s, Soviet computer specialists had a number of major accomplishments to their credit. These include a stored program digital machine, serial production of a small computer, a high-level programming seminar, and the development of one of the first "supercomputers." All occurred within a couple of years after similar achievements in the U.S. and the U.K., and we would consider their efforts fairly innovative and independent.

The reasons for this judgment need to be explained. The fledgling Soviet industry was extremely isolated by a combination of Stalin's policies and Western controls. While a case can be made that the Soviets were aware of, and influenced by, Western work, most of this was via weak forms of technology transfer, and hardware was not closely copied from American and British predecessors.[4] Soviet accomplishments did not exhibit world-class innovation in the sense of greatly transcending anything done in the West. But it is important to recognize that they did some difficult things, in a respectable time frame, and in isolation. This required efforts that should be considered innovative in a local sense, and the fact that similar developments had occurred elsewhere need not detract from them. The distinction between "local" and "global" innovation should be kept in mind throughout this chapter.

This period of an isolated, but fairly strong, domestic computer industry was to be short-lived. Over the next fifteen years, technology transfer activity gradually rose, while the gap in relative capabilities between the Soviet and American industries widened rapidly.[5] The level of innovation grew very slowly during this time, and even the level of local innovation was unimpressive compared with the early 1950s. This was in spite of the much increased attention and priority given to computing in the 1960s. The computer industry of the USSR was not responding well to increasing demands.

On the surface, both the level and relative importance of domestic innovation hit new lows in the late 1960s, and this continued into the late 1970s. As we shall see in our analysis of Overview 3, this is a result of a major disillusionment with the performance of the domestic industry and an attendant massive reorientation toward Western technology. What is hidden is something of a revitalization of local innovation in order to assimilate Western technology. It is one thing to overtly or covertly acquire documentation on or samples of Western computer models. It is quite another to successfully produce functional duplicates in large quantities. The latter requires an enormous amount of on-site development and implementation. These efforts were not impressive compared with Western states-of-the-arts, but they showed substantial progress over the Soviet past. Global innovation was essentially nonexistent.

The massive use of Western technology has resulted in the much improved availability of fairly respectable hardware and software. Given this expeditious fix, an important question now is whether the Soviet industry will be able to keep up the rate of local innovation and produce some serious global innovation. Overall performance through the early 1980s has not been especially impressive. We have yet to identify any major, practical, global innovations. Furthermore, the overall quality of recent Soviet academic, theoretical, computer science is less impressive than some people might have expected.[6]

3. Interest in, and the pursuit of, Western technology

Soviet interest in Western computer technology rose steadily through the mid-1960s, with an extremely sharp rise in the late 1960s that continues into the 1980s. At the risk of some oversimplification, the sharp rise reflects a vote of "no confidence" in the domestic computer industry's capabilities to meet much increased demands, a decision to try to move forward through an extensive functional duplication of successful U.S. hardware systems, and an attendant massive infusion of Western software that this would permit. This policy has determined the character of the Soviet and East European industries for the last 15 years.

The form, intensity, and effectiveness of this technology transfer will be the subject of Sections III, IV and V. However, one important observation should be made here. The largest part of this effort has been focused on U.S. technology. The relative Soviet interest in, and use of, truly domestic West European (i.e., excluding European contributions to U.S. multinationals like IBM) technology declined, and much of this kind of transfer that did occur was into the East European industries. Western Europe's most important role was as a source or conduit for U.S. technology. Interest in Japan was weak for most of this time. However, Soviet interest in Western Europe and Japan has picked up in the last few years, and this is expected to continue.

4. The ability of the Soviet computer industry to absorb acquired foreign technology

Soviet capacities to effectively absorb foreign computing technology have not grown as rapidly as interest in its acquisition. This is to be expected since acquisition is easier than assimilation. To a considerable extent, ease of acquisition depends on the openness and accessibility of Western societies, while the Soviets are more on their own with assimilation. Assimilation also requires a much greater allocation of resources.

If assimilation by the Soviet computer industry is judged primarily by its ability to functionally duplicate important U.S. computer systems, then significant improvement has taken place during the entire period from 1970 into the mid-1980s. There are milestones for two major (a third is coming, but has apparently had some troubles) and two lesser Unified System (ES) undertakings to duplicate IBM mainframe families. There are two or three (depending on how one counts) milestones for major Small System (SM) mini- and micro-computer undertakings that duplicate systems based on the designs of various U.S. manufacturers (DEC-like machines have become dominant, but VAX-like computers have been slow in emerging). The majority of Soviet and East German microcomputers are based on U.S. designs. Similar efforts with regard to peripherals are moving along, but not especially impressively. In fact, the rate of progress in the mass production, modernization, and distribution of a broad range of peripherals may have slowed since the first two Ryad (ES) waves, although many new product announcements have been made. The assimilation of Western software technology continues to lack depth and breadth, especially in applications software, although virtually every Soviet computer center seems to have copies of some Western systems software.

More generally, there is little evidence of very strong forms of assimilation. Examples might include widespread and effective Western-like forms of service and support of fielded machines, or the improvement of R&D and production facilities so that they come out with Soviet equivalents of successive Western systems over notably shorter time intervals. One of the worst arenas for assimilation is telecommunications. We return to these problems in Section IV.

5. The role of Eastern Europe[7]

Soviet-East European relations with regard to computer technology were unimpressive from the early 1950s through the mid-1960s. During this period, the Soviets exploited some domestic East European developments and imported small quantities of equipment but, with few exceptions, technology transfer was weak both qualitatively and quantitatively.

These relations improved dramatically at the end of the 1960s, and progress has continued through the present. This reflects several developments. By far the most important is an extensive, and reasonably successful, partial integration of the hardware and, to a lesser extent, systems software sectors of the CMEA industries. This partial integration comes complete with an interesting division of labor and the effective creation of a common hardware and systems software base through the joint ES and, to a lesser extent, SM programs. Closely related to this is the substantial strengthening of almost all of the East European industries. The East Europeans continue to have better relations with the Western computing world than do the Soviets. However, there has been a notable change of distribution in these relations over the last 15 years, with a relative shift towards the U.S. To some extent this shift may reflect disappointment with hopes that existed for East-West European joint efforts in the 1960s, but it also includes an appreciation of the strengths of the U.S. industry.

The net result has been quite positive from the Soviet standpoint. More Western technology is being transferred through the other CMEA countries. East European trade and computing activities with the USSR have increased well beyond the almost trivial levels that had existed earlier. The fairly impressive rates of increase may have tapered off since the late 1970s, but they still appear to be respectable. Far less impressive has been the progress made toward more comprehensive and deeper forms of integration, especially those involving user communities, over the last half-dozen years. Rhetoric aside, neither the Soviets nor the East Europeans seem particularly enthusiastic about what would have to be done to bring about the next big leap beyond the present level.

6. Soviet progress relative to those countries from which they acquire computer technology

This overview is best conceptualized as consisting of two curves: one for the overall state of computing in the USSR, the other for the overall state in the U.S., Japan, and Western Europe.[8] The trend is measured by the vertical gap between the two curves over time.

The initial gap was small, a tribute to the early, isolated Soviet industry. Starting in the mid-1950s the gap grew rapidly, and it was enormous by the late 1960s. This reflects the discovery of a vast commercial and industrial market for computing by the American industry, and of the far more limited perceptions, effective customer base, and capabilities of the corresponding Soviet ministries. The gap may have closed a little in the early 1970s with the much increased Soviet efforts that were reviewed in the preceding five overviews. This would imply that the slope of the USSR curve was greater than that of the Western curve at this time, but that may not have actually been the case, and the Soviets may have only been losing ground more slowly during that period. The strong Japanese showing since the late 1970s and continued U.S. progress make for another substantial widening, in spite of reasonably good Soviet movement. The various computing "explosions" of the 1980s, notably serious computing for small organizations and the home, and the flowing together of computing and telecommunications, have produced another period of rapid gap expansion.

At the risk of oversimplification, we might summarize the six overviews as follows. Soviet progress in computing has come a long way in terms of their own past and in terms of certain milestone achievements. At the core of this has been a basic decision to intensively pursue Western technology, and the effects of the practical implementation of this policy may be seen in much of the Soviet industry. It is doubtful if this industry would have been able to come as far as it has in the last 15 years solely on the basis of domestic efforts, although the domestic efforts needed to acquire and assimilate Western technology should not be underestimated. Nevertheless, the overall gap between the Soviet and principal Western industries and user communities is growing.

III. Transfer Mechanisms

For almost four decades, the Soviets have used a broad range of mechanisms to acquire Western computer technology.[9] However, the distribution of effort over this range has been skewed. Compared to the set of all possibilities, Soviet activities are heavily biased toward passive, rather than active, and toward covert, rather than overt, mechanisms.[10]

Soviet use of active mechanisms is restricted for three basic reasons. One is U.S. and COCOM export controls.[11] The second is a limited set of suitable and willing Western partners. The USSR does not have the money, high-level expertise, or positive working environment to attract the deep interests of a large number of very good Western companies or individuals over a period of many years. Third are the Soviets' self-imposed constraints. These include restrictions on travel, restrictions on accesses and subject matter, controls on direct relations between the two technical end-parties (e.g., through the use of intermediaries such as foreign-trade organizations or the State Committee for Science and Technology), the lack of interest in large-volume purchases, etc. It is not possible to assign numerical weights to these three factors, but collectively they have severely limited the active mechanisms available to the Soviets.

However, Soviet use of active mechanisms has picked up since the late 1960s. The most commonly used forms have been: academic exchanges and joint projects, detailed contract negotiations, guided plant visits, training for the use or maintenance of purchased products, and attendance at conferences. Without denying the value of these mechanisms, it should be noted that they are usually weak forms of active transfers. Furthermore, the Soviets may downgrade the value of what might otherwise be a fairly active transfer by interposing middlemen, e.g., the KGB or foreign-trade organizations, in the process. While this may serve the interests of the middlemen, it limits direct feedback between the receivers and suppliers of the technology.

A partial list of stronger forms of active transfer includes: transnational "sister plant" relations like those used by IBM, turnkey production facilities, defections of highly trained people, licenses with extensive training, and full-life-cycle joint projects. Most of the few instances of the use of these mechanisms are between East European and Western partners, and are mainly in the form of licensed production. These do not always work out well,[12] although they seem to be more successful in some "average" sense than purely domestic undertakings. There have been a few instances where Westerners, for ideological or academic or monetary reasons, have engaged in extended computer-related technology transfer with the Soviets or East Europeans, but we know of only one case where entire careers were transplanted to the benefit of the Soviet industry.

Perhaps the most singular instance of active U.S.-USSR transfer was the defection of Alfred Sarant, later known as Fillip Staros. Sarant and Joel Barr, later known as Joseph Berg, were American electrical engineers with Communist sympathies who defected to Czechoslovakia during the early 1950s.[13] They later moved to the USSR, where they developed computer systems for military applications, and where Staros was instrumental in the establishment of the Soviet microelectronics industry.[14] By Soviet standards, Staros had a good track record "for getting things done," and there was some innovation in his designs. The computer technology transfer is hard to assess because he had acquired little substantive expertise in the U.S. But he developed such expertise after he left, closely followed Western activities, and found a significant place in the Soviet industry for himself, at least until high-level political changes led to the destruction of his career. His successes and failures are not simply explained by his technical competence. To no small extent, they may have been due as much to an aggressive "American management style." The extent to which he was able to transfer this management style to his Soviet colleagues is not clear.

Passive transfer channels usually boil down to the overt or covert collection of "things": computer systems or subsystems, samples or larger quantities of chips, software in its various forms, vendor brochures, development databases, documentation on standards (the Soviets have also been actively involved with defining committees, and sensibly adopted a number of international standards), books, proprietary reports, detailed design documents, academic journals, etc. The Soviets collect passively, e.g., through mail subscriptions, and more actively, e.g., through the use of intelligence agents who deal with human sources. The latter should not be considered active transfers unless the suppliers and receivers are directly capable of serious technical discussions and have the opportunity for frequent iteration.

Without question, the most widely used technology transfer mechanism is the open literature. Many research institutes are supposedly well-stocked with Western publications, and Soviet computer specialists show familiarity with the content of parts of this literature. It is possible that a very close analysis of Soviet technical publications, an analysis that would discount cliques of domestic researchers and note uncited Western influence, would conclude that the Western literature has had a greater impact on at least this form of domestic R&D than the domestic literature.[15]

Without denying the value of open publications to the Soviets, some limitations should be noted. The best way to do this is to compare Soviet and American opportunities for the use of this literature. Few in-house libraries at Soviet research and development organizations (in industrial ministries, the Academy, or the VUZy) are as well stocked as a major U.S. university. Soviet users usually obtain their copies of Western publications months after Western subscribers. The vast majority of deliveries are institutional; few Soviet computer specialists have individual subscriptions. Library control can be oppressive: check-out times are short, few people are permitted to take Western publications home, advertisements and job descriptions are cut out, photocopying is limited, etc. Centralized abstracting and library services appear to be better at collection than effective dissemination.

There are also more active technology transfer opportunities associated with the use of the open literature, and much of this is denied to the Soviets. Consider an accomplished American researcher at a major university, company, or government laboratory. How might the dynamics of his use of an article in a U.S. journal differ from that of his Soviet counterpart? The chances are good that he knows the author and saw a draft or preprint of the article at least six months before publication, and possibly a year or more before his average Soviet counterpart. He is in a position to deal directly with the author, through an existing professional friendship or through an easily created new one. Not only would he have a good voice phone system to help him do this, but he might do it over a readily available computer network and have additional information sent to him in electronic time over this network. The American researcher might be able to take more advantage of what he read because of the far greater availability of on-site hardware and software. If he did not have the hardware to implement the ideas he read about, he would be in a better position than his Soviet counterpart to order what he wanted, perhaps using the same publication's advertisements to help make a choice. The much vaunted KGB collection capabilities are incapable of providing equally effective substitutes to more than a handful of Soviet institutes.

The Soviet penchant for covert transfers is partly forced on them by export controls, and is partly a result of the more general nature of Soviet relations with foreign countries.[16] It may be argued that the primary value of Western export controls is to limit use of more effective transfer mechanisms. Although there can be, and have been, active covert transfers, most covert mechanisms are passive forms of collecting things (remember: the act of collecting can be active without the technology transfer being so).

It may also be argued that Soviet intelligence agencies have benefitted from the much greater interest in Western technology. Their missions have expanded to the point where the acquisition of technology and products may constitute their single most extensive form of employment in the West.

One fairly common form of illegal product acquisition may be purchased off the floor at trade shows held in the CMEA countries and elsewhere. It is in the interest of Western exhibitors to sell the "used" equipment shown there to avoid the cost and trouble of shipping it back. This is a common and understandable practice all over the world. However, a license to exhibit is not necessarily a license to sell off the floor. Sometimes equipment gets "lost."

Of the various uses for acquired Western hardware, we mention two. The first is the use of a Western unit as the foundation and initial "host" for a Sovietized prototype. A complete copy is produced through the substitution of Soviet-made components and subsystem copies that are tested "in-site" on the operational Western unit. In this way, the original is rebuilt, piece-by-piece, until an entire made-in-the-USSR prototype exists. This process is more suitable for copying large electro-mechanical systems than for microelectronics. The second is the use of Western samples as "place holders" for the design, development, and testing of a larger system. This permits them to move along on the larger system's life cycle before a Soviet-made substitute with the same functional characteristics is available. For example, they might use covertly acquired U.S. microprocessor and memory chips in the pre-fielding stages of the development of a military system. When comparable Soviet-made chips become available, they would be substituted for the U.S. circuits in the serially produced version.

In many ways, the growing complexity of design and manufacture for the computing technologies is making it more difficult and unpleasant for Soviet computer scientists to copy Western technology, although this has not caused them to give up. Increasingly, copying requires more than documentation and samples, even if we only consider passive transfer mechanisms. In the West, the effective development of modern hardware and software is becoming more dependent on comprehensive, sophisticated, integrated, tool environments, which include an interwoven set of computerized tools *and* a working environment built around those tools. Copiers are at an enormous disadvantage without these complete environments. One important example will serve to emphasize this point.

The complexity (element density, functional sophistication, materials handling, etc.) of microelectronic circuit design and manufacture has grown rapidly in recent years. Western industries are learning to pack much more into less space. Not surprisingly, this has become one of the most important applications areas for computer-aided design and computer-aided manufacturing (CAD/CAM). The U.S. and Japanese microelectronics industries have developed very sophisticated CAD/CAM systems. In spite of exceptionally high priority and intensive technology transfer efforts in this area, Soviet systems remain relatively backward and people-based. Soviet computer scientists find themselves with the unenviable task of having to copy chips that have been designed, produced, and tested by highly integrated and automated systems. At best, they may only have part of the CAD/CAM environment used by the original chip developers. The automated systems do not necessarily "think" and operate the same way as a human designer or tester, and they usually operate incomparably faster. For example, a CAD system might enable a manufacturer to design a chip that is strongly optimized in the sense of minimizing internal connection distances. Most humans would tend to design by locating similar functions together. It would be hard to find a Western computer scientist who would relish the thought of reverse engineering a sophisticated, computer-designed chip without a proper set of tools. His Soviet counterparts often do not have a choice.

The Soviets are sensibly giving high priority to the acquisition of CAD/CAM tools, especially for microelectronics. But it is easier for them to acquire pieces than entire environments, and these are integrated environments where the whole is often much greater than the simple sum of the parts. They have also been slow to appreciate the importance of software development environments, an example of a more general underappreciation of software.

Finally, we explicitly consider the desirability of forcing the Soviets to use covert transfer channels. This is another way of viewing export controls to limit Soviet use of some of the more effective, overt mechanisms. As a policy, it is distasteful because it denies direct (but not necessarily indirect) sales to originating Western companies, and because it seems to encourage illegal transfers. However, the transfer of most computer-related technologies is a complex and delicate process. It can easily be upset by lengthening the acquisition chain, and by putting weaker (less knowledgeable or incomplete) links along the chain. Items obtained by covert collectors are more likely to be incomplete or otherwise defective than those bought overtly and directly from the originating company. The collectors are not always in a position to check out the merchandise upon receipt. Collectors are often not the end users, and they may not be overly concerned with getting everything right. The end users may have trouble, perhaps involving more iterations through a long chain, getting the collectors to try again. One might guess that there have been many cases where the value of covertly acquired technology and products has been greatly reduced for these and other similar reasons.

IV. A Partial Assessment of the Soviet Computer Industry

The core of the Soviet computer industry is concentrated in the Ministry of the Radio Industry (MRP), the Ministry of the Electronics Industry (MEP), and the Ministry of Instrument Building, Means of Automation and Control Systems (Minpribor). Because of the confluence of computing and telecommunications in the West, the Ministry of the Communications Equipment Industry (MPSS) and the Ministry of Communications should also be considered. MRP, MEP, and MPSS are represented on the Military-Industrial Commission (VPK). Several other ministries supply equipment whose importance has been underestimated in the USSR: air conditioners, power supplies, magnetic storage media, high quality paper, etc. Our definition of the "computer industry" will also include the research and development communities in the Academy of Sciences (AN) (and the New Department of Information Science, Computer Technology, and Automation) and the higher educational institutions (VUZy), and planning, software, and service organizations scattered throughout the economy.

It is difficult to provide more than crude estimates of the size, rates, and forms of growth of the industry. The reasons for this go beyond those that generally plague assessments of "typical" Soviet industries, including: a large fraction of the core resides in military-industrial ministries, the spread of computing across many ministries and state committees, the mix of a large number of different subtechnologies, problems of separating the industry from the user community, and the partial integration of the Soviet and East European industries.

In spite of these qualifications, and a general reluctance to rely on Soviet statistics (as much for definitional reasons as for concerns about accuracy or falsification), some useful statements may still be made. For our rough definition of the industry, it may consist of several hundred thousand employees in well over a hundred medium and large organizations and a larger number of smaller "pockets." Average growth since 1970 has likely been at least 10 percent per year, and significantly higher for some subtechnologies during certain subperiods.[17]

For the production of general-purpose computers, most of the growth has been via expanding the capabilities of existing facilities. This would include the use of more floor space for manufacturing, the introduction of additional automation to increase productivity, etc. It is not clear if this pattern also holds true for the production of peripherals.

On the surface at least, greater institutional change can be seen in the Soviet software industry. National organizations have been created for such purposes as the coordination of ES systems software research, development, and standardization, and the collection and distribution of applications software. But it would appear that the bulk of the institutional expansion in the Soviet software sector has been in the form of enterprises involved in creating automated management systems (ASU) for other organizations (one could argue that institutes building software exclusively for their own use are not part of the industry). Such enterprises are becoming common in many ministries, where they tend to specialize in ASU development for organizations in their parent ministries, and in USSR-level organizations such as the Academy of Sciences, higher educational institutions, and the GKNT.

The Western imprint on the industry comes in several sizes and shapes. We shall consider: the value of acquired Western equipment and documentation, the impact of technology transfer on Soviet research and development, and Western influence on larger national problems and perceptions.

Western-made computers constitute a tiny part of the total inventory of general-purpose systems in the USSR. Overtly or covertly acquired manufacturing equipment forms a small fraction of such equipment in the USSR. However, these acquisitions have value to the Soviets that transcend crude "fraction of inventory" measurements in at least three ways.

First, there are the direct operational capabilities provided to the end users. Although Soviet and East European-made hardware has improved over the last dozen years, it remains far less reliable than most Western equipment. This is especially true for memory and peripherals. End users who get Western equipment may do so for several reasons: no Soviet-made functional equivalents are available; the simple prestige of having whatever it takes to get Western goodies; but probably the most important is reliability. Receivers are often high-profile or high-priority users who need systems that can be counted on to work. The trade-off of dependence (service and spare parts) vs. dependability for users with heavy clout like the KGB, the Communist Party, or the military may be settled in favor of Western-made systems more often than some people might think. As long as the number of such users does not get too large, the maintenance and spare parts problems are not insurmountable. The availability of complete Western hardware and software systems may also provide both the Soviet industry and end users with technology transfer in the form of hands-on experience with foreign products that may help determine new product programs for the industry.

The second benefit of acquiring Western equipment is that it provides specimens for copying. While it is possible to functionally duplicate computer hardware without samples of the original, it certainly helps to have them. The fraction of Western-made equipment in the total Soviet inventory may be tiny, but the fraction of Soviet and East European-made computer systems that were copied from U.S. designs is large and growing. This statement applies to mainframes, minis, and micros. In this sense, the influence of acquired equipment and documentation has been enormous.

The third benefit is the use of Western-made manufacturing equipment and technology. By far the most important example is design and production equipment and technology for microelectronics. Covert Soviet collection efforts here have been extraordinarily intense. This may be the area of the most concentrated direct dependence on and use of Western equipment. Microelectronics is fundamental to progress in other technologies, and has a vast spectrum of military applications. In some ways, transfers of equipment and technology in this area may be more effective than for other computer-related technologies. Transfers are focused on a fairly small number of high priority receivers, and assimilation tends to be primarily a technical matter, i.e., the interface with the "general Soviet system" presents less of a problem than is the case with other areas like software, personal computing, and telecommunications.

A strong case can be made that Western technology has been a substitute for, rather than a complement to, domestic research and development. Indigenous Soviet hardware designs have almost disappeared, Western systems software is widely used, and the Soviet academic research literature shows little originality. Western technical influence is almost everywhere one looks. It is not unusual to be able to trace an implicitly or explicitly claimed innovation to a close, unacknowledged, Western ancestor. However, it is again important to keep in mind the distinction between global and local innovation. While global innovation is weak, Soviet computer specialists deserve credit for the more limited innovative efforts necessary to bring about the substantial progress that has taken place over the last 15 years.

In this last regard, we consider the software R&D environment, although much of this analysis might also apply to hardware. It would appear that a nontrivial fraction of what the Soviet systems software

R&D community has been doing since 1970 has been in the form of getting Western software to work on Soviet-made machines, or of making minor enhancements to this software. An example of the first kind of task would be the rewriting of parts of Western software systems to accommodate CMEA-made I/O devices. An example of the second is the replacement of English-language error messages with their Cyrillic Russian equivalents.

Let us consider the value of copying/adapting something like a large IBM operating system by a group of bright and energetic people whose previous experience includes nothing comparable. The short-term gains to the State are the accelerated acquisition of an important operational capability and learning experience, through the use of a well-tested Western system and by short circuiting some of the development life-cycle phases, e.g., requirements analysis, design, and some testing.[18] The effort may be viewed more negatively by the R&D people who have to do this work. They may see it as the numbing experience of hacking away at someone else's good and bad work without being allowed to significantly improve it. They may also fear a long-term maintenance task if they are successful—who in the USSR is going to encourage them to go out and build an elegant new operating system of their own design when the technology they adapt from the West is doing what it is supposed to be doing?

Other, similar difficulties are common in both the industry and the user community. Soviet computer center personnel are forced to modify things they did not build or do not fully understand because of local configuration differences and poor vendor support. The vast majority of Soviet users must accept systems as delivered, i.e., they usually have very little say with regard to obtaining tailor-made configurations. Then they must adapt their applications, organizational procedures, etc. to the available hardware or software. They often have precious little help to do this, perhaps no more than translations of IBM or DEC documentation. Even in English, some IBM documentation leaves much to be desired, and the Soviet industry does not seem to have done a particularly outstanding job of improving the Russian editions. More than one IBM customer in the U.S. has had to call for help out of a sense of extreme frustration. However, Western users get good IBM service people and aid from other IBM users to back up documentation in ways that are out of the reach of most Soviet users. These are examples of problems that can be technically devastating. Such problems make managers nervous, and may severely limit their interest in using computers to do what they want done, the way they want it done.[19]

One might argue that the intense Soviet pursuit of Western computer technology has strengthened indigenous capabilities through the investment of greater resources, and pressure to build an industry that is at least capable of acquiring and functionally duplicating Western technology at a reasonable rate. This is a good deal more than what existed in the 1960s. It might also be argued that R&D has been strengthened in other scientific and technical areas because of the increased availability of reasonable general purpose computers.

We conclude this section with brief assessments of selected aspects of Western influence on larger institutional and national problems and perceptions: the broader technical environment, the merging of computing and telecommunications, the role of the military in building the Soviet computer industry, and the prospects for Soviet self-sufficiency.

One of the greatest failings of the Soviet computer industry in the assimilation of foreign technology has been the lack of a detailed appreciation of the broader Western technical computing environment, and the inability to create such an environment, or a comparably effective Soviet-style substitute, for the vast majority of Soviet users. The duplication of U.S. computer systems falls far short of ensuring the productive use of such systems. Notable problems include: the lack of proper ancillary equipment, electrical power, and storage media produced by ministries outside of the industry core, poor availability of service and spare parts,[20] the continuing structural and technical problems with the software sector (although some progress has been made in this area), the poor level of practical training provided by Soviet educational institutions, etc. Progress in all of these areas has lagged far behind that for general-purpose hardware production since the mid-1970s, i.e., since a respectable level of computer equipment has become widely available. It would appear that progress at the core has not had very much "push" influence at the important outer areas of the computer industry.

In this regard, the situation for data communications should be singled out. The Soviets have been talking about gigantic computer networks since the late 1950s. Essentially nothing existed until the mid-1970s, and the "networks" that have been developed since then are unimpressive. The lack of achievement over the last half dozen years is particularly noteworthy because of progress elsewhere in the industry, the advertised importance of networks to Soviet plans, and dramatic practical developments in the West that have been of interest to the Soviets.

The reasons for the poor progress in data communications fall into two categories: technical and behavioral/institutional. We consider only the first; the latter are more complicated and belong more properly in our studies of the Soviet user community. Technically speaking, the USSR is in no position to build broad-based computer networks that could have a significant impact on the national economy. The basic telephone system cannot support extensive data communications. Reasonable dedicated lines exist, but are not generally available. Non-wire two-way communications, e.g., satellite or microwave channels, are even less generally available. Home-to-work data communications are essentially nonexistent for both technical and political reasons. The two communications ministries have done little to seriously improve the overall situation, rhetoric notwithstanding. The problems are enormous. They dwarf those that were overcome to produce Soviet versions of U.S. computer systems.

As noted earlier, many of the problems of the industry stem from the lack of a strong feedback relationship with a world-class user community. The Soviet military is not such a community.[21] The military and the industries and R&D organizations related to the military enjoy privileges: they have advantages over normal civilian organizations with regard to recruiting and rewarding capable people; they may have priority in tasking covert acquisitions and greater exposure to Western technology; military representatives *(voyenpredy)* are in a position to exercise quality control functions at computer production facilities; the Soviet military is in direct competition with Western counterparts in a way that has no strong parallel in the civilian economy, etc. But all of this does not make the Soviet military-industrial establishment a computer-using community comparable to the general-purpose users in the U.S. or Japan.

Consider the following three "meta computing communities": the Soviet military, the U.S. military, and the U.S. civilian communities. The first is the smallest, the most conservative and risk-averting, and the least well-supported. The second is much larger, considerably less conservative in its computer-related activities (e.g., it is inconceivable that the Soviet military would take an ARPANET-like initiative), and is much better supported in every important sense. The third is far larger than the first two combined, extraordinarily diversified across a mind-boggling range of users and applications, is extremely well supported and provides most of the support for the second, and is the main prize of what may be the most singular technological competition in history between the U.S. and Japanese computer industries.

So where does the detailed technological imperative or push for the Soviet industry come from? From the high reaches of the Party-Government pyramid? From the relatively impotent, general civilian user community? From the military? Where does the Party-Government or Soviet military get many of their perceived needs? Some portion comes from the examples provided by the Western military and civilian user communities. Does the Soviet military need a general computing base that is broader and deeper than the one it is capable of building and supporting entirely within itself? Yes, as is evidenced by the way it uses what is available in the West as a surrogate for what it does not have at home. Furthermore, for all its resources and privileges, the Soviet military cannot control what is necessary to build a civilian computing base comparable to that in the West, or even to put pressure on the Soviet computer industry comparable to the pressures that exist on the Western industries. The scope and scale of what is involved is larger and more complex than that for launching a Sputnik.

Finally, Soviet claims that they can achieve world levels across the complete spectrum of computer-related technologies and applications solely on the basis of their own indigenous capabilities are not supported by history, detailed technological assessments, or international trends (see Section V).[22] Soviet computing has been hurt throughout its history by various forms of Western- and self-imposed isolation. In fact, no computing community, including that of the U.S., would be able to move at its current pace if it were to have its contacts with the rest of the world severely restricted. However, the Soviets have achieved a certain form of self-sufficiency in that they run a large industry of their own and produce most of what they use. They have also become less dependent on Western technology in the sense that, if all their overt and covert transfer opportunities were to suddenly disappear, they would be able to function indigenously at a level far above the one that existed in the late 1960s, thanks partly to the transfers that have taken place.

V. Technology Transfer in a Rapidly Evolving Technological and Business World

It might be argued that by far the most important computer-related technology transfer has been the broad exposure to and partial appreciation of Western computing activities at the national level. This helped lead to the change of CMEA perceptions that has evolved over the last two decades and the dramatic changes in policy that affected almost all the trends discussed in Section II, and has had profound influence on the development of the Soviet and East European industries. Western activities are taking place at a rate and on a scale that are impossible to hide from the Soviets. What is most important is most readily accessible to them.

The detailed implementation side of the technology transfer picture is the acquisition, duplication, and assimilation of Western systems, applications, etc. Soviet access to this level of technology has increased dramatically during the last decade, and world technological and business trends are such that this access will continue to increase for some time. These trends include: new system architectures, impressive sustained rates of microelectronic miniaturization, the explosive growth in availability of computing in all sectors of the U.S. economy, the variety and rate of emergence of new products and incrementally innovative ideas, and an increase in the number of capable non-U.S. firms. Collectively, these and other trends are making it easier for the Soviets to find alternate solutions to their needs, to acquire and transport products, and to approach a larger number of potential suppliers for what they want.

But acquisition is not necessarily assimilation, and Soviet progress should be considered in both absolute and relative terms. It may be instructive to view this rapidly changing world from the Soviet side.

The Soviets are observing an incredible range of computer-related activities in the West, particularly in the U.S. and Japan. In roughly the last half dozen years alone, in addition to rapid progress in many "older" areas like microelectronics and disk stores, there has been an extraordinary combination of interwoven technical development and widespread absorption in areas that have "taken off" during this period, including: CAD (Computer-Aided Design), CAM (Computer-Aided Manufacturing), MIS (Management Information Systems) and office automation, data communications and networks, and computing for small organizational and personal use.

All of this makes for an acquisition bonanza. Each year the Soviets obtain many thousands of Western research papers, new product announcements, products, descriptions of new applications, etc. These are being used by the Soviet computer industry more effectively than has ever been the case before. This outpouring of Western activity is making it easier for them to get around Western export controls. But it is also making it necessary for the Soviets to acquire much more just to try to control the rate at which they are falling behind.

The Soviets are increasingly being forced to contend with these pressures and opportunities. But the enormity and range of what is involved precludes getting most of what is needed through a few transfers on the "atomic bomb secrets" or "turnkey plants for the automotive industry" models. What the Soviets are seeing are very broad and rapid rates of incremental innovation, and they are not fully capable of understanding or coping with it. One form of technology transfer used to survive under these circumstances is to watch the West to get an "OK" for the commitment of resources to new directions or specific projects.

Perhaps worst of all from the Soviet standpoint, it is precisely at the level of the national "big picture," where Western computer technology is most exposed and where past claims regarding the advantages of the "Soviet system" were most pronounced, that technology transfer has been least successful. This is also the level where the Soviet industry has been almost impotent in its ability to perform broadly and innovatively. Rhetoric aside, the combination of Soviet leadership, industry, and user community has never been able to generate massive, innovative, new directions in computing such as those described above as "take-off" areas. Furthermore, they have difficulty making the adjustments necessary to move in directions defined by the West, the confluence of computing and telecommunications being an important example. These difficulties seem to have become more pronounced since the mid-1970s[23] and are likely to continue even if the Soviets should be able to become more innovative at the detailed technical level.[24]

NOTES

1. During the last half-dozen years, a respectable English-language literature on Soviet and East European computing has emerged, and there has been an explosive expansion of "computer literacy" in the U.S. and U.K. It is now reasonable to expect readers of this chapter to have some knowledge of computing in general, and of Soviet computing in particular. For the minimum "prerequisite" see Seymour E. Goodman, "Soviet Computing and Technology Transfer: An Overview," *World Politics*, 31, no. 4 (July 1979), pp. 539–70 (coverage through 1977). A fairly extensive listing of post-1976 secondary sources is given in S. E. Goodman, "Computing in the Soviet Union: What Do We Know? What Do We Need to Know? How Can We Find Out?" paper prepared for the Harvard-MIT-Ford Foundation Program on Soviet Science and Technology, November 1983. A good background reference on computing is the *Encyclopedia of Computer Science and Engineering*, Anthony Ralston and Edwin D. Reilly, Jr. (eds.), 2nd ed. (New York: Van Nostrand Reinhold Company, 1983.)

For the purposes of this chapter, "the West" will include Japan. We also note that other East Asian countries, like Taiwan, have strong computer-related connections with the West that involve both legal and illegal technology transfers.

2. Most of our discussion of the user community will be limited to its demand and feedback influence on the industry. Two extensive studies of the absorption of computing into the Soviet economy are in progress at the University of Arizona. William McHenry and John Dolan are the principal researchers. See also S. E. Goodman, "Computing and the Development of the Soviet Economy," *The Soviet Economy in a Time of Change*, vol. 1, John P. Hardt (ed.), Joint Economic Committee, U.S. Congress (Washington: USGPO, 1979), pp. 524–553; and S. E. Goodman, "Computing in the Soviet Union."

3. For more comprehensive assessments of Soviet and East European hardware and software, see Michael Cannon, "A Comparison of U.S. and Eastern Bloc Array Processors," Los Alamos National Laboratory, International Technology Division, September 1983; N. C. Davis, S. E. Goodman, "The Soviet Bloc's Unified System of Computers," *Computing Surveys* (ACM), 10, no. 2 (June 1978), pp. 93–122 (pre-1970 hardware, the first stages of the ES program); S. E. Goodman, "Software in the Soviet Union: Progress and Problems," *Advances in Computers*, 18 (1979), pp. 231–287 (software through 1977–78); C. Hammer, "Soviet Computer Science," Washington, D.C., to appear in 1984 (later stages of the ES program, the SM program, large-scale scientific computers, networks, operating systems, program languages, software engineering, data base management systems, and certain areas of theory); D. J. Kleitman et al., "Soviet Applied Discrete Mathematics," Washington, D.C., 30 November 1982; and Robert Morrison, "Analysis of Soviet Capabilities in the Field of Microprocessor Technology," Los Alamos National Laboratories, draft report, 2 March 1984. Important related technologies have not received the coverage they deserve.

4. By "closely copy" we mean a comprehensive effort at a detailed functional duplication, usually with some form of interoperability in mind. A more

precise definition may vary from subtechnology to subtechnology. For the purposes of this article, the most important example of functional duplication is that for an entire computer system with the intent of achieving a strong form of software compatibility. This involves copying the architecture, the machine language level instruction set, and data interfaces. The term "reverse engineering" will be reserved for a more comprehensive form of copying that would include the duplication of detailed production processes and interoperability down to the component level. Equipment can be functionally duplicated without being reverse engineered. We do not regard the use of general design features or the detailed duplication of a minor feature as "close" copying.

5. It might be noted that the West European industries also fell far behind the U.S. during the same period.

6. Compared with the West, Soviet theoretical research in some fields was arguably stronger in the 1950s and 1960s than it is now. In theoretical areas, East-West technology transfer is relatively uninhibited. Yet much of the Soviet literature over the last half dozen years bears a closer resemblance to Western work of 10 to 15 years ago than it does to contemporary Western research.

7. The modestly successful, partial integration of the CMEA computer industries has been studied elsewhere. See D. A. Mundie, S. E. Goodman, "The Integration of the COMECON Computer Industries: Selected Semi-Technical Appendices," an intermediate report prepared for the National Council for Soviet and East European Research, Washington, D.C., July 1981, 178 pages; S. E. Goodman, "The Partial Integration of the CMEA Computer Industries," Report 624-13b, The National Council for Soviet and East European Research, Washington, D.C., 16 August 1982, 96 pages; S. E. Goodman, "The Partial Integration of the CEMA Computer Industries: An Overview," to appear in *The Economy of Eastern Europe*, vol. 1, John P. Hardt (ed.), Joint Economic Committee, U.S. Congress (Washington: USGPO, 1984).

8. A serious effort to produce detailed, quantitative graphs depicting trends in time is plagued by problems with data (e.g., multiple values, a broad spectrum of reliability over a very large and fragmented collection of sources), definitions, and measurement. By far the most hopeless problem is defining suitable parameters for measuring progress along the vertical axes; another is hidden "apples and oranges" comparisons. With few exceptions, this author believes such tables or graphs to be vulnerable to devastating criticism, and that they tend to give false or misleading impressions of precision. A brief discussion of some of these problems, in the context of comparative U.S.-USSR assessments, is given in S. E. Goodman, "The Impact of U.S. Export Controls on the Soviet Computer Industry," chapter 5 in *The Politics of East-West Trade*, Gordon B. Smith (ed.), (Boulder, Colorado: Westview Press, 1984.)

9. Space does not permit a taxonomy of mechanisms, and our discussion will focus on a few of the most widely used. A taxonomy for overt software technology transfer mechanisms may be found in Seymour E. Goodman, Norman S. Glick, William K. McHenry, John B. McLean, Claude E. Walston, Clark Weissman, "Software Technology Transfer and Export Control," Institute for Defense Analyses, Report N-878, prepared for OUSDRE, January 1981; S. E. Goodman, "U.S. Computer Export Control Policies: Value Conflicts and Policy Choices," *Communications of the Association for Computing Machinery*, vol. 25, no. 9 (September 1982), pp. 613–24. Some specific vehicles for implementing these mechanisms, like the use of Soviet-owned companies, are not listed. We know of no comparable list of covert mechanisms, but it would not be difficult to construct one.

10. Active mechanisms involve direct feedback between a knowledgeable

supplier and a knowledgeable receiver. Passive mechanisms do not. These terms were popularized by J. F. Bucy, Chairman, Defense Science Board Task Force, in an analysis of "Export Control of U.S. Technology—a DOD Perspective," Report prepared for the U.S. Department of Defense, OUSDRE, 4 February 1976.

11. The effect of export controls on the development of the Soviet computer industry has been considered in Goodman, "The Impact of U.S. Export Controls . . ."; some discussion of the possible impact of re-export controls on West-West computer trade may be found in S. E. Goodman and M. R. Kelly, "We Are Not Alone: A Sample of International Policy Challenges and Issues," *The Information Society*, vol. 2, nos. 3–4 (1984), pp. 249–268. Other computer-specific discussions of export control are contained in "Details of Certain Controversial Export Licensing Decisions Involving Soviet Bloc Countries," report by the U.S. General Accounting Office, Washington, D.C., GAO/ID-83-46, 5 May 1983; Charles L. Gold, Seymour E. Goodman, and Benjamin G. Walker, "Software: Recommendations for an Export Control Policy," *Communications of the Association for Computing Machinery*, vol. 23, no. 4 (April 1980), pp. 199–207; Goodman, "U.S. Computer Export Control Policies . . ."; Thomas J. Richards, "An Examination of the Issues Affecting ADP Technology Transfer to the Soviet Union," Ph.D. thesis, George Washington University, Washington, D.C., November 1980 (unpublished).

12. For interesting examples, see Katalin Bossanyi, "The Unintegrated Circuit," *Magyar Hirlap* (Budapest, April 30, 1979), p. 7; "An Assessment of the K-202 Project," *Informatyka* (Warsaw) 9–10 (September–October 1981), pp. 8–17. Perhaps the most successful active transfers have been those between East and West Germany. There is some Western interest in CMEA computer products, but it rarely goes very far. Such relations can turn acrimonious (see *Informatyka* cited above). An interesting Hungarian view of the illegal import of Western computer products may be found in Zsuzsa Lang, "Public Interest—Private Crimes," *Otlet* (Budapest, October 6, 1983), pp. 22, 23.

13. Most of the information on Staros and Berg is from Mark Kuchment, "The Life and Death of Alfred Sarant/Fillip Staros and the Beginnings of Soviet Micro-Electronics," prepared for the Soviet Science and Technology Eyewitness Accounts Seminar on Computing in the USSR, Cambridge, MIT, November 1983. The identifications with Sarant and Barr are not absolutely conclusive, but the evidence is strong. A lesser example of an extended active transfer is Harry Sneed's software undertaking with the Hungarians in Laszlo Kruppa, "The SOFTING Technology: Hungarian Software in the World Vanguard," *Szamitastechnika* (Budapest, September 1981), p. 10; "Interview with Harry Sneed," *Heti Vilaggazdasag* (Budapest, 12 January 1980), pp. 30–31.

14. Several Czech designers, notably Antonin Svoboda and Jan Oblonsky, defected to the West. Svoboda and his students, including Oblonsky, had given Czechoslovakia an early, active, and somewhat innovative computer design group. An in-depth comparison of the post-defection careers of the Staros/Berg and Svoboda/Oblonsky pairs would be welcome. For more information on Svoboda, see Jan G. Oblonsky, "Eloge: Antonin Svoboda, 1907–1980," *Annals of the History of Computing*, 2, no. 4 (October 1980), pp. 284–298.

15. In contrast, almost no Soviet work is cited, or implicitly used, in papers in U.S. or major international computer R&D journals. The reasons are threefold: (1) until recently, the availability and volume of this work was very limited; (2) the U.S. engineering community has a poor history of following foreign efforts (the scientists do better); and (3) much of this work has been relatively weak.

16. The discussion of covert technology transfer in an unclassified publica-

tion presents obvious problems with regard to bibliographic citations. It is our policy never to cite an oral source. Most of the publicly available written information is contained in articles in the popular or computer trade media. The inventory of material on this fashionable subject has become quite large over the last few years, and a bibliography of well over a hundred articles could easily be assembled. A partial summary may be found in Gus Schoone, "The Role of Technology Transfer in Soviet Computing," Draft Report, November 1983.

Such articles should be regarded with more than a little caution. Their authors usually have less topical expertise than is the case with articles on Soviet politics or foreign affairs. Most know little about computing or technology transfer, and do not stick with the subject for a long time. There is also often a chain between original sources and the reporters: an original Soviet source (e.g., a defector), a U.S. intelligence analyst who knows the technology and the Soviet industry, the analyst's boss (the first link in the chain who knows little about the technology), this boss's boss, some higher-level U.S. Government official, the reporter. It is not hard to imagine a substantial information loss along the way.

However, it would be a mistake for these concerns to lead us to discount the available public information on covert technology transfer, or to avoid discussion of the matter entirely. The overall picture of the scope and intensity of Soviet activities painted by these articles is more accurate than the finer-grained details and understanding. Our position is not to give very high credibility to single media sources, but we do value the aggregate.

More generally, our discussion of covert transfer activities should be regarded as necessarily speculative.

17. For example, Soviet industrial production for "computer technology" (undefined, but probably a subset of hardware production) increased by 11 percent from 1982 to 1983. This rate is much higher than those for most of the other sectors reported. See "Industrial Production Figures for the 12 Months of 1983," *RRC Newsletter* (Harvard), 8, no. 6, (6 February 1984), p. 1; also *USSR National Economy in 1982, Statistical Handbook* (Moscow: Finansy i Statistika, 1983).

18. These short-term benefits are not always realized. The overall Soviet track record in this regard may leave much to be desired. We suspect many efforts have failed or have taken the adapters almost as long as it took the original Western developers. Conversely, there have almost certainly been some very successful efforts as well. Much depends on local circumstances, like the quality and motivation of the computer scientists involved, and the quality and completeness of what has been assembled for them to work with.

Another reason for using Western software products is that most have been customer tested to an extent that is inconceivable in the USSR. The importance of this should not be underestimated.

19. The assimilation of computing may come in different forms in different contexts, even within the same organization. For example, consider the absorption of computing in, say, an enterprise in the Soviet aircraft industry. At least two different criteria come to mind: (1) the internal measures of a technically good computer center, e.g., how well they have succeeded in assembling a collection of hardware and systems software, how well the staff does in minimizing down time, etc.; and (2) how well the organization uses its computing resources to support its primary reasons for existing, e.g., CAD/CAM for the design and manufacture of aircraft parts. The two may not be closely coupled.

20. Soviet claims of being unaffected by Western embargoes that include service and spare parts for previously purchased systems sound a bit strained. No doubt, there are installations using Western equipment that are serviced by

highly qualified indigenous maintenance personnel, and covert collectors may be capable of satisfying limited needs for spare parts. One suspects, however, that this covers a small fraction of centers equipped with Western systems, that such an embargo hurts many others, and that it puts a non-trivial additional burden on the covert collectors.

21. A brief discussion of the effort to produce a better mix of the military-industrial and general civilian sides of the industry, for the benefit of both, may be found in S. E. Goodman, "Advanced Technology: How Will the USSR Adjust?" Third Conference of the Series on "The Soviet Union in the 1980s," The Kennan Institute of the Smithsonian Institution, Washington, D.C., 4 March 1983.

22. Claims of this sort have become fairly common since the U.S. has attempted to tighten export controls. A recent example is by Academician Aleksandrov, President of the USSR Academy. See his "A Task Through the End of the Century," *Izvestiya* (19 January 1984), p. 3. Aleksandrov's statement was tacked onto an article concerned primarily with the problem of broadly upgrading computer literacy in Soviet industry—yet he compared the task of achieving computing self-sufficiency with earlier efforts in nuclear and rocket technology.

23. To varying degrees, this statement applies to all of the "take-off" areas noted above. Of course, none of these areas have appeared out of nowhere since the mid-1970s. Most were discussed much earlier, but all experienced rapid recent growth as a result of a combination of commercial opportunities and developments in supporting technologies. Soviet performance and interest in these areas is not uniform, although all are troublesome from the standpoint of the Soviet computer industry's ability to broadly bring these technologies to the general economy. CAD/CAM is perhaps the least problematic in this regard, and the CMEA countries have initiated major programs in these areas. At the other end of this spectrum is personal computing (which involves much more than the availability of microprocessors), and we have seen little beyond announcements of limited hardware and conferences on the subject, e.g., *All-Union Scientific-Technical Conference on Individual Dialog Systems Based on Microcomputers (Personal Computers): Dialog-82-Micro*, Science Center for Biological Research AN SSSR, Pushchino, 25 October 1982.

24. Leading candidates for areas where Soviet scientists may make global, innovative, technical contributions are optical computing and some theoretical subjects. On the basis of the size of the Soviet scientific and technical community, and the time the Soviets have been in computing, it should be inevitable that significant innovations will emerge. What is remarkable is that so little has appeared, especially over the last half dozen years.

We should also expect to see more Soviet activity in certain high profile and heavily publicized areas like "Fifth Generation" computing. See, for example, Paul Walton and Paul Tate, "Soviets Aim for 5th Gen," *Datamation*, 30, no. 10, 1 July 1984, p. 53; V. Mikhalevich, "Information: Its Time Has Come," *Pravda*, 31 July 1984, p. 2.

Technology Transfer in the Soviet Energy Sector

Robert W. Campbell

THE ENERGY sector makes an instructive case for study of Soviet acquisition of foreign technology. A significant amount of transfer has occurred, including examples which have attracted a great deal of attention. Given the problems facing the energy sector, Soviet interest in foreign energy technology is likely to continue. It is, moreover, a sector within which indigenous technological performance and the effectiveness of transfer have varied widely, a circumstance which may help us to understand the many factors that affect the decision to import technology, and the impact of transfers.

As a case study of technology transfer in a specific sector, this chapter attempts: (a) to survey the status of Soviet technology in the energy sector and Soviet needs for technology imports; (b) to characterize the technology transfer that has taken place—its scale, sources, types; (c) to consider the degree of success attained in absorbing the imported technology and evaluate the contribution foreign technology has made to the sector's development; (d) to consider whether technology transfer has stimulated indigenous technical advance or has propagated dependence; (e) to examine how crucial western technology has in fact turned out to be and how the Soviet economy has adjusted when confronted with the U.S. effort to impede Soviet acquisition of technology from abroad; and finally, (f) to describe how Soviet views and policies have evolved in reaction to this experience.

Fortunately, much of this terrain was carefully reviewed a few years ago in a detailed study by the Office of Technology Assessment (OTA) of the U.S. Congress—*Technology and Soviet Energy Availability*.[1] The study enlisted a large number of specialists on Soviet energy to review the status and development prospects of each of the main energy branches, covering its technological level, the extent of Soviet import dependence, and the degree to which the United States might be able to control the flow of western technology to the USSR. A major concern of the study was to elucidate how much difference the West as a whole, and/or the

United States could make to Soviet energy availability by 1990. Additional background regarding the technological level of the Soviet energy economy and technology transfer in the sector is available in other works by the author of this chapter.[2]

Taking advantage of the fact that so much has already been done, this chapter can focus on two main tasks—summarizing the conclusions of previous work, and bringing the picture up to date, concentrating on those aspects of the question that seem especially relevant to the concerns of this volume. The next section reviews the major findings of the OTA study, and the one following that describes developments since mid-1981. Separate sections then take up a number of major technology areas where the prospects for technological transfer seem important, and/or where the record of past transfers helps illuminate some interesting issues.

OTA Findings

We can begin by summarizing the conclusions of the OTA study in rather close paraphrase. The technological level of energy production, transformation, transport, and utilization in the USSR is uneven across branches, but is generally low. The branch in which Soviet competence and technological level is highest is electric power generation, where in some technologies the USSR is essentially even with the West. The Soviet economy has mastered two kinds of nuclear power reactors, and the industry has experimented boldly with such leading-edge technologies as breeder reactors, fusion, use of nuclear reactors for space and process heat, bulk transmission at very high voltages, and magnetohydrodynamic power generation (MHD). Other branches of the energy sector exhibit technological levels appreciably below world standards and in numerous cases technological problems hinder expanded use of particular energy sources or impose very high costs. In the coal industry the USSR is relatively backward across all stages, from production through cleaning and processing to transport and utilization. The USSR has virtually no experience with slurry pipelines, and is only now beginning significant development work. The oil industry suffers from technological weaknesses at all stages from exploration through drilling and production to refining. A special problem is inadequate equipment for lifting the large volumes of fluid from wells in reservoirs that have been produced with massive water injection. The relative importance of oil compared to gas is falling and will continue to do so, and to accommodate this shift, it will be necessary to replace oil with gas in boiler and furnace uses. As use of residual fuel oil is reduced technological improvements to deepen the refining of crude oil and to raise the quality of refined products are vital. Petroleum refining technology in the USSR has traditionally lagged well behind world standards. One strategy for maintaining oil output is to expand offshore efforts. Soviet experience with finding, developing, and producing oil and gas resources offshore is limited, and domestically produced equipment is in short supply and technically inadequate. In gas transport domestic producers have not managed to produce compressor equipment suitable to the task. Cutting across all branches is a general weakness in employing computer technology for control and analysis, as in automating the operation of power plants and systems or in processing the huge amount of seismic information generated in exploration for oil and gas. In a number of cases the scale or geography of the Soviet energy sector is such that it is possible to move ahead only by employing technology at the forefront of development. For example, the extraordinarily large volumes of gas to be transported from Siberia to the areas of concentrated demand in the European USSR mean that the industry should use large diameter lines, powerful compressor units, and pressures higher than those common in world experience. The locations of the best sources for expanding coal output and converting it efficiently into power at mine-mouth plants are in Siberia, requiring that power be transported over distances that call for voltages stretching world technological experience.

To deal with some of these problems, in the 1970s the USSR undertook large-scale purchases of western equipment. By far the largest component of Soviet purchases of foreign technology for the energy sector—about 2.7 billion out of 3.4 billion in 1979—was for the oil and gas sector. According to the study, "the one area in which Soviet petroleum equipment and technological purchases might be described as 'massive' is large diameter pipe and other equipment (compressor stations and pipelaying equipment) for the construction and operation of gas pipelines" (p. 10). Purchases of technological equipment for the coal, nuclear, and electric power sectors, on the other hand, have been small and "appear to have been intended to compensate for specific deficiencies in the quantity or quality of domestic equipment, rather than to acquire new technological knowhow" (p. 10). Regarding possible sources for the kind of equipment the Russians were interested in, the study concluded that "with few exceptions, adequate quantities of the energy equipment sought by the USSR are produced and available outside the United States, and the quality of these foreign goods is generally comparable to that of their U.S. counterparts" (p. 392). It mentioned as important exceptions electric submersible pumps and sophisticated seismic systems for oil and gas prospecting. It also emphasized that though "the USSR is quite dependent on the West for large diameter pipe and the compressor stations it needs to construct gas pipelines . . .

the former item is not produced in the United States and there are multiple alternative suppliers for the latter" (p. 393).

One of the major conclusions was thus that "the immediate leverage of the United States over the Soviet Union in the area of petroleum equipment and technology is probably limited by at least three factors. *First,* the United States is the sole supplier of very few petroleum-related items. *Second,* the USSR has demonstrated some ability to do without these items, at least in the short term. *Third,* and perhaps most important, gas is the energy sector on which the USSR is most dependent for its energy future, and with the possible exception of construction equipment, the United States has little to offer in this area that is unique" (p. 393).

Looking to the future, the study concluded that western technology would continue to be important to Soviet energy development, especially in view of the importance of gas in Soviet energy plans. The extent to which the USSR can capitalize on its tremendous gas potential will depend on its ability to substitute gas for oil, and to add to the gas pipeline network. The rate of construction of new pipelines, both for domestic use and for export, is the most important determinant of the extent to which Soviet gas can be utilized. The study saw little prospect for the Soviet coal industry to make a significant contribution. It considered Soviet targets for nuclear power overly optimistic—not because of lack of know-how or experience with developing the technology of nuclear power—but because of inadequate capacity for producing the required equipment and for constructing power stations. Though it acknowledged large potential savings through energy conservation it concluded that it was doubtful that such savings could be achieved on a large scale. In the long term, western exploration technology and equipment might be crucial to the oil industry.

Recent Changes in the Soviet Energy Situation

The general perspective of the OTA study probably represented a reasonably coherent consensus among the experts. It remains essentially correct in 1984, but there have been slight changes in Soviet energy policy that will probably affect Soviet interest in and priorities for the acquisition of technology from abroad. Soviet priorities for the remaining 15 years of the century have been expressed in "guidelines for the long-range energy program of the USSR." A draft of the program was approved by the Politburo in April 1983, and after nearly a year's delay, the guidelines were published in March 1984.[3] The guidelines help to quantify some major emphases in energy policy and to refine our sense of what the technological bottlenecks are likely to be over the next decade and a half. Also, the early years of the Eleventh Five-Year Plan

(1981–85) have brought some developments that may change slightly our perspective on what the most pressing technology problems are. The major directions of continuity and change emerging from these developments since the OTA study may be described as follows.

In the near term the pressure on the energy sector and the associated technological bottlenecks have been eased somewhat by a general economic slowdown. Growth of total primary energy production was planned at 3.5 percent per year for the Eleventh Five-Year Plan, but growth actually achieved in the first four years of the plan amounted to only 2.5 percent per year. GNP, however, has also grown less rapidly than originally planned, and the under-plan growth of energy output appears adequate to meet domestic needs and to maintain exports at the current level. Nevertheless, the energy sector remains, and is likely to remain in the future, a choke-point for economic growth. It has taken an alarming share of investment in the Eleventh Five-Year Plan (21 percent of all investment in the economy by my calculations compared with 16 percent in the late 1970s[4]). Because of a continuing eastward shift in energy production and worsening natural conditions the situation will get worse, and the only way to contain the investment burden it imposes on the economy is through technical progress to cut costs. One of the interesting features of the long-range energy plan is a forecast that even with a great many improvements expected in technology, it is expected that through the period to the year 2000 energy will continue to take the same high share of all investment as in the Eleventh Five-Year Plan period. Whatever the Soviet leaders may feel about the dangers of reliance on technology transfer from abroad, any failures in domestic programs to meet particular technological needs (and past history suggests there will be such failures) are bound to exert great pressure for acquisition of foreign technology.

The centrality of rapid expansion of gas output as the centerpiece of energy policy in the eighties, and the emphasis on construction of the gas-pipeline network as the technological task that will most stress the technological capabilities and production capacity of the Soviet economy have been corroborated by developments subsequent to the OTA study. Gas output has continued to grow rapidly and has accounted for almost three-quarters of the increment in energy production through the 1984 plan. On the other hand, this success has been bought at a heavy opportunity cost in terms of diverting investment resources away from other needs, both within the energy sector and from other sectors of the economy. Both current policy and long-range plans involve some shift of perspective on the future of gas, and on the relative attention and resource allocation to be devoted to other solutions to energy needs.

The massive commitment to gas in the Eleventh Five-Year Plan was a decision on which Brezhnev spent some of his dwindling political resources at the end of his career, and it is not unlikely, as has been suggested by one western review of the "gas campaign," that his successors may want to ease off somewhat on this commitment.[5] The energy program envisages continued growth of gas output until the mid-nineties, but no further growth after that.

Energy planners probably feel that they must now give more attention to the liquid fuel problem as they look forward. In 1984 it began to appear that oil output may indeed have peaked and is beginning a long-predicted decline.[6] The Russians developed their West Siberian fields with a strategy of forcing output to the utmost by intensive drilling and water injection, and are now facing adverse consequences in the form of a rapid decline in well productivities and the necessity to extract tremendous quantities of water along with the oil.

To stave off a precipitous decline in oil output will require resource inputs and technological improvements on several fronts. These include a doubling of the capacity of drilling organizations, large additions of fluid lift capacity at existing reservoirs, a variety of enhanced recovery technologies, and a serious effort to develop and exploit offshore resources. To handle the increase in drilling, the energy plan envisages radical improvements in the productivity of drilling operations. The best prospect for large additional reserves is probably a massive offshore development program. A couple of months after approving the long-term energy plan (which contains a rather brief outline of the role of offshore development), the Politburo approved what is probably a more operational plan for oil and gas development on the continental shelf to 1990.[7] Interestingly, the particulars of this more detailed plan have not been published as of mid-1984, which may reflect some continuing controversy over priorities as the Twelfth Five-Year Plan is being worked out. But if the Soviets hold to a big offshore effort, it will represent significant new technological challenges. Without going into details, we can say that *all* the strategies mentioned above for coping with declining oil output involve important technological challenges.

Oil and gas together will remain the mainstay of energy output, but over the longer perspective the planners hope to supplement hydrocarbons with a higher share for other primary energy sources. The coal industry has continued the poor performance it recorded in the 1970s into the first half of the 1980s. Output in 1985 will be far below the amount specified in the Eleventh Five-Year Plan, and is likely to be no larger than 1980 output in terms of caloric content. But the planners are apparently still counting on coal to help in the long run. One of the important contributions hoped for from coal is liquid fuel from deep processing of cheap eastern coals. This expectation both reinforces the impression of Soviet pessimism about oil prospects, and poses technological challenges itself. It is doubtful that the Russians will be able to develop a synfuels industry on their own, a point to be elaborated on in a later section.

The concern about a possible pinch in liquid fuel supplies is also revealed in the intention expressed in the plan to devote considerable effort to expanding oil shale output for production of liquid fuel and to establish a methanol industry.

On balance, considering oil, gas, and coal together, the planners appear to expect relatively little growth in fossil fuel output between now and the end of the century. Conservation is to greatly dampen the growth in demand, and such net growth of primary energy output as is required will be met in large part by expanded output of nonconventional sources. Of the latter, the most important is nuclear power. The contribution of nuclear power was already set to grow rapidly, under a plan established in the late seventies that set a target for a capacity of something like 63 million kilowatts by 1990. Despite severe problems in the nuclear power program at the moment, the long-range plan seems to retain a very high priority for nuclear energy, including breeder reactors.

A second development in the energy sector that has improved our understanding of Soviet ability to manage progress without technology from abroad is the Soviet response to the U.S. embargo on export of equipment for the pipeline carrying gas from Urengoi to Western Europe. The Reagan administration did not accept the line of reasoning developed in the OTA study that the U.S. could do little to restrict the flow of technology to the USSR. It has attempted to exploit the USSR's dependence on imports for the oil and gas sector, and to aggravate the economic bind in which the Soviet leaders find themselves by embargoing the export of U.S. pipeline construction and compressor equipment to the USSR. It also tried to force West European firms which had contracted to sell such equipment to the Russians to do the same. The public response from Soviet spokesmen was that the USSR is perfectly capable of solving this technological problem on its own, and that the cutoff of U.S.-produced or U.S.-licensed equipment would not interfere with pipeline construction plans, or the planned gas deliveries to Western Europe. But that claim must be tested against performance, and our first task in bringing the picture up to date is to review how the U.S. embargo has affected Soviet pipeline construction.

It should be emphasized that our concern here is not with the efficacy of the embargo (or the lack thereof) in stopping the pipeline, or in altering West European policies on trade, credit, or technology transfer. The Reagan administration proclaimed that its goal in interfering with the pipeline was to prevent the Europeans from becoming dependent on Soviet gas and supplying large amounts of hard currency to the USSR. Its means for doing so, however—the embargo on equipment—has posed a problem for the Soviet gas pipeline program as a whole. Our question is how effectively the Russians have responded to the compressor cut-off, and how the embargo has affected the expansion of the pipeline system as a whole.

Pipeline Equipment

The background for the pipeline case can be sketched briefly. In the Eleventh Five-Year Plan virtually the entire increment in Soviet primary energy output was to take the form of gas, and virtually all that gas was to come from the Urengoi field in northern Tiumen' oblast' in West Siberia. That implied a tremendous transport job—by 1985 an additional 200 billion cubic meters to be shipped an average distance of 2,500–3,000 km for an increment in transport work of 500–600 trillion ton kilometers. That required the construction of 5 major pipelines to the European USSR, plus an export line, totalling about 20,000 kilometers in length, all of 56-inch pipe. The complex was to have some 180 compressor stations, powered with 13,000 megawatts of compressors. These figures refer only to the main system for the transport of Urengoi gas, and the total pipeline program for the Eleventh Five-Year Plan envisaged construction of 38,000 km of gas transmission pipeline, with 230 compressor stations, with total compressor power of 25,000 megawatts.[8] For the export line, compressor stations and pipe were to be supplied on credit by the West Europeans, to be repaid by exports of gas. The amounts of pipe to be imported in the Eleventh Five-Year Plan from Western Europe (Japan is also an important supplier) far exceeded the amount needed for the export line itself, however. The 4,450 kilometer export pipeline is said to have absorbed 2.7 million tons of pipe,[9] but since the 6 major lines totalled about 20,000 km, the total tonnage of pipe would be over 12 million tons. Only a fraction of that tonnage could be supplied by Soviet pipemills (probably no more than 3–4 million tons). Consequently, the total amount of pipe to be imported in the 11th FYP will run close to 2 million tons per year.[10]

The compressor equipment which the Russians contracted to import from western producers (about 3,000 megawatts) was committed exclusively to the export pipeline, and it was not clear where the 22,000 megawatts needed for the compressor stations planned for domestic lines was to come from. This total implies requirements far above the domestic output levels attained in the Tenth Five-Year Plan, when only about 7,000 megawatts was produced domestically.[11] Moreover, for the large-diameter lines, new models were needed, with larger unit capacities than those already being produced. The unit power of the standard Soviet compressor models available in 1980 was 10 megawatts or less. Compressor stations for 56-inch lines using them would require

8 such units per station, and great savings were possible by designing those stations to use three 25-megawatt units instead. In their explication of Eleventh Five-Year Plan energy plans, Soviet planners provided some rather vague suggestions as to how this equipment was to be supplied, but I never saw any evidence that they had faced up realistically to the task confronting them.

Then in December 1981, in response to the imposition of martial law in Poland, President Reagan widened existing U.S. controls on the export of oil and gas equipment by embargoing the export of any U.S. equipment for the West European pipeline. One of the most important items affected by the ban was U.S.-produced rotors and other components for the gas turbines the European partners were constructing to power the compressor units they were providing under the pipeline deal. In June 1982, these controls were extended to subsidiaries and licensees of U.S. firms abroad, with sanctions to be imposed on foreign companies that violated them. Because the U.S. firm General Electric was the only source capable of producing the rotors in the quantities needed, these actions made it impossible for the West European contractors to supply most of the units promised, though having already received some rotors from General Electric (22 is the figure usually mentioned), they were able, defying U.S. sanctions, to make partial delivery.

The Soviet Domestic Compressor Effort. Because of the political furor the embargo and the sanctions raised among the allies of the United States, the embargo was lifted in November 1982, and controls were further eased in 1983. But we have here an interesting episode that can tell us something about Soviet ability to go it alone in an important technological area. As a result of this disruption in the intended flow of equipment, the Russians faced the prospect of having to rely on their own resources to produce compressor equipment. Their response was to accelerate several programs already under way. These were:

a) development and production of a unit powered by a 25-megawatt gas turbine (the GTN-25) by a consortium of some of the major plants in Leningrad (principally the Nevskii Zavod, the Leningradskii Metallicheskii Zavod, and the Leningrad Turbine Blade Plant, but with numerous other contractors involved as well). The original 1985 output goal of 130 units per year was reaffirmed as an operational first priority, which it had not been earlier.

b) production of a 16-megawatt machine, which has long been under development, at the Khar'kov Turbine Plant.

c) development of a new aero-engine-based unit (the GPA-Ts-16) larger than the aero-engine-based 6.3 megawatt model mastered earlier. The new unit was to use retired NK-4 aircraft engines—i.e., the engine which powered the TU-154 and the Il-62 civilian transport aircraft.

d) expanded production of a 10-megawatt unit powered by a marine turbine (the GPA-10).

e) extensive use of electric motors as prime movers for compressors.

f) in addition, certain models already in production (notably the GTK-10 and the GPA-Ts-6.3) were probably given higher production targets than originally intended.

These programs, especially the first three, were given very high visibility and priority in a Soviet-style campaign in which plants were called on to revise their plans upward, workers volunteered to accept higher obligations, and the press carried frequent reports of mileposts passed in accelerating production. Apparently two defense ministries were called on to make a more serious contribution to this civilian program than previously by supplying gas turbines originally developed for marine and aircraft applications, and by participating in the R&D effort to modify them for pipeline use. Numerous earlier statements emanating from the gas industry had suggested that the Ministry of the Aviation Industry (Minaviaprom) was reluctant to co-operate.[12]

This crash program has now been under way long enough to permit some judgments about how well it has worked. Briefly, the effort to accelerate the domestic supply of compressors has not yet met the need, resulting in a large shortfall in the amount of compressor power available for installation on the new lines. A careful collation of the available information, which I shall not reproduce here, suggests that cumulative output, 1981 through 1984 plan, will be only about 10–11 million kilowatts. Even supplemented by a small flow of imports, this leaves the 25 million kilowatts they planned to have acquired by 1985 far out of sight. Scattered information on the growth of compressor capacity installed on the system leads to the same conclusion. At the end of 1982 it was 23 million kilowatts, and although no figure has been reported for the end of 1983, we know that the plan for 1984 is 3.8 million kilowatts.[13] Assuming that 1983 additions did not exceed 3 million kilowatts, the end-of-1984 total would be 29.8 million kilowatts, and even some acceleration in 1985—say to 5 million kilowatts—would still leave the end-of-1985 total at only about 35, compared to the originally planned 42.6 million kilowatts.

The development and production history of the new models confirms our earlier perceptions of Soviet weakness in this kind of technological advance. There have been serious slippages in the production and testing of prototypes. The first series unit of the GTN-25 after the testing of prototypes was produced in December 1982, and it seems that as many as 15 units may have been produced in 1983. The plan for 1984 is said to be only 30.[14] The goal of 130 in 1985 will certainly not even be approached. The Sumy plant was supposed to produce 55 of the 16-megawatt aero-engine-based units in 1983, and this target may have been met. After the first flush of reports about above-plan assignments in 1983 nothing has been heard about actual outputs under any of these programs. I have not seen one story about the number of units actually produced in 1983 or planned for 1984. I believe this means that there are limited successes to report and that they have backed away from the 1983 priorities. No claims have been made about reliability or any other performance aspects of those installed in 1983. If this case follows earlier experience with new compressor models we will soon hear about problems in use and interruption of production for redesign of these machines, which after all had seen very little testing at the time the decision was made to put them into series production. Soviet sources report nothing at all about the production of the old models, or about the models using electric motors as prime movers.

Compressor stations are not getting built and equipped on schedule on either the export line or the domestic lines. There is a great deal of fanfare about the completion of various lines. The Urengoi-Griazovets line was finished in 1981, the Urengoi-Petrovsk line in March 1982, the Urengoi-Novopskov line at the end of 1982 and the export line in 1983. Reports of completion are usually coupled with a claim that the line involved has been completed ahead of schedule, and has reached its design capacity. These claims, especially the latter, surely contain a large element of puffery. One story states explicitly that when the Urengoi-Petrovsk line was put into service in 1982 it was operated without any compressor stations.[15] When the export line was reported as finished and in operation, there were no compressor stations operating on it. Seventeen of its intended 41 compressor stations were supposed to be in operation by the end of 1983, and it has subsequently been claimed early in 1984 that in fact 19 of these stations were in operation.[16] That is a little difficult to credit given the criticism and sense of disorder in the reviews of the situation at some of those stations appearing in the press at the end of 1983. In some cases the claims may mean that the building had been accepted or that one compressor is in use. As one Soviet commentator says, "although two of the lines from Siberia to the Center were put into operation ahead of the established timetable, a significant volume of work remained before they were completed."[17] Some more recent stories suggest that the strategy has been to try to get two 25-megawatt units installed at the most crucial stations. Gas has been moving through the export line, originally by dint of hooking in some compressor stations on neighboring lines.

Once the embargo was lifted, the West European suppliers began to move ahead swiftly to complete the orders.[18] These units will probably not be received in time to equip the export line, though some may be used on the second round of compressor stations on it (the original 41 minus the 17 finished in 1983).

The consequences may not be as bad as this tale of underfulfillment sounds. It may not really have been necessary to have 42.6 million kilowatts of compressor capacity in operation by 1985, anyway. Soviet designs for compressor stations involve considerable reserve equipment. In a station with three 25-megawatt compressors, only two work at any one time, with the other in reserve. As long as compressors do not fail, design throughput is attainable with two-thirds of the design capacity. Also, throughput on a gas line drops less than in proportion to reduction in compressor horsepower. The pipeline network seems to be succeeding in taking off the increment of gas output at Urengoi, where output is growing according to plan. Deliveries of gas to market, also, seem to be growing as they should.[19] It has been possible to handle and deliver the gas because to some extent line can substitute for compressor capacity. It is this tradeoff that no doubt accounts for the frantic emphasis on completing lines ahead of schedule, so that extra line capacity can compensate for the shortfall in compressor power. Boris Shcherbina, formerly in charge of the Ministry for Construction of Oil and Gas Enterprises (which has the major responsibility for gas pipeline construction) and now a deputy prime minister, is suggesting that it will be possible to complete a seventh line in this Five-Year Plan, rather than waiting until the Twelfth.[20]

The campaign to accelerate compressor development domestically has revealed an interesting glimpse into the process of *internal* technology transfer—i.e., from the military to the civilian sectors of the economy. Two of the new compressor models come in part from ministries in the group co-ordinated by the Military-Industrial Commission (*Voenno-promyshlennaya Komissiia* or VPK) generally thought to constitute the heart of the Soviet military economy. The aero-engine-based GPA-Ts-16 requires significant inputs and help from the Ministry of the Aviation Industry (Minaviaprom) and the turbine for the GPA-10 is produced in the Ministry of the Shipbuilding Industry (Minsudprom). The aviation engines are from the civilian side of Minaviaprom, but I believe the marine turbine must come from a plant largely devoted to military production, since the name of the producing plant has never been mentioned.[21]

The development of the aero-engine-based units was coordinated by an interdepartmental Gosplan commission headed by A. A. Aver'ianov.[22] Aver'ianov recently published an interesting article extolling this experience as a model for technology transfer within Soviet industry.[23] The article is labeled "for discussion" and is couched in rather Aesopian language. Nevertheless, Aver'ianov is clearly asserting that the R&D organizations of Minaviaprom provided important assistance to the R&D organizations in the civilian Ministry of Chemical and Petroleum Machinebuilding (Minkhimmash) which produced the finished compressor unit. He implies that the design bureau in Minkhimmash responsible for the modification of the turbine for the compressor received substantial direct help from some design bureau in Minaviaprom, and says, "the experience accumulated in creating and developing the basic aviation engine made it possible to prepare in a short period an experimental prototype of an aero-based engine for a compressor unit, to spend minimal time readying these prototypes, and to use the existing tooling of the basic engine for series production." He contrasts this experience favorably with the more usual sterile arms-length way in which technological information is transferred through exhibits and literature.

Pipelaying Tractors. The U.S. embargo also covered pipelaying tractors used in constructing pipelines, and American suppliers with orders were unable to obtain export licenses. Specifically, Caterpillar lost a $90 million order for 200 pipelayers.[24] In response to this cutoff, the Russians have resorted to a couple of alternatives. One was to buy from Japanese firms—Komatsu apparently won the orders the American companies could not fill. It is reported that about thirty percent of the pipelayers used in the construction of the export line have been Japanese. In total it is said that the Russians have imported 1500 pipelayers.[25] A highly publicized campaign was also mounted to produce equipment in the USSR. The domestic substitute is a machine called the TG502 produced at the Sterlitamak construction machinery plant, using a 330 horsepower crawler produced at the Cheboksary tractor plant. It is said to be capable of handling up to 50 tons.[26] It was originally expected, before the embargo was announced, that about 1700 of these pipelayers would be needed and despite the publicity given to this as an example of the USSR's ability to substitute domestic for imported equipment, it seems doubtful that they have been able to speed up production beyond the original plan. Number 245 is said to have rolled out of the Sterlitamak plant in July 1982, and the plan for the second half of the year was another 165, which would bring the 1981–1982 total to about 400, of which we know 65 were produced in 1981. The target set for the end of the Eleventh Five-Year Plan was 500 per year.[27] If 1983 output reached 300, 400 were produced in 1984, and the 1985 goal of 500 were met, the total would still be only 1660, i.e., about the planned 1700.

It is probably too early to judge how satisfactory the domestic substitute is. The Russians claim that it is as good as or better than the foreign models, but I suspect that after some more time elapses we will begin to see complaints about its repair record, its capacity, and other shortcomings. It may indeed be somewhat too small. There are plans to introduce a new machine capable of lifting 80 tons, but apparently this depends on getting a 500-horsepower tractor, and as of 1984 this larger model has not yet emerged from the hazards of the development process.

My conclusion is that the Russians were able to make up for the loss of American pipelayers by importing Japanese equipment, but that they have not in fact been stimulated to achieve self-sufficiency by domestic capacity expansion or technological breakthroughs.

Submersible Pumps

A second critical technology for which the Russians depended on imports in the past was U.S.-produced electric-powered submersible pumps. As mentioned earlier, Soviet petroleum production methods rely heavily on reservoir pressure maintenance through water injection, and at a fairly early stage in the life of a reservoir, water makes its way to the producing wells, so that large volumes of water must be lifted for each ton of oil produced. The most productive technology for lifting really large volumes of fluid in these situations is downhole centrifugal pumps powered by electric motors. Soviet-produced pumps of this type, apparently copied from an earlier generation of American equipment received on lend-lease during the Second World War, were too small to handle the fluid volumes involved. They have also been unreliable, working for a comparatively short period of time before they must be pulled from the well and repaired. This is an expensive and labor-intensive process, and inability to handle the amount of repair involved means that large numbers of wells stand idle awaiting repair. In the seventies the Russians tried to meet the problem by importing U.S.-made high-capacity submersible pumps. An earlier study by the author that followed this question through the mid-seventies concluded that the Russians had derived very large benefits from these imports in the form of extra oil output.[28]

The problem of adequate fluid lift capacity has become even more serious since the mid-seventies. In the older fields the water-oil ratio is now staggering. In Bashkiriia in 1980 4.8 tons of water were lifted for every ton of oil.[29] And because they are trying so hard to intensify production from the few big flush fields in Western Siberia by injecting large volumes of water and by maintaining high well flows, these fields also require large amounts of lift capacity. In the oil industry as a whole in 1980 1.38 cubic meters of water was extracted for every ton of oil, and the Soviet forecast is that by 1985 it will be 1.91 cubic meters per ton. The number of wells needing to be equipped with some form of mechanical lift during 1981–85 was to be 37,000.[30]

To meet these additional requirements, the oil industry planners have sought to improve domestic models of electric submersible pumps and expand their output, and to use alternative technologies—notably hydro-piston pumps and gaslift equipment. Some of the gaslift equipment has been imported from France. But progress in meeting the need for gaslift equipment or submersible pumps by domestic production has not been impressive. In a critical review of West Siberian problems in spring 1984, when it appeared that output had peaked, a *Pravda* correspondent said that "the progressive gaslift method for extracting hydrocarbon raw materials which makes it possible to raise the recovery ratio from the formation is being introduced at Samotlor slowly, above all because the Ministry of Oil and Chemical Machinebuilding of the USSR was not oriented early enough to producing the necessary equipment."[31] Nor has Minkhimmash done better on submersibles. I was struck on looking back at my notes from the seventies to find how little has changed. There were frequent statements then that Minkhimmash was about to produce more reliable models and models with capacities matching those imported from the United States (800 to 1,000 cubic meters per day), and in 1975 there was the encouraging news that the new domestic models had successfully passed their field tests. So it comes as something of an anticlimax to find an oil industry spokesman saying six years later in 1981 that some models have now been produced with outputs of 700 cubic meters per day, and that they "expect to master" production of a 1,000-cubic-meter submersible in 1981.[32]

Other sources say that the oil field operators have been disappointed with imported gaslift equipment, but that the capacity of Soviet industry to supply either gaslift equipment or hydro-piston pumps is too limited to meet the numbers required in the Eleventh Five-Year Plan. There is accordingly still great interest in U.S. pumps. A Hughes subsidiary (Centrilift-Hughes) received an order for a $40 million lot early in the eighties, but its export license was held up. The license was finally approved early in 1984, on the grounds that similar equipment is available from other suppliers,[33] and a contract has been signed with the Russians.

In my judgment, the case of submersible pumps demonstrates Soviet inability to match U.S. technology. The reasons are no doubt complex, and probably include production capacity and the vagaries of the local priority system, as well as technological weaknesses. But I imagine that the central problems are suggested in the following quote. "The Ministry of the Oil Industry together with a large group of associated ministries has worked out a complex program of work for creating electric submersible pumps of high reliability. From 1981 on, production of improved designs of electric submersibles will begin on the basis of new materials and technological methods of production."[34] It is an inability to bring together all the pieces from a variety of jurisdictions, rather than any single technological weakness, that is traditionally the roadblock to

technological progress in the USSR. This latest prediction of an immi-
nent solution to the problem should be viewed with some skepticism.

Offshore Exploration

A third area where foreign technology could greatly benefit the
Soviet oil and gas industry is in offshore exploration and production.
The USSR has not used foreign technology extensively for this purpose
in the past, though it has purchased several large rigs abroad, beginning
with the Khazar rig purchased from a Dutch firm in 1968. There have
also been smaller-scale purchases of other kinds of equipment, such as
pipe-laying barges, undersea blowout preventers, and so on. A policy
decision was apparently made to move ahead producing offshore rigs
domestically, notably in the form of the Kaspii-class jack-up rigs copied
from the Khazar, and the Shel'f semisubmersible rigs derived from the
Kaspmorneft' prototype, developed with foreign help. Outside help has
been used in constructing and equipping domestically produced equipment—Armco helped with the Kaspmorneft' and the Finnish firm
Rauma-Repola provided equipment for it and for other rigs of various
types including drilling ships. The USSR has also contracted with western partners to participate in offshore projects in deals in which the
partners provide some of the equipment, e.g., a venture with the Japanese in the Sea of Okhotsk. There is also a co-operative effort with
Poland and East Germany—the Petrobaltika consortium—which is engaged in an exploratory drilling effort in the Baltic, using a western-
supplied platform.[35] Some of the technology involved in these complexes
originates in the U.S., but for the most part the USSR has sought partners from other countries, notably Finland, Norway, Japan, and the
Netherlands.

The strategy of self-supply by copying foreign models appears not
to have worked well. It is probably no exaggeration to say that as an
example of mastering and diffusing an initial injection of foreign technology, it has been a failure. A recent American survey notes very long
delays in getting domestically produced rigs into operation, frequent
breakdowns, very low productivity, and absence of facilities and equipment for repair. In a visit to Azerbaidzhan in September 1982, Brezhnev
is also said to have sharply criticized performance in offshore work.[36]

As indicated earlier, the oil crunch seen in the energy plan for the
remainder of the century justifies a major offshore exploration and
production effort. I believe that a serious offshore program will require
large-scale western equipment imports, both because of Soviet technological weaknesses and because of limited production capacity. The
limited production base is a problem of long standing. In the discussions

leading up to the Eleventh Five-Year Plan one commentator complained that the one yard assigned to producing offshore rigs (at Astrakhan), could not meet the needs of even the Caspian program.[37] A story early in 1984 indicated that at that point planners were still only "considering" plans to provide facilities in the Far East to meet the offshore needs there.[38]

The energy plan guidelines call for domestic producers to supply equipment needed for the offshore program, in particular the Ministry of the Shipbuilding Industry. This may be another case in which an attempt at technological self-sufficiency may come into conflict with military allocations. The President of the Academy of Sciences is reported to have said that the progress of offshore development is slowed "because shipbuilders have to give priority to the defense industry."[39] A plan has recently been announced to fit ships of the Academy of Sciences, the Ministry of Geology and the Ministry of the Gas Industry with a new complex of equipment (the MARS system) to improve Soviet capability to handle oceanic prospecting.[40] The new system will have a more precise location system based on Soviet navigation satellites, and will have improved, real-time data processing capabilities. Limited ability to process the huge amounts of data involved in this kind of work (far behind that in the West) was seen in the OTA study as an important weakness of Soviet oil and gas exploration, and it is difficult to imagine that the new system, using as it does Soviet computer equipment of the Riad series, will involve a significant breakthrough.

Altogether, past experience would suggest little possibility that the Russians can cope effectively with the technological demands of a big offshore effort on their own, especially considering that much of it will have to be in the northern oceans, where conditions are much more demanding than in the Caspian where most Soviet experience has been gained. It is interesting that very little information on the continental shelf program to 1990, approved in spring 1983, has been published. The Soviet leaders are probably well aware that this is an area where they will need to acquire western technology, some of it perhaps from the United States. It is possible that in a policymaking context in which the leadership is trying to avoid dependence, they may be wary of a massive commitment to working offshore.

It seems likely, however, that large deals for offshore equipment will emerge sooner or later, and U.S. suppliers may share in Soviet orders. The approval of the Hughes license application for submersible pumps in 1984 should probably be read as an indication that the Reagan administration will not seek to bar U.S. participation in supplying these needs. It could be a very large market—one estimate is that the USSR will order $25 billion worth of equipment for the Barents Sea work.[41]

Coal Conversion and Slurry Pipelines

A major thrust in Soviet energy policy for the remainder of the century is to make fuller use of the huge resources of lignite found in the Kansk-Achinsk basin along the Trans-Siberian railroad on the border between East and West Siberia. One method for using this low-calorie, nontransportable coal is to convert it to electricity in mine-mouth power plants and to transport the power to the European USSR over high-voltage lines. This is the major approach to using Kansk-Achinsk coal at the present time. The first generating plant has been completed, but progress has fallen far behind the timetable set for developing the power transmission technology needed if the project as a whole is to be completed. An alternative approach is to process the coal into various kinds of energy products—i.e., gas, liquid fuel and semi-coke—with the solid product to be transported to the European USSR either by conventional means or in slurry pipelines. One advantage of the coal conversion approach is that it will add to liquid fuel supplies, and indeed the long-range energy plan sets as one of its goals "meeting the need for motor fuel . . . as the scientific and technical problems are solved, by producing synthetic motor fuel from gas, coal, and oil shale." Experimental work is to be completed by 1990 and commercial production of synthetic motor fuel is to begin in the nineties. The R&D experiments on coal processing pursued so far involve local use of the gas, with the liquid fuel and semi-coke products to be sent to the Urals or to the European USSR perhaps using slurry pipelines. If the liquid fuel can be put in the form of methanol, it can be used as an additive to the slurry mixture to enhance its transportability and ease of combustion directly in boilers.

The USSR has experimented with a variety of coal conversion processes for decades, but its R&D programs in this area have never been focussed on a clearcut objective, nor successful in moving forward to commercially usable processes.[42] The Soviet work gets resuscitated from time to time, and new experimental efforts initiated. The latest is an experimental plant to be built at Tula using Moscow-basin coal.[43] Soviet officials have discussed ambitious projects for coal conversion with the West German Mannesman firm, and with companies in several other countries, including ENI in Italy and Occidental in the U.S. Negotiations with the Germans have been intensive (a joint commission on energy co-operation provides a mechanism) and the negotiations had apparently gone far enough to lead to predictions that an agreement for construction of a million-ton-per-year plant would be signed at the Kohl-Andropov meeting in Moscow in July 1983.[44] That did not happen, however, and one wonders how seriously to take these ambitious plans for synthetic fuel production. It seems highly likely that the Russians use the vision of this project and negotiations over it partly for political purposes, and though it is reported that there is solid support for it in the Soviet bureaucracy, it is difficult to believe that cost considerations can justify a commitment to really large-scale production of synthetic fuel in the near future.

Slurry lines for transporting Eastern coal westward have a rationale apart from synfuel production. If they are to be built, it seems likely that Soviet planners will seek to involve western firms in building and equipping them. State-of-the-art slurry pipeline technology involves pulp characterized by very small particle size, high ratios of solid to liquid, use of additives to enhance stability of the suspension, and direct combustion of the slurry as received without dewatering.[45] Soviet experience with slurry lines is limited to a couple of very short haul lines using older technology acknowledged as unacceptable for the task of moving Siberian coal westward. An experimental project to demonstrate the feasibility of contemporary approaches and to provide information on which to design more ambitious projects was initiated as part of the Eleventh Five-Year Plan, with the goal that it be in operation by 1985. It is intended to move 4.3 million tons of coal per year 250 kilometers from the Inskaia mine at Belovo to a heat and power combine in Novosibirsk. A recent report on the progress of the project suggests, however, that it is hung up on some familiar difficulties in Soviet efforts to move from concept to working innovation. Much of the pipe for the line has been laid, and is all to be in place by the end of 1984, but because of unsettled issues concerning equipment, work had not yet begun as of spring 1984 on the preparation and pumping installations. As a Soviet commentator explains, "over the course of several years the Ministry of Heavy Machinebuilding and its Uralmash combine have dragged their feet on adapting a pump to fit the specifications for the installations, and have attempted to foist on the project an existing mud-pump model despite the fact that tests have shown that it is unsuitable."[46]

Meanwhile development work on slurry line technologies is proceeding rapidly elsewhere in the world. In particular the West German firm Peine-Salzgitter is investing heavily in development work.[47] The Russians have had extensive discussions with several western firms, including Bechtel in the United States as well as the Salzgitter firm, and although such negotiations can be as much an effort to pick the brains of potential suppliers as a sign of serious intent, when the Russians arrive at the crucial decision point to initiate construction of a large-capacity line to move coal from Kansk-Achinsk to the European USSR, they may well find it preferable to contract with foreign companies for equipment and engineering, rather than relying on domestic technology resources.

Conservation

One component of Soviet energy strategy is improved utilization of energy sources (i.e., conservation) and better *structure* of energy sources (i.e., substitution). Both efforts involve large-magnitude expectations. Though quantities are spelled out in the guidelines only in part, it can be estimated that conservation and the substitution of new sources together are to outweigh growth in consumption of the three fossil fuels taken together.[48]

As for conservation, the guidelines forecast that the ratio of energy consumption to national income can be brought down from the 1980 level of 4 kilograms of standard fuel per ruble of national income to the range of 3.32–3.52 kilograms per ruble by the year 2000. This reduction is expected to save 540–580 million tons of standard fuel in 2000. The prospects for accomplishing this depend partly on technology transfer from the West. Soviet equipment designers have not seen energy efficiency as an important consideration in the past because energy has long been priced far below its national-economic cost (as indeed it still is). The major obstacle to conservation is the huge stock of energy-wasteful equipment now in use in the Soviet economy, and massive savings will depend on replacing equipment on a very large scale. For various reasons I need not go into here, Soviet investment decisionmaking has always been biased in favor of building completely new facilities, and against scrapping and replacing existing facilities or their equipment. That bias is deeply ingrained in the system, and is unlikely to change quickly, though the Soviet planners are well aware of the problem and talk a great deal about the need to solve it.

Replacement of old equipment by energy-saving versions involves some new technology inputs, especially insofar as it depends on computers, control apparatus, new materials, and similar refinements, a set of factors which generally represent difficulties for the Soviet system to manage. But for the most part the creation of more energy-economizing technology is something they can handle if they can afford and can implement a policy of accelerated replacement.

A second element in any conservation program has to be substitution of other primary energy sources for the oil that has been so important in meeting the growth of the energy demands of the economy over the last two decades, and the output of which is now certain to fall. The major substitutes will be natural gas for residual fuel oil in boilers and furnaces, electricity for some direct liquid fuel uses, and hydro and nuclear stations for oil-fired power and heat generation. These substitutions are not especially demanding technologically, and I see no great problem with the Russians handling them on their own. A more serious problem is that as dwindling oil supplies are shifted from boiler and furnace use to motor fuel use, there will have to be important changes in the structure of refinery output away from residual fuel oil (which today accounts for about half of all refinery output in the Soviet economy) toward fuels for internal combustion engines. Here I believe the Soviet system will have a much more difficult time in adapting, and may find imported technology very helpful. The oil industry has a poor record in improving refinery technology.[49] It has had a difficult time introducing the sophisticated processes that get more motor fuel from a barrel of crude oil and improve the various quality parameters important for motor fuels such as octane and cetane ratings, pour and freeze points, sulfur content, and so on.

There has been significant use of technology transfer in refining, but Eastern Europe has supplemented what was obtained from Western Europe. A recent western survey found that "much of the refinery upgrading that has occurred in the USSR since the mid-1960's resulted from purchases of 'complete sets of equipment' abroad. Substantial deliveries came from East Germany, Czechoslovakia, Romania, France, Italy, and Japan. In 1982 Czechoslovakia was the largest supplier of refining equipment to the Soviet Union . . . followed by East Germany. Czechoslovakia has supplied 14 complete catalytic gasoline reforming installations . . . designed on the basis of Soviet technical documentation. . . . Also during 1966–83, France supplied a great number of complete installations for the USSR's refining and petrochemical industries."[50] This same survey suggests that the USSR is carrying on extensive domestic R&D work to upgrade refinery technology.

A closely related area of technology is that for processing natural gas, especially the sour gas from the Orenburg and Astrakhan fields. It is interesting that though the Russians tried to use mostly domestic equipment for the earlier Orenburg field, they have put much greater emphasis on foreign technology for Astrakhan, and late in 1983 signed a huge contract with a French firm for equipment and engineering.[51]

My overall judgment would be that though refinery equipment for oil and gas has been less conspicuous than some others as a field for technology transfer in the past, it will become more prominent in the future.

Nuclear Power

Nuclear power is interesting as an area where despite impressive indigenous technological accomplishments, the system still finds that its program goals are in jeopardy because of technological difficulties. The USSR has been technologically self-sufficient in developing a nuclear power industry. Two distinct reactor programs have been brought to the stage of commercial application, one of which has no western counterpart. The industry is far advanced in commercialization of a fast breeder reactor. Soviet nuclear program managers have proceeded rather boldly with such novel ideas as adaptation of nuclear plants for space heating, and heat storage to permit nuclear power stations to operate continuously at full capacity in power systems with load variation. On the whole one would have to say that they have fully demonstrated their technological independence and competence in this area.

When it was decided in the late seventies to give nuclear power a prominent place in energy supply in the USSR and Eastern Europe, the planners undertook to develop capacity to produce the equipment themselves, with appreciable help from Eastern Europe. In the late seventies expansion of the nuclear power industry proceeded rather successfully, but during the Eleventh Five-Year Plan period it has run into serious snags. Output at nuclear power stations grew from 72.9 BKWH in 1980 to 109.8 BKWH in 1983, and 1984 output is planned at 136.5 BKWH, which will constitute nearly 10 percent of total electric power output. This is, however, appreciably behind the pace intended in the Eleventh Five-Year Plan, and it is most unlikely that nuclear power will reach the 230 BKWH output or 14 percent share in total power output projected in the 1985 goals. Generating capacity has grown much slower than planned. Starting at 12.5 million KW at the end of 1980, it was supposed to be augmented by some 22–25 million KW of new capacity in 1981–85. Capacity grew to 18 million KW by the end of 1983 and it seems there is no way it can now reach the 34–35 million KW target for 1985.

The difficulty has been in constructing the generating plants and producing the equipment for them. Construction of the big Atommash plant at Volgodonsk which was to turn out 8 VVER reactors per year when fully finished has proceeded very slowly. It now appears that in a still more serious setback, design errors in the plant have resulted in failure of its foundations, and its operations are apparently at a halt.[52] I am not sure whether there have been equally serious supply problems with equipment for the other reactor system (the RBMK), but in view of the demands that have been laid on the Izhorsk plant to help with the compressor program, it may well have been unable to perform properly its other role as a major supplier of equipment for RBMK plants.

Another obstacle is technological difficulties in producing specialized turbogenerator sets for the nuclear power stations. To cope with the combination of low steam temperature and large size for the very large turbogenerator sets (750–1,000M capacity to match the capacities of the reactors) standard steam turbine designs cannot be used, and the Soviet power machinery industry has not been successful in making these adaptations. Two Russian scientists have recently said that the nuclear program as a whole is on hold because Soviet factories cannot produce the turbines for the generating units. They add that two nuclear power plants sit half finished, with little likelihood they will ever be completed.[53]

At the present time the nuclear program is in turmoil. There has been a reorganization of its administration, and there is apparently a renewed concern with safety problems. The whole nuclear power development is probably at a point where an accumulation of many other technological problems beyond the one with turbogenerators needs to be solved. A recent review by a Soviet planner states that before moving on it is necessary to develop new designs for steam generators, separators, heat exchangers, circulation and feed pumps, and fast acting shut-down fittings.[54]

It is difficult to predict what the implications of this debacle are for technology transfer. I suspect this setback is not likely to lead to imports of foreign equipment or technology. It would probably be difficult to integrate outside elements with the systems already developed in the USSR. If the Soviet Union were going to import nuclear equipment, it would probably be in the form of complete plants. On an earlier occasion Soviet planners expressed interest in Japanese or West German help in building stations, and though nothing ever came of that, it may be relevant as a precedent.

Conclusions

1. The United States has paid a heavy price for the embargo. U.S. producers lost pipelayer exports to the Japanese. There is evidence that Soviet leaders have made it a high priority to avoid technological dependence on the United States, specifying in their negotiations with foreign suppliers that U.S. equipment not be included in project designs. The bidders for the Astrakhan gas deal were told to rewrite their proposals to eliminate U.S. equipment.[55] The political friction with our allies has been a serious cost. These consequences are discussed at length in other contributions to this volume. Hence I need not say more about them here, and will pass on to some points more directly relevant to questions about technological dependence and technology transfer.

2. The Soviet response to the embargo provides interesting substance to the generalization that there are usually substitute ways to carry out any task. Supposed technological obstacles can be skirted by resort to second-best arrangements. Line capacity can be substituted for compressor stations, other prime movers can take the place of gas turbines and so on. These expedients are probably costly, and involve delays, but they can do the job. Past studies and current experience suggest that the costs of second-best solutions (and as a corollary the gains from technology transfers supporting better solutions) may be significant. But it too often seems to be taken as given that technological obstacles are absolute and costs very large.

3. As an example of the costs of second-best solutions, the USSR has found it difficult to make up for the lost or embargo-delayed foreign compressors. The campaign for production of domestic alternatives has

been disruptive and probably costly. As an interesting illustration the director of the Leningrad Metal Plant (LMZ) was severely criticized recently for failing to produce on schedule the gas turbine for a semi-peaking turbo-generator set desperately needed for the Moscow electric power system.[56] Presumably the unproduced unit was a casualty of the high priority the plant was directed to give to the GTN-25. As further evidence, now that the embargo is lifted, the USSR will once more seek compressors abroad. It has been negotiating with the AEG-Kanis firm in West Germany for help in producing rotor kits for the domestic GTN-25. It has even bought some General Electric equipment to replace older compressors on an existing line. In this case the evidence does not support the idea that the Soviet leaders have learned the hard way that it is too dangerous to be dependent. Risky as it may be, importation of technology may still often be their most advantageous course. This conclusion is further buttressed by the submersible pump case. The public statement of policy embodied in the guidelines for the energy plan is that the USSR will continue to develop "mutually advantageous economic and scientific-technical cooperation with developed capitalist countries" [read technology imports] in solving the energy problem. The passage specifically mentions Western Europe and Japan, but pointedly omits the United States.

4. I would judge that the Soviet economy has not come very far in creating an independent technological capability in the production of pipelaying crawler tractors. But it did not really need to, since there was an easy out in the form of an alternative source outside U.S. control.

5. The energy sector is one where technological needs can be served in part by resources from the defense sector, both in the form of R&D assistance, and in the form of actual production of equipment. This aspect of the compressor program was discussed above, and the development of offshore capabilities probably represents another example. Soviet policy on offshore development will thus be a good case to follow to see how the urge for technological independence interacts with the traditional domestic policy of insulating military production from domestic pressures. My evaluation is that there are currently pressures at work to try to reduce dependence on foreign technology by drawing more heavily on the supposedly superior technological capabilities of the defense sector.

6. The energy sector does not seem to have achieved much successful diffusion of imported technology. Submersible pumps are a case in point where imports have failed to shock the domestic R&D people into action, as is also the case of jack-up rigs. There seems to have been an effort to take imported compressor equipment as a model to be copied. The GTN-25 is claimed to be strongly derivative from General Electric models (the Russians have had a very long and relatively close contact

with General Electric) but they have had to come back to West Germany for help with the rotors for the GTN-25.

7. This review of the energy sector provides a reminder that some Soviet imports that get a lot of attention involve very little technology transfer. Large diameter pipe, for instance, is clearly an area of import dependence, but the main motivation for pipe imports is less a Soviet inability to produce large diameter pipe, than the scale of the need. Pipe production is a serious bottleneck domestically, as indeed is steel production as well. There may not be much point in expanding capacity to produce more steel or to cover the especially sharp peak in pipe needed for the pipeline program, considering that this bulge may not last as long as the facilities needed to produce such pipe. What is involved is less a problem of technological capability than of capacity bottlenecks and simple comparative advantage. If steel is to be imported, it might as well be in those forms that require the fabricating capacity in shortest supply, and where comparative *disadvantage* in fabrication is greatest.

The point is that at bottom it is difficult to distinguish between trade motivated by comparative advantage in the usual sense and technology transfer. The resource gains from technology transfer are not in principle different from those obtained from trade in products farther down the production chain, and blocking technology transfer is not much different from economic warfare in the usual sense. The distinction rests on some assumption that technology transfer has a more powerful payoff per dollar's worth of trade, perhaps because the imported goods last longer, or because the effect is multiplied by diffusion.

Disrupting supply to the USSR imposes costs even in the pipe case, and U.S. policy may want to take advantage of that vulnerability. But this is not really a question of technology transfer as much as it is of general import dependence, and policy to exploit it is more in the nature of economic warfare than of controlling technology transfer.

8. The USSR does not seem to have been able to get much help from the East Europeans. It has been suggested that the Russians may turn more to Comecon partners for the equipment they need to overcome problems in all areas of technology since they have concluded that Western firms are not reliable sources. Soviet spokesmen are reported to have passed word of this policy to Comecon. I believe that the possibilities for such shifts are extremely limited. In the area of energy technology, the Russians have made some use of East European help all along. Comecon countries have helped with construction of several of the pipelines, including sections of the export line. Czech firms produce equipment for nuclear power stations and are supposed to build and equip a plant to produce compressors at Uzhgorod. But examination of the relevant categories in the trade statistics shows no noticeable increase in Soviet energy equipment imports from Eastern Europe since 1980.

There is a mechanism for technology transfer from Eastern Europe in the work of the "permanent commissions for co-operation" of Comecon in various fields. A Soviet review of these co-operative activities in oil and gas shows a wide range of things the Russians are interested in, from software for analysis of geophysical data to enhanced recovery from oil fields. But none of them seem to involve the big issues that would solve major problems.[57] Those countries also supply a heterogeneous flow of equipment—we have mentioned nuclear power equipment and the help with the pipeline—and the article cited above mentions a more extended miscellany of equipment for the oil and gas industry. But in the relevant categories that can be distinguished in the Comecon trade statistics,[58] exports from Eastern Europe are small relative to those from Western Europe, and show no sign of accelerated growth or change in share since 1980.

NOTES

1. U.S. Congress, Office of Technology Assessment, *Technology and Soviet Energy Availability* (Washington, USGPO, 1981).

2. Robert Campbell, *Soviet Energy Technologies: Planning, Policy, Research and Development* (Bloomington: Indiana University Press, 1980); *Soviet Technology Imports: The Gas Pipeline Case,* California Seminar on International Security and Foreign Policy, Discussion Paper No. 91, February 1981; and *Trends in the Soviet Oil and Gas Industry* (Baltimore: Johns Hopkins University Press, 1976).

3. The report of the Politburo action was reported in *Ekonomicheskaia Gazeta,* 1983:16, p. 2, and the guidelines were published as an insert in *Ekonomicheskaia Gazeta,* 1984:12.

4. Robert Campbell, "The Economy," in Robert F. Byrnes (ed.), *After Brezhnev: Sources of Soviet Conduct in the 1980s* (Bloomington: Indiana University Press, 1983), p. 8.

5. Thane Gustafson, *The Soviet Gas Campaign: Politics and Policy in Soviet Decisionmaking* (The RAND Corporation, R-3036-AF, Santa Monica, CA, 1983), p. vii. Also an article in the *Oil and Gas Journal,* 4 July 1983, p. 49, cites a Soviet source which projects a much more conservative approach to gas industry expansion than previous official plans indicate.

6. Western discussions of whether the turning point has arrived often overlook an important issue. Soviet oil output figures include condensate as well as crude oil, but in recent years no information has been released on the share of condensate in the total. Moreover, the coverage of "condensate" has never been quite clear and one wonders to what extent the liquid products of gas processing plants may be included. It seems possible that crude oil output actually began to decline in 1983, and that only the growth of condensate output associated with rapid growth of gas output has kept the total up.

7. *Ekonomicheskaia Gazeta,* 1983:29, p. 3.

8. *Ekonomicheskaia Gazeta,* 1981:43, p. 2. Later statements suggested some reduction in these magnitudes.

9. *Pravda,* 11 September 1983, p. 1.

10. There is no firm data in Soviet sources from which to estimate domestic output or imports of 56-inch pipe and these figures, based on Gustafson, *The Soviet Gas Campaign,* should be considered provisional.

11. Robert Campbell, *Soviet Technology Imports: The Gas Pipeline Case,* pp. 21–22, gives imports, and we know from *Ekonomika, organizatsiia i upravlenie gazovoi promyshlennosti,* 1983:5, p. 2, that capacity rose from 8.8 million kilowatts at the end of 1975 to 17,600 megawatts at the end of 1980.

12. See an article in *Planovoe khoziaistvo,* 1980:3, and several speeches by S. A. Orudzhev, then Minister of the Gas Industry.

13. *Stroitel'stvo Truboprovodov,* 1984:1, p. 5.

14. *Oil and Gas Journal,* 12 December 1983.

15. *Ekonomicheskaia Gazeta,* 1982:8, p. 3.

16. *Ekonomicheskaia Gazeta,* 1984:11, p. 2.

17. *Voprosy Ekonomiki,* 1983:4, p. 81.

18. *New York Times,* 29 July 1983. It is a curiosity of this episode that since the lifting of the embargo nothing seems to have appeared in the press about either GE's resumption of deliveries of rotor kits or the West European shipments of compressors.

19. There is a caveat—current performance of the Soviet pipeline system is difficult to follow, since in the early eighties the Russians changed the definition of the series used to report pipeline shipments. One wonders if they are concealing something.

20. *Stroitel'stvo Truboprovodov,* 1982:12, p. 7.

21. For instance, S. A. Orudzhev, *Goluboe zoloto Zapadnoi Sibiri,* Moscow, 1981, p. 10, lists the producing plants for all the other compressor models, but not for this one. The new plant at Uzhgorod which the Czechs are building for the Russians is mentioned as producing the GPA-10 compressor unit, but I believe it only produces some parts and assembles the final product.

22. *Gazovaia Promyshlennost',* 1981:2, p. 33.

23. *Planovoe Khoziaistvo,* 1983:12, pp. 61–64.

24. *Washington Post,* 3 August 1983.

25. *Financial Times,* 5 April 1983, and *Washington Post,* 3 August 1983.

26. *Ekonomicheskaia Gazeta,* 1983:48, p. 3.

27. This output history has been reconstructed from *Stroitel'stvo Truboprovodov,* 1981:5 and 1983:1, *Izvestiia,* 4 August 1982, and *Ekonomicheskaia Gazeta,* 1982:30, p. 4.

28. Robert Campbell, *Soviet Energy Technologies: Planning, Policy, Research and Development* (Bloomington: Indiana University Press, 1980), pp. 221–25.

29. *Neftianoe Khoziaistvo,* 1982:5, p. 7.

30. *Neftianoe Khoziaistvo,* 1981:1, p. 4.

31. *Pravda,* 3 April 1984.

32. *Neftianoe Khoziaistvo,* 1981:7, p. 3.

33. *New York Times,* 7 March 1984.

34. *Neftianoe Khoziaistvo,* 1981:1, p. 5.

35. For details on foreign participation in development of equipment and offshore exploration see *EKO,* 1981:5, p. 94; *Oil and Gas Journal,* 22 August 1983, p. 24; *Gazovaia Promyshlennost',* 1982:6, inside back cover.

36. *Oil and Gas Journal,* 31 December 1982, pp. 34–36.

37. *Current Digest of the Soviet Press,* 31, no. 14, pp. 6–7.

38. *Oil and Gas Journal,* 6 February 1984.

39. *Petroleum Economist,* July 1983, p. 280.

40. *Ekonomicheskaia Gazeta*, 1984:18, p. 16.

41. *New York Times*, 5 October 1983.

42. For a detailed review of the history of Soviet programs in solid fuel conversion see Robert Campbell, *Soviet Energy Technologies*, pp. 175–80.

43. *Oil and Gas Journal*, 23 December 1983.

44. *Chemical Week*, 11 May 1983, pp. 28–29.

45. For a description of current slurry technology, see *New York Times*, 10 May 1984.

46. *Ekonomicheskaia Gazeta*, 1984:19, p. 9.

47. *Coal Age*, February 1983, p. 35.

48. Consumption in 1980 was 1,746 million tons of standard fuel of which 1667 million tons consisted of fossil fuels (Robert Campbell, "Energy" in Abram Bergson and Herbert Levine (eds.), *The Soviet Economy: Toward the Year 2000* (London: Allen and Unwin, 1983, pp. 196–97). The Soviet guidelines do not forecast a consumption figure for the year 2000, but we can get some feel for what the planners have in mind by relating growth in energy consumption to the growth of GNP. Western forecasts for Soviet GNP growth until the end of the century vary considerably, with optimists seeing as much as 3 percent per year as possible, while pessimists see growth averaging below 2 percent per year. If we assume 2.5 percent growth for GNP, energy growth at an equal rate would imply consumption of 2861 million tons of standard fuel in the year 2000. Energy consumption in the USSR has in fact grown as fast as GNP in the last couple of decades, but the planners expect serious conservation efforts to cut the amount of fuel used per unit of output by 12–17 percent, and to be saving 540–580 million tons of standard fuel per year by the end of the century. The midpoint of 560 million tons implies consumption of 2201 million tons of standard fuel in 2000. The plan also forecasts a growth for nonfossil sources of 400–500 million tons of standard fuel, leaving a need for 1801–1901 million tons of fossil fuel in 2000, compared to my 1667 for 1980. This is an average growth rate of about half a percent per year.

49. Robert Campbell, *The Economics of Soviet Oil and Gas* (Baltimore: Johns Hopkins Press, 1968), Chapter 8.

50. *Oil and Gas Journal*, 2 January 1984, p. 27.

51. *Oil and Gas Journal*, 21 November 1983, p. 74.

52. *New York Times*, 29 November 1983.

53. In *Izvestiia*, cited in *Wall Street Journal*, 7 February 1984.

54. *Ekonomicheskaia Gazeta*, 1983:52, p. 2.

55. *Oil and Gas Journal*, 22 November 1982, p. 66.

56. *Ekonomicheskaia Gazeta*, 1983:46, p. 2.

57. *Neftianoe khoziaistvo*, 1982:12, pp. 60–63.

58. See Ministerstvo Vneshnei Torgovli SSSR, *Vneshniaia torgovlia SSSR*, various years. The major headings are code 127, "Equipment for the oil refining industry," 128, "Machines, equipment and rigs for drilling and operation of wells and for geologic prospecting," and 120, "Equipment for underground and surface mining."

Western Technology and the Soviet Defense Industry

Julian Cooper

FEW ISSUES of current East-West relations have aroused such passion and concern as the belief that transfers of Western technology are substantially contributing to the enhancement of Soviet military might. In venturing into this debate one is entering a minefield: the evidence is fragmentary and often based on limited disclosures of classified information; the issues are politically charged with sensitive policy implications. But it is precisely these circumstances that call for a critical independent appraisal of the problem, drawing on the open information available to the academic Soviet studies community and a historically informed understanding of the USSR's economy and technology. This chapter seeks to review and assess the evidence and issues pertaining to the contribution of Western technology to the Soviet defense industry and to situate the problem in a wider perspective. One of the characteristic features of the literature on the topic is its neglect of Soviet sources of information. For understandable reasons, such Soviet evidence is more prolific for earlier years, and for this reason we begin with consideration of the role of Western technology in the development of the Soviet defense industry during the Stalin period. Throughout the following discussion, the West is taken to mean the industrially advanced capitalist countries, including Japan.

Given the sensitivity of the topic, it may be helpful to the reader if the author's own position is made clear from the outset. On the basis of the available evidence it is indisputable that the Soviet Union has in the past acquired from the West technologies which have served to enhance her military might and that such acquisitions continue to take place today. The circumstances of Soviet history have been such that this policy of learning from the West can be a matter of no surprise and from the Soviet point of view has been entirely rational. However, it is also the author's view that the scale of such militarily related transfers and their significance to the strengthening of the Soviet military potential have been widely overstated in the recent discussion, with an associated underestimation of the Soviet Union's capability for independent technological development. For this reason, and also broader considerations set out in the concluding section of the chapter, it is the author's conviction that attempts to further reinforce controls over transfers of technology are misguided and unlikely to genuinely enhance Western security.

The Historical Experience

For Russia, state control and management of arms factories was not an innovation of 1917. The renowned Tula arms factory was established as early as 1712 and by World War I the three government small-arms works of Tula, Izhevsk, and Sestroretsk had established strong traditions of independent gun design and production. This was an evolutionary pattern of technological development through a process of gradual modification of basic designs, supplemented by occasional borrowings from abroad, the most significant being the Vickers "Maxim" machine gun in the decade preceding the War. Characteristically, the "Maxim" design was quickly adapted and improved by the talented specialists of Tula, initiating a program of technical development which continued well into the Soviet period. In the small-arms industry there is a long unbroken tradition of independent design thought extending from the early gunsmiths of Tula to S. I. Mosin, the creator of the famous 1891 rifle, and the eminent designers of more recent years—Fedorov, Tokarev, Degtyarev, Simonov, Goriunov, and Kalashnikov. Of all the branches of the Soviet defense industry, this has probably exhibited the greatest degree of technological self-reliance.

For other types of weapons foreign involvement was more pronounced, especially for those of a technologically complex character. It is easy to forget that before the Revolution Russia had quite strongly developed ship-building, artillery, and even aviation industries (almost 2,000 aircraft were built in 1917). There were also young electrical and communication equipment industries, predominantly foreign-owned, and an embryo motor industry. The private arms factories had strong links with such leading West European armaments manufacturers as Vickers, Schneider-Creusot, Krupp, and Skoda. The Bolsheviks thus inherited a sizeable arms production base; the greatest problem was the paucity of high-level design and engineering skills. During the 1920s, the Soviet defense industry was consolidated and its modern branches formed with extensive resort to foreign technology. Aircraft and engines were purchased from Germany, Italy, France and Britain. The German Junkers company established a factory in Moscow on a concessionary basis, although this proved to be short-lived, lasting only from 1923 to 1927, and the building of tanks and armored vehicles was initiated by the adoption of foreign designs. This was indeed a period when the

Soviet defense industry was dependent on Western technology, but government policy was even then perfectly clear: the technology transfers were to provide a springboard for independent, self-reliant development in the creation and production of weaponry. This process will be illustrated by the example of the aircraft industry.

The young Soviet aircraft industry provides a good example of the successful assimilation of foreign technology and the consolidation of domestic design and production capabilities. In 1930 900 planes were built, the majority Soviet copies of foreign models. But even at this time there were some notable original Soviet designs in production, including the Tupolev TB-1 heavy bomber, the U-2 trainer of Polikarpov, and the R-3 and R-5 reconnaissance planes. The production base was still modest, but expanded rapidly with the construction in the early 1930s of major new enterprises supplied with predominantly imported equipment. Design and engineering skills were initially concentrated in the Central Aerodynamics Research Institute (TsAGI), organized in 1918, and then gradually diffused more widely with the creation of specialized design groups as experience accumulated. A number of foreign designers assisted in this process, including the French specialists P. A. Richard and A. Laville, and the Italian, Roberto Bartini. The Richard design bureau, organized in the late 1920s, was the early school of such talents as Beriev, Kamov, Gurevich, and the rocket designer, Korolev.[1]

One form of technology transfer successfully exploited during the 1930s was the building of foreign aircraft on a license basis. This approach was adopted to fill gaps in the product range when the domestic industry proved unable to meet specific demands, and also to assist in the introduction of more advanced production methods. This experience is of some interest as it serves to illuminate the general problems associated with attempts to reproduce Western technology in Soviet conditions. Flying boat technology proved especially difficult to assimilate and the majority of licenses were in this field. Models built on a small scale included the Italian Savoia, the German Dornier and Heinkel, and, finally, the American Consolidated. For the latter, the transfer process proved difficult; numerous design changes had to be introduced to accommodate the lower skills of Soviet workers and only 27 examples were built in 1939–40.[2] In 1936 a license was purchased for the building of the Vultee light bomber and reconnaissance plane, chosen for the relative simplicity of its all-metal construction. In 1938 36 were built, the first five of American parts. However, it was found that the design lacked adequate rigidity and did not conform to Soviet standards of strength; those built were transferred to the postal service.[3] Of much greater significance for the Soviet aircraft industry, and the most successful of all license purchases, was the building of the Douglas DC-3 (Dakota), known in the USSR as the PS-84, later the Li-2. This was a well-chosen

design, the best passenger aircraft built before the War, and the Soviet
industry learned much from the experience, including the extensive use
in production of molds and templates. As with all American (and British) models, dimensions throughout had to be converted from inches to
millimeters, and in this case all elements were from the outset adapted to
conform to Soviet standards of strength, resulting in a heavier but stur-
dier plane better suited to the rugged conditions of use then prevailing
in the country. The design also had to be reworked to adapt it to the
simpler Soviet production technology, and to accommodate Soviet-built
engines. In itself this was no mean engineering feat. The work of design
adaptation was undertaken at the Douglas works in Santa Monica by a
team of Soviet specialists led by V. M. Myasishchev, later responsible for
the Mya-4 (Bison) bomber, and including M. I. Gurevich, the future co-
designer of the MiG fighter. Over a twenty-year period almost 3,000
were built and some remained in service until the 1970s.[4]

In addition to the acquisition of licenses, there were purchases of
individual examples of foreign models for thorough examination. Perhaps the most striking case was the buying of a range of the latest
German aircraft, including almost all the latest military models, in 1939
and 1940. By this time the development of the new generation of Soviet
fighters and bombers was well advanced and there is no evidence that
close acquaintance with the products of the German industry led to any
substantial changes in the Soviet designs. Stalin instructed the Soviet
industry to "learn how to destroy them."[5] During the 1930s Soviet designers closely monitored Western developments in aircraft design, but
the main volume production military planes were essentially original
Soviet models. Such planes as the Tupolev TB-3 and SB bombers and
the Ilyushin DB-3 bomber and Il-2 armored assault aircraft were major
achievements of the young Soviet industry. The licensed models and
those most obviously derived from foreign prototypes were mainly civilian flying boats and transports. At the same time, a vast range of experimental models was built, revealing considerable design ingenuity and
talent: between 1930 and 1938 no fewer than 350 different prototypes
reached the stage of flight testing.[6] The greatest problem of the industry
was not so much product design as the organization of volume, quality
production; it was in this area that the shortage of skills—engineering,
managerial, and worker—was most acutely felt. The successful designers
were those able to design for relatively simple production technology
and also for the use of less advanced materials than those available in the
West European and American industries.

It was in the field of aeroengines that Soviet dependence on the
West was greatest during the prewar years. This is quite understandable:
aeroengines were probably the most technologically complex of all industrial products at that time. Here again, we find a familiar pattern: the

acquisition of a limited number of foreign licenses with a simultaneous effort to evolve an independent design capability. Once successfully assimilated, the foreign designs were soon modified and uprated, transformed in time into original Soviet variants. In the early 1930s Soviet aeroengine specialists visited a number of foreign producers and studied engine-building practices. At the same time, licenses were purchased for the production of the French Hispano-Suiza (built as the M-100) and Gnome-Rhône (M-85), and the U.S. Wright-Cyclone (M-25 and M-62) models. These acquisitions were associated with the building of new, large, modern factories, including that at Perm in the Urals, which became the base for the Shvetsov design bureau charged with upgrading the Wright radial engines. By the outbreak of war, Shvetsov had created a new, original design, the 1,700 h.p. ASh-82. Meanwhile, in the Central Aviation Engine Institute, created in 1930, Mikulin and other designers strived to develop more original engines with the aim of freeing the industry from foreign dependence. This led to the AM-34, an original blend of foreign design elements, and a series of engines derived from it, some of which entered large-scale production.[7]

During the war the Soviet Union received more than 14,000 aircraft of varied assortment on a Lend-Lease basis,[8] amounting to approximately 10 percent of domestic production during the war years. For the future of the industry, perhaps the most significant acquisition was the sequestration of three B-29 Superfortress bombers, forced to land on Soviet territory in 1944 after running out of fuel on Japanese bombing raids. This led to what was probably the largest reverse engineering exercise in Soviet experience. Under Tupolev's leadership, "over 105,000 items were checked for material specification, functions, manufacturing processes, tolerances and fit and translated into Soviet equivalents with changes by over 1000 draughtsmen. Many parts and subsystems (were) new to Soviet experience, others totally different from established Soviet practice."[9] Again, as with the Douglas DC-3, this was not simply a question of precisely copying the original model; indeed, very few parts of the eventual Tu-4 were identical to their American counterparts. In this case there was no question of obtaining any assistance from the American manufacturer. The first example flew in 1947, and after many problems of assimilating production, approximately 400 were built. The success of this complex exercise was itself testimony to the maturity of the Soviet aviation industry. The experience of reproducing the B-29 facilitated the development of a series of original heavy bombers and transports, including the Tu-20(95) (Bear) and Mya-4 (Bison), both of which entered service in the mid-1950s.

There were parallel developments in other branches of the defense industry. Examples of the latest British (Vickers) and American (Christie) tanks were purchased on a commercial basis in the early thirties and formed the bases of a series of models, at first modifications, later more original designs, culminating in the highly successful wartime T-34 and KV. In this new industry a considerable indigenous development and production capability was built up in a relatively brief period of time. Much has been made by Sutton of the contribution of the Western-built tractor factories in providing a tank-building production base in the prewar years.[10] In the author's view, this contribution has been exaggerated. The principal tank development and production bases were at well-established enterprises: the Kharkov locomotive works, which built the Christie model variants (BT-2, 5, and 7) and created the T-34, and the Leningrad "Bolshevik" and "Putilov" (Kirov) factories (T-26, T-28, and KV). At the time they were built the new tractor factories were well-suited to the building of the then popular "tankettes" (tracked machine gun carriers) and very light tanks; they could then have been considered "dual use" facilities. During the 1930s they had special shops which built light tanks and supplied components and assemblies to the main enterprises, but they were not the principal producers. The Stalingrad tractor factory did organize volume tank building in the immediate prewar years (the T-34) and Chelyabinsk built medium and heavy tanks during the war; in both cases extensive reconstruction and reequipment were required. The largest producer of the war years was another enterprise of the railway equipment industry, the vast Nizhnii-Tagil wagon-building factory, Uralvagonzavod, built during the 1930s. Although it probably incorporated some equipment imported from the West, this appears to have been a largely Soviet-built project; no reference to it can be found in Sutton's work.[11]

Another relatively self-reliant industry was that producing artillery. This was an activity well-established before the Revolution; during the 1920s and early 1930s there was German technical assistance, including training for Soviet engineers and designers.[12] The Soviet industry began by building pre-Revolutionary models, some of foreign origin, then proceeded to develop modifications before embarking on original design during the 1930s and the war. In the shipbuilding industry, foreign technology transfers appear to have been on a more substantial scale and a number of submarines and surface ships were built to German and Italian designs. There is no doubt that imports of foreign production equipment were important for the strengthening of the defense industry during the 1930s, but the capability of the domestic machine tool industry should not be understated. Reflecting their superior innovative potential and higher quality standards, a number of arms factories pioneered the Soviet manufacture of a range of complex, modern machines, including automatic lathes, centerless, internal and surface grinders, and universal milling machines. Again, there was the familiar pattern: the first examples were "Sovietized" versions of leading foreign models, followed by modifications and, later, original designs.[13]

The Four Postwar Programs

At the end of the war, in conditions of massive economic and social dislocation, the Soviet Union embarked on a major program for the technical reconstruction of the armed forces. This covered all the main categories of weaponry, but highest priority was granted to the elimination of the U.S. nuclear monopoly, and the development of three new technologies considered vital to the country's defense—missiles, jet aircraft, and radar. The upgrading of equipment for the ground forces built on the substantial achievements of the war years, and, with the exception of military trucks, this development program owed relatively little to Western technology. The four priority programs shared certain common features: all were based on prior domestic research and development undertaken before and during the war; to varying degrees the programs were accelerated by resort to Western technology; and in all four cases a substantial degree of self-reliance was attained by the early 1950s.

In the immediate postwar period there were two important transfers of foreign technology to the aircraft industry: the acquisition of German aircraft, production technology and expertise, and the purchase and subsequent reproduction of Rolls-Royce aeroengines. Both served to facilitate the transition to jet propulsion, supplementing pre-existing domestic capabilities. Although work on the development of a turbojet engine was initiated by Liul'ka in 1937, it was suspended during the first half of the war and no prototypes were ready for production by 1945. The first Soviet jet fighters were therefore equipped with Soviet-built German engines, the JUMO-004, built as the RD-10, and the BMW-003, as the RD-20.[14] In 1946 the British Rolls-Royce company sold to the USSR 30 Derwent and 25 Nene turbojet engines; this was a normal commercial transaction approved by the then Labour government. The Soviet purchasing delegation to Britain included the MiG designer, A. I. Mikoyan, and the engine designer, V. Ia. Klimov. These engines were rapidly reproduced and put into production as, respectively, the RD-500 and RD-45, the latter powering the MiG-15. The advantage of the British engines was their relative simplicity from a production point of view, but they were not very powerful. A program of design improvement was soon initiated, resulting in the Klimov-designed VK-1 and VK-1F of greater thrust developed by the end of 1948. Meanwhile, Liul'ka, who insisted on pursuing an independent design policy, created the TR-1 in 1947 and went on to create a series of more powerful engines fitted to a succession of Sukhoi aircraft.[15] Simultaneously, a team of German designers was assembled at the Kuibyshev engine works under the leadership of A. A. Mikulin to develop engines based on the Junkers and BMW experience. This work resulted in the AM-3 engine of 1951, at the time the world's most powerful jet engine, and subsequent variants which powered the Tu-16 (Badger) bomber and the Tu-104 airliner.[16]

Soviet radar development began in the early 1930s. Its enthusiastic pioneers exploited a wide range of technical options and had solid achievements to their credit by the outbreak of war, although the level reached was below that attained in Britain, Germany, and the USA.[17] General radio technology and the manufacture of tubes and other components benefited from technical assistance provided by the Radio Corporation of America. In 1943 measures were adopted to strengthen the research and production base for radar development, with the organization of a special council for radiolocation under the chairmanship of Malenkov, and the effective day-to-day leadership of A. I. Berg. An interesting feature of this council was the creation from the outset of a department of scientific and technical information to monitor developments in the field.[18] Soviet specialists closely studied radar equipment supplied by the United States, Britain, and Canada under Lend-Lease, and some items were copied.[19] As Soviet troops entered Germany, Lobanov and other Soviet experts were able to examine on-site examples of German radar installations and detailed technical reports were prepared by a special commission of the radiolocation council based after the liberation in Berlin and headed by A. I. Shokin, the present-day minister of the electronics industry. This study of Western radar technology helped to determine the path of development of Soviet radar in the postwar period.[20] In addition, German radar technicians were assigned to Soviet factories to assist the development effort.[21] From the start, the aim appears to have been to quickly attain technological independence across the range of principal military radar applications, and this was successfully achieved. An emigré radar specialist, Fedoseyev, has observed that: "It was rarely the case that Soviet military designers in my area of research found among Western equipment anything we wanted to reproduce by 'reverse engineering' piece by piece. Basically, we were on our own technologically."[22] In recent discussion of militarily-sensitive technology transfers there has been little reference to radar technology. Acknowledging the excellence of Soviet radar theory, Vorona has claimed that the acquisition of U.S. microcircuitry "no doubt" expedited the creation of the look-down/shoot-down interceptor version of the MiG-25;[23] and the only other frequently cited case relates to the purchase of a radar system for the Moscow Vnukovo civilian airport.[24] Before leaving the radar program, it is worth noting that two of the leading figures in Soviet weapons procurement during recent years had direct association with this successful drive to attain technological independence. N. N. Alekseev, while working for the Main Artillery Administration during the period 1946–51, was actively involved in the creation and testing of radar systems for the army;[25] he subsequently became chairman of the scientific and technical committee of the General Staff (1960–70), and then served as deputy minister of defense for armaments.[26] The career of his successor in the latter post, V. M. Shabanov, was directly associated with the air force radar program from 1945.[27]

The nuclear and missile programs have been discussed elsewhere. In the former case, a lively Soviet research effort of the 1930s, with active participation in the international scientific community, brought the Soviet Union to the forefront of nuclear physics by 1941. Interrupted by the war, research was resumed in the spring of 1943 under Kurchatov's leadership and remained at a relatively modest level until the autumn of 1945. In this case the German contribution was not so significant, but the Soviet program was undoubtedly assisted by information on American nuclear technology obtained through intelligence channels. In Holloway's judgment, informed by detailed research, "The information passed by Klaus Fuchs and other atomic spies was more important for the Soviet effort [than any German contribution] perhaps speeding up the development of the atomic bomb by as much as a year or two. But it is certainly wrong to say that this is how the Soviet Union acquired the 'secret' of the atomic bomb, for, as Niels Bohr remarked, the only secret of the atomic bomb is that it can be built."[28] The fact remains that the development of the Soviet atomic and hydrogen bombs was a major achievement of Soviet science and technology in extremely difficult circumstances; and it is surprising that the CIA should still be claiming in 1982 that "the Soviets stole Western nuclear secrets leading to their development of a nuclear capability."[29]

In the case of rocketry, there was an imaginative research program during the early 1930s which narrowed during the immediate prewar years and the war to focus on aircraft rocket boosters and the successful development of rocket artillery. The postwar program drew extensively on German expertise and technology. Soviet rocket specialists concluded that the V-2 had many design inadequacies, including what they judged to be the unjustified complexity of many of its systems and components. Korolev's proposal for the creation of a more modern rocket of longer range was accepted, but it was decided that its development should be undertaken in parallel with the building of a Soviet version of the V-2 (the R-1) in order to more quickly gain experience in the production, testing and use of large rockets. German designers and engineers were engaged on this latter program; the 300-km. range R-1 entered military service in 1950. Meanwhile, Korolev, drawing on German expertise when required, built up a strong domestic research and design capability. The 600-km. range R-2 was tested in 1950 and entered service in the following year. This development program resulted in the first ICBM, the SS-6, flown in 1957.[30] Again, as with radar, relatively few of the claims of Western technology assisting the current Soviet defense effort relate to nuclear weapons and ballistic missiles: the striking exception, the case of bearings for missile guidance systems, is discussed below. It was noted above that leading figures in Soviet weapons procurement had close association with the radar program. Similarly, Minister of Defense Ustinov headed the council responsible for the rocket program in the postwar period, and Ye. P. Slavskii, since 1957 minister responsible for nuclear weapons development and production, was a deputy head of the administration which managed the nuclear program from 1946. One can only speculate that this experience developed a keen awareness of the benefits to be derived from learning from the West when appropriate, but also a determination not to allow the Soviet defense effort to become dependent in any way on Western technology.

Before leaving this historical review it is necessary to comment briefly on a work which has undoubtedly exerted an influence on perceptions of the domestic technological capability of the Soviet economy. Sutton's three-volume study argues the thesis that "Western technology has been, and continues to be, the most important factor in Soviet economic development."[31] Although primarily concerned with the civilian economy, Sutton does also consider the contribution of Western technology to the defense sector. He finds that the Soviet military and aircraft industries were heavily dependent on transfers from the West in the years up to 1945, but exhibited a greater degree of independence after the war. Overall, he concludes, the defense sector has shown a greater capability for indigenous innovation than its civilian counterpart. However, Sutton's work is not without methodological problems. It relies to a considerable extent on Western source material (not always accurate) documenting transfers to the Soviet Union, but makes little use of Soviet material to establish the host environment and domestic capability. This leads to an understatement of indigenous technological achievements and, in the author's view, a consistent tendency to overstate the contribution of Western technology, not only to the defense sector, but to the economy as a whole. This can be illustrated by Sutton's treatment of the aircraft and tank industries during the period 1930 to 1945.

In his summary of the development of Soviet aircraft during the period, Sutton concludes that they had their origins in U.S. and Italian technology.[32] This conclusion is based on a discussion of some of the technical assistance and licensing agreements, including those for the Vultee bomber and the Douglas DC-3. He also refers to an agreement with the Glenn Martin Company concluded in 1937, and suggests that the Soviet DB-3 bomber was "probably designed in the Baltimore plant by American engineers."[33] This is implausible: the DB-3 was a 1936 version of the TSKB-26, which appeared in 1935.[34] Virtually no consideration is given to the development of the domestic Soviet aviation industry during the period, or to its full product range. The claimed high degree of dependence on Western technology is illustrated by a table suggesting foreign design influence on fourteen fighters and bombers of 1943.[35] This provides a good example of the problems of Sutton's approach and of the lack of rigor which unfortunately characterizes his work. The table in fact covers ten models relevant to 1943, and not fourteen: the Tu-4 (copy of the B-29) was a later, postwar development; the CKB-26 (sic), the DB-3F and the ZKB-26 (sic) were variants of a single model (although Sutton has the first resembling the Douglas DC-2 and the last, the Martin-139!); the I-17 was an experimental model built on a small scale earlier in the thirties (its origin is claimed to be the Submarine (sic) Spitfire, but in fact the I-17, a product of the talented Polikarpov design team, appeared before the Spitfire, in 1934, although Polikarpov may well have been influenced by the earlier Supermarine flying boats). Both the MiG-3 and the Yak-1 are claimed to resemble the British Hurricane fighter, and the Pe-2 and Yak-4 bombers are claimed to be based on the French Potez-63. This simply means that the planes in question shared common design configurations, as did aircraft of other countries at that time. Significantly, Sutton excludes other fighters and bombers of the period, presumably because Western influences could not be traced: a more complete list, giving a different impression of the dependence on Western technology, would include the I-153; LaGG-3; La-5 and 7; Yak-3, 7, and 9; TB-3 and 7; Tu-2; and Er-2.

Similar problems of evidence and the use of sources arise in Sutton's discussion of Soviet tank development in the same period. It opens with a table purporting to summarize the Soviet tank stock and its origins in 1932. This gives a total of 210 tanks, almost all not only of foreign design, but actually built in Western countries.[36] In reality, the Soviet tank stock at the beginning of 1932 was 1,400; while domestic production, principally of British models, amounted to 170 units in 1930 and 740 in 1931.[37] The T-32 tank is described as the basic model of World War II and claimed to be in serial production in 1937; this prototype was, in fact, the immediate progenitor of the T-34, but was not built and tested for production until 1938–39. It is claimed that the T-34 and the American M3 both had the same Liberty aeroengine; in fact, the former had the Soviet designed and built V-2 diesel engine (possibly drawing on an Italian aeroengine design), and not the gasoline Liberty engine. Again, a table is provided summarizing Soviet tanks of 1930–45 and their claimed Western origins.[38] This draws uncritically on German intelligence data, leading to the incorrect identification of enterprises at which some of the models were built and mistaken model designations (e.g., T-32 and BT-28—the latter did not exist). The exclusion of a number of models again leads to a one-sided picture: those omitted include the T-28 and T-38 (both drawing on Vickers designs), the T-40, 50, 60 and 70 light tanks, the T-34, and the KV and IS heavy tanks.[39] In his summary of the period, however, Sutton does correctly acknowledge some independent Soviet technological contribution. This by no means exhausts the errors and omissions in Sutton's account of the role of Western technology in the development of the Soviet defense industry. Unfortunately, the work cannot be considered a dependable assessment of the contribution of Western technology and the domestic innovative capability of the Soviet economy; there remains a real need for a comprehensive study of the history of Soviet technological development which will put the Western contribution in its true perspective.

The Defense Industry

The Soviet defense industry represents an important sector of the socialist planned economy.[40] Most weapons development and production takes place at organizations and enterprises of nine of the twenty industrial ministries responsible for the engineering industry, although many defense enterprises also produce civilian products, and some factories of civilian ministries make weapons. According to the U.S. Department of Defense, some 150 factories and shipyards produce weapons, ammunition, and explosives as end products, supported by more than 3,500 facilities making components and parts.[41] Estimates of the proportion of industrial output devoted to military production show wide variation. The CIA has claimed that one-fifth of total industrial output went to defense in the mid-1970s and that the defense sector consumed approximately one-third of the final product of machine building and metal working between 1967 and 1977;[42] in 1984 the Department of Defense claimed that the military share of total machinery output amounted to 60 percent—I think this is a substantial overstatement.[43] Military-related research and development is undertaken at establishments of the defense industry, and also at some institutes of the Ministry of Defense, the Academy of Sciences, and the higher educational system. The share of defense in total R&D expenditure and manpower is known with even less certainty than the scale of military production, although it can be tentatively estimated that at least sixty percent of qualified scientists and engineers serving industry work in the defense sector.[44]

Since the late 1920s, the development of the Soviet defense industry has been considered a matter of the highest Party and state priority, and while the industry forms an integral component of the planned economy, it also possesses a number of special features which help to secure privileged conditions for its successful operation. This priority is enforced through institutions and procedures which have apparently undergone little change over many years. Coordination and general oversight of the core defense industry and its relations with the rest of the economy are the responsibility of the Military-Industrial Commission of the Presidium of the USSR Council of Ministers, headed for more than twenty years by L. V. Smirnov, a first deputy chairman of the Council. As for civilian industry, plans for the defense sector are drawn up by the State Planning Committee, Gosplan, in association with the ministries and other interested bodies. Within Gosplan there is a special defense industry department, headed by one of its first deputy chairmen. Within the Communist Party Central Committee apparatus there is a defense industry department, headed by I. F. Dmitriev, through which the Party oversees weapons production and the space program. The Military-Industrial Commission and the Gosplan and Central Committee defense industry departments appear to have close relations and at various times leading personnel have switched from one to another. This complex thus forms a substantial center of power at the heart of the Party-government apparatus and must gain added weight when, as usual during the last twenty-five years, one of the Central Committee secretaries also has responsibility for overseeing weapons development and production, especially if this secretary is also a full or even candidate member of the Politburo. Since 1956 occupants of this post have included Brezhnev, Ustinov, and now, it appears, Romanov, the latter having had close association with the sector in Leningrad, an important center of the shipbuilding industry in which he began his career in the early fifties as a designer.

The defense industry faces a single, demanding customer, the Ministry of Defense, which approves the specifications of new weapons and strictly controls the observance of the stipulated quality requirements. The industry's ability to meet these demands is facilitated by its preferential access to material and equipment inputs, in terms of both quantity and quality, and the privileged conditions of employment it is able to offer its work force. Pay scales are higher than in civilian industry and workers appear to have access to better housing and welfare services. While managerial and technical personnel enjoy higher rates of pay and appear to have more opportunities to earn additional bonuses for good work, they also suffer career disadvantages compared with their civilian industry colleagues, e.g., work in conditions of secrecy, and restrictions on foreign travel and the right to publish. For this reason it cannot be assumed that the quality of such personnel is always higher than in the civilian sector. In the military sector there is more effective integration of design, development, and production, which permits more rapid innovation and greater use of program planning and project management techniques that ensure better horizontal coordination than is typical of the rest of the economy. The general designers responsible for missiles, aircraft, and other weapons have substantial command over resources and great managerial authority for expediting the timely completion of priority programs. We are thus considering a relatively successful and innovative sector of the Soviet economy. It would be a mistake, however, to draw too firm a line between the defense industry and its civilian counterpart: the two sectors are interrelated in countless ways, and just as there are effective civilian R&D organizations and enterprises, so must there be less successful and non-innovative components of the defense industry. Uneven performance is, after all, one of the characteristic features of the Soviet economic system.

Western Technology Transfer: The Evidence

In recent years there have been many claims of transfers of militarily-related technology from the West to the Soviet Union, covering a wide range of weapons and equipment for their manufacture. Major sources of evidence include the April 1982 sanitized version of the CIA's report, *Soviet Acquisition of Western Technology,* and the three editions of the Department of Defense's publication, *Soviet Military Power.* In addition, the issue has been discussed at a number of Senate hearings and many examples of transfers have been cited in numerous journal and newspaper articles. In this section we consider some general features of the publicly presented evidence, before turning to a discussion of a number of substantive issues relating to technology transfers and their impact on Soviet weapons production.

The total number of claims relating to militarily significant Soviet acquisitions of Western technology is now quite substantial: the 1984 edition of *Soviet Military Power* refers to an analysis of nearly 800 such cases, of which more than half relate to electronics, computing, and production equipment.[45] Richard Perle, Assistant Secretary of Defense, has claimed that evidence has been found of Western technology in 150 Soviet weapons systems.[46] Of the published claims examined by the author, the most numerous by far are also those concerning microelectronics and computing. Very few relate to strategic systems: the only claims in the field of nuclear weaponry refer to the immediate postwar years, while claimed transfers relevant to strategic missiles concern the "striking similarities" between the U.S. Minuteman silos and those for the Soviet SS-13, and possible acquisitions of guidance and control technology.[47] In relation to aviation technology, there are claims of resemblance between some Soviet transport planes and U.S. models (e.g., the Il-76/ Lockheed C-141 and the Il-86/Boeing 747) and of acquisitions of aeroengine technology. Some Soviet air-to-air and surface-to-air missiles are claimed to contain features of equivalent Western systems (e.g., the Atoll/Sidewinder and SA-7/Redeye). In the case of equipment for the ground forces, with the exception of anti-tank weapons (e.g., RPG-18/ Law and AT-4 and AT-5/Milan), the claims are relatively few, and the single case that has attracted most attention is the KamAZ truck plant, built with the use of Western technology and now supplying trucks to the Soviet army. Claimed naval technology acquisitions relate predominantly to sub-surface and anti-submarine capabilities, although the single most frequently cited case is the military use of two large, commercially purchased, dry docks. Other claimed military acquisitions include signal and information processing technologies, particularly those applicable to air defense systems. As noted, a substantial proportion of the cases relate to electronics and computing: here the claims cover both the copying of computers and microelectronic devices, especially integrated circuits, and legal and illegal acquisitions of computers and electronic component manufacturing equipment. Finally, there is a sizeable set of claims relating to acquisitions of production technology, many concerning pieces of so-called dual-use equipment having the potential of being employed in both military and civilian production.

A characteristic feature of many of the claims is the absence of certainty as to whether advances in Soviet weaponry have stemmed directly from acquisitions of Western technology, or whether items of production technology have actually been employed in the defense sector. Thus, in the reports of the CIA and DOD one often encounters claims of the type: Western technology "A" "may have," "possibly," "very likely," or "probably" led to the development of Soviet weapon "X." It is characteristic of the issue that in the contributions of some journalists, politicians, and propagandists cautious claims harden into dogmatic statements of fact, raising the temperature of the debate. This can be illustrated by considering one of the most frequently cited cases. "U.S. origin grinders . . . produce components for the guidance systems of Soviet ICBMs," declared Commerce Department Assistant Secretary Lawrence Brady at Senate hearings in 1982, echoing a claim repeated on numerous occasions since the appearance of the new generation of Soviet MIRVed missiles in the mid-1970s.[48] Yes, advanced U.S. grinders were eventually purchased by the Soviet Union through legal trade in the 1970s, but similar machines, though of lower productivity, were available from other countries, acknowledges the more cautious CIA report, and, even with its own technology, Soviet industry could have produced missile-quality bearings, albeit with high rejection rates.[49] No one has established any direct link between the purchase of 164 Bryant Centalign grinders, approved by the Department of Commerce in 1972, and the enhanced accuracy of Soviet missiles deployed from 1975. Indeed, as Gustafson points out in his discussion of this famous case, "The official view of the intelligence agencies today is that the Bryant grinders arrived in the Soviet Union too late to have played a crucial gap-filling role in the development of the Soviet fourth-generation missiles."[50] During the 1970s the Soviet machine tool industry successfully developed new, high-productivity equipment for making precision bearings, incorporating original technology widely patented abroad.[51] At the same time, production capacity for making instrument-quality bearings (used in many products besides missiles) was expanded with the building of a new factory, GPZ-24, at Penza, and the expansion of the existing Kuibyshev GPZ-4 and Tomsk GPZ-5.[52] The Kuibyshev works, making bearings for gyroscopes, aeroengines, and other high-precision products, has its own capacity for manufacturing production equipment and without doubt has a substantial technological capability.[53] The persistence of dogmatic claims in this case may stem from the fact that it is almost the only example which impinges directly on the strategic security of the United States.

The same cannot be said of the case of the KamAZ and ZIL truck plants. It has long been known that all the major Soviet truck factories (Moscow ZIL, Minsk MAZ, Gor'kii GAZ, Kremenchug KrAZ and the Miass UAZ) build vehicles capable of serving military purposes— personnel and cargo carriers, prime movers for missiles and tank transporters, rocket launcher carriers, etc. These specialized military variants are built either at the main production plant, or at separate facilities, e.g., some of the heavy-duty MAZ prime movers are built at Kurgan in the Urals and some military variants of the ZIL truck are built at Bryansk. The initial construction of some of the major truck plants was undertaken with substantial resort to foreign technology, the Gor'kii GAZ being the outstanding example, built with Ford technical assistance in the early 1930s. But for most of the postwar period, these enterprises have been equipped with predominantly Soviet technology, supplemented by periodic, selective purchases from the West and Eastern Europe.[54] This applies to the Moscow ZIL works, which in recent years has served as a development center for new production technology in close association with institutes of the Ukrainian Academy of Sciences.[55] At the same time, this leading enterprise of the motor industry has acquired equipment from the West, including computers for its management information system. But this does not justify such claims as: "Russia's ZIL truck complex . . . built with the aid of American exports,"[56] or, "These two sprawling plants (KamAZ and ZIL) were built in the early 1970s, largely with U.S. and European-supplied machinery and know-how."[57] This tendency to exaggerate the Western contribution to the KamAZ works is widely met in the literature. According to the DOD's *Soviet Military Power* of 1983, it was built "almost exclusively" with Western technology; according to de Borchgrave, it is an "American built project."[58] In reality, the overall plan for the project, the design and construction of most of the shops, much of the general-purpose equipment, and the design of the truck were Soviet; the Western contribution took the form predominantly of specialized equipment and associated layout plans. In 1980, the then Director of the Defense Intelligence Agency stated that the U.S. contribution represented one-eighth of the total cost of the project, the total Western contribution one-quarter.[59]

A feature of some of the claims is that they take the form: Soviet weapon "X" has undergone rapid development in recent years; the USSR is believed to be deficient in the technologies related to this type of weapons; therefore, Western technology must have been utilized, even though no positive evidence is available that such transfers have taken place. In particular, this applies to the improved accuracy of Soviet missiles during the 1970s, to recent observations on the development of a Soviet modern cruise missile, and to some of the advances in microelectronics. This is a procedure of dubious validity. It extends the list of claimed Western transfers, but it also betrays an unwillingness to acknowledge that the Soviet defense industry may be capable of successful innovation in areas of the most advanced technology. Another feature of some of the claims is that they involve assertions of similarity between specific items of Western and Soviet military hardware. Again, this type of evidence is by no means unproblematic. What kind of resemblance is at issue—the general concept, a design configuration, a precise design reproduction, the copying of detailed engineering features. . . ? What is the time lag involved? Is the lag so brief as to suggest possible access to Western design documentation, or delayed to the extent that knowledge of the Western equivalent was in the public domain at the time of the alleged duplication? Were actual physical examples of the hardware available to the Soviet industry? Unfortunately, the nature of many of the claims is such that these questions cannot be answered. For some of the cases cited in the literature time lags can be established as follows:

C5A Galaxy, first flight 1968	: new Soviet heavy transport, under development, 1980s
C-141 transport, first flight 1963	: Il-76, 1971
Boeing 747, first flight 1969	: Il-86, late 1976
Redeye AA missile, in service 1964	: SA-7, c. 1967
Sidewinder A-to-A missile, 1953	: AA-2 Atoll, early 1960s
Law M72 anti-tank weapon, in prodn. 1962	: RPG-18, early 1980s
Tow and Milan anti-tank missiles, 1970–72	: AT-4 and AT-5, c. 1977
M-16 5.56-mm rifle, used in Vietnam, 1962	: AK-74 5.45-mm rifle, 1978

From this it can be reasonably concluded that whether it was used or not, substantial information was available in most cases at the time when equivalent Soviet development programs were initiated. In some cases, the USSR is known to have acquired examples of weapons captured in Vietnam, the Middle East, and elsewhere. There should be no surprise that these were thoroughly analyzed and tested for applicable design concepts and technical features; the United States does exactly the same when Soviet weapons are obtained. Exclusion of the serendipity of war and revolution would probably greatly reduce the list of allegedly copied weapons. It should not be forgotten that "copying" is a two-way process: some Western systems owe their origin to original Soviet innovations. Two examples will suffice. Multiple rocket launchers developed in Western Europe and the United States have been inspired by the Soviet "Katyusha" and its subsequent variants; and the American mechanized infantry combat vehicle, the Bradley, which has been under development for the army, is the equivalent of the Soviet BMP first seen in 1967. Finally, in no case has it been claimed that a Soviet weapon is a precise, detail-for-detail reproduction of a Western system. As noted above in the discussion of the prewar aviation industry, it is doubtful whether this is a practical option even when design documentation is available.

Two further points about the evidence are worth noting. First, while occasional reference is made to Soviet interest in obtaining technology in order to devise countermeasures to Western systems, the general assumption is that the Soviet Union acquires technology from the West in order to apply it directly in the creation of new weapons. But just as the United States and other NATO powers continually attempt to obtain militarily-related technological information and samples of actual hardware in order to monitor developments on an intelligence "need-to-know" basis, not necessarily with practical application in mind, then so must the Soviet Union. And insofar as the USSR can be assumed to have at its disposal less sophisticated electronic-communications intelligence than available to the U.S. National Security Agency and other wings of the intelligence service, greater reliance has to be placed on more traditional forms of technological information gathering.[60] Second, it is notable that many of the claims refer to the licit and illicit transfer of specific items of hardware. This is interesting in the light of the findings of the 1976 Bucy Report, the Defense Science Task Force Report on Export of U.S. Technology, which led to the adoption of the critical technologies approach to the control of transfers. It was a basic premise of that report that "Communist nations are now [as opposed to the pre-1970 situation] chiefly interested in acquiring design and manufacturing know-how so that they may permanently improve their national capabilities, rather than rely on product imports from the West."[61] It could be argued that hardware figures so prominently in the list of claimed acquisitions simply because it is more visible than know-how; nevertheless, it is surprising that this central pivot of the Bucy Report has been accepted so readily.

In concluding this review of the evidence for transfers of militarily-related Western technology, it must be stressed again that we are not denying that the Soviet Union has acquired such technology or that it has played a role in strengthening its military capability. But we are making a plea that the evidence for claimed acquisitions should be presented in an honest manner with appropriate qualifications, and with provision of adequate information for informed independent assessment of the credibility of the claims and hypotheses advanced.

Channels of Acquisition

The Soviet defense industry obtains Western technology in many forms and through a variety of channels. The 1976 Bucy Report provided a convenient summary of the principal transfer mechanisms and their relative effectiveness, drawing the useful distinction between passive and active mechanisms. The former include technical information derived from trade exhibitions, commercial catalogues and other literature, simple license purchases without know-how, and the sale of products; these forms are considered of low effectiveness. More active and effective are considered to be such mechanisms as commercial visits, the transfer of processing equipment without know-how, licenses with know-how, consultancy and the provision of engineering documentation and technical data. Most effective of all, are considered to be the sale of processing equipment with know-how, training in high-technology areas, technical exchanges with on-going contact, joint ventures, licensing with extensive teaching effort, and, finally, turnkey factories.[62] For the Soviet defense industry, some of the options are not available, or are available to only a limited extent; and an additional distinction must be drawn between open, legal acquisitions and those realized through illegal or espionage channels. The problem facing the Soviet Union is that it is precisely the most effective, active transfer mechanisms that are the least accessible. Not only COCOM controls and national export regulations, but also the general unwillingness of reputable Western companies to become involved in active, on-going projects of a militarily-sensitive nature, effectively bar access to many of the most effective channels of technology acquisition. Therefore, the Soviet defense industry is forced to exploit the less effective, passive transfer mechanisms, and its system of acquisition can be understood as one geared to deriving the maximum benefit from such second-best options.

In the author's view, the single most important channel of Western technology acquisition for the defense industry is probably the collection, analysis, and domestic dissemination of published foreign scientific and technical information in all its forms, including books and journals, commercial literature, government reports, conference proceedings, patents and standards, supplemented when required (and possible) by equivalent information of a less open nature obtained through a variety of channels, not excluding the efforts of intelligence agencies. This is a passive form of transfer, but one well-suited to the conditions of the Soviet planned economy: "scientific and technical information" is effectively a sub-branch of the economy, with its own mechanisms of planned production and distribution.[63] Most of the principal national organizations of this system are subordinated to the State Committee for Science and Technology, the most important being the All-Union Institute of Scientific and Technical Information (VINITI), under the directorship since 1956 of A. I. Mikhailov, who for the preceding twenty years worked in various branches of the defense industry.[64] Other major national agencies include the All-Union Research Institute for Patent Information, the State Public Scientific and Technical Library, which has a special department of industrial catalogues acquired through such channels as foreign trade organizations, exhibitions, and contacts with Western firms, and the All-Union Center for Translations, which services the entire economy with translations of foreign technical literature. The whole national system employs some 200,000 people, over half with higher education. It can be assumed that these agencies service both the civilian and defense sectors, but the latter also has its own organization, the subordination of which has not been revealed.[65] The All-Union Institute of Interbranch Information (VIMI), under the directorship of G. T. Artamonov, appears to serve as an informational agency for the defense industry as a whole and as a channel for the transfer of information from this sector to the civilian economy.[66] According to one author, VIMI acts as a processing and distribution agency for the information acquired by a variety of collectors, including the scientific and technical intelligence sections of the KGB and the military intelligence directorate (GRU) of the Ministry of Defense. Information requirements are identified and prioritized by the defense industry ministries and the Military-Industrial Commission and communicated to the relevant collectors.[67] Within the defense industry ministries there are central informational agencies and departments at research organizations and enterprises designated as special information services, which handle and analyze the acquired information.[68] In both the civilian and defense industry ministries foreign scientific and technical information, including patents and standards, forms an important input into the project selection and planning process. It is a source of ideas and specific technical solutions and serves to provide parameters against which the technological level of proposed domestic developments can be assessed. This could be considered one of the means through which competitive market and military pressure is brought to bear on Soviet industry.[69]

According to Admiral Inman, about seventy percent of all Soviet acquisitions of militarily-useful Western technology have been accomplished by the Soviet and East European intelligence services, using clandestine, technical, and overt collection operations, and of the remaining 20–30 percent, most significant have been legal purchases of open-source literature.[70] It is not easy to see how these proportions were determined: open-source information may well serve as an important input into the defense project selection and planning process on an ongoing basis without there being any positive evidence of its use in the eventual weapons systems created. A rather different picture is presented in the 1984 edition of *Soviet Military Power:* here it is stated that "while the illegal and covert technology collections have been important, it should be noted that the majority of Soviet acquisitions of Western technology have been achieved through legal means."[71] Inman also acknowledges that only a small percentage of acquisitions come from direct technical exchanges conducted by scientists and students. In view of the justified concern generated by recent attempts to impose restrictions on some forms of scientific publication and the holding of scientific conferences, it is worth recalling that on this occasion Inman declared that "I have a perception that the leakage from basic research is minimal. There is little. But the Soviets themselves have difficulty in applying that. I would go very slowly in that category where one is dealing with the open publication of basic research."[72]

Informational transfers are not the sole form of acquisition of Western technology. The Soviet Union attempts to purchase and otherwise obtain examples of weapons and militarily-useful production technology from COCOM members and non-members alike. COCOM controls relate in the main to precisely this form of acquisition, despite its claimed low level of effectiveness as a transfer mechanism. Unfortunately, there is little evidence on the overall scale of acquisitions in this form, and the situation is complicated by the existence of so-called dual-use technologies, capable of either civilian or militarily-related application. One author notes that "minicomputers designed for routine lab work can be used to control nuclear weapons production; laser technology exported for manufacturing purposes can be modified for exotic satellite-killing weapons; computers for weather forecasting and air-traffic control can be programmed to direct missile launches, special drill bit machinery for oil and gas exploration can be used to make armor piercing warheads. The list goes on."[73] And, as Khrushchev once observed, buttons can be used to hold up soldiers' trousers.[74] Insofar as the Soviet Union has a genuine economic need for minicomputers, lasers, drill bits, and other dual-use technologies there can be no clear distinction between strategic technology denial as such, and more general economic warfare. The attempt to tightly control such technologies leads to some of the absurdities witnessed in recent months, e.g., talk of controlling the circuitry of advanced washing machines, and the imposition of export controls on mass-produced home computers.

The Use of Western Technology in the Soviet Defense Industry

Why should the Soviet defense industry wish to exploit Western technology? What are the benefits? What also are the costs and drawbacks? Is there any detectable general strategy of acquisition? This section will attempt to provide answers to these questions taking account of the known characteristic practices and procedures of the Soviet defense industry.

Ever since the war, the United States has set the pace of military technological innovation—as the frequently heard argument for the maintenance of U.S. qualitative technological superiority testifies. This does not mean that there have been no Soviet "firsts," but, in general, the Soviet weapons designers and producers have faced the task of emulating Western initiatives while having a weaker general economic base to draw on. In these circumstances it is not surprising that they have resorted to Western technology to facilitate the catching up process. By doing so, there are obvious advantages in terms of cost and time. Insofar as a proven design concept or configuration is available, it may be possible to reduce the required research input and minimize the risk of costly failure. As indicated, familiarity with Western developments is probably of particular value in the early stages of the procurement process, for drawing up a requirement for a new system and in formulating initial design concepts at the project selection stage. For all concerned, risk minimization must be an important consideration. The issue is not one of Soviet technological capability in some absolute sense, although this impression is sometimes conveyed in the literature. The Office of Technology Assessment is surely correct in concluding that "although the USSR has undoubtedly realised savings from pursuing the strategy of a 'technological follower,' nowhere has it been demonstrated that it has obtained any technology from the West which it could not have developed itself, given adequate incentive and resources."[75]

An appreciation of the Soviet weapons design and development process and its evolution over time provides grounds for arguing that substantial resort to Western technology will be avoided if at all possible. A key actor in the process is the design bureau and its associated trial production plant, headed by a general or chief designer. One of the characteristic features of the Soviet defense industry is the stability of these design teams and the long, unbroken leadership of their heads. Leading designers are often well-known figures in Soviet society, and can expect to become members of the Party Central Committee or the Supreme Soviet.[76] These design organizations develop their own traditions and practices, not necessarily conducive to the assimilation of externally generated innovations. One factor that probably should not be discounted is the designer's professional pride: no designer of any real talent and ability in the Soviet Union as elsewhere would wish to reproduce the designs of others. There are indeed documented cases of leading designers having explicitly rejected the option of copying foreign weapons and technology.[77] The design procedures characteristic of established branches of the defense industry would also appear to work against dependence on Western technology. Soviet aircraft, tanks, small arms, etc., tend to undergo evolutionary development with stress on design inheritance and commonality. New models frequently incorporate many systems and assemblies lifted from those they replace: a policy which reduces time, cost, and risk.[78] In the aircraft industry, and probably elsewhere, design and production methods are strictly regulated and standardized by the leading central research organizations of the ministry, to the extent that aircraft of different design bureaus will share common features and configurations, e.g. the variable-sweep wing which has predominated in the 1970s on military planes.[79] Thus for any given new design one would not expect the incorporation of much new technology derived directly from the West, and even when foreign ideas are adopted they probably undergo an extensive prior process of "Sovietization." For this reason, incidentally, the time and cost savings associated with the use of Western technology may not be as great as often imagined. These procedures are such that one would not expect to find many "smoking gun" examples of copies of Western weapons.

Another important consideration is the well-known reluctance to become dependent on foreign technology in any priority sector of the economy. The drive for self-reliance has been a feature of the defense industry from its earliest days. For this reason, one would not expect to find the practical application of any important new technology acquired from the West for which there is not already a certain minimum background research and development capability in the Soviet Union. This would apply with particular force to the use of acquired items of hardware: without a potential for replacement, adaptation, and further development, the defense industry and armed forces would become dependent on the possibility of making similar acquisitions in the future. Such a risk is unlikely to be acceptable.

Taking a longer-term view, a general pattern does emerge. During the "normal" evolutionary stages of development of any given type of weapons system, resort to Western technology acquisitions appears to be relatively modest and restricted in the main to general monitoring of foreign developments and selective borrowing of new ideas for technical improvement. But for completely new systems, based on original principles, the position appears to be somewhat different. At a certain point when a decision has been made to seriously embark on a new path of development pioneered in the West, there is often resort to acquisitions in order to accelerate the process, while simultaneously a domestic capability is built up. Obvious examples are the transition to jet aeroengines, the use of German experience in the creation of the first ballistic missiles, and, more recently, the copying of proven Western microprocessors. An important point to note is that the assimilation of the Western technology appears often to have been regarded as a training process: while at least one design bureau was engaged in reproducing the foreign technology, other design teams were engaged in efforts to forge a more independent path of development, drawing on the experience of their colleagues. This was certainly the case for both jet engines and missiles, and there is evidence that a similar approach has been adopted in the field of microelectronics. It is this approach which sometimes allows the Soviet Union to create original systems earlier than Western specialists believed likely. As a rule, once the Western technology has been successfully assimilated, a process of progressive modification and adaptation is quickly initiated, and the design may undergo substantial transformation in a relatively brief period. The prewar development of tanks provides an excellent example: less than a decade separated the purchase of the original Christie model from the United States and the successful creation of the T-34, the best tank of World War II, bearing little resemblance to its design progenitor. On the other hand, it would be a mistake to conclude that breakthroughs to new types of weapons and militarily-related technology must necessarily await injections of Western technology: the Sputnik and other Soviet space successes provide adequate testimony to this.

To the extent that these patterns are valid, they underline the need to see Soviet acquisitions in a broader perspective. At any given time certain types of weapons incorporating specific key technologies will be decisive for the armed forces of the major powers. During the 1930s, mechanization and aviation were of crucial importance; in the early postwar years, nuclear weaponry and strategic delivery systems. In all these cases Western technology made a significant, though not decisive, contribution to the initial acquisition of the capabilities in the Soviet Union; once acquired, subsequent development was based to a considerable degree on domestic resources. More recently, microelectronics has become the crucial technology for across-the-board improvement of weapons systems of all types. Once again, the Soviet Union has resorted to an injection of Western technology, but historical experience would suggest that this may be a transitional process, preparing the way for indigenous innovation, aided by the expertise possessed by East European countries. What the next key technology will be and when it will break are not entirely clear, but it is worth noting that in laser technology the Soviet Union already possesses a strong domestic capability.

In this connection it is of some interest to consider briefly the Soviet electronics industry and its innovative potential. The modern Soviet electronics industry owes its origins to the wartime and postwar radar program and for a long time its development took place within the combined radio-electronics ministry. It gained its organizational independence under the leadership of A. I. Shokin in 1961, becoming a ministry in 1965. It is a highly specialized, self-reliant ministry, producing a very high proportion of all electronic components used in the Soviet economy, and also much of its own production equipment and special materials. The ministry (MEP) was one of the first to go over to the corporate structure of organization based on associations and science-production associations, creating conditions for the effective integration of research, development, and production. Most of the large production associations on which information is available have a research capability and frequently possess facilities for the development and manufacture of production equipment. Some of the well-known associations engaged in integrated circuit production are directly subordinated to the ministry, eliminating the intermediate tier of administration characteristic of most of Soviet industry.[80] This facilitates the rapid resolution of problems by direct reference to the ministry and gives the association greater scope for initiative in decision making.

As an industry experiencing rapid technical change, MEP has been forced to give serious attention to questions of organization, planning, and management for rapid innovation. It has created a central research and training complex at Zelenograd near Moscow, supported by a large network of institutes and science-production associations. In addition, it has drawn on the research capability of the Academy of Sciences and the higher educational system. With the recent formation of a new Academy division for informatics, computing technology, and automation, the basic research effort is being upgraded with the creation of a number of new institutes. These include an Institute for Microelectronics at Yaroslavl, under the directorship of K. A. Valiev, formerly head of MEP's own Zelenograd microelectronics institute, and an Institute of Microelectronics Technology and Super-pure Materials, with attached design, development, and production facilities.[81] Deepening the industry's basic research capability at this time accords well with the strategy outlined above.

With large associations new intra-organizational arrangements have been pioneered by "Svetlana" in Leningrad since 1971, with the creation of specialized "science-production complexes," integrating design, development, and production units for specific types of new products. The leadership of the design bureau within the complex has responsibility for the entire cycle from research to production, which is managed and planned on an integrated basis.[82] Wide use is made of temporary project groups and, in general, one gains the impression that the ministry has been more successful in evolving flexible organizational forms than is usual in Soviet industry. MEP has also devoted much attention to planning and project selection techniques, with strong emphasis on program planning methods and scientific and technical forecasting. Western practices have been closely studied and propagated widely. During the 1970s the ministry created a new branch system of quality control and management, involving the formation of a Main Quality Inspectorate at the level of the ministry, and a strong central research institute, "Elektronstandart." Large associations have deputy directors for quality and bonuses are linked to the reduction of rejection rates.[83] The ministry also has its own experimental system of incentives, designed to encourage the adoption of high output targets, rapid innovation, and the effective use of labor, assets, and materials.[84] Whether all these measures will be adequate to generate the required rates of innovation remains to be seen, but they do provide evidence of serious intent.

Over the last decade the product range of the industry has undergone substantial change and this cannot have escaped the attention of the Soviet consumer. The production of large-scale integrated circuits was started in the mid-1970s, "Svetlana" being one of the first publicly acknowledged producers. At about this time "Svetlana," the Voronezh "Elektronika" and Kiev "Kristall" began making microcalculators on a volume basis: by 1980 the annual production rate exceeded 2 million units of 30 different models.[85] From 1975 the Minsk "Integral" began making digital watches. The first traced Soviet report of microprocessor development dates from 1976, when Shokin described the creation of a set of microprocessors as a great achievement of the preceding five-year plan.[86] In 1977–78 there were reports of microprocessor production at "Svetlana" and "Elektronika," and also of new microcomputers made by the same associations. In 1977 it was claimed that three different microprocessor sets had been created; by 1980, about ten, rising to approximately fifteen sets by 1983, covering all the main types of microchip technology, with many of the sets in both ceramic and plastic packaging.[87] Some Western accounts give the impression that Soviet microprocessor production takes place on a small scale only, concentrated at Zelenograd. This is clearly not the case: several large associations are without doubt engaged in volume production, including "Svetlana," "Elektronika" and "Kristall." More recently, microprocessor production has started up in the communications equipment ministry at the Riga

"VEF" association, which has also announced that a personal computer is entering production.[88] The Soviet Union is now on the threshold of the home computer era: two models have been announced for production in 1984.[89] Microprocessors have now been incorporated in a wide range of products, including machine tool and robot control units, control and measuring instruments, communications equipment, optical instruments, and, recently, some consumer goods and toys.[90] The incorporation of microprocessors in consumer products would seem to suggest that the basic problems of volume production have now been overcome.

In developing microprocessor technology, representatives of the Soviet electronics industry have explicitly acknowledged a strategy involving three main directions: firstly, the reproduction and further improvement of the best foreign models, secondly, the creation of original Soviet microprocessor sets, and, thirdly, the development of a unified system of microprocessors known as the ES MP.[91] By implication, these directions are being pursued in parallel. Of the three most widely met microprocessor sets, the K580, K589, and K587, the first two have strong resemblance to U.S. Intel designs dating from 1974.[92] It can be deduced that the K580 is being manufactured at the Kiev "Kristall" association. The K587 set forms the basis of the "Elektronika NTs" series of microcomputers and to the author's knowledge neither has been identified as a Western design. Both appear to be products of the Zelenograd Scientific Center; of the microcomputer families discussed in the Soviet literature the "NTs" series would appear to be the best-suited for military and space applications.[93] Thus, as suggested above, the development of microelectronics appears to be following a familiar pattern of assimilation of Western technology.

The extent of the indebtedness of the Soviet electronics industry to Western technology is difficult to determine. According to the 1984 edition of *Soviet Military Power,* more than one-third of all known Soviet integrated circuits have been copied from U.S. designs; but this must mean that up to two-thirds have not, which is contrary to the impression created by many recent press accounts. There is no doubt that the Soviet Union has acquired production equipment for the industry from the West through both legal and illegal channels, but it would probably be a mistake to underestimate the domestic capability and that of the Soviet Union's CMEA partners. In the GDR, for example, Karl Zeiss of Jena produces equipment considered to possess the potential for fabricating the most advanced microcircuits, including the 256K random access memories. Some of the Jena equipment has been purchased by the Japanese electronics industry.[94] Moreover, the GDR is itself a large-scale producer of microprocessors: the "Mikroelektronika" combine is reported to have achieved an annual output of 135,000 units, compared with only 2,200 in 1978.[95] Despite the progress achieved, the Soviet Union still lags behind the USA and Japan in microelectronics and probably to an even greater extent in computers and their application. The available evidence suggests, however, that the lag may not be as great as widely perceived and that the domestic capability for future advancement is rather more substantial than assumed in much of the recent discussion of export controls.

One dimension of the technology transfer problem which has received little attention is the reverse flow of technologies of potential value for weapons production offered for sale to Western countries by the Soviet Union, either as export goods or as licenses. The limited evidence available does suggest that the USSR has a more relaxed attitude to such transfers than the United States. Kiser, one of the few Western specialists to have examined the issue, has remarked that the Soviet bloc is "surprisingly liberal" about what it is prepared to sell to the West. Technologies are offered for sale, which, "if the shoe were on the other foot, the U.S. government would be unwilling to export to the Soviet Union."[96] Among the original production technologies offered as licenses are some developed by organizations of the Soviet defense industry ministries. Kaiser Aluminum and Reynolds Aluminum of the United States are two of the Western firms which have acquired licenses for electromagnetic casting of aluminum alloys, developed at the Kuibyshev metallurgical works of the aviation ministry.[97] Other Soviet metallurgical processes of potential use in military production include electroslag remelting, cold rolling of tubes (used by Universal Oil Tubes to make hydraulic tubing under an Air Force contract), and titanium sponge production technology: all have been offered for sale in the West.[98] Other items offered include a range of lasers and laser-based production processes, advanced welding technologies, and electronic components, including integrated circuits. For understandable reasons, Western companies are not very forthcoming about their use of Soviet technologies in weapons production, but it is known that General Dynamics has used high-precision optical equipment from the GDR in building the F-16 fighter.[99]

Conclusion: Technology, Transfers, and Security

In this chapter it has been argued that on a selective basis the Soviet defense industry has successfully exploited acquisitions of Western technology to accelerate the development of new weapons; at the same time, the general strategy has been one of securing a minimum level of dependence on the West. The assimilation of Western technology has not been either trouble- or cost-free: for use in Soviet conditions all things of alien origin must undergo "Sovietization," a necessarily time-consuming process.[100] Close monitoring of the course of technological development in the capitalist world has not only facilitated the selection of projects for priority attention and the choice of technical solutions, but also provided external reference points for assessing domestic progress in an economy characterized by weak internal mechanisms of competition. Examination of the pattern of acquisitions over time suggests that resort to Western technology has been particularly important in the early stages of the transition to completely new weapons systems pioneered in the West. In such cases the technology transfers have accelerated Soviet development programs, but have not been decisive to their success. The assimilation of the foreign technologies has served a training function, helping to generate an independent capability such that subsequent development has proceeded with less need to draw directly on the expertise of the West, although subsequent Western advances have still been subject to attentive scrutiny. For well-established types of weapons, exemplified by small arms and traditional forms of artillery, Soviet resort to Western technology has been much less evident; indeed, for many such systems the Soviet Union has long been at the forefront of world technological development.

It must be stressed that these conclusions are provisional. We are still at the stage of advancing tenable hypotheses requiring further research for their translation into substantiated theses. This review of the available evidence does suggest, however, that it may be possible to arrive at firmer conclusions through independent research, despite the fact that much of the relevant information is considered to be of a sensitivity requiring classification, both in the East and the West.

It was not the purpose of this chapter to address directly the vexed issue of the control of strategic technology transfers. The general thrust of the argument presented here nevertheless would appear to point in the direction of a more relaxed approach, focusing only on actual weapons systems and those technologies demonstrably vital to the creation of completely new systems. However, the wisdom or otherwise of imposing controls should involve a broader set of considerations; not simply pragmatic questions of what technologies should be restricted and by what means, but more fundamental issues of the relationship between technology and national security, and the impact of controls on both East-West relations and intra-West relations. For the entire postwar period it has been an almost unchallenged axiom that the security of the West is crucially dependent on the maintenance of technological superiority over the Soviet Union. We now live in a world in which security is indivisible: no major power can be genuinely secure if that security is purchased at the price of the insecurity of other major powers. There is now wide recognition that nuclear strategic parity offers greater mutual security than one-sided advantage. It cannot be ruled out that in the future, not only Western security, but also the survival of humanity, may be best served by tolerance of broad East-West military technological parity in the framework of mutually agreed quantitative arms limitation, with a depoliticization of the whole issue of technology transfers.

NOTES

1. V. B. Shavrov, *Istoriia konstruktsii samoletov v SSSR do 1938 g.* (Moscow: Mashinostroenie, 1978), p. 379; B. Gunston, *Aircraft of the Soviet Union* (London: Osprey, 1983), p. 255.

2. Shavrov, p. 386; V. B. Shavrov, *Istoriia konstruktsii samoletov v SSSR 1938–1950 gg.* (Moscow: Mashinostroenie, 1978), p. 125 (Hereafter, Shavrov, Vol. 1 and 2).

3. Shavrov, Vol. 2, pp. 122–23.

4. Shavrov, Vol. 2, pp. 123–24; D. Gai, *Nebesnoe pritiazhenie* (Moscow: Moskovskii Rabochii, 1984), pp. 59–64; Gunston, p. 165. During the war some military variants were developed.

5. See A. S. Iakovlev, *Tsel' zhizni* (Moscow: Politizdat, 1967), pp. 217, 227, and 236; A. I. Shakhurin, *Kryl'ia pobedy* (Moscow: Politizdat, 1983), pp. 75–78. Models acquired included the Messerschmitt 109 and Heinkel 100 fighters and the Junkers 88 and Dornier 215 bombers.

6. Shavrov, Vol. 1, p. 567.

7. *Razvitie aviatsionnoi nauki i tekhniki v SSSR* (Moscow: Nauka, 1980), p. 166.

8. R. H. Jones, *The Roads to Russia* (Norman: University of Oklahoma Press, 1969), Table II (no pagination).

9. Gunston, p. 323.

10. A. C. Sutton, *Western Technology and Soviet Economic Development*, Vol. 2 (Stanford: Hoover Institution Press, 1971), Ch. 5.

11. This image of the Soviet tractor industry as being "dual use," heavily committed to tank production, lives on: Senator Armstrong: ". . . the reason why the Soviets want to buy American pipelayers instead of building their own is because their tractor plants are all pretty much full up—building tanks" (*East-West Trade and Technology Transfer*, Hearings before the Subcommittee on International Finance and Monetary Policy of the Committee on Banking, Housing, and Urban Affairs, United States Senate, 14 April 1982 [Washington, D.C.: USGPO], p. 13).

12. See *Sovetskii tyl v Velikoi Otechestvennoi voine*, Vol. 2 (Moscow: Mysl', 1974), p. 117; V. Grabin, *Oktiabr'*, 1973, no. 10, pp. 124–30.

13. See J. M. Cooper, *The Development of the Soviet Machine Tool Industry, 1917–1941*, Ph.D. thesis (University of Birmingham, 1975).

14. *Razvitie aviatsionnoi nauki i tekhniki v SSSR*, p. 198.

15. See L. M. Kuz'mina, *General'nyi konstruktor—Pavel Sukhoi* (Moscow: Molodaia Gvardiia, 1983), p. 100; L. M. Kuz'mina, *Ognennoe serdtse* (Moscow: Moskovskii Rabochii, 1983); M. Arlazorov, *Vint i krylo* (Moscow: Znanie, 1980), pp. 133–34.

16. Sutton, Vol. 2, p. 264; *Razvitie aviatsionnoi nauki i tekhniki v SSSR*, p. 202.

17. M. M. Lobanov, *Razvitie sovetskoi radiolokatsionnoi tekhniki* (Moscow:

Voenizdat, 1982); M. M. Lobanov, *My—voennye inzhenery* (Moscow: Voenizdat, 1977); *Krasnaia Zvezda*, 25 May 1984.

18. Lobanov (1982), pp. 155 and 158.

19. Lobanov (1982), p. 162, and A. Fedoseyev, *Design in Soviet Military R & D: the Case of Radar Research in Vacuum Electronics,* Papers in Soviet Science and Technology, No. 8 (Harvard University, Russian Research Center, May 1983), p. 2. Fedoseyev, a leading designer of magnetrons for radar apparatus, notes that this was "my first and last work in the area of copying Western equipment."

20. Lobanov (1982), pp. 162–63.

21. A. Lee (ed.), *The Soviet Air and Rocket Forces* (London: Weidenfeld and Nicholson, 1959), p. 121.

22. Fedoseyev, p. 3.

23. *Transfer of United States High Technology to the Soviet Union and Soviet Bloc Nations,* Hearings before the Permanent Subcommittee on Investigations of the Committee on Governmental Affairs, United States Senate, May 1982 (Washington, D.C.: USGPO, 1982), p. 112.

24. "U.S. Builds Soviet War Machine," *Industrial Research and Development,* July 1980, p. 53.

25. Lobanov (1982), pp. 188 and 190.

26. *Sovetskaia voennaia entsiklopediia,* Vol. 1 (Moscow: Voenizdat, 1976), p. 145.

27. Lobanov (1982), pp. 170, 212, and 231; *Voennyi entsiklopedichekii slovar'* (Moscow: Voenizdat, 1983), p. 812.

28. D. Holloway, *The Soviet Union and the Arms Race* (New Haven and London: Yale University Press, 1983), p. 23.

29. G. K. Bertsch and J. R. McIntyre (eds.), *National Security and Technology Transfer* (Boulder, Colorado: Westview Press, 1983), p. 98.

30. *Tvorcheskoe nasledie Akademika Sergeia Pavlovicha Koroleva (Izbrannye trudy i dokumenty)* (Moscow: Nauka, 1980), pp. 395–99; D. Holloway in R. Amann, J. M. Cooper, and R. W. Davies (eds.), *The Technological Level of Soviet Industry* (New Haven and London: Yale University Press, 1977), pp. 455–59.

31. A. C. Sutton, *Western Technology and Soviet Economic Development,* 3 volumes (Stanford: Hoover Institution Press, 1968, 1971, and 1973). See also A. C. Sutton, *National Suicide—Military Aid to the Soviet Union* (New Rochelle, New York: Arlington House, 1973).

32. Sutton, Vol. 3, p. 368.

33. Sutton, Vol. 2, p. 222.

34. Shavrov, Vol. 2, pp. 27–28.

35. Sutton, Vol. 2, p. 225.

36. Sutton, Vol. 2, p. 240. Note, one of the two sources cited by Sutton is the authoritative R. M. Ogorkiewicz in B. H. Liddell Hart (ed.), *The Red Army* (1956), but examination of this work reveals that it provides no support for the data presented in the table.

37. *Istoriia vtoroi mirovoi voiny,* Vol. 1 (Moscow: Voenizdat, 1973), pp. 214 and 270.

38. Sutton, Vol. 2, p. 243.

39. For a well-informed summary of Soviet tank development, see *Tanks of Other Nations: USSR* (The Royal Armoured Corps Tank Museum, Bovington Camp, Dorset, 2nd ed., 1976).

40. See D. Holloway, "The Soviet Union," in N. Ball and M. Leitenberg (eds.), *The Structure of the Defence Industry* (London: Croom Helm, 1983).

41. U.S. Department of Defense, *Soviet Military Power,* 1st ed., Sept. 1981, p. 10 and 3rd ed., April 1984, p. 93.

42. U.S. Central Intelligence Agency, National Foreign Assessment Center, *Estimated Soviet Defense Spending in Rubles* (Washington, D.C.: USGPO, May 1976), p. 16 and *Estimated Soviet Defense Spending: Trends and Prospects* (Washington, D.C.: USGPO, June 1978), p. 2.

43. *Soviet Military Power,* 3rd ed., April 1984, p. 101. The methodology employed is not revealed, but may be similar to that used by Lee (W. T. Lee, *The Estimation of Soviet Defense Expenditure, 1955–1975. An Unconventional Approach* [New York: Praeger, 1977]). Lee estimated that military durables represented 40 percent of machine-building final demand in 1970, rising to 48 percent in 1975.

44. See M. Acland-Hood, "Military Research and Development: Some Aspects of Its Resource Use in the USA and the USSR," in Stockholm International Peace Research Institute, *World Armaments and Disarmament. SIPRI Yearbook 1983* (London: Taylor and Francis, 1983), pp. 213–43 for a convenient summary of the various estimates and methodological problems; J. M. Cooper, "Scientists in Soviet Industry: A Statistical Analysis," *CREES Discussion Papers,* Series RC/B17, University of Birmingham, 1981.

45. *Soviet Military Power,* 3rd ed., April 1984, p. 108.

46. *The Times* (London), 24 March 1984.

47. Bertsch and McIntyre, pp. 99 and 101. The similarity of the missile silos was apparently revealed by reconnaissance photographs, but it is not clear that the claim, if valid, has much practical significance. The solid-fueled SS-13 appeared in 1965 four years after the Minuteman I and only 60 were deployed, compared with approximately 1,000 of the contemporaneous liquid-fueled SS-11s.

48. *East-West Trade and Technology Transfer,* p. 58.

49. Bertsch and McIntyre, p. 101.

50. T. Gustafson, *Selling the Russians the Rope? Soviet Technology Policy and U.S. Export Controls,* Rand R-2649-ARPA (Santa Monica, 1981), p. 10.

51. Gustafson, pp. 10–14.

52. *Avtomobil'naia Promyshlennost',* 1977, no. 1, pp. 3–4. Gustafson incorrectly locates the latter two works in Leningrad and, contrary to his belief, the Leningrad creators of the new equipment did receive a State Prize for their work in 1979 (*Trudovoi pul's Leningrada* (Leningrad: Lenizdat, 1982), p. 63). More recently, Leningrad and Ivanovo machine tool builders have developed more precision-bearing production equipment, earning another State Prize in 1983 (*Pravda,* 7 November 1983).

53. *Pravda,* 24 April 1984.

54. U.S. Central Intelligence Agency, National Foreign Assessment Center, *USSR: Role of Foreign Technology in the Development of the Motor Vehicle Industry* (Washington, D.C.: USGPO, 1979).

55. *Izvestiia,* 14 August 1980; *Pravda,* 11 October 1981.

56. *US News and World Report,* 17 March 1980, p. 51.

57. "U.S. Builds Soviet War Machine," p. 52.

58. *Soviet Military Power,* 2nd ed., March 1983, p. 78; A. de Borchgrave and M. Ledeen, "Selling Russia the Rope," *New Republic,* 13 December 1980, p. 14.

59. See *USSR: Role of Foreign Technology,* pp. 20–21; *Allocation of Resources in the Soviet Union and China—1980,* Hearings before the Subcommittee on Priorities and Economy in Government of the Joint Economic Committee, U.S. Congress (Washington, D.C.: USGPO, 1981), pp. 14 and 51. According to Soviet accounts, some 70 percent of all the equipment installed is of Soviet origin (*Soviet Weekly* [London], 9 August 1975).

60. It is notable that a comprehensive review of the relevant literature has yielded only two references to the possibility that the Soviet Union may obtain militarily related technological information through communications intelligence channels.

61. *An Analysis of Export Control of U.S. Technology—A DOD Perspective,* A Report of the Defense Science Board Task Force on Export of U.S. Technology, 4 February 1976 (Washington, D.C., 1976), p. 27.

62. *An Analysis of Export Control of U.S. Technology,* p. 6.

63. For a comprehensive review of the information system, see B. Parrott, *Information Transfer in Soviet Science and Engineering—A Study of Documentary Channels,* Rand R-2667-ARPA (Santa Monica, 1981).

64. See his biography in *Nauchno-tekhnicheskaia Informatsiia,* series 1, 1975, no. 1, pp. 25–26 (hereafter, *NTI*).

65. This silence suggests that it is either directly under the Council of Ministers or the Military-Industrial Commission.

66. According to a recent Soviet work, "To VIMI is assigned the creation, selection, processing, and dissemination of information of an interbranch character for a group of branches of industry, and research into the most important questions of informational activity" (G. Kh. Popov [ed.], *Upravlenie nauchno-tekhnicheskim progressom* [Moscow: Ekonomika, 1982], p. 53). Regnard is explicit that VIMI serves the military production branches (H. Regnard, *Défense Nationale,* December 1980, p. 114). On VIMI's servicing of civilian ministries, see *NTI,* series 1, 1975, no. 7, p. 24 and G. Artamonov, *Pravda,* 18 March 1975.

67. Regnard, pp. 113–16.

68. VIMI has been concerned recently with developing centers of analysis of information within industrial ministries. See *NTI,* series 1, 1977, no. 5, which includes some discussion of the arrangements in the electronics industry. In this article, Artamonov makes reference to the fact that in some branches leading research institutes have the status of special information centers, *spetsinformtsentry.*

69. This is one important reason, inter alia, why it may be mistaken to think that Soviet acquisitions of Western technology are always for direct use or reproduction; the monitoring of Western developments through the obtainment of examples of hardware or detailed technical data provides an input into the planning process in circumstances of limited involvement, not necessarily from choice, in the international division of labor.

70. *Transfer of United States High Technology to the Soviet Union and Soviet Bloc Nations,* p. 236.

71. *Soviet Military Power,* 3rd ed., April 1984, p. 108.

72. *Transfer of United States High Technology to the Soviet Union and Soviet Bloc Nations,* p. 242; S. H. Unger, "The Growing Threat of Government Secrecy," *Technology Review,* February/March 1982, pp. 31–39 and 84.

73. "U.S. Builds Soviet War Machine," p. 51.

74. Some types of buttons were actually on the U.S. export control list until 1966, together with wigs and false beards, caps for cap pistols, and woolen underwear! (*Columbia Law Review,* 1967, p. 823).

75. Office of Technology Assessment, *Technology and East-West Trade: An Update* (Washington, D.C.: USGPO, May 1983), p. 76.

76. Among those elected to the Supreme Soviet in 1984 were aircraft designers Antonov, Beliakov, Novozhilov, Tupolev, and Iakovlev; aeroengine designers Lotarev and Solov'ev; missile and rocket designers Chelomei, Glushko, Makeev, and Utkin; and small-arms designer Kalashnikov (*Pravda,* 7 March 1984).

77. For example, Liul'ka rejected the copying of German jet engines (*Tekhnika i Nauka*, 1983, no. 9, p. 38), and the rocket designer Isaev is reported to have opposed the copying of the V-2 rocket engine (*Novyi Mir*, 1979, no. 7, p. 216).

78. See V. M. Sheinin and V. M. Makarov, *Rol' modifikatsii v razvitii aviatsionnoi tekhniki* (Moscow: Nauka, 1982).

79. See R. D. Ward, "Soviet Practice in Designing & Procuring Military Aircraft," *Astronautics and Aeronautics*, September 1981, pp. 24–38.

80. Including the Leningrad "Svetlana," Voronezh "Elektronika," and Minsk "Integral" (*Leningradskaia Pravda*, 26 February 1984).

81. *Vestnik Akademii Nauk SSSR*, 1984, no. 2, p. 139.

82. See *Ekonomicheskaia Gazeta*, 1977, no. 25, pp. 11–14; *Pravda*, 17 March 1984.

83. *Standarty i Kachestva*, 1976, no. 5, whole issue on the MEP system.

84. *Ekonomicheskaia Gazeta*, 1977, no. 11, p. 10.

85. Estimated from *Izvestiia*, 11 July 1980; *Pravda*, 3 November 1980.

86. *Trud*, 21 May 1976.

87. *Electronics Weekly*, 7 December 1977, p. 6; E. P. Balashov and D. V. Puzankov, *Mikroprotsessory i mikroprotsessornye sistemy* (Moscow: Radio i Svyaz', 1981), p. 318; *Mikroprotsessornye komplekty integral'nykh skhem: sostav i struktura* (Moscow: Radio i Svyaz', 1982), pp. 13 and 179–82. All the early sets had only ceramic packaging, better suited to military applications.

88. *Sotsialisticheskaia Industriia*, 12 January 1984.

89. *Sotsialisticheskaia Industriia*, 3 January 1984; *Trud*, 1 January 1984.

90. *Pravda*, 17 May 1984, 20 September 1981; *Pribory i Sistemy Upravleniia*, 1983, no. 12, pp. 37–40; *Radiotekhnika*, 1983, no. 1, p. 5; *Trud*, 4 April 1984, 7 June 1984; *Kommercheskii Vestnik*, 1983, no. 24, p. 18.

91. Balashov and Puzankov, p. 292.

92. *Radiotekhnika*, 1983, no. 1, p. 11; R. Heuertz, "Soviet Microprocessors and Microcomputers," *Byte*, April 1984, pp. 351–62.

93. "NTs" probably stands for *Nauchnyi Tsentr* (scientific center); just as the "Elektronika S" series is produced by "Svetlana" and the "K" by "Kristall" in Kiev.

94. R. Wohl, "Soviet Research and Development," *Defense Science and Electronics*, vol. 2, no. 5, September 1983, pp. 11–19.

95. *Pravda*, 15 June 1984.

96. J. W. Kiser III, *Washington Post*, 14 August 1983.

97. The invention and use of this process are described in *Metallurgi—vchera i segodnia Kuibyshevskogo metallurgicheskogo zavoda imeni V. I. Lenina* (Kuibyshev: Kuibyshevskoe knizhnoe izdatel'stvo, 1979), pp. 130–31 and 243–44. Its creators received a State Prize for technology in 1973 (*Pravda*, 7 November 1973).

98. See Kiser and J. W. Kiser III, *Report on the Potential for Technology Transfer from the Soviet Union to the United States* (prepared for the Department of State and the National Science Foundation) (Washington, D.C., July 1977), pp. 29–37. Soviet titanium sponge was used in the building of the "Tornado" multiple-role combat aircraft until questions were raised in the British Parliament (*The Times* [London], 29 October 1976).

99. Kiser (1983).

100. This also applies to Western techniques of management when applied in the Soviet economy; see the author's observations on this question in R. Amann and J. M. Cooper (eds.), *Industrial Innovation in the Soviet Union* (New Haven and London: Yale University Press, 1982), pp. 506–7.

Soviet Trade in Agricultural Commodities and Technology

Anton F. Malish

AT FIRST glance, a case study of Soviet-Western trade in agricultural products and related technology would seem remarkably out of place in the context of trade and technology transfers in sectors usually thought more sophisticated such as energy, computers, weaponry, and automobile production. Yet only two commodities, wheat and corn, exported from the United States to the USSR, routinely account for more than half of the value of all trade between the two countries. In 1978 and 1979, a "bumper" and an average year for Soviet domestic agricultural output, agricultural commodities alone accounted for more than one-quarter of all Soviet imports. In 1979, the grain tonnages moving from U.S. ports to the USSR would have required three average-sized ships every two days. In the 1978–79 grain marketing year, the United States was supplying nearly three-quarters of Soviet grain imports and about 5 percent of its domestic grain consumption. Although the U.S.-USSR Long-term Grain Supply Agreement of 1975 (LTA) imposed a treaty-equivalent obligation on the United States not to interfere with up to 8 million tons of the USSR's grain import requirements, this kind of concentration invited the manipulation of such trade for foreign policy ends (in the United States, it also built a constituency against such efforts), and both the United States and the USSR have made such attempts. Thus, when faced with the Soviet invasion of Afghanistan, which President Carter called the "most dangerous act of international aggression since World War II," he chose an embargo on most agricultural exports to the USSR as his most potent response. In turn, Soviet grain-buying practices during 1983 suggested that they were using trade to enhance their leverage during the negotiations on the second LTA.

Anton F. Malish is Chief, East Europe-USSR Branch, International Economics Division, Economic Research Service, U.S. Department of Agriculture. The views expressed are those of the author and not necessarily those of USDA. Sandra Josephson and Carolyn Duff compiled the tables covering Soviet trade in agricultural technology and provided other research assistance.

Although discussions of Soviet agricultural trade naturally tend to focus on grain trade and specifically on USSR grain imports from the United States, this trade has been a consistent feature only since 1972. In contrast, the USSR has been, almost from the beginnings of the Soviet state, an important recipient of agricultural technology. Lenin is quoted as saying that "of all the forms of [American] aid, the aid to our agriculture and improvement of its technical methods is the most important and valuable for us." And later, during the 1960s and 1970s for example, the Soviets turned to Western sources to upgrade availabilities of mineral fertilizers, particularly phosphates. The expansion of their poultry industry and large-scale cattle fattening complexes seem based on U.S. prototypes, and their imports of insecticides and herbicides include Western-developed compounds.

Nonetheless, the Soviet leadership viewed its always-smoldering consumer discontent over food supplies and its reliance on imported grain as a weakness with strategic implications. Beginning in 1980, they began to formulate a "Food Program" as a long-term solution. Basically a package of institutional changes intended to make agriculture more efficient by tightening the links between the farms and the inputs and distribution sectors, it is intended to be in effect through the remainder of the decade. Its aim is to secure quality foodstuffs for the population "without any interruptions" and with the "greatest possible self-sufficiency."[1]

A successful Food Program could alter the composition of Soviet imports in ways besides diminishing the demand for imported grain. If its less-costly management changes work, it would seem essential to restructure investment in the agro-industrial complex, particularly in the marketing and distribution areas, and in providing agriculture with more and better inputs. Imports of agricultural technology embodied in machinery, insecticides, herbicides, the techniques and components for their manufacture, hybrids, and breeding stock could increase in importance.

There is some evidence that the composition of Soviet imports is already changing. A very preliminary examination of Soviet statistics—which probably captures only *a minimum* of embodied technology (and at best only a part of the unembodied technology, such as the cost of seminars, purchased production licenses, design assistance, etc.)—shows that Soviet imports of "agricultural technology" tripled between 1975 and 1983, while the much larger imports of agricultural commodities "merely" doubled.

The U.S. experience has been that the Soviets are especially interested in obtaining the results of research in genetic engineering, remote sensing, swine hybridization, poultry breeding, and soil mechanics. They have been anxious to learn more about the use of soybean meal in animal rations, the use of soy isolates as meat extenders, and a wide range of technologies dealing with cultivation and soil conservation, veterinary medicine and instruments, mechanized cultivation and harvesting of row crops, plant protectants and growth regulators, and automatic control systems for meat-packing plants and dairies. While the United States is generally regarded as the leader in agricultural technology, with few exceptions (such as superphosphoric acid), the kinds of technology that would be attractive to the Soviets are widely available.

The most important long-run influence on U.S.-Soviet agricultural trade seems to be Soviet domestic economic policies, and specifically a Soviet decision to rapidly increase livestock numbers and animal product consumption. This expansion was linked to an anticipated rapid growth in domestic feed supplies, the erratic nature of which then proved insufficient to sustain a rapidly increasing animal inventory. This underlying feed/livestock relationship is expected to remain the primary force driving U.S. exports to the USSR in the immediate future. Yet, the natural fit between the United States as the world leader in agricultural technology, on one hand, and the USSR's ambitious plans to better supply its citizenry with high-quality foodstuffs, on the other, suggests a mutuality of economic interests reaching beyond agricultural commodity trade. Whatever the prospects for trade in other sectors, U.S.-USSR trade in agricultural technology is likely to expand.

This chapter surveys Soviet agricultural technology, and patterns in USSR trade in agricultural commodities and technology. It primarily examines Soviet imports, and pays close attention to those areas of agricultural technology where the United States could be an important supplier. Finally it examines the policy implications of such trade for both countries.

Soviet Agricultural Technology

One way to judge the potential for U.S.-Soviet trade in agricultural commodities and technology is to briefly review selected indicators of agricultural performance.

Four years of poor harvests lead one to forget that the USSR is a major agricultural nation. Even in 1980, a very poor year for Soviet domestic production, the USSR was, according to the United Nations Food and Agricultural Organization (FAO), the world's largest producer of wheat, barley, oats, and rye. Among non-grain crops, it was the largest producer of sunflower seeds, sugar beets, potatoes, and seed cotton. Its inventories of cattle and hogs exceeded those of the United States. It was the world's largest producer of cow's milk, mutton, and lamb; the second largest producer of beef and veal; and the third largest producer of pork and poultry.

While USSR statistics would indicate that Soviet citizens are among the world's best-fed people when total available calories are counted, the Soviets have long been without the high-quality food products that accompany rising living standards. Shortages of meat, dairy products, and fruits and vegetables have been an increasing cause of consumer discontent. This situation became so prevalent that by 1981 General Secretary Brezhnev admitted "the problem of food is, on the economic and political level, the central problem of the whole [1981–85] 5-Year Plan." Under Brezhnev's successors, high priority has remained on raising the standard of living of the Soviet people.[2]

The Soviets attributed their food problems to four main causes. First, Soviet money incomes increased while food prices remained stable. The result was a greater consumption demand than the distribution system could handle. Second, the outflow of agricultural workers to urban areas exceeded productivity gains on the farms and reduced the resource base. Third, the remaining rural inhabitants increased purchases of food from the state trade network rather than relying on their own production. Finally, the general inefficiencies in the agro-industrial complex, particularly the waste and losses occurring in the procurement, storage, transportation, processing, and trade of agricultural products, prevented distribution of what was produced to the dinner table.

On the production side, mechanization of Soviet agriculture remains at an insufficient level, and existing machines are of a low technical standard and are poorly utilized. The situation for mineral fertilizers and herbicides is similar.

The Technology Gap between U.S. and Soviet Agriculture

Although institutional factors are at the core of many Soviet agricultural problems, problems such as low-quality machinery, insufficient fertilizers and plant protectants, and pressures on the distribution system, probably stem from a technological cause. One study showed the fixed assets per Soviet farmer at 6,200 rubles (about $8,600 at official exchange rates) while the fixed assets per industrial worker were reported at 11,100 rubles ($15,400). Similar U.S. figures would put the value of fixed capital per farm employee at $36,600 contrasted to $23,300 per worker in manufacturing. In reporting these data, USDA noted it was significant that a Soviet farmer has only about half the plant and equipment available to an industrial worker while a U.S. farmer has about 60 percent more, even if the data could not be compared with precision.[3] In essence, Soviet agricultural machinery is spread over a larger area and has to work harder with the probable result that it cannot perform planting and harvesting tasks with the timeliness enjoyed in the United States. Yet, the shorter Soviet growing season puts a higher premium on meeting optimum seeding and harvesting dates.

One of the most striking differences between U.S. and Soviet agriculture is the low number of trucks and roads in the USSR. The Soviet truck fleet is just 40 percent the size of ours, and in terms of each 1,000 economically active persons in agriculture, barely 4 percent of U.S. figures. The United States enjoys a kilometer of hard-surfaced rural road for each 45 hectares of arable land, and averages a truck per kilometer. In the USSR, the ratio for *all* roads is 314 hectares per kilometer and the truck fleet is about half as dense. This critical truck and road shortage in the USSR isolates communities and imposes an additional transportation task on the tractor fleet.

According to Soviet sources, the USSR applied 84 kilograms of fertilizer (nutrient weight) per hectare of cropland in 1980. The United States applied 117, England, 319, and West Germany, 480.[4] In the production of insecticides and herbicides, the Soviet level was but two-thirds of that in the United States.

With the exception of cotton, grown entirely on irrigated land in the USSR while much of the U.S. crop is dry-land farmed, USSR yields of principal crops during 1979–81 were generally within the range of a third to three-quarters those obtained in the United States. Livestock productivity was well below that of the United States, and despite serious efforts to improve efficiency and intensify livestock production by increasing mixed feed production, by paying greater attention to breeding, and by investing in feed-harvesting equipment, storage, and livestock facilities, the Soviets achieved little or no improvement in feeding efficiencies throughout the 1970s. Their increases in product output remained largely based on larger numbers of low-productivity animals.[5]

In the most recent definitive examination of Soviet agriculture against climatically analogous areas, D. Gale Johnson and Karen Brooks concluded that Soviet resources—land, labor, machinery (horsepower), fertilizers, and animals—produce only approximately half as much as the same bundle of resources produces in climatically similar areas of North America.[6] In other words, the Soviets could lower production costs, or alternatively, increase output by recombining existing resources, upgrading the quality of existing inputs, and carrying out agricultural tasks in a more timely manner. Put another way, the potential for technological improvements is very high.

Soviet Marketing and Distribution

The Soviet marketing and distribution system is a complex one that has come under increased scrutiny as a source of waste and losses. Soviet economists have reported serious inefficiencies at virtually each step from farm to store. V. Tikhonov, writing in the 10 December 1980 issue of *Literaturnaya gazeta*, noted that grain is hauled to state elevators that do not always have adequate storage capacity. Then, "when the procurement rush ends, at least 35–40 percent of the grain is loaded into trucks and hauled back to the state and collective farms as feed." He calculated that as many as 20 million truck trips—in a country with an acute shortage of agricultural trucks—were spent hauling grain back and forth.

A second economist, V. Tereshchenko, criticized the entire processing network in a single article: "It is no secret that some of the produce never reaches the consumer . . . Agricultural production is developing at a faster rate than the sectors which procure, process and market field and livestock unit products." According to Tereshchenko, storage and primary processing are still weak sectors lacking mechanical ventilation and refrigeration facilities. Tomatoes, in short supply in northern cities, are left to rot in the southern Ukraine for lack of packing materials.[7]

The Soviet and East European press has occasionally reported the extent of waste and losses in the marketing and distribution chain. The reports are frequently inconsistent with one another but they are always high. Potato and vegetable losses reportedly amount to 15–20 percent of annual output. A study by East German specialists put losses in CMEA countries due to spoilage in the entire production process at 30 percent of red meat, 10 percent of meat products, 20 percent of poultry, 60 percent of fish, 25 percent of eggs, 27 percent of potatoes, 38 percent of vegetables, and 18 percent of fruit, with the bulk of the losses occurring in the Soviet Union.[8]

Patterns in Agricultural Trade and Technology

The long-standing technological gap between U.S. and Soviet agriculture—only briefly touched on here—suggests a choice of strategies for increasing Soviet efficiency. They could concentrate on importing commodities while devoting their internal development resources towards other (and presumably more productive) sectors.[9] Alternatively, they could increase investment in domestic agriculture, in part relying on imported technology to overcome particularly difficult bottlenecks. Such clearly delineated options may, of course, be an overstatement, but, in any case, Soviet actions suggest they have been trying to do both, and curiously, sometimes followed courses that seemed inconsistent with their policy statements.

Documentation from the 24th Party Congress (1971) indicates that the Soviets intended to support a rapidly expanding livestock sector from domestic resources. On the one hand, the Brezhnev era saw a rapid run-up of capital investment in the agro-industrial complex (during 1971–75 investment was some two and a half times what it was in 1961–65). They had a history of promoting development by acquiring Western agricultural technology, and they banked heavily on further acquisition of input-related technologies through the 1970s. On the other hand, the erratic nature of Soviet domestic grain production compromised this strategy. Hence, when they began, Soviet grain imports were essentially unplanned, but once under way, a fortunate combination of world economic and political events made reliance on Western—mainly United States—grain production and reserves an acceptable policy.

Trends in Commodity Trade

Tables 1 and 2 at the end of this chapter show USSR trade in agricultural commodities between 1975 and 1983.[10] The rapid expansion of Soviet agricultural imports put the USSR among West Germany, Japan, and the United States as the largest importers of agricultural commodities. Its agricultural exports, on the other hand, have remained modest, about the size of those of Ireland.

USSR agricultural imports, which had been valued at $9–10 billion in the mid-1970s, began a significant increase, peaking near $21 billion in 1981 before declining to about $18 billion in 1983. In 1981, they represented 28 percent of all imports. The trends generally corresponded to domestic agricultural performance as shown in Table A.

Four commodity groups have generally accounted for 60–75 percent of Soviet agricultural imports. In 1981, grain and grain products made up 41 percent of the total; sugar, 19 percent; meat and dairy products, 9 percent; and fats and oils, 6 percent. These groups were generally responsible for the increase between 1979 and 1981; grains and sugar (in 1983) led the subsequent declines.

The increase in total agricultural imports was accompanied by an increase in the share paid-for in hard currency, from 27 percent in 1970, to 66 percent in 1980.[11] Grains, refined sugar, and oilseed and oilseed meals are typically commodities requiring payment in hard currency.

Grain Trade and Policy. For most of its history, the USSR has been a net exporter of grain. In setting his goal of 16 million tons of meat by 1965, First Secretary Khrushchev anticipated domestic grain production gains of from 38 to 50 percent above the 1959 level thus reaching 164–180 million tons by 1965. During the 1970s, this policy, by then involving conversion of the Soviet livestock economy to an industrial basis, showed itself in a 20-percent increase in total animal units (i.e., all livestock and poultry inventories converted to cow equivalents on the basis of feed requirements). But Soviet grain production did not keep up with the expansion. Both the 1972 and 1975 crops (and especially the latter), even when supplemented by record grain imports, proved insufficient to maintain animal herds, particularly hogs. The 1975 crop, which led to the 20-percent reduction in hog inventories, totalled only 140 million tons, nearly a third less than the previous year's outturn. Hog inventories were so reduced that it took 4 years just to recover to 1975 levels.

Table A

USSR Production and Import Trends, Selected Commodities, 1978–1983

Item	1978	1979	1980	1981	1982	1983
Production:						
Gross agricultural output (billions of 1973 rubles)	128.3	124.3	122.0	120.7	126.0	133.8
Grains (MMT)	237.0	179.0	189.0	158[a]	180–185[b]	190–195[c]
Meat and fat (MMT)	15.5	15.3	15.1	15.2	15.4	16.0
Sugar beets (MMT)	93.5	76.2	81.0	60.8	71.5	82.0
Oilseeds (MMT)	11.0	10.6	10.4	10.6	11.2	11.1
Imports:						
Total agricultural commodities (billions of current rubles)	7.0	8.8	11.2	15.0	14.0	13.3
Grain and products (MMT)	23.6	28.4	31.4	45.7	40.3	33.0
Meat (TMT)	184.0	611.0	821.0	980.0	939.0	985.0
Sugar (raw equivalent, MMT)	4.0	4.1	5.0	5.2	7.4	6.0[b]
Oilseeds, meal (SBE, MMT)	.8	1.5	1.4	1.7	2.8	3.9[b]

[a] Unofficial USSR sources. [b] Author's estimate. [c] Author's estimate.
MMT = million metric tons; TMT = thousand metric tons; SBE = soybean meal equivalent.
SOURCES: Adapted from official USSR reports. 1983 partly estimated.

Quite clearly, this kind of distress slaughter if periodically repeated would virtually guarantee that Soviet diets would remain deficient in high quality foodstuffs. Of course, the policy of maintaining (at least nominally) state-store retail prices for food staples and shortages of consumer goods in general intensified meat availability as an indication of Soviet well-being.

Within the 1972–75 period, Soviet policy makers had experienced two harvest shortfalls when they needed more than 20 million tons of grain from the world market. The Soviet desire to improve standards of living, an unreliable domestic feed base, an easing of East-West tensions, Western expectations of a growing Soviet market, and a new attractiveness for Soviet oil, gold, and arms exports formed a powerful combination that drew the USSR to the world grain market.

Despite U.S. government supply-related interventions in 1974 and

1975 to restrict Soviet access to U.S. grains, the USSR came to rely on the United States as a guarantor of its livestock herds. The relationship was cemented in the U.S.-USSR Long-term Grain Supply Agreement of 1975 (LTA), which obligated the USSR to purchase at least 6 million tons of wheat and corn from the United States during each October–September period for 5 years beginning in 1976. The Soviets could buy up to 8 million tons without further consultations, and the United States could offer more, or the Soviets could request more, in semi-annual consultations provided for under the agreement. By 1979, the United States supplied nearly 70 percent of Soviet grain imports. In turn, U.S.-USSR trade consisted primarily of the flow of U.S. agricultural commodities from the United States to the USSR (Table 3). In 1979, for example, agricultural commodities accounted for almost 80 percent of all U.S. exports to the Soviet Union, about 96 percent of which was grain and soybeans.

Overall, the USSR came to rely more on the United States to fill its agricultural import needs than the United States relied on the Soviet Union as a market for U.S. agricultural exports. The United States sold as much as 8 percent of its agricultural exports to the USSR only once (in 1979) while the USSR bought as much as 22 percent of its agricultural imports from the United States. This trend, shown in Table B, might have continued had it not been disrupted by the 1980 embargo.

The 1980 Embargo

The existence of a grain-supply treaty obligation, a recognition on the part of many in both the Administration and in Congress that an exercise of U.S. grain market power would probably be ineffective, and an outstanding offer of 25 million tons of grain for the fourth agreement year, provided a strong counter argument to those who saw the grain trade as a diplomatic lever to be exploited for foreign policy objectives. Yet the notion persisted that such sales could be used to force modifications in Soviet behavior. Accordingly, when the Administration sought a response to the Soviet invasion of Afghanistan, a grain embargo was an option high on the list.

Under the regulations adopted to enforce the embargo, those commodities that could "contribute significantly" to the Soviet feed/livestock economy were denied validated export licenses. Products in this category included wheat and corn (except for the 8 million tons specified in the LTA), soybeans, soybean meal, mixed feeds, and end-products such as meat. Commodities that might substitute for grains or livestock output under certain circumstances—tallow, hides and skins, etc.—were placed under a case-by-case licensing review. Those products not related to the feed/livestock economy, such as fruits, nuts (except peanuts) and

Table B

Total Soviet Agricultural Imports and U.S. Share
(millions of U.S. dollars)

| | | U.S. share | |
Year	USSR agricultural imports[a]	Dollars	Percent
1975	9,146	1,170.3	13
1976	9,331	1,604.8	17
1977	9,131	1,052.8	12
1978	10,241	1,765.1	17
1979	13,331	3,000.1	22
1980	17,232	1,137.8	7
1981	20,904	1,684.7	8
1982	19,327	1,850.3[b]	10
1983	18,016	1,457.0[b]	8

[a] Converted from official Soviet exchange rates prevailing in each year.
[b] Not adjusted for transshipments.
SOURCE: Adapted from official U.S. and USSR statistics.

berries, could be shipped but would be closely monitored. In February, U.S. exports of superphosphoric acid and phosphates to the USSR were also embargoed.

The embargo denied the Soviets about 12 million tons of U.S. grain during the 1979/80 July–June marketing year. The Soviets were expected to import 2–2.5 million tons of soybeans and soybean meal from the United States during the 1979/80 soybean marketing year; the embargo left the Soviets about 1.2–1.7 million tons short. By searching the world for additional supplies and paying higher prices, the Soviets were able to make up about half the grain shortfall and probably all the soybean and soybean meal from non-U.S. markets. By the 1980/81 marketing year, the Soviets were importing a record amount of grain despite the embargo. The U.S. share, which had been running at about 70 percent, fell to 50 percent in 1979/80 and to about a quarter in 1980/81 as shown in Table C.

U.S. policymakers indicated that the USSR would suffer the entire loss of the 17 million tons (i.e., the difference between the 25 offered and the 8 covered by the agreement) of grain caught by the embargo. The Vice President stated that this grain "ordered by the Soviet Union will not be delivered" and its loss would extract a "heavy price" for the Afghanistan aggression.[12] White House officials were forecasting a 20-percent decline in Soviet meat production (about 3 million tons).[13] Had Soviet per capita meat consumption fallen by 20 percent it would have dropped to about that of Libya. One official even alluded to the possibility of a bread shortage, though, in fact, a threat to bread supplies was not even a remote possibility.

These predictions seemed to overlook the availability of Soviet grain stocks (while their exact level is not known in the West, it would be safe to think that the bumper crop of 1978 provided a carryover that could be used to maintain animal feeding) and to assume that other grain exporting nations would not make up for the denied U.S. grain. This second assumption may have been reinforced by a series of meetings held at the USDA Under-Secretary level. Under-Secretary of Agriculture Dale Hathaway testified that a meeting with other exporting nations on 12 January 1980 resulted in "general agreement among the export representatives that *their governments* [emphasis added] would not directly or indirectly replace the grain that would have been shipped to the Soviet Union prior to the actions announced by President Carter." With respect

Table C

USSR Imports of Wheat and Coarse Grains 1978/79–1982/83 July–June Marketing Years

Source	78/79	79/80	80/81	81/82	82/83
	(Million Metric Tons)				
U.S.	11.2	15.2	8.0	15.4	6.2
Canada	2.1	3.4	6.8	9.2	8.9
Australia	.1	4.0	2.9	2.5	1.0
Argentina	1.4	5.1	11.2	13.3	9.6
EC	.2	.9	1.5	2.4	3.8
Others	.1	1.8	3.6	2.2	2.5
Miscellaneous grain (all sources)	.5	.6	.8	1.0	.5
Total	15.6	31.0	34.8	46.0	32.5
	(Market Share in Percent)				
U.S.	72	49	23	34	19
Canada	13	11	20	20	27
Australia	1	13	8	5	3
Argentina	9	16	32	29	29
EC	1	3	4	5	12
Others	1	6	11	5	8
Miscellaneous grain (all sources)	3	2	2	2	2
Total	100	100	100	100	100

Source: Compiled from USDA, Foreign Agriculture Circular, FG-20-83, 13 July 1983

to oilseeds, Hathaway noted the United States had "received assurances" from Brazil and Argentina that they "would not seek commercial advantage."[14]

As Under-Secretary Hathaway also noted in his statement, however, the Argentine position was that it would not "alter artificially the current demands of the different markets." In other words, private grain traders in Argentina were left to make whatever sales they wanted, and they were quickly moving toward doubling their grain sales to the USSR. In March, Canada announced a 2-million-ton sale of grain to the USSR which it indicated was in keeping with its traditional level of sales and therefore, despite the unusually large size of the sale, was consistent with Canadian support of U.S. policy. The Soviets, of course, were also seeking grain from a variety of non-traditional grain exporters including Sweden, Brazil, Thailand, and others.

The Administration undercut its embargo with some actions of its own. On 29 April 1980 the United States announced that it would honor its commitment to supply 6–8 million tons of grain in the fifth grain agreement year beginning 1 October 1980. Under Article II of the agreement, it could have attempted to negotiate a release of its treaty-equivalent obligation, although it is unlikely that the Soviet Union would have accepted such a proposal. On 20 June U.S. grain companies, which had been asked to refrain from selling third-country grain to the USSR, were told that they could now do so consistent with the policies of those third countries. The announcement in October 1980 of a new U.S. long-term grain supply agreement with China was almost certain to have weakened further Australian and Canadian resolve to participate in the embargo.[15]

By the fall of 1980, the embargo had become an election year issue and U.S. domestic support for it was fading. Among its last acts, the Carter Administration extended it into 1981 as a "vigorous and far-reaching action" in defense of U.S. national interests.

On 24 April 1981, President Reagan announced his decision to terminate the embargo on agricultural commodities and phosphates. He announced that his decision followed a full study that took into account national security, foreign policy, and agricultural needs.

The Aftermath

The Soviets reacted to the embargo with indications that they considered their reliance on the United States for feedgrains a weakness with strategic implications. Statements indicate that the Food Program, with its emphasis on improving management and eliminating waste and losses, was in part a result of the embargo. Internationally, they moved to secure their new sources of supply with new agreements—with Argentina in 1980, with Canada (May 1981) and Brazil (July 1981)—that committed them to purchase about 10 million tons annually from U.S. competitors. Coupled with the expansion of competitors' grain-exporting capacity, U.S. agribusiness interests feared that the United States had been reduced to a residual supplier role and that in some years, it might export no grain at all to the USSR.[16]

Within the USSR, heavier-than-normal slaughter of livestock (primarily of hogs) occurred in the first two months of 1980. Both cattle and hogs were slaughtered at lighter weights during 1980. But overall, the Soviets decided to preserve animal numbers, and meat output fell. Meat imports significantly increased. Disturbances related to food shortages of commodities that were the target of the embargo were reported in some Soviet cities. USDA research characterized the embargo as a "troublesome element" for Soviet planners and the impact as "more than trivial."[17] But these events cannot be isolated from the effects of the Soviet Union's poor 1979 and 1980 harvests, and the ability of the Soviets to import more grain in 1980 than in the previous year suggests the domestic problems of Soviet agriculture greatly outweighed the impact of the embargo.

Soviet data do not permit an assessment of the embargo's economic costs, although some must have been associated with the higher prices of Argentinian grain in the spring of 1980, disrupted shipping schedules, and port congestion in the USSR. The Soviet press treated the embargo primarily in terms of its damage to the U.S. economy; however, a few glimpses suggest it led to a more costly restructuring of crop and livestock production. For example, the director of the USSR's crop department in the Ministry of Agriculture admitted:

> This country takes into account the principles of the worldwide division of labor. In some cases it's more profitable for us to ship grain from America to our Far Eastern regions than to transport grain across this huge country. It is also cheaper for us to buy a certain amount of soybeans and corn from other countries since our climatic conditions are not as favorable to these crops as that of the United States, for example. But if necessary we are quite capable of growing these products ourselves, although it will be more expensive.[18]

Within the United States, a series of actions severely compromised the possibility of future use of grain embargoes. The Agriculture and Food Act of 1981 (22 December 1981) included an embargo protection provision that would trigger 100-percent parity payments to U.S. producers of selectively-embargoed agricultural commodities to markets that represented 3 percent or more of U.S. exports of the embargoed commodity. Parity payments of 100 percent on grains would be prohibitively expensive; by one estimate, depending on grain prices, it could run as much as $50 billion in Federal expenditures. Soviet imports of only about 2 million tons of either wheat or corn each year would set the trigger for these domestic payments. Since a complete embargo would be needed to avoid the embargo protection provisions, agricultural interests sought for and obtained a Presidential commitment (22 March 1982) that a complete embargo would be used only in extreme situations threatening U.S. national security and only if cooperation with other nations could be obtained. In January 1983, the President signed the Futures Trading Act of 1982 which contained a "contract sanctity" provision stipulating that if an embargo was declared, the President could not cancel shipments of grain or other commodities that have been privately contracted until 270 days have passed. The restriction would be automatically suspended only if the President declares a national emergency or if the Congress declares war. This combination of domestic legislation and Administration commitments, according to Marshall Goldman, meant "that we have now been denied what has probably been the most effective tool in our nonmilitary arsenal."[19]

In terms of U.S. economic costs, an investigation by the United States International Trade Commission put the minimum cost to the U.S. government of the 1980 embargo at $475 million, the loss incurred by the Commodity Credit Corporation (CCC) in the purchase and resale of commodity contracts—primarily grains and soybeans, but also frozen whole broilers—interrupted by the embargo.[20] The Schnittker Associates brief (see note 16) put the cost of the embargo measured in lost output of goods and services economy-wide at $11.4 billion. The long-run impact of the embargo is said to include depressed grain prices, a declining share of world grain trade held by the United States, and exceedingly high U.S. and world grain stock levels.

The flexibility associated with U.S. grain-exporting institutions and transportation systems meant that some portion of future Soviet grain imports would probably still originate in the United States. Nevertheless, projections of future increases in Soviet grain production and gradually decreasing import needs held the possibility that the United States—as a residual supplier that the USSR was eager to characterize as "unreliable"—might supply no grain at all in some future years. This concern led the United States to approach the USSR for a second long-term grain agreement (the 1975 LTA had been extended twice for additional one-year periods). That agreement was signed in August 1983. While similar to the 1975 agreement, it raised the Soviet annual minimum commitment to 4 million tons each of corn and wheat, plus an additional million tons of either grain. In addition, it provided for a Soviet option of importing either soybeans or soybean meal which could be counted against the additional million tons at a ratio of two tons of grain to one of soybeans or meal. The Soviets could buy up to 12 million tons of grain without consultations. Other changes included eliminating the "escape clause" article that had permitted the United States to ship less than the minimum in the event of a massive U.S. crop failure. That article had never been used in the 7-year history of the original agreement. An article providing for the use of U.S. government "good offices" to be "of assistance" on questions of grain quality was added. Like the old agreement, the transactions would be with private U.S. firms at the market price prevailing and in accordance with normal commercial terms. The agreement is to be in force until 1988.

Other Products

The USSR has been the world's largest sugar importer. Although the Soviets have imported raw sugar primarily from Cuba, they have increasingly supplemented this trade with smaller, but still significant tonnages from Brazil, the Philippines, Thailand, and other countries. Soviet imports of refined sugar also have increased dramatically, primarily from the European Community.

The sharp increases in meat imports in 1981–1983 similarly placed the USSR as the world's leading meat importer. Principal suppliers of red meat have been Romania, Argentina, New Zealand, and Australia. Leading suppliers of poultry meat were Hungary, Brazil, and Bulgaria.

In the mid-1970s, the Soviets relied on Brazil for their oilseed imports. The Soviets would probably have preferred to maintain this relationship, but because of concerns about possible swine fever contamination in Brazilian soybeans (nearly all Soviet imports of oilseeds are soybeans) they shifted purchases to the United States. By 1978 and 1979, the U.S. share of these imports was 95 percent or more. The 1980 embargo disrupted this trade; Soviet purchases switched back to Brazil, and Argentina became a new supplier. The United States regained its principal supplier status in 1982, but at only a 43-percent market share.

For some time, experts had been predicting that soybean meal should have been among the fastest growing agricultural commodities imported into the Soviet Union as it could provide a quick improvement in the long-recognized protein imbalance in livestock rations. This trade proved slow in developing, however, possibly because soybean meal is more difficult to handle than grain, possibly because those at working levels in USSR feed mills and on farms have little experience with the commodity, or possibly because the Soviets were attempting to deal with the protein shortage through an expansion of other protein sources including output from its microbiological industry. In any case, the U.S. embargo resulted in a higher Soviet priority for improving feeding efficiency and reducing the "overconsumption" of grain in rations. These imports finally began to develop rapidly in 1980, with Brazil and the Netherlands as the principal suppliers. Despite marketing efforts by U.S. firms, the United States has not participated in the expansion of

Soviet soybean meal imports. The Soviet reason often given has been that the "unreliability" of the United States as a trading partner discouraged USSR interest.

Unlike agricultural imports, Soviet agricultural exports have remained valued at about $2.7 billion since 1977 with little year-to-year variation (although 1983 was lower). Natural fibers (virtually all cotton) routinely made up about half the value. In 1982 and 1983, however, problems with the quality of the Soviet crop interfered with these exports. The USSR, one of the three leading world producers, had to purchase cotton, including some from Australia and the United States, to meet part of its export commitments.

The Soviets also report exports of grain and grain products, usually valued at between $400 and $700 million. Because of the USSR's foreign trade accounting, some of this trade includes purchases made in third countries for delivery to client states.

Trade in Agricultural Technology

The Soviets have a long history of relying on imported technology to expand their production of agricultural products. During the late 1920s and early 1930s, agricultural machinery and parts reached up to 40 percent of all USSR imports from the United States. In 1931, two-thirds of all U.S. exports of agricultural equipment went to the USSR.[21] This trade ended as the Soviets developed their own manufacturing capability, a capability based on the assistance and equipment that U.S. firms had provided to establish the first Soviet tractor plants in Chelyabinsk, Kharkov, and Volgograd.[22] The new Soviet state also benefited from technical assistance from American specialists demonstrating the advantages of large-scale mechanized farming techniques.[23] Before World War II, meat packing plants in major Soviet cities were built with attention paid to previous U.S. experience.

During the mid-1950s, a Soviet delegation returning from a two-month visit to the United States and Canada published a virtual encyclopedia covering what they had learned about crop and livestock raising techniques, farm equipment design and specifications, equipment applications, and possible adaptations to be incorporated in Soviet agriculture. At that time, the Soviets were especially impressed with trailing equipment that could be operated by the tractor driver, self-feeders for hogs and cattle, manure-removing equipment for stock barns, the use of specialized farms and installations for seed production, and feedlot operations.[24]

Today, Soviet interest in obtaining Western agricultural technology is probably as great as it was in the 1950s if not greater. In remarks made in Canada during his May 1983 visit, Mikhail Gorbachev (the Politburo member with responsibility for agriculture) noted a role for "trade and economic and scientific and technological relations with other countries" in implementing the Food Program. In a speech at the November 1982 meeting of the U.S.-USSR Trade and Economic Council, N. S. Patolichev, the Soviet Foreign Trade Minister, virtually invited U.S. firms to participate in the USSR's Food Program, particularly in food processing, farm machinery engineering, and equipment for processing and storing agricultural products.

An assessment of the amount of trade in agricultural technology from either Western or Soviet statistics is especially difficult. However, on the basis of a preliminary examination of Soviet trade statistics covering embodied agricultural technology (Tables 4 and 5), this trade has been growing much more rapidly than trade in commodities. In those tables, "agricultural technology" was defined very broadly as *including* agricultural machinery, tractors and spare parts, mineral fertilizers, agrochemicals, and equipment for their manufacture. Also included was equipment for the food processing industry. This definition, incidentally, is very much broader than that, for example, which would be used to identify "high technology" imports. Data were excluded in categories where the bulk of the trade reported was likely "industrial" in nature (for example, while the category "equipment for the fur and skin industry" probably included some trade in embodied agricultural technology, that category was excluded because it also covered shoe manufacturing plants where most of the trade was likely to occur). Thus, on the basis of this statistical search, which probably captured *a minimum* of embodied technology, and at best only a part of unembodied technology, Soviet imports of "agricultural technology" tripled between 1975 and 1983; increasing from $970 million to $3.1 billion.[25] This trade has also tended to be better balanced than trade in agricultural commodities. Soviet imports of agricultural commodities, on the other hand, were much larger, but "merely" doubled, from $9.1 billion in 1975 to $19.3 billion in 1982. Thus, Soviet data would suggest that imports of agricultural technology trade are about 10–15 percent of Soviet imports of agricultural commodities (by value) with much of it unreported. Soviet exports of agricultural technology, with the same data limitations noted above, have increased so that in 1983 they exceeded the level of USSR agricultural exports.

This statistical approach would have been even more useful if the sources of the agricultural technology trade could have been better identified. Unfortunately, Soviet trade data are not so precise. In general, however, by far the bulk of USSR imports of agricultural machinery originated from CMEA member countries. On the other hand, significant portions of insecticides and herbicides came from non-CMEA sources as did imports of equipment of the food processing industry. In 1981, about 24 percent (by weight) of pesticides and about the same percentage (by value) of food processing equipment came from outside the CMEA group.

Data from the U.S. Department of Commerce suggest that the U.S. share of this trade in agricultural technology could be in the range of 10–15 percent in each of the last two years. U.S. exports to the USSR of most agricultural inputs and technology were relatively modest, except for fertilizer raw materials, of which superphosphoric acid was by far the most important.

In the last five years, the United States exported more than $750 million worth of fertilizers to the USSR, most of it in the last two years. Over the five-year period, the United States exported to the USSR $13 million in farm machinery and parts, $7 million in meat, poultry, and other food processing and food service machinery, and $4 million in pesticides.

Tractors, Agricultural Machinery, and Trucks

In 1982, the USSR tractor and agricultural machinery industry turned out 550,000 tractors, 110,000 grain harvesters, 10,000 cotton harvesters, and "hundreds of thousands" of other types of machinery and implements. These production levels would exceed the combined totals of the United States, Great Britain, and France. Soviet demands for agricultural machinery are largely fulfilled by domestic production, and in some specialized applications (minitractors, tractors for vineyards) by long-term cooperative production and trade arrangements within CMEA.[26] Yet, the constant theme of machinery breakdowns, spare parts shortages, and high scrappage rates indicates that the Soviet machinery pool is still insufficient to cope with peak planting and harvesting tasks. A deputy minister of the USSR Ministry of Tractor and Agricultural Machine Building reported that "the technical level of many types of agricultural equipment does not always meet the growing demand and, in a number of cases, is inferior to those produced abroad." Ample evidence suggests the Soviets are seeking Western technology to overcome these shortcomings.

During the Tenth Five-Year Plan (1976–1980) Western industrialized countries provided the Soviet agricultural machine building industry with equipment for manufacturing spray atomizers, equipment for manufacturing industrial tractors, gas welding machines, and items from metal powder, among others.[27]

High-horsepower tracklaying tractors and parts have been an important U.S.-USSR trade item, amounting to nearly $300 million in U.S. exports between 1980 and 1983. These tractors, however, are probably not intended for agricultural uses. The few instances of imports of agricultural tractors (some purchased from displays in trade shows) are likely used for engineering studies in the USSR. While some features might be incorporated in later Soviet production models, most experts would not see tractors or agricultural machinery as candidates for "reverse engineering." In the USSR, the kinds of skills needed to convert machinery back into production specifications and blueprints are probably reserved for high-priority projects where the possibility of obtaining either large quantities of the desired import, or design assistance, production licenses, and turnkey factories for its manufacture, is remote. In the case of civilian trucks, tractors, and agricultural machinery (and indeed for most agricultural technology items), Soviet trade organizations and Western firms have arranged such transfers. Interestingly too, the literature and discussions with U.S. businessmen do not suggest Western exporters of agricultural machinery or technology are particularly concerned about facing Soviet versions of their own equipment on the export market. The USSR's large internal demand apparently makes export competition in agricultural machinery an unlikely prospect.

The Food Program envisages the design and production of some 600 types of tractors and agricultural machines of "up-to-date requirements as to reliability and service life." The Soviets report efforts with Finnish firms for cooperative production of certain harvesters, seed drills, trailers, and other types of machinery. The Soviets also evidence interest in U.S. technology for the production of agricultural field equipment, such as grain harvesters, and in certain specialized equipment such as potato diggers, beet thinners, and fruit harvesters.

One would also think that the Soviets would want a modern spare parts/maintenance program for their machinery, although the development of a U.S.-modeled computerized parts-inventory control system would probably require a significant redirection of resources (and could be one of the areas in agricultural technology where significant "dual use" military capability could exist).

Agricultural Chemicals

Khrushchev's plans for overtaking the United States in per-capita meat consumption required a rapid expansion of the USSR chemical industry to support grain and feed crops. This expansion was seen as "a way to protect Soviet agriculture from the vagaries of nature," and in the late 1950s and early 1960s the USSR began to purchase a "sizable number" of chemical plants and technology from the West.[28]

Again, during the 1970s, the USSR undertook a major expansion of its manufacturing capability for fertilizer raw materials. Central to this expansion was the construction of about 40 large ammonia production facilities, which by 1982 would have nearly doubled Soviet ammonia production capacity. The Soviets contracted to buy at least 31 of these plants from Western firms. The technology, machinery and equipment, design services, etc., would be paid for, in part, by the export of ammonia.

The largest of these barter agreements was the 1973 twenty-year, $20 billion agreement with Occidental Petroleum.[29] In brief, Occidental agreed to build ammonia plants in the USSR, to build a 1,600-mile ammonia pipeline from Togliatti to Odessa (and related port facilities), to purchase ammonia, urea, and potash during a 20-year period beginning in 1978, and to export superphosphoric acid to the USSR. These exports of superphosphoric acid were to reach 1 million tons in 1980 and continue at that level until 1997.

The Soviets have admitted to a considerable reliance on imported technology for the manufacture of mineral fertilizers. During the Tenth Five-Year Plan, imported equipment was used for manufacturing 65 percent of nitrogen fertilizers, including 70 percent of ammonia, 74 percent of carbamide (urea), and 54 percent of sulphuric acid. The Occidental-built pipeline would not only deliver ammonia for export but would deliver highly concentrated sulphuric fertilizers for direct soil application to some 13 grain-growing regions. The nutrient equivalent of one million tons of superphosphoric acid, according to Soviet sources, would provide them an additional 5 million tons of grain (7 million tons by some Western analyses). In short, the yield expansion in grain production under the Food Program was quite clearly linked to Soviet fertilizer production and its related imported components and raw materials.[30]

The Soviets planned to use the superphosphoric acid as a raw material in seven plants especially designed for the production of liquid fertilizers. In addition, superphosphoric acid is considered an ideal raw material for production of phosphate animal feed supplements.

The United States is the only large-volume exporter of superphosphoric acid. This USSR-Occidental countertrade was just developing (it had reached 543,000 short tons valued at $93 million in 1979) when, in February 1980, phosphate materials were included in the embargo—the only agricultural input to be so included. The reason given was that the continued sales of phosphates, while commodities for the feed/livestock economy were halted, would have been incompatible with the objectives of the embargo.

Indeed, the denial of the superphosphoric acid may have been as important in its effect on the Soviet feed/livestock economy as the denial of grain. If the embargo denied the USSR a million tons of superphosphoric acid, it probably cost the USSR about as much domestic grain production as the trade embargo cost them in imports. But while the Soviets were able to find alternative sources for much of the denied grain, they had fewer alternative sources of superphosphoric acid. The option of converting the chemical plants to use more widely available merchant-grade phosphoric acid would have been time-consuming, and it would have required a reversion to a lower level of technology.

The embargo on phosphates ended on 24 April 1981. Since then, superphosphoric acid has become the leading non-agricultural U.S. export to the USSR, with shipments valued at $268 million in 1982 and $215 million in 1983.

The massive infusion of imported technology was a contributing factor to the tripling of Soviet fertilizer output between 1965 and 1980. Nevertheless, production in 1980, at 104 million tons (standard units), was well under the 143 million tons originally planned. Production was to reach 150–155 million tons in 1985, but output was still only 109 million tons in 1981—suggesting that the Eleventh Five-Year Plan target is compromised. Despite reported consumption of phosphorus fertilizers at levels comparable with those in the United States, phosphorus fertilizer production in the USSR is still far short of supplying Soviet needs. And, of course, Soviet "consumption" data actually reflect a "delivered to agriculture" concept that masks numerous opportunities for waste and losses before application to crops.

The Soviets report some 100 million hectares being phosphorus deficient. Significant phosphorus deficiencies exist in the Volga regions, the North Caucasus, both important grain areas, and in the Far East. Soils in these regions contain only about 5 milligrams of phosphorus per 100 grams of soil, while high-yielding crops require 20 or more milligrams. In addition, low phosphorus levels reduce the effectiveness of nitrogen and potassium fertilizers.[31] These kinds of data suggest the potential for further arrangements regarding fertilizer manufacturing processes and technology is not yet exhausted.

A further opportunity for Western technology might also be in improving the crop response when fertilizer is applied. U.S. firms have developed soil supplements to enhance plant growth, stimulate soil microbial action, and reduce requirements for nitrogen fertilizers by more than half. Growth regulators can also be used. On the other side, Soviet journals cite violations of agrotechnics, failure to optimize fertilizer mixes, and losses in shipping, storing, and use as reasons for the less-than-expected response of potatoes, sugar beets, cotton and vegetable crops to fertilizer applications. This prompted a delegation of Soviet specialists to visit the United States in July 1983 to meet with American firms producing fertilizing equipment and methods of fertilizer application (such as anhydrous ammonia applicator systems).[32]

Despite missed overall production targets in most years, the Soviets are major exporters of mineral fertilizers and fertilizer raw materials.

These two categories make up about half of the value of USSR exports of "agricultural technology," and exceed fertilizer imports by about four to one.

But the Soviets are major net importers of pesticides. These are often complex compounds, difficult to manufacture, store, and apply, and whose chemical basis remains proprietary. Their application generally increases with the adoption of energy-saving and erosion-reducing no-till and minimum-tillage farming, both of which should be expanding in the USSR. Not surprisingly, therefore, Soviet reports have shown an increasing concern about insufficient quantities of plant protectants, related losses, environmental damage from pesticides, and the relationship between plant protectants and the success of the Food Program.

The Soviets report problems with presowing treatment of seeds, concern with smut, rust, downy mildew, blight, wilt, weed infestation, and pest damage from shield bugs, beet webworms, grain beetles, Hessian fly, flea beetles, and Colorado potato beetles. In 1982, plant protection work was carried out on 181.5 million hectares: 103.4 million were treated for pest and diseases, 71.7 million were applied with herbicides and 6.4 million hectares were applied with defoliants and dessicants. Yet, a seminar on plant protection reported that requirements were not being fully met, particularly for selective herbicides and insecticides for use on grains, oilseeds, and vegetables.[33] The seminar noted the production of 37 new pesticide preparations being developed, but also reported that 22 preparations had been retired because of environmental concerns. And obsolete preparations were still in production. These can be of little use as the pest target normally develops a resistance after prolonged contact with the same agent.

The Soviets have reacted by importing a number of Western pesticides. From the United States over 60 toxic materials and feed additives have been entered (probably in 1980–82) and many of them recommended for use in the USSR.[34] Known imports from the West include "trifluralin," a complex chemical for weed control in soybeans, "atrazine," a well-established herbicide for use on corn, "zolone," a trademarked insecticide for use on fruits and nuts, "mikal," a trade-marked systemic fungicide for fruits and tobacco, "reglon," a trade-marked broad-spectrum herbicide used as a drying agent, and "lindane." Perhaps not surprisingly, a report on the Agribusiness-USA exposition noted that companies selling agricultural chemicals were "among the most satisfied group of exhibitors."[35]

Agrochemical producers have factories sited in numerous Western countries. This diversity reduces the possibility of agrochemical trade being disrupted by the policies of any one country and this might encourage the Soviets to rely on imports. Still, should the Soviets follow the practice developed in mineral fertilizers, they can be expected to approach Western firms to build turnkey plants for the production of agrochemicals (including plant growth regulators), probably on the basis of countertrade agreements.

A closely related area of possible technology transfer is the application techniques and equipment of insecticides and herbicides. Research by Vladimir Treml shows an unusually high death rate in the USSR from poisoning by pesticides and herbicides.[36] In the United States in 1978, 31 such deaths were recorded while the Soviet number was 3,010. These striking differences may reflect less-stringent exposure standards in the USSR, inexperience in handling sometimes highly toxic compounds, possibly lower quality application technique or equipment, or other reasons not immediately evident. In any case, the Soviets have indicated an interest in U.S. organization and methods for supplying farms with agrochemicals. Similarly, application equipment is likely to be sought after.

Food Processing Equipment

The better distribution to the consumer of what is produced on Soviet farms is a key element in the Food Program. Waste and losses of the high-quality food products in greatest demand would suggest particular efforts at improving techniques in meat processing plants and dairies, and in other areas of food processing.

Two recent articles by the former USSR Minister of the Meat and Dairy Industry give some idea of the opportunities for utilizing Western technology. More than 70 million animals (excluding poultry)—more than 40 percent of the number slaughtered—are currently butchered outside state enterprises specialized for that purpose. These animals are often slaughtered under primitive conditions, without adequate refrigeration being available, with consequent loss of slaughter-house by-products, and with lower quality of primary products. By their own admission, the technical proficiency of Soviet large-scale refrigeration plants lags behind Western standards, and the scale of output associated with deep-cold, fast-freezing techniques "remains insignificant."[37]

During the Eleventh Five-Year Plan (1981–85), the Soviets plan to build 170 major enterprises for the meat and dairy industry. The plan calls for 26 new meat-packing plants, 70 dairies, 10 meat-processing factories, 27 cheese-making and 15 churning plants.[38] It also envisions the reconstruction and modernization of an unknown number of existing facilities, and the gradual termination of on-farm slaughtering.

In December 1981, the USSR Ministry of Meat and Dairy Industry signed an agreement on scientific and technical cooperation with Iowa Beef Processors, a subsidiary of Occidental Petroleum, providing for the exchange of information on meat processing and joint feasibility studies. The Soviets report that design assistance for a meat processing plant is involved, as well as study of "wasteless" meat processing. A 1983 contract with a Finnish firm calls for a port project near Tallin involving cold-storage and packing facilities for meat and fruit.

Moreover, the Soviets have indicated interest in virtually every phase of meat processing, beginning with specialized vehicles to transport animals from the farm to killing-room floor, through slaughtering, cutting, packaging, freezing, and by-product processing. Interests in dairy equipment and technique cover the entire spectrum of processing whole milk products, cheese, ice cream, and dry milk products. Automated and computerized control of the entire processing and packaging operation has attracted Soviet interest. Known Soviet contracts with Western firms cover the procurement of entire milk bottling lines, sausage making lines, poultry processing lines, a venison processing factory, complete dairies and equipment for milk separators, and cooling and pasteurizing plants.[39]

In a related technology, the Soviets have contracted with two U.S. companies for the delivery of soy isolates and textured proteins to the USSR. These products, commonly known as meat extenders, are easy to handle and make a direct contribution to human nutrition. As such, they seem especially suited for the Soviet market. The Soviets reported their own first "experimental" plant for manufacturing protein powders went into operation at Chernovtsy, Ukraine during the summer of 1983.[40]

Outside the sector of livestock processing, the Soviet food-processing industry seems unable to turn out the necessary equipment. According to one report, in 1981 the Soviets manufactured only two lines to process and pack fruits and vegetables into cans and glass containers, and a machine to produce *bliny* (pancakes) has been in the design stage since 1964. Production amounts to 20 machines annually against a need of thousands.[41] These kinds of shortcomings suggest considerable market potential for Western firms. The Soviets have been important importers of a wide array of food and tobacco processing equipment for many years, and Western firms have helped engineer and equip plants whose output has ranged from baby food to cigarettes.

Livestock Production

Probably no area of agricultural science offers more avenues for technological advances than does livestock production. Efficiencies can be obtained by altering the animals themselves through specialized breeding (which now may involve artificial insemination and embryo transfers), by changing the animals' environment, by improved rations optimized for each stage of an animal's development, and by new animal health and veterinary practices including the introduction of vitamins and amino acids as feed additives. The Soviets have imported agricultural technology in each of these areas.

In the early 1960s, they purchased equipment and techniques for a large broiler operation from a U.S. firm. This acquired technology may have set the stage for the development of a large-scale poultry industry that the Soviets undertook in 1964.

During the Ninth Five-Year Plan (1971–75), the Soviets began a major construction effort to build 1,170 specialized livestock enterprises. In 1972, they reached an agreement with a U.S. firm for the construction of three prototype feedlots for beef cattle. The U.S. firm would provide the equipment, supervise the construction, and provide operation assistance. These large-scale cattle fattening operations now number over 3,000. Another U.S. firm had contracted to construct 20 plants for the production of protein feeds.[42]

During the Tenth Five-Year Plan the USSR continued to import complete sets of machinery and equipment for cattle and poultry farms. According to the V. Burmistrov article cited earlier, it imported about 2,150 sets of equipment for poultry farms, four poultry plants and four cattle breeding complexes. For the current plan period, the Soviets have continued to purchase mixed feed factories and complete cattle breeding facilities.

While the Soviets rely primarily on their CMEA partners for some 90 percent of their imports of complete sets of agricultural equipment (cattle breeding complexes and poultry farms come mainly from the GDR and Hungary) they have continued importation of feed factories and feedlot technology from Western sources. Exhibits at the Agribusiness-USA trade fair in Moscow would indicate interest in U.S. technology in veterinary techniques, biological and chemical veterinary medicines and their production, veterinary instruments, and livestock and poultry feeding systems. Their interests in animal nutrition are directed at learning more about the use of soybean meal in livestock rations. Currently, about 95 percent of the imported soybean meal in the USSR is used in the poultry industry, although it has obvious application in hog rations as well.

The prospects for further breed improvement based on "foreign genetical potential" are reported in Soviet agricultural newspapers. A role for biotechnological methods and genetic engineering is envisioned. The Soviet livestock herd still is characterized by mixed breeds and dual-purpose cattle, rather than cattle specialized for milk or beef production. Northern European, U.S., and Canadian varieties could make further contributions toward improving the quality of Soviet livestock assets.

Miscellaneous Technologies

Efforts to reduce waste and losses extend to other areas of agricultural production. During 1981–85, the Minister of Procurements reports that the USSR will need about 200 new grain storage units, these to be built first of all in the grain-producing areas and at river and sea ports. Present grain storehouses and grain dryers and cleaners were classed as outmoded and not used regularly.

A number of U.S. firms are world leaders in technologies for grain storage, monitoring grain losses, and grain drying. These would seem to have obvious potential in the Soviet market. The Tallin harbor project mentioned earlier includes a grain section designed for the loading, unloading, and storage of some 300,000 tons of grain. Besides the portion of the project contracted to Finnish companies, other Western firms will supply some of the grain-handling equipment.

The Soviets are engaged in an expansion of their microbiological industry. This industry produces yeasts from purified liquid oil paraffins to be used as protein sources in livestock rations, antibiotics, vitamins, microbiological fertilizers, and plant protectants. Although microbiological feed proteins have not been considered competitive in the West with soybean meal, the Soviets embarked on an expansion that took production from 675 thousand tons in 1975 to 1.1 million tons in 1982.

Nor have the Soviets neglected technology transfer in agricultural management. In October 1983, they entered into a three-year trial experiment whereby Imperial Chemical Industries of the United Kingdom would furnish fertilizer, equipment, management technique, and possibly seeds for four 500 hectare wheat plots in various locations in the USSR.[43]

Space does not permit more than a broad-brush treatment of other agricultural technologies likely to find their way to the USSR during the Food Program. The Soviets have shown an interest in new seed varieties including hybrid sorghum, high lysine corn, wheat varieties, and seed processing and presowing techniques. Improved selection and new varieties of seeds are considered the main means of increasing yields and in furthering the intensification of agriculture. Methods of fruit and vegetable storage in gasses and electron-ion fields are contemplated. U.S. firms can provide machinery and equipment for on-site construction of storage bins for fruits and vegetables, an area where the Politburo recently announced a construction program based on "light metal materials" for 1986–90. The potential for technology transfer exists for irrigation equipment and technique, land leveling and drainage, packaging materials, cotton harvesting and ginning equipment, machinery and equipment for production and storage of fodder, and soil desalinization. Opportunities for trade in these technologies seem feasible as well.

U.S.-USSR Exchanges of Agricultural Research

In June 1973, the United States and the USSR signed a five-year agreement covering cooperation in the field of agriculture. This agreement is automatically renewable and is now in the third five-year period.

The agreement provides for expanding "existing cooperation" in agricultural research and development, applying "new knowledge and technology" in agricultural production and processing, and broadening relationships in agricultural trade including the "exchange of information necessary for such trade." These purposes are to be pursued under two working groups, one covering economic matters, and the other covering research and technology. Under the latter, programs were developed for bilateral exchanges in plant science, livestock science, soil science, and mechanization.

Exchanges under the agreement halted following the Soviet invasion of Afghanistan. One of the U.S. sanctions then taken was the reduction of high-level government contacts with the Soviets, and this policy remained in effect through 1983. Although exchanges could have continued under the agreement's executive secretariat (and a minor exchange did occur in 1982), the Soviets have refused to continue without first meeting at a higher (joint committee) level.

From 1973 through 1979, scientific exchanges with the USSR involved 61 U.S. and 64 Soviet delegations including 219 U.S. scientists and 252 Soviet scientists. Under agreement activities, the Soviets were especially interested in U.S. research in genetic engineering, remote sensing, swine hybridization, poultry breeding, and soil mechanics. They would probably want to encourage exchanges in these areas should activities resume.

The policy-procedural impasse under the agreement, of course, does not deny Soviet scientists access to U.S. agricultural research. Since 1980, they have taken part in visits and technical seminars worked out directly with U.S. firms and institutions (generally, these are related to trade-promotion activities), and access to U.S. journals is easily obtained.

Conclusion

The juxtaposition of Soviet trade in agricultural commodities and prospects for future trade in agricultural technology leads to important foreign and economic policy considerations in both the Soviet Union and the United States.

For the Soviets, the strategic implications of sustaining their livestock assets on the basis of grain imported from an adversary became immediately evident in 1980. The U.S. embargo, coupled with the contemporary rise of the Solidarity Union in Poland, jolted the Soviet leadership into an awareness of its continuing vulnerability over food policy issues. The resulting Food Program combined such a variety of institutional reforms that it suggested a desperate effort to improve efficiency in the agro-industrial complex. On the one hand, it included typically Soviet measures, such as the creation at the Council of Ministers level of a Commission for the Agro-Industrial Complex. This commission, expected to result in better inter-sectoral cooperation, seems to duplicate a previously successful Soviet management technique, the creation of a Military-Industrial Commission to coordinate the military and civilian sectors in the fulfillment of the USSR's defense plans. On the other hand, the Food Program incorporated more "radical" reforms, establishing rayon (district) "associations" for the agro-industrial complex, setting up "collective contract teams" on state and collective farms, and expanding the initiatives for private plot production. These reforms are intended to diffuse decision-making and to link individual incomes more closely to performance. As a follow-up effort, the Soviet government issued a series of decrees in 1983 aimed at the well-recognized weaknesses of low-quality farm machinery and inadequate economic incentives. Based on press reports, agriculture was the most important domestic issue discussed at the highest levels of the USSR during 1983.[44] In such a broad-fronted attack, some improvement in agricultural efficiency would almost certainly result, and gross agricultural output—spurred by an especially good performance in the livestock sector—surpassed the 1978 record for the first time. Agricultural commodity imports were some 13 percent below the 1981 peak.

Apart from the institutional changes, the Food Program should have resulted in increased capital investment in the agro-industrial complex, particularly in the industries serving agriculture and in those where an infusion of foreign technology would seem especially helpful. Possibly because of the agro-industrial sector's already major claim on total capital investment funds (33 percent, 27 in agriculture alone), however, such an increase in investment in the industries serving agriculture does not now appear likely before the Twelfth Five-Year Plan begins in 1986. One rationale for this may be that a reform of the agricultural management system was considered an essential precondition for the efficient absorption of new technology. By this reasoning, the Food Program and increased utilization of foreign agricultural technology would be complementary efforts, the program first creating a proper institutional setting, which would then be followed in 1986–90 by investment allocations to the industries serving agriculture and increased expenditures for foreign technologies. The storage construction program being worked out for 1986–90 would be consistent with this hypothesis.

From the U.S. government's point of view, agricultural technology trade is generally viewed as militarily nonsensitive and therefore not likely to be impeded by national security controls under the Export Administration Act (EAA).[45] However, the continuing tendency to use sophisticated electronic and precision instruments in agricultural applications could restrict some U.S. exports.[46]

As for the foreign policy controls permitted under the Act, U.S. agricultural technology exports to the USSR are more exposed to disruption than agricultural commodities. The major U.S. agricultural technology export to the USSR, superphosphoric acid, was covered by the 1980 embargo, and the safeguards against future selective embargoes—the triggering of parity price supports, Presidential commitments, and contract sanctity legislation—all apply only to agricultural commodities. This more-favorable treatment for agricultural commodities has led some to argue that more-expansive contract sanctity provisions should be "the keystone" of a renewed Export Administration Act (although both the Senate and House passed bills to amend and extend the EAA, a compromise version had not been agreed upon as of July 1984).[47] Alternatively, some researchers have indicated that a "Long-term Comprehensive Agreement" between the United States and the USSR, one that would extend the same kind of guarantees to trade in agricultural equipment and processes that the existing LTA extends to wheat and corn, could be used to assure a reliability of supply and thus promote trade.[48]

The constituencies favoring trade in agricultural commodities with the USSR are likely to be less ardent when agricultural technology is involved and some of them could feel directly threatened. Thus, the U.S. government could face a dilemma over favoring strategies that promote trade in commodities and those that promote competing technology exports. In either instance, however, the Administration argument that Soviet payments for agricultural materials diverts their hard currency from more dangerous uses would seem applicable to farm machinery and most other agricultural technologies as well. And finally, while the United States is generally recognized as the leader in many areas of agricultural technology, the production techniques for agricultural machinery, chemicals, and food processing machinery are widely available. Even if some non-U.S. items were not competitive in the leading Western markets, their suitability for use in the Soviet Union would still be substantial. In short, while the potential for foreign policy interference in an expanding U.S.-USSR trade in agricultural technology might be greater than for commodities, the economics would suggest little reason for doing so.

Table 1

USSR Agricultural Imports, 1975–1983, by Value

Commodity	1975	1976	1977	1978	1979	1980	1981	1982	1983
					Million dollars[1]				
Meat and dairy products	526.6	413.5	733.9	292.7	894.5	1459.3	1790.4	1583.6	1461.8
Grain and grain products	2866.8	3158.6	1609.4	2636.2	3814.9	5674.9	8366.1	6720.9	5362.5
Fruit, vegetables, and nuts	783.7	765.1	970.8	1018.8	1199.3	1441.4	1466.3	1453.1	1303.5
Sugar	2185	2071.6	2464.6	3130.6	3177.1	3863.7	3940.2	4366.5	4025.3
Tobacco and products	524.1	526.4	562.5	589.5	649.6	759.4	865.4	919.5	923.2
Oilseeds and oilmeal	138.6	454.7	397.7	273.1	559.3	512.3	911.5	903.2	1219
Fats and oils	120.7	101.4	198	199.1	523.3	864.3	1155.2	980.8	892.8
Other	2000.1	1839.6	2194.2	2101.3	2513.2	2657.1	2409.3	2399.5	2827.8
TOTAL	9145.6	9330.9	9131.1	10241.3	13331.2	17232.4	20904.4	19327.1	18015.9

[1]USSR official data converted at average official rate of exchange for given years.
SOURCE: Vneshnyaya torgovlya SSSR, 1975–83.

Table 2

USSR Agricultural Exports, 1975–1983, by Value

Commodity	1975	1976	1977	1978	1979	1980	1981	1982	1983
					Million dollars[1]				
Meat and dairy products	85.5	85.5	74.9	91.6	91.3	97.6	150.8	91.3	89.2
Grain and grain products	681.9	399	680.3	390.8	788.5	537.8	695	553.9	428.6
Fruit, vegetables and nuts	31.6	24.9	29.5	28.5	31.7	47.2	46.2	43.2	48.3
Sugar and confectionaries	36.7	35.6	33	58.9	72.3	76.3	104.9	107.1	55.1
Furs, hides, and natural fibers	1038.5	1162.7	1510.9	1401.7	1423.2	1570.3	1634.1	1646.6	1347.1
Fats and oils	391	234.8	218.5	185.9	179.4	172.6	136.9	132.6	127.2
Other	161.2	135.7	171.5	176.9	200.3	210.1	208.5	203.2	206.9
TOTAL	2426.3	2078.2	2718.6	2334.3	2786.7	2711.8	2976.4	2777.9	2302.4

[1]USSR official data converted at average official rate of exchange for given years.
SOURCE: Vneshnyaya torgovlya SSSR, 1975–83.

233

Table 3

U.S. Trade with the USSR, 1972–1983*

Year	Total	U.S. exports Agricultural	Nonagricultural	Total	U.S. imports Agricultural	Nonagricultural
			(Million dollars)			
1972	542	430	112	88	4	84
1973	1,191	920	271	204	5	199
1974	607	300	308	334	9	326
1975	1,834	1,133	701	243	7	236
1976	2,306	1,487	819	215	8	206
1977	1,621	1,037	584	221	11	210
1978	2,249	1,687	563	530	12	517
1979	3,604	2,855	749	873	15	858
1980	1,510	1,047	463	431	10	421
1981	2,430	1,665	765	357	12	345
1982	2,589	1,855	734	229	11	218
1983	2,002	1,457	545	341	10	331

*Not adjusted for transshipments.
SOURCE: Compiled from official statistics.

Table 4

USSR Agricultural Technology Imports, 1975–83, by Value

Commodity	1975	1976	1977	1978	1979	1980	1981	1982	1983
					Million dollars[1]				
Agricultural machinery, equipment, and tractor spare parts[2]	477.0	648.3	730.8	896.5	1020.9	1192.8	1154.9	1219.1	1404.5
Mineral fertilizers and equipment for fertilizer production	28.1	10.2	10.6	406.8	551.7	162.7	203.9	330.8	369.7
Pesticides and herbicides	143.0	134.0	143.2	176.5	213.7	369.0	339.0	332.9	398.8
Equipment for the food processing industry	309.7	308.5	322.3	385.1	507.2	701.2	615.0	740.3	898.4
Other	15.4	6.8	13.3	73.0	86.4	91.0	23.5	56.1	54.5
TOTAL	973.2	1107.8	1220.2	1937.9	2379.8	2516.8	2336.3	2679.2	3125.9

[1] USSR official data converted at average official rate of exchange for given years.
[2] For 1977–83, spare parts for all agricultural machinery and equipment.
SOURCE: Vneshnyaya torgovlya SSSR, 1975–83.

Table 5

USSR Agricultural Technology Exports, 1975–83, by Value

Commodity	1975	1976	1977	1978	1979	1980	1981	1982	1983
					Million dollars[1]				
Agriculture machinery, equipment, and tractor spare parts	575.1	693.6	822.7	903.6	987.5	1044.2	1070.6	1021.0	986.3
Mineral fertilizers, ammonia & phosphorus	518.4	426.3	495.1	623.0	706.9	1149.7	1404.3	1272.9	1321.6
Pesticides and herbicides	17.2	13.4	20.6	21.5	20.1	25.7	33.9	40.3	41.0
Equipment for the food processing industry	87.9	110.1	126.8	144.8	173.8	184.3	166.1	199.5	152.0
Other	74.1	103.9	113.5	130.4	166.6	181.0	124.8	155.0	121.9
TOTAL	1272.7	1347.3	1578.8	1823.3	2055.0	2584.8	2799.6	2688.7	2622.8

[1] USSR official data converted at average official exchange rate for each year.
SOURCE: Vneshnyaya torgovlya SSSR, 1975–83.

236

NOTES

1. Briefly, the Food Program addresses questions that have engaged the Soviet government's attention since at least 1965. The program envisages creating an integrated agro-industrial complex to coordinate the planning, financing, and management of the agricultural sector, those industries serving it, and downstream production and marketing facilities. Its main elements include:

Management Reorganization—the creation at the Council of Ministers level of a Commission for the Agro-Industrial Complex, and at republic, oblast, and rayon levels, regional agro-industrial associations, to overcome the bureaucratic barriers that compartmentalize agricultural management.

Farm Level Reforms—the creation of "collective contract teams" so that wages of farm workers are more closely tied to harvest results.

Private Plot Initiatives—an effort to increase the high-quality foodstuffs in short supply by, for example, allowing individuals to keep as many animals as they want so long as they contract the output to state and collective farms.

Price Reforms—an increase in procurement prices for certain commodities plus a bonus system tied to increased payments when output exceeds the annual average of that obtained in the Tenth 5-Year Plan. This way, bonus payments go to those who increase production, not just to those who meet (possibly too low) targets.

Agricultural Trade Policy—the U.S. embargo probably prompted an effort to take domestic action to reduce their exposure to pressure exerted through foreign grain sales.

2. To the extent that the Food Program was a creation of the collective leadership of the Communist Party, and apparently ingrained in long-range planning, it is unlikely that future successors would bring about drastic shifts in either the program or its foreign economic implications. The new General Secretary Konstantin Chernenko was an extremely ardent supporter of the Food Program (he called it "a profound reconstruction of the national economy") before Andropov became General Secretary, and has supported it in language remarkably similar to Brezhnev's.

3. USDA, *USSR, Review of Agriculture in 1981 and Outlook for 1982*, p. 17.

4. USDA, *USSR World Agriculture Regional Supplement, Review of 1982 and Outlook for 1983*, p. 17.

5. See ibid., pp. 4–6.

6. D. Gale Johnson and Karen Brooks, *Prospects for Soviet Agriculture in the 1980's* (Bloomington: Indiana University Press, 1983).

7. *Pravda*, 2 September 1981.

8. Reported in *Zycie Gospodarcze*, 28 March 1982 and quoted by Yuri Markish and Anton F. Malish, "The Soviet Food Program: Prospects for the 1980's," *ACES Bulletin*, Spring 1983, p. 60.

9. Jan Vanous, writing in a 10 September 1982 Wharton Econometric Forecasting Associates Newsletter, has argued that such a strategy would be in keeping with the Soviets' "comparative advantage." He argues that "in the Soviet Union the ruble value of resources required to produce 1 metric ton of oil is estimated to be the same as the ruble resources required to produce 0.3 metric tons of grain. Thus, . . . the Soviet Union would be better off reallocating resources from grain production to oil production, so that they could produce and export more oil and import more grain." According to Vanous, the Soviets do not fully take advantage of the oil-grain trade-off because of "political and strategic reasons," i.e., they do not want to be dependent on the West for grain.

10. These tables are adapted from those prepared by USDA's East Europe-USSR Branch, which converts officially reported Soviet data (from *Vneshnyaya torgovlya SSSR*) to U.S. dollars at the officially reported average exchange rates for each year. The categories reported approximate the SITC for agricultural products (excluding natural rubber and some minor crude material categories). Data for 1983 are partial estimates. The Soviets report exports and imports on an f.o.b. basis. They also record as imports items purchased abroad, even if they actually never enter the USSR. Thus, for instance, Canadian flour purchased for delivery to Cuba appears in Soviet trade statistics as both an import and an export.

11. Joan Parpart Zoeter, "USSR: Hard Currency Trade and Payments," in U.S. Congress, Joint Economic Committee, *Soviet Economy in the 1980's: Problems and Prospects*, Part 2 (Washington, D.C.: USGPO, 1982), p. 502.

12. Press release, 7 January 1980.

13. John Roney, "Grain Embargo as Diplomatic Lever: A Case Study of the U.S.-Soviet Embargo of 1980–81," in *Soviet Economy in the 1980's: Problems and Prospects*, Part 2, 1982. Mr. Roney's account of the decision-making process leading to the embargo is particularly fascinating.

14. Statement of Dale Hathaway, Under Secretary of Agriculture for International Affairs and Commodity Programs, to the Subcommittee on International Finance, Committee on Banking, Housing, and Urban Affairs, United States Senate, 22 January 1980.

15. Sir Leslie Price, chairman of the Australia Wheat Board, was quoted as saying that at the January meeting the United States had given assurances to other grain-exporting nations that it would not sell wheat surpluses arising from the embargo on the established markets of other wheat traders. According to Sir Leslie, this counter-assurance is what prompted Australia and Canada to agree to the U.S. request to limit sales to the USSR (*Journal of Commerce*, 28 October 1980).

16. "Effects of the 1980 and 1981 Limitations on Grain Exports to the USSR on Business Activity, Jobs, Government Costs, and Farmers," Brief prepared for the National Corn Growers Association by Schnittker Associates, 12 February 1982.

17. USDA, *The U.S. Sales Suspension and Soviet Agriculture, An October Assessment* (Washington, D.C.: USGPO, 1980).

18. Radio Moscow North America Service, 8 February 1980.

19. Marshall Goldman, "Interaction of Politics and Trade: Soviet-Western Interaction," in *Soviet Economy in the 1980's: Problems and Prospects*.

20. United States International Trade Commission, *U.S. Embargoes on Agricultural Exports: Implications for the U.S. Agricultural Industry and U.S. Exports*, Report on Investigation No. 332-157 Under Section 332 of the Tariff Act of 1930, December 1983.

21. Mikhail V. Condoide, *Russian American Trade, A Study of the Soviet Foreign Trade Monopoly*, 1946, p. 98.

22. Earl M. Rubenking, "The Soviet Tractor Industry: Progress and Problems," in U.S. Congress, Joint Economic Committee, *Soviet Economy in a New Perspective* (Washington, D.C.: USGPO, 1976), p. 607.

23. E. Shershnev, *On the Principle of Mutual Advantage, Soviet-American Economic Relations*, 1978, p. 38.

24. V. V. Metskevich, "Report of the Soviet Agricultural Delegation on its Trip to the United States and Canada," Moscow (unattributed translation found in EE-USSR Branch files), 335 pages, 1955.

25. Soviet export statistics seem to include license fees, and supervisory and other personnel costs in the exportation of complete plants. The accounting of these service costs in the importation of complete plants is less certain. Soviet imports of intangibles such as design and production licenses, exchanges of agricultural research findings, and technical information, if not included in complete plants, have not been recorded in import statistics since at least 1975 (see Vladimir G. Treml and Barry L. Kostinsky, *Domestic Value of Soviet Foreign Trade: Exports and Imports in the 1972 Input-Output Table*, Foreign Economic Report No. 20 , U.S. Department of Commerce, October 1982, pp. 29–32).

26. V. Burmistrov, "Traktoroexport's Assistance in Accomplishing Tasks of the USSR Food Program," *Foreign Trade*, no. 11, 1983.

27. Vladimir Sushkov, "Foreign Trade for the Agro-Industrial Complex," *Foreign Trade*, no. 1, 1983.

28. Bruce Parrott, *Politics and Technology in the Soviet Union* (Cambridge: MIT Press, 1983), p. 147.

29. This agreement has been well covered in numerous sources. See, for example, United States International Trade Commission, *Anhydrous Ammonia from the USSR*, Report to the President on Investigation No. TA-406-6, Under Section 406 of the Trade Act of 1974, April, 1980.

30. Vladimir Sushkov, "Foreign Trade for the Agro-Industrial Complex," *Foreign Trade*, no. 1, 1983.

31. USDA, *USSR, World Agriculture Regional Supplement, Review of 1982 and Outlook for 1983*, May 1983, p. 17.

32. *Journal of the US-USSR Trade and Economic Council*, 8, no. 3.

33. *Zashchita rasteniy*, no. 6, June 1983, translated in JPRS, 25 October 1983, *USSR Report: Agriculture*, no. 1406.

34. Interview with Boris Runov, Deputy Minister of Agriculture in the USSR and Soviet Chairman of the U.S.-USSR Joint Committee on Agricultural Cooperation, as reported in *Moscow News*, no. 22, 1983.

35. Robert S. Krause, "Agribusiness Report," *Journal of the US-USSR Trade and Economic Council*, 8, nos. 4/5.

36. V. Treml, "Fatal Poisonings in the USSR," *Radio Liberty/Radio Free Europe Research*, Y90/82, 7 December 1982.

37. S. Antonov, *Kommunist*, no. 4, March 1983.

38. S. Antonov, "The Soviet Food Program," *Journal of the US-USSR Trade and Economic Council*, 8, no. 3.

39. *Journal of the US-USSR Trade and Economic Council*, 8, no. 3.

40. Radio Moscow, 10 June 1983 as monitored by the BBC.

41. *Business Eastern Europe*, 16 March 1984, p. 85.

42. David M. Schoonover, "Soviet Acquisition of U.S. Technology for Agricultural Production," FDCD Working Paper, USDA, April 1975. This short monograph provided an excellent summary of the theory and application of technological transfer in agriculture to the USSR in the early 1970s.

43. John Hardt, "Long-term Agreement (LTA), Some Considerations for Agricultural Trade," Paper originally prepared for a Conference on East-West Trade, Technology Transfer, and U.S. Export Control Policy, Institute of International Studies, University of South Carolina, 1–3 March 1983.

44. Office of Soviet Analysis, Central Intelligence Agency, Joint Economic Committee Briefing Paper, *USSR: Economic Trends and Policy Developments*, 14 September 1983, p. 22.

45. One of the clearest statements of U.S. policy on this issue is in a letter from the Secretary of Commerce to C. William Verity where the Secretary states:

"American and Soviet interests are well matched in agribusiness, and the technology involved is generally of a nonsensitive nature." *Journal of the US-USSR Trade and Economic Council*, 8, no. 2.

46. On 28 May 1984, the *Washington Post* reported that an official of the U.S. Defense Intelligence Agency had indicated that, if the United States were the sole supplier, some exports of equipment designed for gene-engineering research could be restricted because of that technology's potential use in Soviet biological and chemical warfare research.

47. C. William Verity, Jr., "US-USSR Trade: A Vital Need?" *Journal of the US-USSR Trade and Economic Council*, 8, nos. 4/5.

48. Hardt, "Long-term Agreement (LTA), Some Considerations for Agricultural Trade."

PART III

The United States and Western Trade with the USSR

American Politics and Trade with the USSR

Gary K. Bertsch

Introduction

WE HAVE witnessed in the 1970s and early 1980s a changing and confusing set of U.S. policies governing Soviet-American and East-West trade.[1] For example, shortly after a presidential commission reported to President Nixon that the volume of U.S. trade with the East was small and likely to remain so for the 1970s, the Nixon administration undertook an expansive East-West trade program. To initiate this program, U.S. Secretary of Commerce Stans traveled to the USSR in November of 1971 to explore improved commercial relations. In May of 1972, President Nixon arrived in Moscow and signed a list of "basic principles of relations" between the two superpowers. The seventh principle held that "the USA and the USSR regard commercial and economic ties as an important and necessary element in the strengthening of their bilateral relations. . . ."

However, the commercial element in the superpower relationship never approached the euphoric declarations of the signatories. First, the Nixon Administration lost control of the commercial issue as an assertive Congress led by Senator Henry Jackson imposed some significant restrictions on the trade relationship. By the end of the decade, commercial relationships were soured further when the Carter Administration continued to link U.S. trade to Soviet domestic and foreign policy behavior. Although confirming the importance of U.S.-Soviet trade at the 1979 Vienna summit, the Carter Administration sought to use trade as a foreign policy tool, and in response to the Soviet invasion of Afghanistan, imposed a series of economic sanctions against the USSR. As a result, the U.S.-Soviet trade relationship deteriorated sharply.

The Reagan Administration also displayed mixed signals on the issue of U.S.-Soviet trade. Shortly after taking office in 1981, President

I would like to express my appreciation to John Hardt, Martin Hillenbrand, Loch Johnson, Henry Nau, William Root, and the contributors to this volume for their comments on an earlier draft.

Reagan lifted the agricultural embargo, yet simultaneously sought to tighten controls on technology sales. Later, President Reagan announced a list of economic sanctions against the Soviets for their complicity in the repression of Poland, and generally worked through 1984 to lower the level of Western commercial relations with the USSR. In 1983, however, the United States signed a major long-term grain agreement with the Soviet Union. These newsworthy highlights—first, marking the end of the generally consensual Cold War policy of economic warfare, and second, the more contentious rise and fall of economic detente—draw attention to the complexity and volatility of U.S. trade policy with the Soviet Union. On the basis of a cursory review, such developments reflect confusion and incoherence; below the surface, however, they reflect the complex political dynamics of the pluralistic American system.

Why has U.S. trade policy with the Soviet Union grown more conflictual in the 1970s and 1980s and been described by informed observers at home and abroad as *ad hoc,* spasmodic, and incoherent? Why has the policy been so confusing and volatile? Unfortunately, there is no clear and simple way to explain the complex and changing U.S. policies. These changes are, to some extent, a consequence of global and international forces such as the East-West rivalry and competition, macroeconomic forces, and alliance politics within an uneasy partnership. They are also the products of U.S. responses to regional problems and Soviet involvement in such places as Angola, Afghanistan, and Poland. And they are certainly influenced by personalities and domestic forces and politics, including growing differences within the United States about the East-West relationship, and the fluctuating political strength of the American presidency. A comprehensive analysis of the U.S. politics of East-West trade should capture these and other relevant forces. This chapter will attempt to do so by describing what has transpired in the 1970s and early 1980s, and by analyzing these events and the major issues through the perspective of political pluralism.

There are many theories, perspectives, and ideas for explaining the domestic politics of U.S. foreign economic policy.[2] Political pluralism, the dominant explanation of American politics, views the political process in terms of competing coalitions of interests (both private and public) and multiple centers of power. This chapter will argue that the relatively high level of ideological consensus and structural centralization of political power governing U.S. trade policy with the Soviet Union and Eastern Europe during the Cold War period has been replaced by ideological dissension and structural pluralism. During the last decade the U.S. political system has been characterized by an unfortunate lack of agreement on the basic premises governing East-West trade, and by competing coalitions and centers of power often guided by different premises and pursuing opposing interests.

To examine these issues and premises as they define the U.S. politics of Soviet-American and East-West trade, we will examine the Nixon, Carter, and Reagan presidencies. In addition to an overview of each period, we will examine the major actors, the different political coalitions and centers of power, and the political dynamics describing each period. Particular attention will be paid to the *economic, security,* and *foreign policy* premises underlying U.S.-Soviet trade policy. First, how do the relevant actors view the *economic* costs and benefits of trade with the Soviet Union? Second, how do they see the *strategic,* or *national security,* implications? Third, what do they expect in terms of the *political,* or *foreign policy,* consequences of trade with the Soviet Union? The analysis will show the relative absence of a viable consensus upon which a coherent policy of U.S.-Soviet trade might be based.

The Nixon Years: Politics and Policy during the Period of Detente

After the election of President Nixon, the first major East-West trade item to be placed on the new administration's agenda was the Export Control Act, which was to expire in the fall of 1969. Substantial congressional support for liberalizing the Act was demonstrated at hearings held from April through July of 1969. Senators Walter Mondale, Edmund Muskie, and William Fulbright, among others, argued that the Cold War was over and that the restrictive U.S. trade policy was counter to our economic interests and causing suspicion and tensions in East-West relations. On 3 June 1969 the *New York Times* described the Act's restrictions as "self-defeating," "cold war policies," and "inconsistent with the Nixon Administration's theory that it is time to move from an era of confrontation into one of negotiation and cooperation."[3]

At this point the Nixon White House was apparently unwilling to loosen trade restrictions and expand East-West trade. Kissinger describes his and Nixon's views in the following terms:

> Given Soviet needs, expanding trade without a political *quid pro quo* was a gift; there was very little the Soviet Union could do for us economically. It did not seem to me unreasonable to require Soviet restraint in such trouble spots as the Middle East, Berlin, and Southeast Asia in return. Nixon had similar views, with a political edge. He did offer Dobrynin increased trade for help on Vietnam but he was doubtful that the Soviets would take the bait. If not, he saw no sense in antagonizing his old constituency by accepting liberalizing legislation. On the contrary, given the "soft" position he was taking on Vietnam he used East-West trade to refurbish his conservative credentials.[4]

While the Department of Defense generally supported the White House position, the other two major bureaucratic actors—the Departments of State and Commerce—favored trade liberalization. The Department of State felt that increased trade would improve the political atmosphere and the Department of Commerce viewed it as good for the economy.

During the first months of the new administration, Kissinger sent President Nixon a briefing paper summing up his and the agencies' recommendations (the Departments of State and Commerce were for trade liberalization; the Department of Defense opposed it) on the revision of the Export Control Act and related East-West trade issues. Although the briefing paper generally recommended, according to Kissinger, a liberalization of policy, Nixon went against the recommendations. In May of 1969, President Nixon decreed that the Administration would oppose all legislative efforts to liberalize Soviet trade.[5] As Kissinger notes, however, this did not stop the pro-trade agencies within the bureaucracy, particularly the Department of Commerce, from continuing to push for the liberalization of trade within the existing law. Subsequently, in December, Congress liberalized the law by passing the Export Administration Act of 1969. This act declared that although there are reasons for controlling U.S. exports (specifically to protect national security, further foreign policy, guard against short supply, and oppose terrorism), unwarranted restrictions can and have adversely affected foreign trade and the balance of payments. Overall, the new act represented a shift in favor of the expansion of non-military trade with the Soviet Union and Eastern Europe.[6]

However, the Nixon Administration continued to take a hard-line attitude on trade and, according to Kissinger, intended to use trade concessions as a "political instrument, withholding them when Soviet conduct was adventurous and granting them in measured doses when the Soviets behaved cooperatively."[7] Kissinger describes Soviet behavior as cooperative during this period, noting the conclusion of agreements on Berlin and accidental war, the breakthrough on SALT, and the general thaw in U.S.-Soviet relations. Apparently, by the spring of 1972, the White House was rather pleased with Soviet policy. On 22 May President Nixon arrived in Moscow and (1) signed an agreement covering cooperation in science and technology, including the establishment of contacts and arrangements between U.S. firms and Soviet enterprises; (2) issued a communique establishing a Joint U.S.-USSR Commercial Commission to monitor commercial relations and negotiate a trade agreement; and (3) signed a text of "Basic Principles of Relations," one of which noted that "the U.S.A. and U.S.S.R. regard commercial and economic ties as an important and necessary element in the strengthening of their bilateral relations and thus will actively promote the growth of such ties. They will facilitate cooperation between the relevant organizations and enterprises of the two countries and the conclusion of appropriate agreements and contracts, including long-term ones." In July 1972 the two countries moved further to liberalize trade relations: They signed a three-year grain agreement covering the sale of up to $750 million of grain; the United States undertook to make credit available through the Commodity Credit Corporation; and the first session of the U.S.-USSR Joint Economic Commission was held in Moscow. On 18 October of the same year President Nixon and Soviet Trade Minister Patolichev signed a comprehensive trade agreement which called for an expansion of trade, and included a settlement of the USSR Lend Lease debt to the United States in exchange for the granting of most favored nation (MFN) status.[8] During this period, the U.S. and USSR also began to seriously consider cooperation on large natural gas projects (i.e., North Star and Yakutsk). For a time, it appeared that the United States was out front of its allies on trade with the Soviet Union.

While the pro-trade forces in government and the private sector were now mobilized and prepared to expand significantly the trade relationship, there were some powerful actors who had other objectives in mind. In October 1972, Senator Henry Jackson introduced an amendment—to become known as the Jackson-Vanik amendment—to U.S. trade legislation linking the Nixon promise of MFN status to Soviet emigration policy.[9] Senator Jackson's move brought together a rare coalition from the left and right—Kissinger described it as being like an eclipse of the sun—and set in motion a variety of developments that would prove to have a deep impact on future U.S. policy.

The subsequent two-and-one-half-year struggle surrounding the Jackson-Vanik amendment demonstrates several significant aspects of pluralistic politics in the American system. Many influential actors and competing centers of power representing the executive branch, Congress, and the private sector became involved in the struggle. The actors in the executive branch, in addition to the President, included Henry Kissinger, then Presidential Assistant for National Security Affairs, and George Shultz, Secretary of Treasury and the chief American representative on the U.S.-USSR Joint Commercial Commission. Although there were some bureaucratic differences on the Jackson-Vanik amendment issue within the executive branch—e.g., Secretary of Commerce Peter Peterson was known as a strong advocate of East-West trade and a vigorous opponent of the amendment while Defense Department officials were reluctant supporters of U.S.-Soviet trade and the President's position—the high degree of foreign policy centralization within the White House effectively overcame interagency differences, resulting in strong opposition to the Jackson-Vanik amendment.

The key actors in the Congress were (1) Senator Henry Jackson, who took particular interest in U.S.-Soviet relations and the trade question and understood the relevance of the issue to his upcoming presidential bid; (2) his assistant, Richard Perle, who spearheaded the amendment effort; (3) Senators Jacob Javits (R-N.Y.) and Abraham Ribicoff (D-Conn.), Jackson's closest allies, both Jewish and from states with large and influential Jewish constituencies; and (4) Republican Representative Charles Vanik, who introduced the Jackson amendment in the House. While the White House supported presidential linkage of trade and MFN status to Soviet *foreign* policy, these congressional actors wanted to link MFN explicitly to Soviet *domestic* policy, and most specifically, to the emigration of Soviet Jews. The executive branch and key congressional actors were now locked in an acrimonious struggle over the making of U.S.-Soviet trade policy.

There were also a variety of important interest groups involved in this episode. Among the most influential and active groups opposed to the Jackson-Vanik amendment were (1) the National Association of Manufacturers (NAM), which lobbied extensively against the amendment, (2) the U.S. Chamber of Commerce, (3) the National Foreign Trade Council, and (4) the East-West Trade Council. On the other side, supporting the amendment were (1) the AFL-CIO and its President, George Meany, who felt that trade with the Soviet Union was a costly economic mistake with benefits lopsidedly in favor of the Soviets; (2) a number of American academic organizations, such as the Federation of American Scientists, the National Academy of Sciences, and the American Psychiatric Association, all of which were concerned with the repression of dissidents in the USSR; and (3) a variety of active Jewish organizations and leaders of American Jewry.

The Jackson-Vanik amendment brought these actors and the Soviets themselves into intense and lengthy negotiations. Jackson and his forces wanted the Soviets to give specific assurances about the number of Jews who would be allowed to emigrate. Nixon and Kissinger wanted to conduct "quiet diplomacy" and use trade to build "a web of constructive relationships." The pro-trade, business groups wanted the government to stay out of trade, and the Jewish groups wanted the U.S. government to use trade to force the Soviets to open the gates to Jewish emigration. After interminable negotiations and hearings, the issue came to a head in the summer and fall of 1974. Following an exchange of letters between Kissinger and Jackson in which the conditions concerning Jewish emigration were spelled out, members of the administration and Congress worked out a set of principles that empowered the President to grant MFN and credits to the Soviet Union for an initial period of up to eighteen months. Then, through the Trade Act of 1974 and the Export-Import Bank Amendments of 1974, Congress placed significant limits on the amount of Eximbank's credit and financial guarantees for exports to the Soviet Union. The Soviet leaders reacted harshly to the conditions imposed by Congress and to the public assertions in the United States that they had agreed to increase Jewish emigration in exchange for MFN, and on 10 January 1975, they noted that as far as they were concerned the 1972 Trade Agreement with the United States was null and void.

Although there were some pro-trade developments during the Ford Administration period—for example, the 1975 Grain Agreement setting a minimum of 6 million metric tons of corn and wheat to be purchased annually by the Soviets—U.S.-Soviet trade had suffered a great setback. In response to the Soviet nullification of the trade agreement, Kissinger announced that the United States would not take steps to expand trade with the Soviet Union as called for in the agreement. Kissinger's interest in U.S.-Soviet trade was further soured by Soviet complicity and use of Cuban proxies in the Angolan civil war.

What had happened during the Jackson-Vanik episode? Significantly, a number of important domestic and foreign policy issues became entangled in a manner that led to confusion and political disarray. Although originally reluctant to expand U.S.-Soviet trade, the subsequent Nixon-Kissinger initiatives were based upon the idea that U.S.-Soviet trade was an "important and necessary element in strengthening bilateral relations" between the superpowers. The White House came to feel, primarily for political motives, that the trade relationship might prove to be a useful instrument in building a more constructive relationship with the Soviets. The White House and State Department felt that trade could be used to influence Soviet foreign policy, but unlike Senator Jackson, they were circumspect about trade's impact on domestic issues and changing the Soviet system;[10] finally, they hoped to keep American domestic politics out of their East-West policy. Senator Jackson had other ideas. Not only did he want to use trade as an instrument to try to change Soviet emigration policy, but he recognized the importance of the issue to the U.S. political process, and to his bid for the Democratic presidential nomination. Hence, he was eager to raise the U.S.-Soviet trade issue in the domestic arena in his effort to garner Jewish support for his presidential bid. In this environment, domestic political considerations began to transcend the interests and objectives of foreign policy. Other Congressmen were supportive because they saw in this issue an opportunity to challenge Nixon and Kissinger and reassert the role of Congress in the making of American foreign policy.

The Jackson-Vanik episode, then, demonstrated some significant elements of the U.S. politics of East-West trade. Included is the power that different actors and groups can assume under certain conditions. Reacting to centralized foreign policy-making in the Watergate era, powerful congressional actors—Senators Jackson, Javits, and Ribicoff—and their staffs, led by such personalities as Richard Perle, were able to do battle with the "imperial presidency" and win. One can envision other possible outcomes for U.S.-Soviet trade in the 1970s if the timing had been changed, or if the personalities had chosen to play it differently. But, as it turned out, U.S.-Soviet relations became a hostage of domestic politics and East-West economic relations were dealt a serious blow.

The political elements of the trade relationship clearly dominated during the period. Although some in the private sector and the Department of Commerce called attention to the economic benefits of trade, and some in the Department of Defense called attention to security considerations, the major centers of power debated, and the issue was largely decided on political grounds. The White House came to support an expansion of trade for foreign policy reasons; Senator Jackson and others opposed it for domestic political reasons. Largely because of the Vietnam and Watergate experiences and the decline of presidential power, a resurgent Congress became a dominant center of power determining U.S. policy during this contentious period. Largely absent were arguments and calculations—and a center of power—based upon the economic considerations that had become of fundamental importance among America's allies. The Department of Commerce and pro-trade Congressmen were much less active and powerful than were their counterparts in Europe. Also generally absent among both U.S. and allied considerations were the national security implications of trade and technology transfer that were to become of paramount importance during the Reagan Administration.[11] Overall, there was little comprehensive thinking and no national consensus on the fundamental economic, security, and foreign policy premises of U.S.-Soviet and East-West trade.

The Carter Years: Economic Diplomacy and the Deterioration of U.S.-Soviet Relations

The issues of arms control and human rights dominated the Carter Administration's Soviet agenda during the first year. The administration made two SALT II proposals in the early months, and on 30 March 1977 the Soviets rejected them both. Brezhnev and the Soviet leaders took no more kindly to President Carter's human rights initiatives than they did to his proposals for arms control. There were obvious confusion and mixed signals in the new administration's Soviet policy. Some initiatives, associated with Secretary of State Cyrus Vance and his advisors within the Department of State, appeared conciliatory and cooperative; other signals, associated with National Security Advisor Zbigniew Brzezinski and his NSC staff, seemed more hard-line and confrontational.[12] But although there was some uncertainty about the administration's broader East-West policy, by the summer of 1978 an identifiable White House approach to U.S.-Soviet trade began to take shape.

The strategy was to some extent a consequence of a review of the U.S.-Soviet strategic balance conducted by Harvard professor Samuel Huntington. Huntington, a former university colleague and collaborator of Brzezinski's, had joined the NSC staff as Coordinator of Security Planning. The outcome of the review was Presidential Review Memorandum 10. Brzezinski describes the memorandum as "mixed," registering concern about Soviet military strides but "relatively sanguine about our overall ability to compete politically, economically, and ideologically with the Soviet Union."[13] This review memorandum led in August 1977 to Presidential Directive No. 18. Concerning economic relations with the USSR, the document said that "the United States must take advantage of its economic strength and technological superiority to encourage Soviet cooperation in resolving regional conflicts, reducing tensions, and achieving adequately verifiable arms control agreements."[14] In this vein, at a June 1978 U.S. Military Academy Conference at West Point, Huntington noted that it was time:

> to untie our hands so that we can capitalize on our economic resources in our relations with the Soviets, either to induce them to be cooperative, where that is possible, or to compete with them more successfully, when that is necessary. I am not issuing a call for a return to economic warfare; nor am I espousing economic *laissez faire* in our relations with the Soviets. I am saying that we should be prepared to engage in economic diplomacy.[15]

In an article published in *Foreign Policy* a few months later, Huntington expanded on the issue of economic diplomacy:

> In short, economic capabilities and economic relations must serve the basic U.S. foreign policy objectives of encouraging East-West cooperation, containing Soviet expansion, and promoting American values.[16]

About the same time, the United States began to impose export controls to react to Soviet behavior and in anticipation of using these controls to influence Soviet policy. In July 1978, to protest the harsh Soviet treatment of dissidents, the arrest of a U.S. businessman, and the trial of two American reporters in Moscow, the United States denied an export license for a Sperry Univac computer ordered by TASS for use at the 1980 Olympics. On 1 August 1978, the United States placed foreign policy export controls on Soviet purchases of oil and gas equipment, using the Huntington argument that such controls were necessary as flexible instruments of foreign policy. On 31 August President Carter called for a review of a license issued earlier to Dresser Industries for export of a drill bit plant to the USSR. Although he reaffirmed the granting of the license on 6 September 1978 he withdrew it in November of 1980 in response to the Soviet invasion of Afghanistan. The "Dresser case" was an obvious portrayal of what George Shultz at the time disparagingly referred to as a naive policy of "lightswitch diplomacy;" that is, turning trade on and off to influence Soviet behavior.[17]

The White House policy of "economic diplomacy," closely associated with Brzezinski and Huntington, was not uniformly and eagerly supported throughout the executive branch. During the 1978–80 period, I conducted over 200 interviews, throughout the U.S. government as well as with many representatives of the private sector, about the making and nature of U.S.-Soviet trade policy. Officials within the Department of State were skeptical about the expected impact of economic diplomacy. Although they perceived some positive foreign policy consequences from economic relations with the Soviet Union, they considered the expectation of fundamental changes in Soviet foreign and domestic— for example, human rights—policies naive.[18]

Most officials in the Departments of Commerce and Treasury were also troubled by the Carter policy of economic diplomacy. Concerned with the deteriorating U.S. export performance, these officials were aware of the economic costs of "lightswitch diplomacy." Secretary of Commerce Juanita Kreps and Secretary of the Treasury Michael Blumenthal also stressed the fact that a healthy economy was a necessary factor in U.S. national security and that an erosion of U.S. power and influence could come from a failure to meet the export challenge.[19] Aware of the trade competition of America's allies, they were concerned that U.S. exporters would be viewed as unreliable and be considered by the Soviets as suppliers of "last resort." Deeply resentful of Brzezinski and his staff, and the fact that they "had the President's ear," these officials considered the over-emphasis on fuzzy political and strategic considerations as damaging to U.S.-Soviet trade and, in turn, the U.S. economy. Some in the Department of Defense, under the leadership of Harold Brown, were also somewhat skeptical of the policy, although for very different reasons. Although supportive of a hard-line policy on trade with the Soviet Union, most Defense officials were not enamored of the idea of "conditioned flexibility." That is, they wanted to see strict controls on technology transfer and strategic trade regardless of the state of U.S.-Soviet relations or the treatment of Soviet dissidents. Stressing the need to protect U.S. technological "lead time," and spurred by the 1976 Defense Science Board Report on the Export of Technology (commonly called the Bucy Report after its chairman, J. Fred Bucy of Texas Instruments), the Department of Defense was motivated by the need, and U.S. governmental capabilities, to control the transfer of critical technologies for reasons of national security.

The U.S. Congress was divided on the issue. Senator Jackson, and others earlier supporting the Jackson-Vanik amendment efforts, wanted the Carter Administration to be even more restrictive. Jackson warned that the Soviets were acquiring technology that bore directly on the military balance; he described our export controls on militarily relevant technology as "acute hemorrhaging."[20] However, Representative Bingham and Senator Stevenson, chairmen of the primary House and Senate's subcommittees concerned with export control policy, were deeply troubled and fearful that economic diplomacy would do further damage to the United States' declining export performance. The private sector was also divided. Businesses with interests in the Soviet market were outspokenly critical of the policy. Agreeing with Shultz's critical characterization of the policy as "lightswitch diplomacy," they wondered how it would be possible to engage in meaningful business ventures with the Soviet Union under such political uncertainty. On the other hand, the Jewish groups were highly supportive of the President's policy and lauded his efforts to pressure the Soviets.

Even though the White House with its activist NSC advisor Brzezinski was the primary U.S. center of power influencing U.S.-Soviet relations during this period, they were not effective in formulating a unified national policy. A typical response from government officials to my queries about U.S. trade policy with the Soviet Union was: "What policy? We don't have a policy; or if we do, it changes almost daily." Resentment of the NSC role, a lack of presidential leadership, and deep bureaucratic differences resulted in considerable infighting, delay, and uncertainty. Nowhere was this more apparent than concerning the issue of trade promotion and export controls.

One of the high priorities of the Carter Administration was the promotion of U.S. exports. In an anti-inflation speech in April 1978 President Carter called for a cabinet-level task force to increase federal incentives to export and to remove unwarranted trade barriers, including unnecessary export controls. This pro-trade program occurred at the same time that Congress began to review the Export Administration Act (EAA) of 1969, which was due to expire in the fall of 1979. Although the 1969 Act represented a far-reaching liberalization of its predecessor, the Export Control Act of 1949, there was considerable opinion in government, and even stronger feelings in the private sector, that the United States should do more to remove trade barriers and promote exports. Concerning export controls, many in Congress and the export community felt that the EAA of 1969 should be revised to reduce unnecessary controls (e.g., export controls imposed for reasons of foreign policy) and streamline the lengthy, time-consuming licensing process. Following extensive hearings throughout the spring of 1979, four major bills were introduced in Congress to renew the EAA of 1969. The Senate Banking Committee, under the direction of Senator Adlai Stevenson (D-Ill.), introduced a bill that would have significantly reduced U.S. controls and streamlined the licensing process. The House Committee on International Relations, under the leadership of Representative Jonathan Bingham (D-N.Y.), introduced a similar pro-trade bill. A third bill, introduced by Congressmen Barber Conable (R-N.Y.) and Sam Gibbons (D-Fla.), was even more strongly pro-trade and proposed sweeping changes in the licensing structure and administration of export controls. However, a fourth bill, introduced by Congressman Lester Wolff (D-N.Y.) and Clarence Miller (R-Ohio), and supported by Senator Jackson, was intended to tighten controls and move primary licensing authority from the Department of Commerce, which was considered too lax, to the more security-conscious Department of Defense.

The U.S. government became deeply divided on the question of East-West trade and export controls. On the one side stood those in favor of reducing and streamlining controls, and expanding trade. Included were the key congressional actors, Senator Stevenson and Representatives Bingham, Conable, and Gibbons. Also included were the more pro-trade arms of the executive branch, the Departments of Commerce, State, and Treasury, although these agencies were divided within, because of both conflicting internal responsibilities—for example, within DOC, the Bureau of East-West Trade was responsible for promoting trade with the Soviet Union while the Office of Export Administration was authorized to control it—and varying degrees of support for the mixed signals coming out of the White House. The White House was also divided. There were those concerned with the strategic balance who wanted to control technology transfer more tightly and use trade and technology to bargain with the Soviets, and there were those who wanted to reduce export barriers and promote U.S. trade performance worldwide. Because of these divisions, the White House did not play a leading role in the review of the Export Administration Act and the bureaucracy remained divided.

Supportive of reducing trade controls and active in the congressional review were many trade associations representing the high technology industries (computers, electronics, petroleum equipment, etc.); also involved were the National Association of Manufacturers, the Emergency Committee on American Trade, the National Governors' Association, and other interest groups supporting an expansion of American trade. These groups worked effectively with the pro-trade members of Congress; together they represented a formidable coalition and center of power in the 1979 review of U.S. export control policy.

There were also important actors concerned with maintaining or even tightening export controls on East-West and U.S.-Soviet trade. The Department of Defense and the Department of Energy, then under the direction of Secretary James Schlesinger, were both control-oriented, as were key White House actors such as Zbigniew Brzezinski and certain members of the NSC staff. However, the mood of the country and Congress was clearly pro-trade in 1979 and although there were modifications to some of the more radical elements of the pro-trade, anti-control bills, the new Export Administration Act, signed into law by President Carter in September 1979, was intended to minimize controls and facilitate the licensing of exports. The act noted, among its findings, that restricting exports "can have serious adverse effects on the balance of payments" and urged that export trade be "given a high priority."

These hopeful signs for U.S.-Soviet trade were short-lived. A few months later, in December 1979, Soviet troops moved into Afghanistan. No nation committed to world peace and stability, President Carter said, "can continue to do business as usual with the Soviet Union." On 4 January 1980 President Carter announced the following sanctions against the USSR: (1) an embargo on future grain exports (and other livestock and feed-related products), involving cancellation of an offer of 17 million metric tons (mmt) of wheat and corn, but excluding the delivery of the 8 mmt covered under the 1975 Agreement; (2) suspension of licensing of all high technology and other products requiring validated export licenses as well as all outstanding licenses, pending a review of licensing by an interagency committee chaired by the new Secretary of Commerce, Philip Klutznick; (3) reduction of Soviet fishing privileges in U.S. waters; and (4) limitation of Aeroflot service to the United States.

On 9 January 1980 the International Longshoremen's Association (ILA) announced a boycott of all Soviet cargo and/or ships at ports from Maine to Texas. This led over the next year to a sharp reduction of Soviet liner service to the East Coast and Gulf ports, and the shifting of bulk cargoes to third-flag vessels. On 18 March the Department of Commerce announced that a review of export control policy had been completed and that the President had decided on more restrictive criteria to be used in controlling exports of high technology to the Soviet Union. The administration began a case-by-case review of outstanding export licenses and pending applications. On 28 March Secretary Klutznick announced that at the direction of the President he was barring exports of U.S. goods and technology to be used at the 1980 Summer Olympics in Moscow as well as other transactions and payments associated with Olympic-related exports.

The use of trade sanctions in the aftermath of the invasion of Afghanistan was economic diplomacy in action and gutted the pro-trade intentions of the EAA of 1979. President Carter was clearly the key player in imposing the sanctions. He quotes from his diary:

> We discussed how far we wanted to go with economic measures against the Soviet Union. I want to go the maximum degree—interrupting grain

sales, high technology, cancelling fishing rights, reexamining our commerce guidelines, establishing a difference in COCOM (an international
committee which set rules for trade with communist nations) between the
Soviet Union and China, cancelling visits to the Soviet Union, restricting
any sort of negotiations on culture, trade and so forth.[21]

Although the President acted decisively in using economic sanctions to
respond to the Soviet invasion of Afghanistan, he was unable to forge a
unified policy within the U.S. government and the Western alliance.
Domestically, his policy of economic diplomacy and use of trade sanctions met with considerable resistance even though the Soviet invasion
brought widespread condemnation throughout all sectors of American
society. Although economic warfare was a policy based upon widespread
consensus in the 1950s, President Carter's movement in that direction in
the 1980s, even in view of provocative Soviet foreign policies (not only in
Afghanistan, but also in Cuba, the Horn of Africa, and other places as
well), brought about contentious domestic conflict. There was even considerable division in the White House.[22] Although Secretary Vance and
the Department of State surprised both President Carter and Brzezinski
in recommending harsh economic reprisal in response to the Soviet
invasion, the decisions brought about "acrimonious" debates within the
White House.[23] Vice-President Mondale opposed the grain embargo,
and others felt the United States would be acting alone without the
support of her allies. The executive branch was deeply divided with
splits within and between the various departments. Congress, the private
sector, the academic community, and the broader public were also divided.[24] Some felt that the President's actions were appropriate; yet
others considered them misguided and likely to fail.

What is important to note is that although there was widespread
dissatisfaction in the United States with the Soviet Union's domestic and
foreign policies—and particularly with the invasion of Afghanistan—
the U.S. government could not create a unified policy of economic reprisal. There are several important reasons for this. First, the period of
detente saw considerable dissolution of the Cold War mentality (or ideology) upon which the policies of economic diplomacy and warfare might
be based. Although many Americans and important political actors still
subscribed to these beliefs, many others felt that trade and economic
relations between East and West were important, for both economic and
political reasons, and ought to be preserved even in the face of abhor-
rent Soviet policies. Once again, the U.S. government was acting without
a consensus on the fundamental economic, security, and foreign policy
premises of U.S.-Soviet trade.

Second, not only had America's Cold War ideology weakened, but
so too had its presidency. A weakened presidency in the aftermath of

Vietnam and Watergate, combined with a new president inexperienced in foreign policy, often getting conflicting advice from his Secretary of State and National Security Advisor, made it extremely difficult for President Carter to forge a policy of consensus. My interviews during this period found many who felt that the President, the White House and NSC staff, and the broader executive branch mishandled the issue. The Carter Administration evinced mixed signals, too little and ineffective consultation, and a lack of executive leadership.

Third, U.S. economic needs and problems, and the political interests they generated, established a political climate in which economic sanctions were not easily accepted. The business community had been mobilized to support the President's National Export Policy and they had invested considerable time and resources in fighting for a liberalization of the Export Administration Act and U.S. export controls. When the President decided to wage a battle of economic warfare, many in Congress, the executive branch, and the private sector, and in allied countries as well, remained wedded to a policy of economic detente. By the end of the Carter Administration, the United States and the Western alliance were deeply divided on the issues of U.S.-Soviet and East-West trade.

The Reagan Years: 1981–84

The domestic political context at the outset of the Reagan Administration can be described in terms of three elements: the inherited interests and cleavages concerning U.S.-Soviet and East-West trade; the deteriorating U.S.-Soviet relationship; and the conservative, anti-Soviet philosophy of the new administration. Among the traditional interests were the business and farming lobbies which supported trade for economic reasons. Some business groups were not particularly interested in the importance of Soviet trade *per se* but felt rather that America's unfavorable record in U.S.-Soviet trade could jeopardize its reputation as a reliable supplier and its competitive position, trade performance, and profitability worldwide. Others supported U.S.-Soviet trade for foreign policy reasons. Some valued the "stick" (negative linkage), thinking that trade provided the United States bargaining power over the Soviets; others preferred the "carrot" (positive linkage), feeling that trade would encourage the Soviets to play a more responsible role in international affairs. The anti-traders took an even keener interest in U.S.-Soviet economic relations during the Reagan period. Some opposed trade on moral grounds, believing that the U.S. should not do business with the "evil empire" under any conditions. Others criticized trade on economic grounds, considering the U.S.-Soviet commercial relationship a "one-way" street with the Soviets deriving most of the benefits. Others opposed economic relations with the Soviet Union for national security and strategic reasons; U.S. and Western trade was seen as contributing directly to the Soviet military buildup. These and other considerations continued to compete for popular and political support.

The positions of the anti-traders were strengthened by the deteriorating U.S.-Soviet relationship. Continuing criticism of the Soviets' occupation of Afghanistan, their complicity in the Polish crisis, their involvement in regional crises such as the Middle East and Central America, and their continuing military buildup and firm positions on arms control provided increased ammunition for those critical of the trade relationship. The promises of those in favor of economic detente, the anti-traders argued, had been disproven by Soviet policies in the late 1970s and early 1980s. The Soviets, in their opinion, had become more adventurous abroad and more repressive at home.

President Reagan, and many joining him in the new administration, assumed office in January 1981 with a strong inclination toward the anti-trade points of view. In terms of foreign policy, they saw no evidence of the positive impact of trade on Soviet behavior. Economically speaking, they saw the United States as having to invest extra resources in developing new defense capabilities in order to respond to Soviet military advancements resulting from their access to Western technologies. Furthermore, excessive Western credits, often subsidized by U.S. allies, were seen as providing Soviet leverage over their Western creditors. Finally, and perhaps most important of all, President Reagan and some members of the new administration were purportedly concerned about the contribution of Western equipment and technology to the Soviet military buildup.

The Reagan Administration sought to develop and implement a comprehensive policy on East-West trade. The policy was to be consistent, prudent, and predictable. It was to be both restrictive and based on the idea of linkage; trade was not to be conducted in a vacuum but would be conditioned by Soviet behavior and the international environment. National security and strategic considerations were to loom large in this policy. There would be a tightening of strategic/military trade controls said to contribute (both directly and indirectly) to Soviet military capabilities, and an effort to avoid trade in areas that might result in excessive Western resource dependencies (e.g., natural gas) and excessive financial exposure. The Reagan strategy grew out of an NSC paper that outlined a "prudent approach" to East-West economic relations. The approach argued that economic relations with the Soviet Union and Eastern Europe should be conducted within the context of the broad political-security objectives of the Western Alliance. Included in these objectives were the needs to right the strategic balance and bring about NATO modernization. Concerning economic relations, the "prudent approach" sought to (1) review the adequacy and improve the enforcement of COCOM strategic trade controls; (2) convince the allies that export controls for reasons of foreign policy are necessary in contingency planning and in responding to crises; (3) foster alliance discussion of dependencies on Eastern resources and markets, and develop collective measures to guard against Western vulnerabilities; and (4) gain Eastern adherence to the rules of economic relations as practiced in the West. Although the Reagan Administration had great hopes about articulating and implementing this prudent approach in concert with America's allies, domestic and alliance politics intervened. The ensuing political conflict was indicative of the pluralistic nature of U.S. and alliance politics and raged in a variety of issue areas.

Grain and Agricultural Trade

During the 1980 campaign President Reagan had opposed the grain embargo "because American farmers had been unfairly singled out to bear the burden of this ineffective national policy."[25] After several months of intense discussion within the new administration, President Reagan on 24 April 1981 moved to honor his campaign pledge and lift the grain embargo. Responses to a Congressional inquiry corroborate my interview findings of an interagency split on this sensitive issue.[26] The Department of State was in favor of preserving the embargo for the time being; State felt that the embargo was having a significant impact on Soviet grain imports and bringing about declining meat production.[27] The Department of Agriculture disagreed and argued that "the embargo on the USSR had not been effective in terms of its impact on the USSR, while here at home it has represented a serious burden for American farmers."[28] There were also interagency disputes about whether the United States ought to demand a *quid pro quo* for lifting the grain embargo (which it did not), about the question of timing, and about sending ambiguous signals to the Soviets and our allies. Following the President's announcement, there was considerable division in other quarters of American government as well.

Congressional reaction ran along the traditional lines. Legislators from the farm states supported the President's decision. Senators Robert Dole (R-Kan.), and Roger W. Jepsen (R-Iowa) applauded the President's action; Jepsen said that it "sent a message to the world that this administration will keep its promises."[29] Opponents of the action, both Democratic and Republican, were critical of the message the United States was sending to the Soviets and to our allies. Senate minority leader Robert Byrd (D-WVa.) said lifting the embargo now gives our nation "an image of softness and vacillation."[30] Senator Charles McC. Mathias Jr. (R-Md.) noted: "The worst thing we could do is give any indication that we are accepting the occupation of Afghanistan as a normal situation."[31] Representative Bingham found the President's actions "amazing," "truly astounding" and sought to reimpose the embargo.[32] Moreover, Congressmen from industrial and high technology districts considered lifting of the grain embargo and simultaneous tightening of industrial and technology trade controls as unfair to their constituencies.[33]

Even more critical on these grounds were America's allies. The vigorous efforts of the Reagan Administration to slow industrial and technological trade, particularly that associated with the Urengoi (sometimes called the Yamal or Yamburg) natural gas pipeline, while simultaneously ending the grain embargo, approving large above-agreement agricultural sales, and finally in 1983, signing a new long-term grain agreement did not sit well with America's allies. The Reagan Administration hoped the Europeans would see these actions as evidence that the United States was not out to end all trade with the USSR; however, the President's actions were widely denounced by Western leaders, by NATO Secretary Luns, and by the European press. The perception of a double standard in U.S. policies in this regard provoked the European response that "what is good for the American farmer is also good for Western European workers."[34] The Reagan Administration responded to these charges by arguing that there was a fundamental difference between agricultural trade and the gas pipeline project; grain exports drain the Soviet Union of hard currency, are non-strategic and consistent with the administration's policy of promoting non-strategic, while restricting strategic, East-West trade. Furthermore, the Reagan Administration argued that the Urengoi controls hurt the United States as much as the Europeans, noting that each side had about the same value of contracts at stake.

The Reagan Administration endured the domestic and alliance pressures and strains and set about placing U.S.-Soviet agricultural trade on a sound commercial footing. President Reagan warned a group of farmers on 22 March 1981 that there might be times when U.S. national security is threatened and he might declare an agricultural embargo, but he promised not to do so unless it was part of a complete boycott having the cooperation of other nations. His commitment corresponded with the intent of the new Agricultural and Food Act of 1981, which significantly increased the compensation to farmers in the event of an agricultural restriction which is not imposed on all U.S. exports.

One of the major issues on the President's agenda was now the extension of the 1976–81 grain agreement with the Soviet Union. On 3 August 1981 the United States and the Soviet Union agreed to extend the agreement for one year and seek to negotiate a new long-term agreement. When the negotiations were delayed due to the Polish crisis, the two parties agreed to extend the agreement for another year in 1982.

The questions of extensions and signing a new agreement generated considerable controversy and division inside and outside of the U.S. government. The Reagan Administration was being cautious. It did not want to foreclose agricultural trade with the USSR, but it wanted the Soviets to know that it was not eager to normalize trade relations under the present state of political relations. Even those who generally supported agricultural trade with the Soviet Union—for example, the wheat and grain associations and their Congressional representatives—were divided on the question of extending the old or signing a new long-term agreement. Farm associations such as the National Association of Wheat Growers and the U.S. Wheat Associates normally oppose government-to-government trade agreements, although both recognize that a special situation exists with the USSR. The Cargill Grain Company—one of the largest grain exporters in the world—surprised the agricultural community in the summer of 1982 by publicly opposing the renegotiation of another long-term agreement. Cargill contended that such arrangements do not create new demand because they do not add new consuming units or induce countries to buy more grain than they originally intended. Instead of bilateral agreements, Cargill argued, the United States should guarantee to customers the sanctity of negotiated contracts. The American Farm Bureau Federation and the American Soybean Association also opposed long-term bilateral agreements, insisting that "free market" principles should apply to the sale of all U.S. farm goods. On the other side, the Wheat Growers' Association, the National Grain and Feed Association, and the National Corn Growers' Association all supported the negotiation of a new long-term grain agreement.

Due to the Soviet involvement in Poland and the deteriorating U.S.-Soviet relationship, President Reagan delayed the negotiation of a new agreement for over two years, calling attention to self-imposed restraint. However, wanting to enhance America's image as a reliable supplier, President Reagan finally proposed to the Soviet Union in April of 1983 that they negotiate a new agreement. The discussions proceeded quickly and in August, Agriculture Secretary John Block and Soviet Foreign Trade Minister Nikolai Patolichev signed a new five-year agreement which imposed a minimum annual level of Soviet imports of nine million metric tons of wheat and corn. Referring to Block's description during the Moscow signing ceremonies of President Carter's embargo as distasteful, Zbigniew Brzezinski quipped: "What is truly distasteful is Secretary Block crawling on his knees to Moscow."[35] Seeing its share of Soviet grain imports dropping from around 70 percent at the time of the embargo to about 20–25 percent in 1983, the Reagan Administration moved to reestablish the U.S. share of agricultural exports in the Soviet market.

The question of agricultural exports, like other East-West trade issues, generated considerable political conflict during the Reagan years. There was division inside and outside of government. The most powerful actors appeared to be the farm lobbies and their Congressional representatives. President Reagan's campaign pledge, his ability to rationalize agricultural exports as non-strategic trade costly to the Soviets, and the power of the pro-trade elements of the bureaucracy—particularly the Department of Agriculture—encouraged the administration to act in a way that would expand U.S.-Soviet agricultural trade. As we shall see, the intent and thrust of this pro-trade decision was unique when placed alongside the President's other actions intended to reduce the level of U.S.-Soviet and East-West trade.

The Polish Sanctions and the Pipeline Imbroglio

Soviet involvement in the Polish crisis and the imposition of Polish martial law gave President Reagan cause to further restrict non-agricultural East-West trade. On 29 December 1981 President Reagan imposed a number of sanctions, citing heavy and direct Soviet responsibility for the repression in Poland. U.S. sanctions on the Soviet Union consisted of: (1) suspension of Aeroflot services; (2) closing of the Soviet purchasing commission; (3) postponement of negotiations on a new long-term grain agreement; (4) suspension of negotiations on a new maritime agreement; (5) suspension of the granting or renewal of validated export licenses to the USSR; (6) expansion of the list of oil and gas equipment and technology requiring a validated export license, and suspension of the granting of such licenses; (7) continuation of the "no exemption" policy for the USSR in COCOM; and (8) non-renewal of some exchange agreements on energy and technological cooperation.

The President's actions stirred immediate response pro and con. Noting that it took the Polish crisis to "energize the U.S. government," Senator Henry Jackson attacked the administration for still being far away from a vigorous program to meet the Soviet danger.[36] He criticized the administration for the earlier licensing of energy equipment and technology, claiming that it told our allies and the Soviets that the United States did not consider oil and gas production strategic items. He went on to recommend that:

> The Administration should immediately prohibit the use of any American technology in connection with the pipeline. It should promptly convene meetings at the highest allied level to develop alternatives for Western European energy. It should provide substantial assistance in developing such alternatives, including technological and financial measures. And it should provide strong incentives for our allies to develop Western energy supplies rather than Soviet ones.[37]

Lurking beneath the surface of this and related statements, and intensely debated in the U.S. government, was the issue of moving further to extend extraterritorially the sanctions to include equipment produced by U.S. subsidiaries abroad, as well as equipment produced abroad under license arrangement with U.S. companies.

Although the President appeared to act decisively when imposing the sanctions in December, the administration was divided then, and in subsequent months, on this crucial question. The Department of State, typically sensitive to the views of the allies, was opposed to moving once again to discourage European participation in the natural gas pipeline project. Secretary of State Haig preferred an alternative package of sanctions in the credit field that might be more acceptable to the allies. Haig and others at State were afraid of putting undue pressure on the allies to the point that it would weaken the alliance and shift attention from the Polish crisis to the likely divisions that would result in the Atlantic Alliance. The Department of Defense, and the National Security Council and White House staff, on the other hand, pushed for extending the controls. These groups argued that even if the allies were not forced to come along, at least they would come to understand how seriously the Reagan Administration considered the issue.

Concerning the broader question of East-West energy cooperation, certain members of the Reagan Administration—particularly Secretary of Defense Caspar Weinberger—had been deeply concerned about the question of Western participation in Soviet energy development from the outset of the new administration. Now the Polish crisis provided them with one more opportunity to try to discourage it. At issue from the beginning was the Urengoi gas pipeline which would deliver gas from the Soviet Union to Western Europe. At the Ottawa Summit in the summer of 1981 President Reagan had urged the allies to reassess the advisability and security implications of the pipeline and to consider pursuing energy alternatives. The President went on record to say that he opposed the pipeline in principle if not in practice. The West Europeans informed the President of their intentions to proceed with the pipeline, the so-called East-West trade deal of the century.

During the summer and fall of 1981, U.S. officials continued to warn the allies about the security implications of the pipeline, particularly the issue of West European vulnerability to Soviet gas leverage. In July of 1981, high officials in the Department of Defense proposed opposing the pipeline in practice, but were overruled by the President. They and others in the Reagan Administration were also concerned about the boost the pipeline would provide to the Soviets' hard currency earnings. State Department official Myer Rashish then led a delegation of U.S. officials to Europe to discuss U.S. proposals for energy alternatives.

Hard-liners in the administration blame Haig for not pursuing this course of action vigorously enough. Although always interested in considering energy options, the Europeans remained committed to the Urengoi pipeline project.

In February 1982 Undersecretary of Commerce Lionel Olmer disclosed that the U.S. government was now considering sanctions that would (1) prohibit subsidiaries of U.S. firms from exporting non-U.S. oil and gas equipment and technology to the USSR and (2) prohibit export to the USSR of products made abroad using technology exported from the United States before the imposition of the U.S. controls. The decision to apply these sanctions was left in abeyance pending a summer mission to Europe to get allied support for tighter credit and financial conditions, led by Undersecretary of State James Buckley, and President Reagan's participation in the June 1982 Versailles summit. Although the Buckley mission and Versailles summit proceeded independently, the U.S. pressed the allies to raise credit rates and tighten financial supports for East-West trade in both. When the allies failed to fully support the President's proposals, Reagan returned from the summit and startled both the allies and many informed observers by announcing on 18 June the extraterritorial extension of the U.S. controls noted above. These controls appeared to be directed more at the U.S.'s European allies than at its adversaries.

The President's actions unleashed political storms both at home and within the alliance. Senate Foreign Relations Committee Chairman Charles Percy (R-Ill.) said it "is difficult to see how this action will do any more than split the NATO alliance and give the Soviet Union an opening to further divide us."[38] The U.S. Chamber of Commerce said the "unprecedented blanket prohibition over U.S. subsidiaries and affiliates and control of previously licensed U.S. technology pose serious questions concerning the present direction of U.S. international economic policy."[39] Former Undersecretary of State George Ball called the sanctions a "great affront" to U.S. allies, saying that the administration's claim that it was blocking the pipeline to pressure the Polish government to ease repressive measures was "mere shadowplay."[40]

Congress was soon drawn into the fray as well. After listening to Undersecretaries Olmer and Buckley defend the President's actions, a House subcommittee approved legislation on 4 August 1982 to terminate the Reagan Administration's controls on the export and reexport of U.S. oil and gas technology to the Soviet Union.[41] The House Foreign Affairs Committee said the President's controls add "substantially to both the perception and the fact that the U.S. controls are more of a sanction upon Europe than upon the Soviet Union."[42] On 10 August the Committee voted 22-12 to abolish the President's controls. The House bill was introduced in the U.S. Senate on 13 August by Senator Paul Tsongas (D-Mass.) who said the President's policy "is driving a wedge between the United States and Western Europe, to what must be the obvious delight of the Kremlin."[43]

The Reagan Administration fought back and gathered more ammunition to support its policy. Secretary of Defense Weinberger revealed that the Soviets may have been using slave labor on the pipeline project. Supporting the administration's position, Rep. William Broomfield (R-Mich.) told the House of Representatives of additional reports of slave labor including one noting that some 10,000 Vietnamese had been sent to work on the pipeline to offset Vietnam's debt to the Soviet bloc.[44] Although these and related actions severely weakened the House bill, those critical of the administration's policy still managed to pass (209-197) and send to the Senate a bill intended to overturn the President's sanctions.

The allies also registered their strong dissatisfaction with the President's policies. In June 1982 the Foreign Ministers of the European Community threatened court action against the U.S. sanctions and called them "contrary to the principles of international law, unacceptable to the Community, and unlikely to be recognized in courts in the EC."[45] In July the European Community lodged a formal protest calling on the Reagan Administration to reverse its decision. The protest was preceded and followed by more stiff criticism from the EC Foreign Ministers and European heads of state.

Citing "substantial agreement" among the allies on an economic strategy toward the Soviet Union, President Reagan announced on 13 November 1982 the lifting of the extraterritorial controls.[46] Although the President noted that the allies agreed not to engage in trade arrangements which contribute to the military or strategic advantage of the Soviets, or serve preferentially to aid the "heavily militarized Soviet economy," the so-called agreement was of questionable significance. Within hours the French tried to disassociate themselves from it by saying in a communique that France was "not a party to the agreement" announced in Washington. On the more positive side, the agreement did result in the series of alliance studies concerning the broader issues of East-West economic relations (described in Angela Stent's chapter).

Although the White House sought to be the primary center of U.S. power during this episode, the furor in Congress and within the Western Alliance had forced the Reagan Administration to rescind the controls. The President rationalized the lifting of the extraterritorial controls in terms of the new resolve of the allies to consider the strategic dimensions of East-West trade. Little had really changed, however, and the Europeans went ahead with their East-West trade deal of the century.

Strategic Trade and Multilateral Export Controls

President Reagan and some key members of his administration assumed power in 1981 with a deep suspicion of the strategic and military consequences of East-West trade and technology transfer. The point man in raising these concerns, Secretary of Defense Caspar Weinberger, warned: "The Soviets have organized a massive, systematic effort to get advanced technology from the West. The purpose is to support the Soviet military buildup."[47] In the 1981 Department of Defense white paper, *Soviet Military Capabilities,* a section on the "Soviets' Quest for Technological Superiority" warned of the West's shrinking technological advantage and the contribution of U.S. technology to Soviet military capabilities.[48]

Key appointments in the Department of Defense and other agencies gave broader support and exposure to this point of view. Richard Perle, Senator Henry Jackson's former assistant and key actor in the Jackson-Vanik amendment episode, was appointed Assistant Secretary of Defense for International Security Policy. An active and articulate supporter of more restrictive export controls, Perle was a highly visible supporter of the President's policy.[49] Another key appointment was Lawrence Brady as Assistant Secretary of Trade Administration in the Department of Commerce. Brady had already established his credentials for tighter export controls during the Carter Administration when, as acting director of the Office of Export Administration (OEA), he went against the administration's policy (and that of his boss, Secretary of Commerce Juanita Kreps) and warned Congress of the hemorrhaging of U.S. and Western export controls. Describing the Carter Administration's export control policy as "a total shambles," Brady sought to tighten the controls during the Reagan period. Both Perle and Brady felt greater control of East-West trade and technology transfer was necessary to protect America's superiority in military technology and, eventually, her freedoms.

During the early Reagan period, the new administration proposed a package of measures to curtail the eastward flow of military-related technology. The measures included strengthening of U.S. and allied (COCOM) export controls, increasing efforts against foreign industrial espionage, expanding the control list of "militarily critical technologies," and getting the academic community to reduce Soviet access to the free exchange of ideas in U.S. scholarly research.[50] The President hoped for and expected allied support and cooperation on these measures. The President's most meaningful opportunities to press these issues in multilateral fora were at the Western economic summits. In the 1981 summit at Ottawa the President's East-West trade concerns were relegated—by Pierre Trudeau at Helmut Schmidt's insistence—to the final minutes of the conference. Although the allies did agree to follow-up discussions within the COCOM forum, the allies were skeptical of U.S. motives to upgrade and tighten the COCOM export control system. One of the reasons for the lack of U.S. success was the inability of the U.S. government to agree on what should be done and how it ought to go about it. This was a result of continuing interagency and broader domestic disputes about the nature of U.S.-Soviet trade policy.

The question of strategic trade controls has traditionally generated political conflict, both at home and within the Western alliance;[51] it soon became an explosive issue in the Reagan administration. The Department of State, the lead U.S. governmental agency for the administration of export controls within the multilateral COCOM system, placed considerable importance on working quietly and cooperatively with the allies to improve the COCOM system. Sensitive to demanding too much, attempting to be realistic about what was possible within an uneasy partnership where U.S. allies valued highly their trade with the Soviet Union and East European states, most State Department officials took great care to avoid antagonizing U.S. allies on the issue. They sought export controls limited to what was clearly defined as strategic.

The Department of Defense, on the other hand, was in favor of broadening the controls and pressuring the allies to shore up what it perceived as the hemorrhaging COCOM control system. In a January 1982 briefing to the President's Export Council Subcommittee on Export Administration, Assistant Defense Secretary Perle argued:

> I don't believe we have made a sufficiently determined effort yet to bring our allies along. I am under no illusions about how easy it will be to dissuade them. In fact I rather doubt that they can be dissuaded by argument alone. But a combination of argument and pressure—a good deal more pressure than we have applied in the past—ought to be able to cut down significantly on their willingness to transfer advanced technology to the Soviet Union.[52]

Perle went on to discuss specific forms of pressure, noting that one U.S. ally (most likely, West Germany) was interested in acquiring some U.S. military technology but was told they should not expect to get it until they improved their strategic export controls. Under these circumstances, controls on West-West technology transfer became a hotly contested issue both in U.S. and allied governmental circles.

The Department of Defense was clearly the lead agency during this period in pressuring the allies, the U.S. Congress, and the responsible U.S. agencies—particularly the Office of Export Administration within the Department of Commerce—to tighten export controls. It gained surprising support in this effort from the Department of Commerce. Commerce has traditionally had something of a split personality on East-West trade due to its dual trade promotion and control functions. The

general orientation of the Department of Commerce is pro-trade; however, the Office of Export Administration within the Department is responsible for export controls. During the Reagan period, with the
control-oriented Lawrence Brady in overall charge of export administration, the Department went much farther than usual in emphasizing
the control side of its dual functions, particularly when it came to the
issue of trade with the Soviet Union. Illustrative of this, on 20 May 1982,
Secretary of Commerce Baldrige warned that current export control
enforcement efforts were inadequate.

> One of the Reagan Administration's most important achievements so far
> is the initiative to significantly improve the multilateral system of strategic
> trade controls that restrict the flow of sophisticated Western technology
> which could contribute, directly or indirectly, to the improvement of
> Soviet military capabilities.[53]

On the same day, Commerce Undersecretary for International Trade
Lionel Olmer warned of "a hemorrhage . . . of a national heritage" if
more were not done to carefully control the export of high technology to
the Soviet Union.[54] While Baldrige and Olmer were also sensitive to the
importance of U.S. export performance, they generally joined the Department of Defense and the White House on the issue of tightening
export controls. With this support, the Reagan Administration pushed
on a variety of fronts to combat the technology drain. Included were
greater restrictions on academic research with military relevance, efforts
to stem illegal transfers of outbound cargo through U.S. borders (Operation Exodus), and more emphasis on intelligence, enforcement and
prosecution.

Congress, representing the diverse interests of American economic
and political life, was divided, as usual. There were the traditional anti-
Soviet legislators who were concerned that the United States and the
West were "selling the rope." There were others like Senator Sam Nunn
(D-Ga.) who spearheaded detailed Congressional and CIA investigations
and hearings and made a serious effort to look into the transfer of U.S.
technology to the Soviet Union.[55] Then there was a growing group of
Congressmen, representing high technology constituencies, who were
fearful of the economic impact of more restrictive controls. As discussed
in greater detail below, these Congressmen were organized to oppose
what they perceived to be excessively restrictive controls damaging the
global competitiveness of U.S. technology exporters. Trade associations,
business lobbies and individual businesses joined congressional efforts to
oppose many of the administration's policies.

Representatives of the academic community also organized to oppose what they perceived to be growing restrictions on the free exchange
of ideas. On 27 February 1981 the presidents of Stanford, Cal Tech,

MIT, Cornell, and the University of California-Berkeley wrote to the Secretaries of Commerce, Defense, and State to express concern over what they saw as attempts to extend unnecessary export restrictions to the academic community. The presidents and other academic organizations continued to express their deep concern about the Reagan Administration's attempts to apply export administration regulations and other controls to universities.[56] A subsequent study by the National Academy of Sciences warned that there were greater costs than benefits in trying to unduly restrict the flow of academic research; the study concluded that restricting access to basic research would require casting a net of controls over wide areas of science that would be extremely damaging to overall scientific, economic, and military progress.[57]

On the other side, a variety of conservative, private organizations like the Heritage Foundation and the Institute on Strategic Trade acted to publicize the Soviets' purported thirst for U.S. technology and the national security costs of weak controls. Miles Costick, President of the Institute on Strategic Trade, wrote and traveled widely to inform the American people and the Western allies of the strategic implications of East-West trade. Although having little direct policy impact, these and other anti-trade actors and associations heightened the American public's concern with the issue, and created a more favorable environment for the policy goals of the Reagan Administration.[58]

The Reagan Administration's efforts to tighten multilateral East-West trade controls, and the bureaucratic politics surrounding these efforts, exploded into public view in the early fall of 1983. Claiming that the "arrogance of the U.S. government is rapidly eroding the effectiveness of controls on the export of strategic equipment and technology," William A. Root, longtime Director of the Department of State's Office of East-West Trade, resigned in protest in an open letter to the President and the U.S. Congress. In the letter, Root wrote that those who "proclaim the loudest" the need to strengthen strategic trade controls (i.e., Department of Defense) "are doing the most to weaken them."[59] In heading up the U.S. office which had to negotiate export control issues (such as the COCOM review of the embargo list) with the Western allies, Root had been continually frustrated by the Department of Defense's advocacy of proposals which were entirely unacceptable to U.S. allies. The difficulties finally came to a head in 1983 when Defense (1) decided to remove itself from the U.S. interagency deliberations concerning the COCOM list review; (2) proclaimed that COCOM was an inadequate forum to negotiate such important issues (e.g., controls on computer exports); and (3) contended that the real negotiations should take place later in an unspecified forum at which a senior Defense official should represent the United States. Fundamental divisions such as these in the U.S. government did not allow the development of a national position and made the problem of forging an alliance consensus impossible. These and related developments were part of the broader political environment in which the Export Administration Act (EAA) was once again reviewed.

The Politics of Export Administration Act Renewal

Despite the major overhaul and expected rationalization and improvement of U.S. export control policy in the Export Administration Act of 1979, implementation of the Act by the Carter and Reagan Administrations drew criticism from various quarters. Anti-trade and defense-oriented critics considered the controls too lenient; pro-trade, business-oriented critics felt the controls were too restrictive and unpredictable and were doing great damage to the credibility and performance of U.S. exporters. With the 1979 Act to expire on 30 September 1983, the renewal of the legislation turned out to be a highly politicized and drawn-out affair.

Although there were differences in the broader administration, the Reagan White House was critical of recent (i.e., Nixon and Carter) export control policy on a number of counts. First, they saw export controls for reasons of national security as excessively lax and allowing the transfer of strategic technologies making significant contributions to Soviet military capabilities. Second, export controls applied for foreign policy reasons (e.g., in response to the Soviet invasion of Afghanistan) discriminated unfairly against some U.S. exporters (i.e., agricultural exporters); furthermore, these controls were applied in a way that was perceived to have little impact on the Soviet Union. Third, the Reagan White House was critical of the lack of predictability in U.S. export controls; exporters were subject to unpredictable regulations and were not given clear signals about what could and could not be exported. Finally, the United States had inadequate control over the exports and re-exports of subsidiaries, licensees, and affiliates in other Western countries.

These issues and the legislation required to update the Act in 1983 represented something of a dilemma for the Reagan Administration. The administration was faced with reconciling its free market orientation and its desire for unfettered free trade with its intention of more strictly controlling the transfer of technology aiding the Soviet military buildup. In addition were the difficulties and dilemmas surrounding foreign policy controls. Although the administration believed that export controls should be linked to Soviet foreign policy behavior, they recognized that such a policy introduced the unpredictability that they sought to reduce; the administration was therefore loath to spell out its exact policy on when foreign policy controls would be applied. The administration was also confronted by other difficult problems when it came to revising the EAA and U.S. export control policy: how to utilize and apply the "critical technologies approach" as required by the 1979 Act;[60] how to coordinate U.S. controls with those of the allies; whether to apply U.S. controls extraterritorially; whether to impose import controls on U.S. allies who did not comply with U.S. controls; how to apply controls differentially to various Communist countries, and notably, how to relax export controls on the People's Republic of China while tightening them on the USSR.

Concerning the issue of foreign policy controls, the EAA of 1979 retained the President's traditional authority to use export controls to achieve U.S. foreign policy goals—the United States remains the only member of the alliance with foreign policy controls—but mandated major revisions in the administration of such controls. The 1979 Act stipulated the criteria the President must consider before using foreign policy export controls. The Act also required the President to inform Congress when imposing, increasing, or extending foreign policy controls; to justify such controls to the public; and to extend annually the controls lest they should expire. Despite these requirements intended to limit presidential use of foreign policy controls, the Carter and Reagan Administrations subsequently initiated major controls on exports to the Soviet Union, and, in so doing, violated at least the spirit if not the legal requirements of the Act.

Consequently, foreign policy controls emerged as one of the central issues in the 1983 review and extension of the EAA. On 4 April 1983, President Reagan sent to Congress proposed legislation to amend and reauthorize the EAA of 1979. Responding to concerns and criticisms that America's use of foreign policy controls was making U.S. exporters unreliable suppliers, the administration's bill contained a provision concerning the sanctity of contracts in force when foreign policy controls were imposed. Some in Congress and the private sector, however, criticized the administration's proposal on contract sanctity, noting that it did not go far enough. They noted that the administration's proposal was limited to contracts requiring delivery of goods or technology within 270 days after the control is imposed; furthermore, the critics complained that the administration's proposal would still allow the President to prohibit exports for which contracts had already been signed if such contracts would prove detrimental to overriding U.S. national interests. The administration's bill did little to allay the concerns of the pro-trade coalitions.

In October of 1983 the U.S. House of Representatives passed a bill, sponsored by Representative Don Bonker (D-Wash.), to extend and amend the EAA of 1979 that was much more to the liking of the pro-trade actors in Congress and the private sector. The House bill had an alternative provision on contract sanctity which would have prohibited the President from imposing foreign policy controls on exports for which contracts had already been signed; however, escape clauses permitting the President great latitude still concerned the pro-traders. Also responding to U.S. and allied complaints about the extraterritorial application of foreign policy controls, the House bill would have prohibited the application of such controls to companies outside the United States. A Senate bill sponsored by Senators Jake Garn (R-Utah) and John Heinz (R-Pa.) was also intended to make important changes in the President's authority to impose foreign policy export controls, and had real contract sanctity, although it was considerably tougher than the House bill on the question of national security controls.

Concerning the question of national security controls, the EAA of 1979 provided for the control of exports which make a "significant contribution" to Soviet military potential. Defense-minded Congressmen and members of the Reagan Administration were concerned that the 1979 Act was still allowing the sale and transfer of "dual use" technologies (those with both civilian and military applications) that had at least indirect, if not direct, impact on the Soviet military buildup. They were concerned that Soviet civilian acquisitions were allowing them to release resources to the Soviet military sector and allowing civilian/military interactions leading to the overall improvement of the technological level in the military sector.

The Reagan Administration's proposed amendments to the EAA of 1979 were intended to address these national security concerns. Among other provisions, the administration provided presidential authority to prohibit imports into the United States from violators of U.S. national security controls; authority for stronger enforcement measures and penalties for violators of export control laws; and other proposals for tightening national security controls. The more pro-trade House bill included some measures for improving enforcement of national security goals, but included many other provisions that were far less restrictive than the administration's proposals. The more security-oriented Senate bill also contained a number of provisions that might have led to more restrictive national security controls, including a provision allowing the president to impose import controls if a majority of the nations belonging to COCOM agreed that the foreign company was in violation of U.S. national security controls. The provisions and bills were changing continuously as the political infighting passed the 30 September 1983 legislative deadline and dragged on into 1984.

There was no one center of power during this ongoing imbroglio but rather multiple centers of power competing to see their interests served. Dividing the various centers and actors were some new and highly sensitive issues (e.g., contract sanctity, extraterritoriality, and import controls) generated by the Carter and Reagan Administrations' active use of export controls. On the issues of import controls and ex-traterritoriality—i.e., the power to apply U.S. export controls to U.S. subsidiaries, licensees, and other affiliates abroad—the Reagan Adminis-tration sought to extend U.S. export controls in the form of a U.S. import ban on the products of foreign companies which violated U.S. controls by allowing unauthorized reexport of U.S. origin items, as well as unauthorized exports by U.S. subsidiaries of non-U.S. origin items. The private sector, and some of its representatives in Congress, vigor-ously opposed the Reagan policy, fearing that such an extension of ex-traterritoriality would further damage U.S. export performance as Western companies would avoid reliance on U.S. technology due to the uncertainties of the politically motivated and often changing use of U.S. export and, now, import controls. Critics cautioned that U.S. insistence on extraterritorial jurisdiction could mean an end to the U.S. multina-tional corporation and to the multilateral system of export controls.

The trade interests of the U.S. export community were represented by Congressman Bonker and other pro-trade congressmen who op-posed the administration's initiatives. Bonker wanted no presidential authority for import controls; no licenses of U.S. exports to allied COCOM countries; and requirements on the president mandating specific Congressional approval (i.e., legislation) prior to imposing ex-traterritorial controls on U.S. subsidiaries, licensees, and other affiliates abroad. Furthermore, to combat the administration's reluctance to guarantee contract sanctity, Bonker and others sought to reduce the president's discretion and provide for full sanctity, meaning that existing contacts would not be broken by foreign policy controls.

The deep and continuing differences between the Congress and administration, and within both the administration and Congress, were reflected in the amount of time Congress devoted to the legislative re-view. Unable to agree on the new act before the expiration of the old on 30 September 1983, Congress extended the 1979 act to 14 October 1983. Still unable to take action, Congress let the 1979 act expire on 15 October, requiring President Reagan to invoke the International Emergency Economic Powers Act to continue his authority to administer U.S. export control policy. Still unable to act before adjournment, Con-gress voted on 18 November to extend the 1979 act once again to 29 February 1984. The debate and differences continued through the spring and summer of 1984. As Americans went to the polls in the fall of 1984, they were still without a new Export Administration Act.

The delay and confusion were consequences of the presence of competing centers of power and the absence of a viable national consen-sus on East-West trade and export controls. The interested actors were divided and unable to agree on the basic premises required for national policy. The pro-traders in the private sector were upset because they were losing business.[61] Labor was upset because of their distaste for the Soviet attitude toward organized labor; they felt East-West trade and technology transfer were weakening the U.S. industrial base and technological superiority and saw the need for further export controls on the sale of American technology.[62] The General Accounting Office was critical because it found many export control regulations to be excessive and ineffective.[63] Some Congressmen were upset because they saw the U.S. "selling the rope;" others saw excessive national security and unpredictable foreign policy controls destroying America's credibility as a reliable supplier. The governmental bureaucracy was divided and the Reagan White House was unable to forge a unified export control policy.

Conclusion

U.S. trade with the Soviet Union has been an instrument of and a hostage to American foreign policy throughout the postwar period. Initially, trade was largely viewed as an instrument of economic warfare; subsequently, in the late 1960s and early 1970s, it began to be seen by some as an instrument of detente. More recently, trade remains a hostage of politics as these and other perspectives compete in the pluralistic American system. During the Nixon period, the executive branch and the U.S. Congress considered significant changes in a number of vital areas of American policy. First, the Congress decided to liberalize its export control policy governing trade with the Soviet Union and other controlled countries. Second, President Nixon agreed to go to Congress to seek a change in U.S. policy, which denied MFN treatment to Soviet goods. Third, the President agreed to make the Soviet Union eligible for loans from the U.S. Exim Bank, facilitate the sale of grain, and form a U.S.-USSR Commercial Commission to ensure that there would be high-level attention to the matters of U.S.-Soviet trade. Not all of these policy changes were fully realized, but they represented an indisputable movement away from a policy of economic warfare and towards a policy of economic detente.

This period had significance beyond the policy changes themselves. In addition, it represented the passing of the former Cold War ideology and the relatively high level of consensus on East-West trade (calling for economic warfare) and the rise of greater divisions and dissension surrounding the new policy of economic detente. During the Cold War period, both the executive and legislative branches viewed trade and Western technology as values to be denied the Soviet Union. The denial of trade and technology transfer was seen by most as a weapon to inflict damage on the Soviet economy. Subsequently, as the Cold War ideology weakened in the 1960s and 1970s, the basic premises surrounding East-West trade, which had previously generated a relatively high level of consensus, became issues of greater division and debate. However, although the Cold War ideology had been discredited, it was not fully replaced. Many began to support a new ideology of expanded trade, coexistence, and detente, but they were unable to generate a reasonable level of agreement on the guiding principles of U.S.-Soviet relations and East-West trade. The lack of agreement on basic premises has been the defining characteristic of the American politics of East-West trade over the last decade. Some major actors and centers of power have been guided by the premises of economic detente, while others still cling to the principles of economic warfare.

The first premise generating disagreement and dissension in the American system concerns the *economic consequences* of East-West trade. There is no agreement in the United States about expected economic benefits, both to the Soviet Union and to the United States, resulting from trade. There are some, and many in the Reagan Administration, who believe that trade should be deemphasized unless the benefits are clearly to the U.S. advantage. And since they see little need for or benefit from U.S.-Soviet trade (except perhaps in agricultural trade), they feel trade should be denied and used to create stress in the Soviet economy, to make the Soviet people more restless and less governable. Some of these anti-traders ignore the U.S. benefits from East-West trade, or if they do acknowledge them, consider them minuscule compared to those derived by the Soviet Union.

On the other hand, there are the pro-traders who contend that trade benefits both the United States and the Soviet Union. Some of the pro-traders cling to the 1960s "bridge building" and 1970s "detente" viewpoints feeling that a healthy Soviet economy and less restless populace will make the Soviet leaders more secure and less assertive abroad. Aware of the declining export performance in the United States, many of these proponents also value the U.S. economic benefits derived from East-West trade and cite the relationship between American export performance there and U.S. competitiveness around the globe.[64] These and other viewpoints concerning the economics of East-West trade continue to divide the American political system in the 1980s.

A second premise defining the American system concerns the *strategic* and *security* implications of U.S.-Soviet trade. Although no responsible American official supports trade which would clearly make a significant contribution to Soviet military capabilities, there are deep differences within the United States today about indirect contributions and the broader security implications of East-West trade. There are some, again dominant in the Reagan Administration, who claim that broad sectors of industrial trade, and particularly both legal and illegal technology sales and transfers, make significant contributions to Soviet military capabilities. Reagan Department of Defense officials such as

Secretary Weinberger and Assistant Secretary Perle contend that much more should and can be done to stem militarily relevant trade and technology transfer. Although not a politically significant force today, some still cling to the more extreme Cold War premise and would go so far as to restrict all trade because of its indirect contribution to Soviet military capabilities.

On the other hand, a politically significant viewpoint and coalition drawing together important actors from the private sector and the U.S. Congress today challenges both this and the Reagan Administration viewpoints. Although conceding that there are strategic and security implications of East-West trade, they argue that efforts to restrict trade are often counterproductive. Citing many unintended consequences of the denial approach and restrictive export controls, these actors note: first, that Western embargo lists may represent priority or shopping lists to Soviet planners, who then concentrate massive resources on both espionage and the indigenous development of the equipment and technology apparently deemed important by the United States and her Western allies; second, by attempting to restrict militarily relevant trade, U.S. export controls impede nonmilitary trade in a way that does considerable damage to U.S. export performance.[65] Overall, the former Cold War perspective that all East-West trade is strategic trade has weakened; yet, there is no new consensus about the security and strategic dimensions of East-West trade.

A third premise, also characterized by dissension and disagreement in the United States today, concerns the *foreign policy* implications of East-West trade and technology transfer. Some perceive a powerful link between trade and political relations; they expect foreign policy benefits from East-West trade. Nixon and Kissinger, among others, expected trade to contribute to a web of constructive relationships that would serve to restrain the less desirable features of Soviet foreign policy. Although U.S.-Soviet trade did not grow significantly because of the Jackson-Vanik and Stevenson amendments, which means that this relationship was never really tested, many still expected increased European-Soviet trade to moderate Soviet behavior. The Carter Administration pursued a more activist form of linkage policy, believing that trade ("the stick") could serve a policy of economic diplomacy; trade leverage could be used to influence Soviet behavior, both foreign and domestic, and serve American values. However, following the Soviet invasion of Afghanistan, Soviet complicity in the Polish crisis, and the shooting down of the KAL flight, critics of East-West trade argued that increased Western trade with the Soviet Union had done nothing to improve Soviet behavior. Again, another fundamental premise of East-West trade is now characterized by division and dissension.

There has never been, of course, total agreement about the defining principles of American foreign policy. However, the Cold War ideology of the 1950s brought considerable support for a policy of economic warfare. As the ideology of that period weakened and support for a policy of economic detente strengthened, it appeared in the early 1970s that detente would build a new consensus around a set of premises supporting East-West trade. This never happened, however, for reasons discussed earlier in the chapter. Instead, the 1970s represented a decade marked by debate and confusion on the issue of trade with the Soviet Union and other communist states. Then, with the inauguration of the Reagan Administration, and the deteriorating U.S.-Soviet relationship, there were efforts to build a neo-Cold War consensus around a policy that looked something like the economic warfare of the past. However, because of the increased decentralization of American foreign policy-making power, the efforts of the Reagan Administration met with stiff resistance.

The old axiom that American "politics stops at the water's edge," suggesting that the United States has a bipartisan foreign policy, has little relevance to the recent period. There was no consensus on the issue of East-West trade, and given the pluralistic structure and process of American government in the contemporary era, there may be little hope of building one. There are a number of reasons for this development, far too complex to analyze here, but they do include the weakening of presidential power in the post-Vietnam and Watergate eras; the increasing assertiveness of a Congress disposed to recapture its constitutional role in American foreign policy; a declining role for the U.S. Department of State in international economic policy; rapid turnover in the bureaucratic actors with responsibility for East-West trade policy; the increasing importance and power of U.S. commercial, and particularly agricultural, interests in a period of declining export performance; and U.S. reactions to Soviet foreign policy intrigues in such places as Angola, Afghanistan and Poland. Of significance and to be discussed here, however, is the fact that a decline in the Cold War consensus was combined with an increasingly pluralistic political system marked by more political actors and centers of power with access to the making and implementation of U.S. foreign economic policy.

This development had significant implications for each of the periods of East-West trade policy considered in this chapter. Although initially reluctant to break with the old Cold War consensus, the Nixon Administration eventually undertook an expansive East-West policy that was based on a new set of premises. It appeared that the Nixon-Kissinger team was moving toward a policy of economic detente that recognized that U.S.-Soviet trade could be of mutual benefit, could improve political relations by providing the U.S. a bargaining tool and leverage, and would not—through the effective use of strategic trade controls—make dangerous contributions to Soviet military capabilities. However, because of the Watergate episode, Senator Jackson's concern with Soviet emigration policy and presidential ambitions, Soviet complicity in Angola, the lingering anti-Soviet premises of the Cold War, and the politics of American pluralism, the Nixon and Ford Administrations achieved little success in building a new consensus.

The Carter Administration had even less success as the differences between the pro- and anti-trade forces became even more pronounced. The pro-trade coalitions in Congress and the private sector fought hard for a liberalization of the Export Administration Act in 1979. Their legislative victories were limited to hortatory language which did nothing to deter the Carter Administration's use of trade sanctions as the primary response to the Soviet invasion of Afghanistan in 1980. The uncertain and confusing Carter strategy of economic diplomacy moved U.S. policy in the direction of economic warfare.

President Reagan assumed the presidency sympathetic to the Cold War roots of this policy, but at the same time, sympathetic to the principles of free trade and wary of the evils of governmental regulation. Cold War personalities, the politics of pluralism in an America that had swung to the right, and a deteriorating East-West environment interacted in complex, confusing and sometimes bewildering ways. Policy reflected this and was changing and also sometimes inconsistent. While honoring his campaign pledge to drop the grain and agricultural embargo, President Reagan simultaneously moved to further restrict most other sectors of East-West trade; after initially allowing licenses for the sale of American equipment to be used in the European-Soviet natural gas pipeline project, the Reagan Administration reversed itself, expanded export controls, applied them extraterritorially to U.S. allies as well, and then dropped them before removing itself from the pipeline fray.

There was no integrated policy governing East-West trade during the Reagan Administration because there was no national consensus. The government and broader populace remained divided on the fundamental economic, foreign policy, and security premises required for a national policy. Unfortunately, the likelihood of a coherent policy in the future appears remote. Political pluralism remains the defining characteristic, the hallmark, of the American system. Ideological dissension continues to characterize our attitudes on U.S.-Soviet trade. Competing coalitions of interests holding conflicting beliefs about the premises of East-West trade will continue to vie for power in the making and implementation of American foreign economic policy.

The development of an integrated, coherent U.S.-Soviet and East-West trade policy appears unlikely. It will be difficult to forge an anti-trade policy of economic warfare because of the powerful coalitions of

U.S. exporters and the pro-East-West trade interests of America's allies. It will be equally difficult to develop a pro-trade policy of economic detente because of the lingering values of the Cold War in an East-West divided world. However, if U.S.-Soviet relations continue to deteriorate as they have in the late 1970s and early 1980s, U.S. trade policy toward the USSR could continue to move in the direction of economic warfare. Conversely, if there were a major arms control agreement and a significant improvement in U.S.-Soviet political relations, economic relations might also improve. Under both scenarios, trade is likely to remain a hostage of politics. Accordingly, a changing, spasmodic, unpredictable, and often inconsistent U.S. policy may have to be recognized as an unfortunate reality of the contemporary era.

NOTES

1. Although U.S. trade relations with the Soviet Union have often been volatile, policy was more consensual and trade virtually nonexistent from 1949 to 1959. Trade began to grow in the 1960s, particularly with the 1963 Soviet crop failure and U.S. grain sales to the Soviet Union, and the former policy of economic warfare became an issue of considerable debate and conflict. For background, see Marshall Goldman, *Detente and Dollars: Doing Business with the Soviets* (New York: Basic Books, 1975); and Jozef Wilczynski, *The Economics and Politics of East-West Trade* (New York: Praeger, 1969).

2. See, for example, Robert A. Pastor, *Congress and the Politics of U.S. Foreign Economic Policy, 1929–1976* (Berkeley: University of California Press, 1980), pp. 26–60.

3. Noted in Henry Kissinger, *The White House Years* (Boston: Little, Brown and Company, 1979), p. 152.

4. Ibid., pp. 152–53.

5. Ibid., p. 154.

6. For a fuller review of these issues, see Gary K. Bertsch, "U.S. Export Controls: The 1970s and Beyond," *Journal of World Trade Law*, 15, no. 1 (1981), pp. 67–82.

7. Kissinger, *The White House Years*, p. 840.

8. See the chronology of U.S.-Soviet trade, 1971–83, in this volume for these and related developments.

9. The following discussion of the Jackson-Vanik amendment draws heavily upon, and is discussed in considerably more detail in, Paula Stern, *Water's Edge: Domestic Politics and the Making of American Foreign Policy* (Westport, Conn.: Greenwood Press, 1979); and Dan Caldwell, "The Jackson-Vanik Amendment," in John Spanier and Joseph Nogee (eds.), *Congress, The Presidency and American Foreign Policy* (Elmsford, N.Y.: Pergamon Press, 1981), pp. 1–21.

10. Nixon notes: "I have never had any illusions about the brutally repressive nature of Soviet society. But I knew the more public pressure we placed on the Soviet leaders, the more intransigent they would become. I also knew that it was utterly unrealistic to think that a fundamental change in the Soviet system

could be brought about because we refused to extend MFN status." Richard
Nixon, *The Memoirs of Richard Nixon* (New York: Grosset and Dunlap, 1978),
p. 876.

11. Security considerations did perhaps play a role in some decisions. For
example, Secretary of Defense Melvin Laird attacked Henry Ford II in 1970 for
considering a Soviet request to build a diesel truck assembly plant. Although
Secretary Laird ended Ford's participation, other U.S. businesses became major
participants in the Kama River enterprise with, interestingly, Laird's concur-
rence.

12. See, for example, President Carter's more conciliatory Charleston July
1977 speech as compared with the more hard-line speech at Wake Forest in
March of 1978. Even within each speech there seem to be more cooperative
stances, attributed to Vance, and more confrontational, associated with
Brzezinski.

13. Zbigniew Brzezinski, *Power and Principle* (New York: Farrar, Straus,
Giroux, 1983), p. 177.

14. As noted by Samuel Huntington, "Trade, Technology and Leverage:
Economic Diplomacy," *Foreign Policy*, 32 (Fall 1978), pp. 64–65.

15. U.S. Military Academy, *Integrating National Security and Trade Policy: The
United States and Soviet Union*, Final Report (West Point, N.Y.: U.S.M.A., 1978),
p. 25.

16. Samuel Huntington, "Trade, Technology and Leverage: Economic Diplomacy," p. 65.

17. George P. Shultz, "Lightswitch Diplomacy," *Business Week* (28 May 1978).

18. For a fuller discussion of the policy of economic diplomacy and related
questions, see Gary K. Bertsch, "U.S.-Soviet Trade: The Question of Leverage,"
Survey, 25, no. 2 (1980), pp. 66–80.

19. In testimony before the Senate Banking Committee in 1979, Secretary
Kreps noted: "Our physical security and foreign policy interests are, of course,
paramount. But economic performance and political and military power are
ultimately inseparable. In today's world, our economic vitality is increasingly
dependent on our ability to export. Today's environment requires that we take
more seriously than ever before the erosion in our power and influence that can
come from a failure to meet the export challenge." U.S. Congress, Senate Banking Committee, *U.S. Export Control Policy and Extension of the Export Administration
Act*, Hearings, 96th Congress, 1st Session, p. 37.

20. U.S. Congress, Senate Permanent Subcommittee on Investigations,
Transfer of Technology to the Soviet Union and Eastern Europe, 95th Congress, 1st
Session, September 1977, p. 2.

21. Jimmy Carter, *Keeping Faith: Memoirs of a President* (New York: Bantam
Books, 1982), pp. 475–76.

22. Brzezinski, *Power and Principle*, p. 433.

23. Carter, *Keeping Faith*, p. 476, and Brzezinski, *Power and Principle*, p. 431.

24. See, for example, U.S. Congress, Hearings before the Subcommittee on
International Finance, *U.S. Embargo of Food and Technology to the Soviet Union*, 96th
Congress, 22 January and 24 March 1980.

25. Statement by the President, Office of the Press Secretary, 24 April 1981.

26. See U.S. Congress, Joint Economic Committee, *East-West Commercial Policy: A Congressional Dialogue with the Reagan Administration*, 16 February 1982,
pp. 40–47.

27. Ibid., p. 41.

28. Ibid.

29. *International Trade Reporter: U.S. Export Weekly*, 28 April 1981, p. A-3.

30. Ibid.

31. Ibid.

32. Ibid., 5 May 1981, p. A-1.

33. Ibid.

34. For a discussion of German views, see Heinrich Vogel, "The Politics of East-West Economic Relations Reconsidered: A German View," *Osteuropa Wirtschaft*, 27, no. 3 (1982), pp. 230–37.

35. *Herald Tribune*, 27–28 August 1983.

36. *International Trade Reporter: U.S. Export Weekly*, 16 February 1982, pp. 533–34.

37. Ibid., p. 534.

38. Ibid., 29 June 1982, p. 454.

39. Ibid., 20 July 1982, p. 558.

40. Ibid., 10 August 1982, p. 671.

41. Ibid., 17 August 1982, pp. 699–700.

42. Ibid., 24 August 1982, p. 748.

43. Ibid., 17 August 1982, p. 699.

44. Ibid., 5 October 1982, pp. 6–7.

45. Ibid., 29 June 1982, p. 454.

46. Ibid., 16 November 1982, p. 259.

47. *Wall Street Journal*, 12 January 1982.

48. *Soviet Military Capabilities* (Washington, D.C.: USGPO, 1981), pp. 71–81.

49. For an illustration of Perle's views see Richard Perle, "Technology and the Quiet War," *Strategic Review* (Winter 1984), pp. 29–35.

50. For a fuller discussion, see Gary K. Bertsch, *East-West Strategic Trade, COCOM and the Atlantic Alliance* (Paris: The Atlantic Institute for International Affairs, 1983). COCOM stands for Coordinating Committee, is based in Paris, and represents NATO (minus Iceland and Spain) and Japan's multilateral body for strategic trade controls.

51. See Gunnar Adler-Karlsson, *Western Economic Warfare, 1947–1967* (Stockholm: Almqvist & Wiksell, 1968).

52. *International Trade Reporter: U.S. Export Weekly*, 2 February 1982, p. 468.

53. Ibid., 1 June 1982, p. 323.

54. Ibid.

55. See U.S. Congress, Report made by the Permanent Subcommittee on Investigations, *Transfer of United States High Technology to the Soviet Union and Soviet Bloc Nations*, 15 November 1982; and Hearings, before the same subcommittee under the same title, 4, 5, 6, 11 and 12 May 1982.

56. See James Ferguson, "Scientific Freedom, National Security, and the First Amendment," *Science*, 12 August 1983.

57. National Academy of Sciences, Committee on Science, Engineering and Public Policy, *Scientific Communication and National Security*, 2 vol. (Washington, D.C.: National Academy Press, 1982).

58. For a fuller treatment of the issues raised in this section, see Gary K. Bertsch and John R. McIntyre (eds.). *National Security and Technology Transfer: The Strategic Dimensions of East-West Trade* (Boulder, Colo.: Westview Press, 1983).

59. *International Trade Reporter: U.S. Export Weekly*, 27 September 1983, p. 915.

60. The "critical technologies" approach grew out of the Report of the Defense Science Board Task Force, *An Analysis of Export Control of U.S. Technology—A DOD Perspective* (Washington, D.C.: Office of the Director of Defense and

Research Engineering, 1976). For the requirements of the EAA of 1979 concerning critical technologies, see Janet Ecker, "National Security Protection: The Critical Technology Approach to U.S. Control of High-Level Technology," *The Journal of International Law and Economics*, 15, no. 3 (1981).

61. See, for example, the testimony provided in the Hearings before the Subcommittee on International Finance and Monetary Policy, U.S. Senate, *Reauthorization of the Export Administration Act* (Washington, D.C.: USGPO, 1983).

62. *International Trade Reporter: U.S. Export Weekly*, 7 December 1982, p. 403.

63. *Export Control Regulation Could Be Reduced Without Affecting National Security* (Washington, D.C.: U.S. General Accounting Office, 1982).

64. See, for example, the views expressed in Margaret Chapman and Carl Marcy (eds.), *Common Sense in U.S.-Soviet Trade* (Washington, D.C.: American Committee on East-West Accord, 1983).

65. For a careful exposition of these viewpoints, see Marshall Goldman and Raymond Vernon, "U.S. Economic Policies toward the Soviet Union," in Joseph Nye (ed.), *The Making of America's Soviet Policy* (New Haven: Yale University Press, 1984).

East-West Economic Relations and the Western Alliance

Angela E. Stent

Introduction

THE UNITED States and its partners have in the past disagreed over East-West economic relations, but in the last few years this issue has played an unprecedentedly divisive role in the politics of the Western alliance. Indeed, the economic relationship with the USSR has ceased to be primarily an East-West problem. It is arguably as much, if not more, of a West-West than an East-West issue because it involves the fundamental question of the extent to which Europe and Japan should follow U.S. policies with which they disagree. The U.S. interest in economic relations with the USSR lies almost exclusively in the agricultural export sector whereas its allies' interest lies in the industrial and energy sector. Yet America has tried to restrict the flow of European and Japanese industrial goods to the Soviet Union, and this policy has provoked considerable opposition among its allies. There appears to be an asymmetry between the relatively minor role that economic relations with the USSR play in any Western economy and the amount of polemics this subject has engendered within the alliance. Moreover, NATO was originally established as a military organization, and the United States has met resistance in attempting to broaden its functions in the East-West trade area. It is, therefore, of great importance to Washington to seek a more viable modus vivendi with its partners on these issues.

America's allies have a greater economic stake in their ties with the USSR than does the United States because they are far more trade-dependent than is the United States and because the USSR is a natural market for some of their products. Hence it is inevitable that there will be a difference between the United States and its allies on how to conduct business with the USSR. From a U.S. perspective, the European and Japanese willingness to engage in non-agricultural trade with the USSR represents a potential danger to Western security because some of the civilian technology sold to the Soviets may have military applications.

Even if the equipment is strictly civilian, there is concern that by selling technology to the USSR, the West enables the Soviets to maintain a constant or increasing defense budget because the Soviets do not have to construct themselves what they import from the West and do not have to divert precious resources to manufacture products that they cannot produce themselves. The Europeans and Japanese reject these arguments, largely because they are convinced of the mutually beneficial effects of commercial relations with the Soviet Union. These kinds of disagreements lie at the heart of the recent pipeline dispute. However, as a result of the pipeline conflict, the United States and its allies have made a concerted effort to find a more viable consensus on East-West economic relations.

This chapter will examine both the areas of agreement and disagreement between the Western allies on the issue of East-West economic ties. It will analyze trade with and technology transfer to the Soviet Union as an alliance issue, focussing on the policies of the key allies of the United States—the Federal Republic of Germany, France, the United Kingdom, and Japan—by examining their attitudes toward and policies on four central questions:

—What should Western policy toward the Soviet Union be? How should one deal with the Kremlin, and how does one balance the interests of alliance cohesion against the need to preserve an East-West dialogue?

—How do the various nations in question view the pros and cons of East-West economic relations? In particular, what is the relative importance of exports to and imports from the USSR, what are credit policies, and how do domestic lobbies for or against East-West trade operate?

—What is the role of technology transfer to the Soviet Union, and does this issue raise questions that are different from those involved in East-West non-technological trade?

—What is the linkage between economics and politics in relations with the Soviets? Should trade be politicized, and if so, in what way, with what goals?

These issues represent the core of U.S.-European and U.S.-Japanese disputes. I will discuss the Urengoi pipeline as a case study in these differing perspectives and policies, and then examine future prospects, taking into account various allied studies that have been undertaken since the ending of the U.S. sanctions against the pipeline, to see what possibilities for better alliance coordination exist.

East-West trade disputes between the United States, Western Europe, and Japan can only be understood within the wider context of allied debates over how to deal with the Soviet Union in general and what defense strategy to pursue in particular. The United States and its allies had different expectations from the evaluations of detente with the USSR in the early 1970s. These diverging assessments of Soviet policies have spilled over into the economic realm. What is less clear is whether disputes over policy toward Moscow are over means or ends. On the surface, it would appear that the disagreements are over means, over how best to contain Soviet power while diminishing the Soviet military threat. When it comes to discussions over economic relations, however, there are disagreements between those who believe that it is in the long-run interest of the West to have an economically weak USSR and those who consider that an economically strong Soviet Union with a stake in material well-being for its population would be more beneficial to Western interests. These debates carry arguments over means to the point where the ends of policy are in dispute.

As a global power engaged in global competition with the USSR, the United States had rather broad expectations of detente—or at least this was how detente was presented to the American public and to the Congress.[1] When the USSR stepped up its intervention in the Angolan Civil War and then in Ethiopia, Afghanistan, and Central America, and increased its conventional and nuclear military buildup, those American politicians who considered that the Soviets had thereby violated an agreed-upon code of conduct pronounced detente dead. The Europeans, by contrast, had more limited, regional expectations of detente. In particular, the West Germans expected to stabilize the situation in Europe through their Ostpolitik treaties of the early 1970s recognizing the postwar status quo. From their perspective, despite the deployment of Soviet SS-20 missiles, Moscow has abided by its commitments in Europe even though it may have broken an American-defined set of rules. Europeans tend to judge Soviet behavior by Moscow's conduct in Europe, whereas the United States judges it on a global scale.

Although West-West economic relations will not be dealt with in this chapter, it is important to note that East-West trade disputes are also part of a wider U.S.-European and U.S.-Japanese debate over America's domestic economic policy—particularly high interest rates, a growing deficit, and increasing protectionism—and its impact on the U.S.'s economic relations with its allies and competitors in NATO and Japan and on their own economies. Thus, disagreements over commercial policy toward the USSR and technology transfer to members of the Council for Mutual Economic Assistance (CMEA) have been exacerbated by other West-West tensions within the alliance. It is in this context that the dispute over the construction of the Urengoi export pipeline for natural gas from West Siberia to Western Europe assumed such a disproportionately disruptive role in NATO.

The focus of this chapter is the Western alliance. Yet the USSR has not been a passive bystander in the disputes. To some extent, Western quarrels over East-West commerce reinforce Soviet preconceptions of the nature of capitalism, where Western countries compete to sell to the

USSR. Given the Soviets' long-term goal of dividing the alliance while profiting from the West's desire to engage in East-West trade, Moscow has both threatened individual Western countries about the dire consequences of following restrictive U.S. policies and wooed them with attractive offers, trying to play different European countries off against each other and against Japan. Although the USSR did not create the divisions within the alliance, it has certainly profited from them. This is another factor that the United States and its partners must consider in reassessing their policies.

The United States' Perspective

The United States pursues a restrictive policy on non-agricultural East-West commerce, has a broad definition of security, a comprehensive set of laws governing the transfer of non-military technology, and a tendency to use trade for political purposes. On all of these points, it has met increasing resistance from its allies.

Although the foreign and domestic determinants of U.S. East-West trade and technology transfer have been dealt with in other parts of this volume,[2] it is instructive to highlight certain aspects of U.S. policy that are of particular relevance to the alliance. First, there is, of course, no "U.S." position, but there is a spectrum of views both within the U.S. government and between various governmental agencies, the Congress, and the business community.[3] This not only creates problems within the United States, but makes it far more difficult for Washington to coordinate plans with its allies, who have a much more unified view of East-West commerce. Spokesmen in Europe and Japan reply to questions about American policy with, "Which American policy?" The variety—some would call it cacophony—of views within the United States also provides ample opportunity for America's allies to procrastinate about taking decisive action because they can use the excuse that they do not know what "U.S." policy is.

Having underscored the difficulties of forging a "United States" position, I shall nevertheless outline what have been broadly accepted premises of various administrations in the past twenty years. Although the United States has traditionally been suspicious of East-West commercial ties, the disillusionment with detente has intensified the criticism of non-agricultural exchanges with the Soviets. The current U.S. attitude—prevalent since Ronald Reagan became President—is that the United States must build up its military strength and pursue a resolute, assertive policy toward the USSR, playing down the elements of cooperation. In this world view, the allies are seen as a partial obstacle to the further containment of Soviet power, because they continue to stress the two-track policy toward the USSR outlined in the 1967 NATO Harmel Report—building up military strength and encouraging cooperation at the same time.[4] There is in certain parts of the Reagan Administration a suspicion about the extent of the allies' commitment to their own defense against the USSR. The exigencies of combatting Soviet power are perceived in Washington to take precedence over the need to listen to the allies, although this policy has been somewhat modified over the last year.

These views have influenced U.S. attitudes toward East-West commercial ties and America's approach toward allied cooperation. The United States has traditionally viewed East-West commercial ties as essentially political, disproportionately beneficial to the Soviet Union and morally questionable. As Walt Rostow, head of President Kennedy's Policy Planning Council, wrote in 1962:

> The major issues of our trade control policy are political—not strategic, economic, or commercial. From the standpoint of the USSR, the political significance of the U.S. restriction policies has been out of all proportion to their importance on the Soviet economy or strategic position. The principal reason for this is that they serve as a symbol of U.S. unwillingness to grant the USSR full respectability as an equal in the postwar world order, a symbol that the U.S. dares to discriminate against the USSR under contemporary conditions.[5]

Compare this with the State Department's early 1982 statement:

> Our economic or trade relations with the Communist world, and particularly with the countries of the Warsaw Pact, have a different dimension from our economic relations elsewhere. Economic relationships with these countries cannot be divorced from our broad political-security objectives. U.S. economic policies must support the overriding foreign policy goal of deterring Soviet adventurism, redressing the military balance between the West and the Warsaw Pact, and strengthening the Western Alliance.[6]

These quotations show the shift from symbolism to security as the chief preoccupation. The American concept of security is overwhelmingly military in nature, whereas that espoused by the Europeans is equally economic. As one leading European businessman wrote, "It is impossible to prove—with the exclusion of a few high technology areas—that East-West trade adds more to Soviet power than it contributes to the well-being of Western economies."[7] Moreover, to the extent that the allies agree that high technology exports pose a military threat to the security of the West, they disagree on where to draw the line. Europeans agree with the United States on the need to control exports that have a *direct* application to Soviet military power, that is, items that could be diverted to actual use in the conduct of war. But Washington has recently broadened its definition of security controls to include goods and technologies that contribute *indirectly* to the conduct of war—namely exports that serve to strengthen the entire Soviet industrial base. It has returned to the pre-1969 definition of security controls. The United States now has a narrower definition of what contributes to national security and a broader definition of what threatens it than does Western Europe. Moreover, the American concern with technology transfer covers three areas—trade, scientific exchange, and espionage—and these three issues get confused.

The belief that all trade with the USSR builds up its military-industrial base is shared by people outside the administration, in particular, in the Congress. The logical implication of this policy is that all trade with the USSR should cease; yet there are few advocates of this viewpoint in responsible positions. For instance, an exception has always been made for grain exports since the United States first sold grain to the USSR in 1963. The State Department, in a memorandum justifying the grain sale (at the same time as the United States was pressuring its allies not to sell equipment to the USSR for the construction of the Friendship oil pipeline) argued that

> it would appear certain that a [wheat] sale by the U.S. would be advantageous to U.S. foreign policy interests. It would advertise the superiority of our agricultural system over the communist system in a most dramatic fashion—it would be a further step toward the reduction of East-West tensions.[8]

U.S. governments have always differentiated between agricultural and non-agricultural exports to the USSR. This view arouses a certain amount of skepticism among America's allies, who argue that grain exports also strengthen the Soviet economy. Indeed, in an ironic reversal of positions, in 1963 Chancellor Konrad Adenauer bitterly opposed U.S. grain sales to the USSR, claiming "only the stupidest cows choose their own butcher."[9]

America has traditionally taken a restrictive attitude toward non-agricultural exports to the USSR. Despite legislation that permits the granting of official credits to the USSR, these have rarely been given, largely for political reasons. Although there have been various business groups that have in the past lobbied on behalf of trade with the USSR, their activities have been surprisingly muted, given the clout that business lobbies have in other areas of the U.S. political system. This is because there also exist powerful ethnic and religious lobbies and organized labor that argue against commercial ties with the USSR unless they are tied to certain political conditions. Given the prevaling climate of U.S.-Soviet ties, the anti-trade groups receive a more sympathetic hearing than the pro-trade groups.

Unlike its allies, the U.S. does have a well-defined concept of technology even if it is difficult to implement legally. The 1976 Department of Defense Bucy Report gives a concise definition of what technologies should not be transferred. Differentiating between "evolutionary" and "revolutionary" technology, the Bucy Report recommends severely restricting the export of design and manufacturing know-how while lessening export controls on certain machinery. Export controls should focus on the intrinsic use of the product, and not on its "intended end-use," if the latter is clearly non-military.[10] Moreover, technology transferred through indirect means may be more significant than technology transferred directly by the sale of a good. The critical technology approach is predicated on the assumption implicit in the Bucy Report that "one can select the subset of technologies of significant military value on which our national military technology superiority can be presumed to be most dependent."[11] The Bucy Report assumes that it is possible to differentiate between technology and equipment, and recommends more extensive export controls on the former, while lessening controls on the sale of end products. Most European countries question the validity of the "critical technologies" approach as a means of establishing criteria for export controls. The Bucy concepts are now incorporated in the 1979 Export Administration Act (EAA) in the Militarily Critical Technologies List (MCTL). However, the MCTL is classified (it is also over 700 pages long!), meaning that U.S. and foreign businessmen have to guess at its contents.

From the point of view of U.S.-allied relations, domestic U.S. legislation such as the EAA affects Europe and Japan through the licensing process and through the possibility of taking sanctions against foreign corporations that violate U.S. definitions of what can and cannot be transferred to the USSR. No other Western country has such legislation. The heated debates over the renewal of the 1979 EAA in 1983–84, and the lobbying by European groups to mitigate some of the provisions reveal how much disagreement there is over the implementation of the U.S. concept of technology transfer. In particular, some proposals in the bill suggest that the U.S. not export high-technology items to its allies unless there are convincing guarantees that this technology will not be diverted to third countries.[12] Although there are other provisions in the EAA that disturb the Europeans and Japanese, the attempt to apply U.S. concepts extraterritorially to its allies has evoked a strong response from the European Community.

Finally, the American attitude toward the link between politics and economics differs from that of its allies. According to the U.S. State Department, economic ties with the CMEA are "a key component of our overall relationship and contribute to our goal of encouraging evolutionary change, the increased assertion of national self-interest, and greater governmental respect for the rights of individual citizens."[13] Certainly one strand of American opinion has viewed trade as an incentive for better Soviet political behavior. Another has viewed trade denial as a means of influencing Soviet behavior. Unlike its allies, America still believes that sanctions can be effective, if properly coordinated.[14] Indeed, the EAA embodies the concept of politicized trade. Foreign-policy controls in the Act exist to enable the President to react to Soviet behavior of which he disapproves and, through the extraterritorial application of those controls, to impose this policy on allied governments. These foreign-policy controls are unique in Western legislation and apply to non-technological areas. Successive American administrations have believed that it was possible to modify Soviet behavior in domestic or foreign policy through the use of trade carrots and sticks. Other officials have realized that while sanctions may not alter Soviet behavior, they are an important moral and symbolic statement of disapproval on the part of the U.S. government. President Carter, for instance, did not believe that the grain embargo would remove Soviet troops from Afghanistan, but he imposed the embargo to demonstrate to the USSR that the United States was willing to make an economic sacrifice because it considered the Soviet invasion unacceptable. Thus, there has been a persistent tradition of linking politics and trade in U.S. economic ties with the USSR.

The Federal Republic of Germany

Of the various East-West trade policies of the allies of the United States, that of the Federal Republic is the most important. Germany has a long historical tradition of economic relations with Eastern Europe and Russia, and these economic contacts flourished even in times of tense political relations. Of all the NATO countries, the Germans have by far the greatest political stake in relations with the USSR and also the largest economic stake, even though trade with CMEA nations forms less than 8 percent of total German trade. The Federal Republic has been the USSR's most important capitalist trading partner for some years. Although Germany's East-West trade policy is not that different from that of its other European Community (E.C.) partners, it has come under special scrutiny from the Reagan Administration for a variety of political reasons. The United States has traditionally expected West Germany to be more compliant on these issues than, say, France, because of Washington's perceived special relationship with and special influence in Bonn. Since West Germany is the European nation most exposed to Soviet power and because of the division of Germany, Bonn is still expected to adopt a distanced stand from the USSR, to dispel lingering Western suspicions about the possibility of West Germany exchanging its membership in the Western alliance for reunification on Soviet terms.

The Federal Republic's economic relations with Eastern Europe and the Soviet Union have been determined by its special geographical and political place in Europe. One-half of a divided nation, West Germany depends on the United States for its security and on the USSR for its continued relationship with the German Democratic Republic. West Germany has, since 1949, been more beholden to United States policy on East-West economic relations than have its European partners because of its political dependence on Washington; yet at the same time, it has a greater political stake in these economic ties than do any of its allies because of the division of Germany and the presence of ethnic Germans in most CMEA nations. More than any other Western nation, Germany has sought to use its economic ties with CMEA for political purposes, and has to some degree succeeded.

While Bonn has eschewed the use of economic sanctions since 1969, it continues to believe in the efficacy of trade incentives to elicit certain political concessions in the humanitarian field. Moreover, it has become clear since the fall of the Social Democrat-Free Democrat (SPD-FDP) government in 1982 that the Christian Democrats-Christian Social Union (CDU-CSU) share their predecessors' commitment to a stable East-West economic relationship. A positive attitude toward economic relations with the USSR has been the hallmark of continuity in German policy over the last fifteen years. This policy has been productive for Germany's Ostpolitik, but has become increasingly problematic in Bonn's relations with Washington.

Underlying U.S.-West German disagreements over East-West trade policy is a different evaluation of the outcome of detente.[15] Detente has worked for West Germany, inasmuch as the intra-German relationship has vastly improved over the past fifteen years and continues to do so despite the deployment of U.S. Pershing missiles on West German soil. The CDU-CSU government is as committed to pursuing an active Ostpolitik as was its predecessor, the SPD, because of the perceived need to maintain contacts with the population of East Germany. As long as the Soviet Union continues to sanction the intra-German dialogue, Bonn will continue to develop its relationship with the USSR. Nonetheless, West Germany is well aware that its relationship with the U.S. must take priority over all other ties, and it is constantly confronted with steering a delicate line between its Ostpolitik and its Westpolitik.

Germany is, therefore, politically predisposed to favor East-West economic exchanges. It also favors them for sound economic reasons. Probably the most important source of the FRG's interest in East-West trade is its desire for export markets. With the highest postwar unem-

ployment rate, particularly in the steel sector, a trade-dependent economy like that of the FRG must be concerned to maintain or to increase
exports and thereby guarantee employment. Indeed, for Germany, as
for all other European countries, a viable economy is an essential component of national security. Germans argue that economic health and ex-
port-led employment have been the foundation of their postwar stability.
Whereas the United States is relatively self-sufficient, West Germany is
trade-dependent. The FRG considers guaranteed export markets a cor-
nerstone of security and therefore a prerequisite for the survival of a
democratic way of life. Trade with the USSR accounts for 2.2 percent of
total German trade, the latter providing about 100,000 jobs.[16] Yet despite
its relatively small contribution to overall German exports, politicians
from all parties stress that this trade is economically important for certain sectors. Moreover, it is linked to political benefits.

German spokesmen reject the argument that non-agricultural exports to the USSR are potentially a security threat because they build up
the Soviet industrial economy. They stress the mutually beneficial impact
of economic relations, claiming that whatever damage is done to their
security by strengthening the Soviet economy is more than offset by the
benefits of this trade for their own economy. For instance, the USSR and
Eastern Europe are the single largest export market for the West German machine-tool industry; approximately one-third of machine-tools
go to the CMEA nations. The same is true for firms producing large-
diameter pipe. Trade with CMEA is disproportionately important for
this sector, and 25 percent of all steel pipe goes to CMEA. There is,
therefore, a positive attitude toward exports to the USSR for both economic and political reasons. In November 1983, the German-Soviet Economic Commission discussed new projects, particularly in the electronic
field.[17] In December the Germans were awarded a major contract with
the Finns to construct a new Baltic port in Tallinn, and other deals—for
instance a coal slurry pipeline—are under discussion.[18]

West German credit regulations differ from those of many Western
countries. The West German government does not officially subsidize
interest rates on credits, although there are various informal ways in
which the government can influence commercial rates of interest. In
general, however, West German interest rates are higher than those of
other NATO countries, and the Soviets complain about this. Sometimes,
as with the pipe-natural gas deals, the banks charge a rate of interest
lower than the current market rate (in the Urengoi pipeline case ranging from 7.5 to 9.18 percent), but the companies will charge the Soviets a
higher price for the products, and will reimburse the banks for the
difference between the market rate and the rate of interest charged.[19]
Commercial bank credits are readily available to communist countries,
and are mostly guaranteed by the government.[20] They are administered

by the Hermes credit insurance company, a private corporation that acts on behalf of the government.

Hermes credits have become a controversial issue between the U.S. and Germany. After the invasion of Afghanistan, Washington put pressure on Bonn to cease granting Hermes guarantees to the USSR, but Germany refused. The Hermes issue has received further attention since the Reagan Administration came into office. The U.S. argument is that while it is technically correct that the German government does not officially subsidize interest rates, Hermes guarantees are cheaper than those in the private market and therefore represent an indirect subsidy. The Germans dispute this view. Without Hermes, they argue, there would be no private credits to communist countries. Private firms would not be able to provide credits without guarantees, and these would be prohibitively expensive were they not underwritten by the government. So there is no such thing as private market guarantees that are allegedly more expensive than Hermes guarantees, because these private guarantees do not exist in reality. Thus German spokesmen strongly dispute U.S. assertions that Hermes credits represent a form of subsidy. The Soviet debt to the FRG is currently about 4.1 billion DM[21] and the total East European debt is about 25 billion DM, or a quarter of the communist countries' total debt to the West.

There is a basic consensus within West Germany over East-West economic issues. All major political and economic groups favor these ties, and only a few minority fringe groups oppose East-West economic relations. The major lobbying group is the *Ostausschuss der deutschen Wirtschaft* (German East-West Trade Committee) which operates under the Federation of German Industry and has existed since 1952. It represents exporters, banks, and importers, and has close links to the government. The major trade unions, unlike those in the U.S., favor East-West commercial ties for the jobs they create. There are some economic interest groups that have protested against unfair competition from the smaller CMEA nations' imports in the textile and clothing area, but these groups are relatively unimportant.[22]

In general, the West German interest in East-West economic relations is as significant on the import as on the export side. Indeed, in 1982 the Germans had a $603 million trade deficit with the USSR. West Germany is deficient in indigenous energy resources; as such one of its prime national security goals is the diversification of energy resources and the securing of new suppliers. Energy imports meet 5o percent of the FRG's primary energy demand, and future forecasts suggest that Germany will remain overwhelmingly dependent on imported hydrocarbons. The FRG imports 96 percent of its oil and 62 percent of its natural gas. The USSR appears to be an especially promising supplier of natural gas because it has the world's largest natural gas reserves and because it is eager to sell this gas to Western Europe for hard currency. Currently, West Germany imports 16 percent of its natural gas and 6 percent of its oil from the USSR. Whereas oil exports from the USSR are expected to decline in the next decade, natural gas exports are predicted to increase significantly. Today, 25 percent of coal imports, 13 of platinum, 56 of palladium, and 25 of asbestos come from CMEA.[23]

Unlike the U.S. and like its E.C. partners, West Germany does not differentiate in principle between trade relations with the USSR and technology transfer. The Federal Republic agrees that no technology with direct military applications should be exported to the Soviet Union, but it takes a somewhat more skeptical view of the significance of civilian technology for the Soviet economy and of the USSR's ability to absorb and diffuse Western technology. Germany belongs to CoCom (the Paris-based Allied Coordinating Committee that controls East-West exports) and therefore participates in the multilateral export control system; but it does not have guidelines as elaborate or as clearly defined on West-East technology transfer as does the U.S.[24] It has, like its European partners, never developed a theoretical framework such as the U.S.'s militarily-critical technologies approach to economic relations with the USSR. Whereas there is no national German debate any more over the desirability of economic ties with the East, there is a national debate over how far Germany should follow U.S. policies on these issues. The current discussions suggest that the Germans are unwilling to adopt a more restrictive policy, except on technology transfers that have demonstrable direct military applications.

West Germany is the U.S.'s only ally that still believes that economic ties with the USSR can produce political results. Yet its attitude toward linkage is different from that of the U.S. Before 1963, successive German governments followed the U.S. policy of using economic relations as negative linkage—denying trade to the USSR in the hope that this might change Soviet behavior. However, a decade of experience showed that negative linkage was unproductive. It had failed to alter Soviet behavior on issues of vital concern to the Federal Republic and the USSR such as the status of West Berlin and intra-German ties.[25] Since the beginning of the new Ostpolitik, in the late 1960s, West Germany has ceased to accept the principle of economic sanctions or trade denial as a means to induce changes in Soviet behavior. Most German officials and specialists reject the use of sanctions because they do not alter Soviet behavior and because they impose economic and political costs on the country that introduces them.[26]

The Federal Republic does, however, believe that positive linkage can be productive, and this is part of its Ostpolitik. This is particularly important in the intra-German relationship, where the West German government has concluded a variety of economic agreements with the

East German government—from paying for autobahns that run from parts of West Germany to Berlin to paying for the release of political dissidents to guaranteeing a DM one billion loan in June 1983 and a DM 750 thousand loan in July 1984—because these agreements reinforce the East German government's commitment to improving human contacts between the two Germanys.

The Germans believe that economic and political relations reinforce each other and even that, in times of political crisis, economic relations are one channel of cooperation that can exist even when other aspects of the relationship are strained.[27] Since the USSR has traditionally sought to separate its economic and political relations with Western countries and to avoid being the object of Western linkage, in order to maximize the benefits of these economic ties, it too has sought to sustain the economic relationship with the Federal Republic irrespective of the political situation.

The Federal Republic has therefore found it increasingly problematic to support U.S. policy on expanded sanctions toward the USSR and Poland. The German government has argued that the invasion of Afghanistan, however reprehensible, should have been viewed primarily as a problem between the USSR and the less developed nations and not as essentially an East-West conflict. Germany pledged not to undercut U.S. sanctions, but refused to introduce its own after the invasion of Afghanistan or after the imposition of martial law in Poland. Thus, by 1979, the Schmidt government had made it clear that it would give higher priority to maintaining its economic ties with CMEA than to complying with the U.S. East-West trade policy, and the Kohl government appears to be committed to the same policy, although it has not as yet been tested. Thus, Germany has a dual approach toward the politics of East-West economic relations. It links politics and economics in a positive sense whenever possible. However, it rejects linkage whenever that linkage threatens to impede economic relations. This is, to some extent, the result of a more complex perception of Soviet intentions and responses than that which is accepted in the United States.

France

France's East-West trade policy is different from that of both the United States and the Federal Republic of Germany. France is less dependent politically on either the United States or the USSR than is West Germany, and can afford to take a more independent stance toward East-West commercial ties. France has a smaller political and economic stake in these ties than does Germany, although it has a greater stake than does the United States. Moreover, France's Gaullist traditions have influenced every French government over the past twenty years, of whatever political persuasion, and have meant that Paris has been committed to diversifying its international political and economic links as much as possible, has been averse to mixing economics with politics, and has resisted American attempts to influence its policy. France has used economic relations with CMEA as part of its strategy of building an autonomous world role, but has had few illusions about their political pay-off.

Under the government of President Mitterrand, France's attitude toward the Soviet Union has been closer to that of the United States than has Germany's; yet the government's critique of Soviet policy in Afghanistan and Poland and the Soviet military build-up has not extended to restricting economic relations with the East. Unlike Germany, France is not dependent on the Soviet Union on issues such as Berlin and intra-German relations. However, France has always found it useful to pursue a relationship with the USSR as a means of maintaining its independence from the United States. The French reluctance to admit that the allies had agreed to review their East-West trade policies in return for lifting of the pipeline sanctions reflects the French aversion to cooperating publicly with America on these issues.

The government of Francois Mitterrand has become increasingly critical of the detente policies of President Giscard D'Estaing and has admitted that detente, as originally conceived, was flawed. This argument may in part be a product of Mitterrand's perceived need to distance himself from the four communists in his cabinet, but it may also be part of a longer-term tougher stance toward the USSR.[28] The French have been far less concerned than the Germans to maintain what are perceived as questionable gains from detente and Mitterrand's position on the USSR has resembled that of Reagan more than Schmidt or Kohl. However, this skepticism about relations with the USSR and support of the deployment of U.S. missiles in Europe does not extend to following U.S. policy toward the USSR on any other matters.

Despite its hardening stance toward the USSR, France is a firm supporter of East-West commercial relations. Its main concern is not with limiting trade but with encouraging it, since France's overall share of OECD trade with the USSR has been declining over the past few years.[29] Indeed, the French took over some contracts that were denied American firms after the invasion of Afghanistan and the subsequent U.S. sanctions. French spokesmen, like their German counterparts, reject the idea that non-agricultural trade strengthens the Soviet economy and represents a security risk. They also stress the mutually beneficial aspects of that trade. France's export sector, like that in other E.C. countries, is suffering in the current recession, and CMEA represents an attractive and growing market for precisely those industries in the greatest trouble, for instance, the steel industry. East-West trade is disproportionately important for this sector, as for the machine-tool sector, even though trade with CMEA represents less than 4 percent of France's total trade. For instance, the steel firm Creûsot-Loire sells between one-quarter and one-third of its total export production to CMEA nations.[30] In 1980, 50.4 percent of France's steel pipe exports, 41.3 of compressor exports, and 30 of sheet-iron went to CMEA.[31] In November 1983, France signed a long-term grain agreement with the USSR, in apparent contravention of the European Community's Common Agricultural Policy. Moreover, at the November 1983 and February 1984 meetings of the Franco-Soviet Trade Commission, the USSR agreed to increase its purchases of French steel, chemicals, and agricultural products.

The French government subsidizes interest rates on credits to communist nations and has stated quite clearly that it will not raise those rates beyond the current OECD consensus.[32] France grants subsidized export credits to all countries, including the United States, and has refused in its credit policy to differentiate politically between countries since the mid-1960s. There is, therefore, little prospect that France will cooperate with the U.S. attempt to tighten substantially credit terms for communist nations.

As in Germany, there are few domestic groups that argue against economic ties with the CMEA nations, although some French intellectuals have become more critical of trade policy since the invasion of Afghanistan. In general, however, all major business groups, government bodies, and trade unions—in particular, the communist-led Confédération Générale du Travail—support a policy of expanded exports to the USSR.

France has import interests similar to those of West Germany. It seeks to diversify its energy imports for national security reasons and considers the Soviet Union an important source of energy supplies. Although it has, unlike Germany, been able to push ahead with the development of nuclear power, it still needs to diversify its sources of imported energy and reduce its dependence on OPEC oil. It currently imports 17 percent of its natural gas from the USSR and considers the Soviet Union a reliable and desirable supplier. However, it is concerned to reverse its $1.3 billion trade deficit with the USSR in 1982.

The French position on technology transfer is somewhat different from that of the Federal Republic, although it is in general much more difficult to obtain information on these issues from the French than from the United States or the Germans. The French have recently become more aware of the security implications of technology transfer, and in October 1981 established a commission charged with protecting sensitive French technologies.[33] In 1983, France expelled forty-seven Soviet diplomats, accusing them of spying and trying to steal technological secrets. There is considerable evidence that the French have become increasingly concerned about technology leaks. Yet, since their system is not discussed publicly, it is difficult to discern whether they have produced a new set of criteria for evaluating technology transfer. Certainly, they do not have as elaborate a system as the U.S. critical technology concept.

Under the Giscard administration France appeared to endorse the view that closer economic ties with the USSR had a beneficial effect on political relations. Since the invasion of Afghanistan, and in particular, the crackdown in Poland, the French are publicly more skeptical about linkage. They still believe, as do their E.C. allies, that economic relations with the smaller CMEA members can be politically beneficial in that they encourage East European independence from Moscow. However, there is far greater skepticism about the beneficial implications of trade with the USSR. In general, the French seek to separate economics from politics in their relations with the USSR and have largely succeeded in compartmentalizing the two aspects of their relationship. As Lionel Jospin, General Secretary of France's Socialist Party, recently put it, one must "separate the logic of human rights from the logic of economics."[34] In rejecting the politicization of East-West economic relations, France has also refused to comply with U.S. sanctions against the USSR. Indeed, Foreign Minister Cheysson spoke of a "progressive divorce" between the United States and France after the pipeline sanctions were imposed. France's disinclination to link politics and economics extends both East and West, and is part of its more distanced stance from both of the superpowers.

The United Kingdom

Britain's policies on East-West commercial relations resemble those of France rather than those of Germany and the United States. Like France, Britain is not beholden to the USSR politically in the same way that Germany is. However, unlike France, Britain has always stressed its special Atlantic relationship with the United States and publicly values its close ties to America more than does France. Like France, Britain is skeptical of the political value of trade with the USSR, but insists on its right to pursue East-West trade for economic reasons. Whereas it has publicly been more willing to cooperate with the United States in trying to find a new allied consensus on East-West economic relations, in practice it has not been particularly cooperative in altering its policy.

The government of Prime Minister Margaret Thatcher has been rather critical of detente and has been much more willing to support the U.S. view of the Soviet Union than have any other of the allies of the United States. Among the population at large, particularly those involved in the anti-nuclear movement and those in the Labor Party, there is a more benign view of the USSR and a greater willingness to blame the problems of detente on the United States; but on the government level, the British view of the Soviet Union and of detente has been critical and uncompromising.

As with the French, this cooling of relations with the USSR over the past five years has not extended to economic ties, although there were some attempts to take symbolic restrictive measures after the invasion of Afghanistan in conjunction with the European Community.[35] Like France's, Britain's share of the CMEA market has been declining over the past decade, and it is concerned to increase its exports to the region. London does not admit that trade with the USSR is in principle a security risk because it strengthens the Soviet economy. Trade with CMEA accounts for only 2.5 percent of British trade, but it is disproportionately important for certain sectors.[36] In 1982, CMEA accounted for 1.5 percent of British exports and 1.9 percent of its imports. The major exports were of machinery and chemicals, and the major imports of petroleum and diamonds.[37] The significance of exports to the USSR was graphically illustrated when, defying the U.S.'s extraterritorial pipeline sanctions, Prime Minister Thatcher herself went to Scotland to show solidarity with the firm John Brown, which was shipping rotor parts manufactured under American license for compressors to the USSR in contravention of the U.S. sanctions. After years of declining U.K.-CMEA trade, the British anticipate that their trade with the region will improve in 1984.[38] The British, like the French, subsidize rates of interest on export credits to communist nations and have said that this practice will continue.

There is also a broad domestic consensus within Britain that East-West exports should be promoted, particularly in such difficult economic times with the highest postwar unemployment rate. Business, unions, and government are agreed on this policy, and there is little internal debate on the issue. The weekly *Economist* went further than most publications in questioning the desirability of the Urengoi pipeline,[39] but the mainstream of British opinion favors increased East-West commerce, although there is growing concern about CMEA imports. Indeed, Britain has for some time had a balance of trade deficit with the USSR (it reached $502 million in 1982) and seeks to reverse this deficit. Although Britain does have significant indigenous energy resources, it imports a considerable amount of oil and oil products from the USSR and also petrochemical products.

The British have been somewhat more receptive than the U.S.'s other allies to the idea of differentiating between economic relations with the USSR in general and technology transfer in particular. Although the government does not necessarily accept the militarily critical technologies approach, it has become more concerned about the transfer of dual-use items to the USSR. Export licensing procedures have been tightened up domestically, and recently, the Customs and Excise set up a special East-West trade unit to keep a closer watch on questionable shipments from Britain to the USSR.[40] However, Britain, like its E.C. partners, tends to follow the U.S. lead in CoCom instead of developing a distinctly national technology transfer evaluation system.

The British attitude toward the linkage of trade and politics resembles that of the French. In principle, the British have always separated trade and politics wherever possible, so that deteriorating political relations will not have a negative impact on economic ties. The British doubt that economic relations with the USSR can improve political relations, although some officials in the Thatcher government appear to feel that economic ties are one means of retaining a channel of cooperative communication in an era when political relations have worsened. Where the British are dubious about the positive political impact of trade, they definitely reject the principle of sanctions, and they always have. The response to the U.S. imposition of extraterritorial sanctions on the Urengoi pipeline stressed Britain's sovereignty and the inadmissibility of extraterritorial sanctions, gave economic reasons why the United Kingdom needed to fulfill its export contracts, and claimed that sanctions do not change Soviet behavior and are a useless tool.[41] Indeed, the government invoked the 1980 Protection of Trading Interests Act to compel its corporations to defy U.S. sanctions.

While Britain may have more political reason than France for cooperating with the United States, its foreign economic interests and serious economic situation domestically make it highly unlikely that the United Kingdom will restrict trade with the USSR or other CMEA nations, except perhaps in certain limited high-technology areas.

Japan

The Japanese position on economic relations with the USSR is both similar to and different from those of America's other allies. Given its close proximity to the USSR and its consciousness of the growing Soviet naval and military buildup around its borders, Japan is particularly sensitive to the Soviet military presence.[42] It is probably more immediately aware of the Soviet Union than is any other U.S. ally, with the possible exception of the Federal Republic of Germany. Yet like West Germany before 1972, Japan has outstanding territorial claims against the USSR, since the Soviets occupied the Northern territories, and the USSR and Japan have not signed a peace treaty. The unresolved territorial issues give Japan a stake in securing tolerable relations with the USSR in order not to close off the possibility of the return of the islands. As one diplomat has written, "Geographically, Japan has an interest in maintaining stable and correct relations with the Soviet Union."[43] Moreover, Japan, like America's other allies, used to separate politics from economics in its relations with the USSR. Since Nakasone came into office, he has linked the Northern Territories issue to East-West trade. Since Japan is more trade-dependent than any other major Western economy and is highly dependent on imports of energy and raw materials, it is particularly sensitive to the need to diversify its trade links, including those with the USSR. However, it implemented sanctions against the Soviets after the invasion of Afghanistan which are still in place. Japan's disagreements with the United States over East-West trade policy must also be seen in the context of disputes with America over West-West trade, particularly over Japanese automobile and computer exports to the U.S. The United States has had a more strained economic relationship with Japan than with any other of its allies, and this has complicated Washington's attempts to secure Japanese cooperation on restricting trade with the USSR.

Japan's relationship both with the United States and with the USSR is different from that of the other allies of the United States. Japan is, of course, dependent on the United States for security protection, and although it has increasingly cooperated with the alliance, it is not formally a member of NATO. Moreover, with a strong postwar pacifist tradition and a reluctance to increase military expenditures, Japan has also come into conflict with the United States over its own defense posture, since the Reagan Administration began to pressure it to spend more on defense. This is also true of America's NATO allies, but the difficulties between Japan and the United States have been exacerbated by growing U.S. protectionism. As far as the USSR goes, Japan is in a unique position in that it has been courted by China, and has in the past decade been able to play off China against the USSR to some extent, culminating in the 1978 Sino-Japanese Friendship treaty, which the USSR has denounced.[44] Yet Japan's ability to play the China card has been restricted by the consciousness of Soviet proximity and displeasure.

The Japanese attitude toward the USSR and toward detente has been changing in the past few years, particularly under Prime Minister Nakasone. Despite the Japanese predisposition to conduct normal relations with the USSR, the conventional and nuclear Soviet buildup, the increase of visible Soviet power in the Sea of Okhotsk, the interference with Japanese shipping rights and the rhetorical intransigence over the Northern territories issue have had a detrimental effect on the Japanese public's view of the Soviets.[45] Moreover, the deployment of Soviet SS-20's toward Asia has also begun to have an effect on public opinion. As one observer points out, "Japan has long been a passive partner in her alliance with the United States, particularly in the area of security."[46] As Washington has put more pressure on Japan to increase its defense spending and take a harder stance toward Moscow, Tokyo has responded by changing its posture toward the USSR. The Japanese attitude toward security, like that of America's European allies, is economic as well as military. However vulnerable Japan feels to the Soviet military buildup, it is equally vulnerable to a potential Mideast oil cutoff, since it is highly dependent on energy imports. Japan seeks to diversify its energy imports, and cooperation in developing and importing Soviet energy resources is perceived to be in its security interests.

Although Japan's policy toward the USSR is changing somewhat, its attitude toward economic relations with the Soviets has remained constant in the past fifteen years. Japan favors the development of economic ties with the USSR. Poor in raw materials, it is interested in the development of natural gas, oil, and pulpwood in Eastern Siberia and Sakhalin and in fisheries. The USSR is equally interested in Japanese participation and financial and technical cooperation in Eastern Siberia. Although the optimism about Japanese-Soviet economic relations in the early 1970s has largely evaporated, Japan nevertheless has a continuing interest in these economic relations. It has been the USSR's second largest capitalist trading partner for some years and is committed to increasing economic ties. The Japanese in general share the European view that non-agricultural trade with the USSR is mutually beneficial and does not represent a security risk. Trade with the USSR is important for Japan's steel, machine-building, and chemical industries, and the employment effects of such exports are considered to be a vital component of Japan's national interest. Like its European allies, Japan grants subsidized credits to the USSR and has until recently resisted restricting such credits. There is domestic support of these economic relations, coordinated by the Ministry of International Trade and Industry (MITI) which acts as a spokesman for the main business interests. Despite the growing public discussion over Soviet intentions and the security threat, there has been no challenge to the prevailing view that economic links with the USSR are desirable. Japan, unlike many European nations, enjoys a positive balance of trade with the USSR—$2.5 billion in 1982.

Japan has recently been the USSR's most important OECD supplier of high technology, and it does not normally differentiate between trade with the USSR and technology transfer. This is partly because MITI is responsible for the transfer of technology to other nations, and MITI's function is to promote, not restrict, trade. Japan's Defense Agency, unlike similar bodies in the other allied countries, has little input into licensing decisions. The most widely cited example of the precedence of economic over security considerations in Japan is the "floating dock case": the Japanese sold the USSR a "floating dock" that not only helped the Soviet shipbuilding industry but also had significant military applications.[47] Nevertheless, under Nakasone MITI has become more concerned with the security aspects of technology transfer. Indeed, Japan may have calculated that it would rather restrict its technology exports to the USSR than confront U.S. import quotas, and it may have an informal agreement with the United States on this issue. Given Japan's style of negotiation and its relationship with the United States, Japan is likely to follow a strong allied lead on restricting technology transfer. It is, however, unlikely to develop its own technology transfer concepts.

The Japanese have traditionally also been reluctant to link political and economic relations and have sought to insulate their economic ties from deteriorating political relations.[48] However, this has changed under Nakasone, who has said publicly that closer economic ties with the USSR will be linked to better political relations. The Japanese were willing to give some support to U.S. post-Afghanistan sanctions. Japan suspended but did not cancel credits for ongoing Siberian projects and has given no official credits for new projects since 1979. Prime Minister Ohira said in 1979 that Japanese participation in any Western embargo of equipment shipments to the USSR would depend on prior European and American initiatives. Thus, Japan is unlikely to further restrict its economic relations with the USSR unless there already is in place a firm allied consensus on the issue.

Pipelines—Past and Present

U.S.-allied differences over East-West economic relations have at various times in the past twenty years developed into a public confrontation over specific issues, in which the United States has sought to change its partners' policies and has not succeeded. Two of the most significant examples of these disagreements are the pipeline embargoes of 1962 and 1982. A comparison of the striking parallels between them and the continuity of issues in these quarrels illustrates the key points over which the U.S. seems bound to disagree with its allies.

The 1962–63 NATO Pipeline Embargo

In November 1962, the United States introduced in NATO a resolution forbidding the export of large-diameter pipe to Soviet bloc countries. The immediate focus of U.S. efforts was the construction of the Friendship oil pipeline from the USSR to Eastern Europe. At that time, three German steel concerns had signed contracts for the delivery of large-diameter pipe to the USSR, and other countries were also interested in supplying pipe. The United States used the NATO forum instead of CoCom because CoCom rules require unanimity, and the British had indicated that they would veto such a stipulation. After many months of exerting strong political pressure on all its allies, but particularly the Germans, the United States managed to persuade the government of Chancellor Konrad Adenauer to force the German corporations to cancel their contracts. This caused an outcry within the Federal Republic, where the Chancellor was severely criticized for violating the sanctity of contracts. None of the other U.S. allies complied with the order, and Britain and Italy continued to sell pipe.[49]

In 1962, as in 1982, U.S. motivations were a complex mixture of preoccupation about the USSR itself and frustration with its allies for their lack of solidarity on policy toward the Soviet Union. This mixture of East-West and West-West motives has been a constant feature of U.S. attempts to change the policies of its allies. In 1962, the United States (like the USSR) was concerned about the Franco-German rapprochement, later cemented in the January 1963 Franco-German treaty. The United States interpreted this as an anti-American act, and feared that the Germans might be won over to the French position of opposition to the proposed multilateral nuclear force. The United States was also concerned about Germany's more flexible Ostpolitik under Foreign Minister Schroeder. Thus, to some extent, the pipe embargo was part of a larger attempt to realign Germany with American policy toward the USSR.

As for the pipeline itself, U.S. objections were twofold. On the one hand, Washington feared that, by selling pipe to the Soviets, the West would help to build up the Soviet energy infrastructure and that, as a Senate Committee darkly warned,

> Ever since the Soviets came to power in 1917, they have looked for ways to undermine the free world. . . . It is now becoming increasingly evident that [Khrushchev] would also like to drown us in a sea of oil if we let him get away with it. . . . If these tactics continue to succeed, there is danger that Western countries will become increasingly dependent on Soviet oil supplies for vital defense as well as industrial activities. The danger such a situation would pose to the security of the free world cannot be overstated.[50]

At that time, Soviet oil exports, European dependence, and Soviet hard currency earnings were all of concern.

The other American argument concerned a broader security issue. Building a pipeline from Baku to Eastern Europe would, it was argued, be used to supply fuel to the Red Army and enable it to strengthen its presence in Eastern Europe. The NATO resolution, unlike the pipeline sanctions in 1982, demanded no specific concessions from the Soviets but was designed to deny the Soviets the wherewithal to improve their economic—and therefore ultimately military—position.

From the point of view of America's allies, the main question then, as in 1982, was how to balance economic interest against the perceived need to comply with the U.S. directions. With the exception of West

Germany, every other NATO member decided not to comply with the NATO order. Only Bonn, because of its special dependence on the United States at that time, felt constrained to defy its own economic interests. As Foreign Minister Schroeder said, in defending his government's decision to cancel the contracts,

> My heart is completely with the iron and steel industry, with full employment and with the full utilization of our capacity. . . . But I must choose here between the interests of foreign policy and the interests of the economy. Thank God only in a limited sphere. So I am choosing foreign policy.[51]

The lessons of this pipeline embargo suggested the futility of America's trying to impose its policies on reluctant allies—a lesson that was apparently forgotten twenty years later. Perhaps the most successful aspect of the embargo was that West Germany complied. However, other allies continued to sell pipe to the USSR, and not only was the Friendship pipeline built, but the USSR developed its own—albeit limited—capacity to manufacture large-diameter pipe as a result of the embargo. Moreover, German compliance with the United States soured German-Soviet relations for some time, a fact that the Germans frequently mentioned during the 1982 pipeline embargo. Finally, far from producing greater allied harmony on these issues, U.S. attempts to prevent its partners from trading with the Soviets caused greater alliance friction, spilling over into other issues that were not connected to East-West economic relations. Moreover, a year after the embargo was imposed, the United States began to sell grain to the USSR, and justified these exports as beneficial for the U.S. farmer while refusing to accept that pipe exports were beneficial for the German steelworker, even though both grain and pipe undoubtedly did strengthen the Soviet economy.

The 1982 Pipeline Sanctions

The 1982 pipeline embargo concerned the construction of the natural gas export pipeline from the Urengoi peninsula in the USSR to Western Europe. The United States viewed the pipeline, which had been under discussion for some time, as a symbol of the dangers of too close East-West economic cooperation, particularly while the USSR was occupying Afghanistan and Poland was under martial law. After the imposition of Polish martial law in December 1981, the U.S. government refused permission to the General Electric Company to export components for the pipeline for use in Western Europe by firms manufacturing compressor station equipment under U.S. license. In June 1982, citing the Polish situation, President Reagan extended the ban on the export of rotor parts for turbines to all foreign companies using U.S.

licenses. He used an extraterritorial U.S. action as opposed to a multilateral forum because of allied resistance to his policies. In practice, this
would have meant that no West European company would have been
able to manufacture the compressor station parts. None of America's
allies complied with these extraterritorial sanctions. The British and
French have laws that forbid their corporations to comply with the sanctions. The Germans do not (although they are currently considering
introducing such legislation) but nevertheless, the government made no
attempt to prevent its firms from exporting the components, unlike the
situation in 1962–63. Eventually, in November 1982, before the lifting of
Polish martial law, the U.S. rescinded the sanctions, saying that the allies
had agreed to reconsider the issue of East-West trade, and in March
1984 it approved the sale of U.S. energy equipment to the USSR.[52]

Many of the considerations behind U.S. policy in 1962 were present
in 1982. First, the United States and its allies increasingly disagreed over
policy toward the USSR. The invasion of Afghanistan divided the allies
over how to react to Soviet aggression; the United States favored sanctions and other punitive measures, while the Europeans and Japanese
were reluctant to respond with sanctions. Moreover, there was an even
greater reluctance to react to the crackdown in Poland with anything
more than rhetorical criticism. Despite the 1979 NATO Two-Track decision to deploy intermediate-range U.S. missiles in Germany, Britain, and
Italy if arms control negotiations failed, the United States was concerned
about the increasing questioning of the wisdom of this decision among
the populations of Europe and especially within the West German SPD.
Thus, there was a growing disjunction between the Reagan Administration's view of how to deal with the USSR and that of its allies. This,
together with the fact that Europe was far more dependent on Soviet
energy supplies in 1982 than in 1962, and had a far greater economic
stake in relations with the USSR, influenced the U.S. decision to select
the pipeline as an issue.

If one examines the U.S. rationale for the pipeline sanctions, then
the reasons changed over time. The initial explanation had to do with
responding to Polish martial law; subsequently the reasons shifted to
concern over both Soviet hard currency earnings and dependence on
Soviet gas and on exports to the USSR. Finally, when President Reagan
lifted the sanctions, he justified his move not by alluding to Poland but
by saying that the allies had now agreed to reexamine the question of
East-West economic relations.[53] As several European journalists pointed
out, one might indeed question what the real, as opposed to the apparent, reasons for the pipeline sanctions were.[54] It appears that the West-
West dimensions—the desire to punish the allies for their policies and
possibly to secure greater allied agreement on a strategy toward the

USSR—had as much to do with the sanctions as the East-West issue—concern about the security impact of the pipeline itself.

From the U.S. standpoint, there were four basic objections to the construction of the pipeline, which lie at the heart of U.S.-European and U.S.-Japanese disputes over East-West economic relations, and were all present in the previous pipeline debate too, although not as directly articulated. The first was, is it in the interest of the West to develop Soviet energy resources? In a sense, this is a specific example of the more general debate about whether *all* East-West trade strengthens the Soviet industrial base, thereby making it potentially a more dangerous adversary. Critics who held this view argued that to participate in the development of Soviet energy resources was to make the USSR a more formidable antagonist by strengthening its economic infrastructure and by increasing its ability to affect world energy markets. Moreover, opponents also dismissed the argument that if the West helped to develop the Soviet energy sector, the USSR was less likely to look to the Persian Gulf states for future energy supplies. The USSR, they argued, had traditionally pursued expansionist political and economic goals in the Persian Gulf, and increasing Soviet energy supplies would not in the long run moderate Soviet ambitions in that part of the world.

Most European and American supporters of the pipeline did not argue from this narrow security point of view. They claimed that, although there appeared to be a temporary world oil glut, in the long run, the energy crisis would not evaporate.[55] It was therefore to the benefit of Western security to develop as many alternative supplies of energy as possible, and the USSR clearly appeared to be a major supplier. Proponents of the pipeline stressed that it was in the West's interest to promote the expansion of the Soviet energy infrastructure and thereby to prevent another devastating oil shock. Moreover, some experts argued that an energy-short Soviet Union would be more likely to turn its sights—and troops—toward the Persian Gulf than a USSR that was accelerating the development of its energy resources with Western equipment.

The second set of arguments, related to the first, concerned the hard currency question. Was it in the West's interest to pay the USSR for its increased exports of natural gas, thereby strengthening the Soviet economy? The Reagan Administration argument was that the hard currency earnings that the Soviets would gain from the extra natural gas exports constituted a security risk. The Soviets would use the hard currency to purchase more Western equipment to build up their industrial infrastructure and this might ultimately force the West to increase its defense expenditures to counter Soviet military moves. President Reagan cited two reasons for continuing grain sales, against which he contrasted the issues involved in the pipeline: "Grain, the Soviets can get in other places, if they want it. . . . The other element is that grain will result in the Soviet Union having to pay out hard cash."[56] This dual argument—that the Soviet Union had alternative suppliers and that grain imports deprived it of needed hard currency, whereas it did not have many alternative suppliers of rotors for pipeline compressors and selling it pipeline equipment enabled Moscow to increase its hard currency earnings—was technically correct. However, it appeared somewhat contrived in view of the Reagan Administration's avowedly anti-Soviet policy.[57] It was obvious that the real reason for lifting the embargo was domestic and electoral, namely, to gain the support of farmers.

The European and Japanese response to this argument was that the potential security threat posed by the hard currency earnings would be more than balanced by the economic gains that the pipeline exports would bring to Western Europe.

A third argument concerned the possible doubling of some Western European nations' dependence on Soviet gas supplies. There was much concern about the potential Soviet political leverage that could be derived from Western Europe's increased "addiction" to Soviet gas. The worst-case scenario was that the USSR might suddenly cut off the flow of gas in conjunction with perhaps another Middle East oil embargo, cause economic havoc in Europe, and press Soviet political demands on a reluctant Europe. Even if this scenario was extreme, critics argued that the USSR might well use the threat of "interruptions" in gas supplies to blackmail Western Europe. In particular, the threat of a gas cutoff to residential users, for instance, in Bavaria, could cause major problems for the Germans.

In Europe the response to the import dependency concern was varied. On the one hand, the USSR had until then never employed energy exports as a form of political leverage in its relations with E.C. members and, proponents of the pipeline argued, the USSR was dependent on Western supplies of equipment and spare parts, as well as on continued hard currency earnings. Moscow would have to think very hard before jeopardizing any of these by using gas exports as a political lever. However, most Europeans recognized the need to develop a safety net, so that there were sufficient alternative supplies to deter the USSR from any gas blackmail. The safety net involved the following arrangements: interchangeable gas networks, developing more gas from the North Sea and other sources, increasing interruptible contracts with industry, increasing the number of dual-fired burners, and enlarging underground storage. Clearly, none of these alternative arrangements were foolproof, and the possibility for Soviet leverage would always exist. It is undeniable that a Bavarian householder dependent on Soviet gas supplies is more vulnerable to Soviet pressure than a Soviet pipeline construction worker who is dependent on European equipment is to West German pressure.

The final element inherent in transatlantic disputes over the pipeline involved credits whose rates of interest were below market rates. The United States had attempted to secure OECD agreement to cease subsidizing credits to communist countries. The United States maintained that subsidizing any credits distorts free trade and is in principle undesirable. There appeared to be little economic rationale for making credits cheaper as long as U.S. interest rates remain high and the West experiences economic difficulties. Moreover, there was a political aspect to this argument. Washington considered it wrong to subsidize credits to one's political adversaries since that eases their economic burdens.

The Europeans rejected these arguments. They claimed that subsidized credits were a feature of European trade with the whole world, including the United States, and represented a subsidy to domestic industries as much as to the USSR. Moreover, in many deals, such as the pipeline, lower rates of interest were offset by higher equipment charges.[58] This did not, however, answer the political question about the desirability of subsidizing credits to one's antagonists while the West experiences economic problems.

From the allies' point of view, the issue involved in the imposition of U.S. sanctions was, as it had been in 1962, whether to place foreign policy interests over economic interests—that is, was it more important to comply with the United States than to pursue their own economic goals. Unlike twenty years earlier, the U.S. had used legal means—the extraterritorial imposition of U.S. law—to try and force the allies to comply with its policies. This time, as in 1962, the Europeans chose their economic and political relationship with the USSR—which was much greater than in 1962, particularly for West Germany—over the perceived need to support U.S. policy. After all, they argued, they had supported America on the really crucial missile issue. The major change from 1962 was that the Germans, by now more emancipated from the U.S. and with their own Ostpolitik, refused to comply and were indeed highly critical of U.S. policy. As Chancellor Schmidt said, "The Americans should know that they are destroying the alliance in the name of Poland."[59] Moreover, the U.S. sanctions came at a time of increasing U.S.-European and U.S.-Japanese strains over West-West trade, which exacerbated the allies' difficulties with the sanctions. America's allies generally agreed that the sanctions had a more detrimental impact on U.S. relations with its partners than on the Soviet Union.

A comparison of the two pipeline embargoes indicates that East-West trade problems between the United States and its allies have increased over the past twenty years. This is partly because political expectations have changed. The Europeans and Japanese consider themselves more equal partners with the United States and less obliged to subordinate their interests to those of Washington. Moreover, their economic interdependence with CMEA has grown over the past two decades and they are unwilling to jeopardize these ties in a period of economic recession. European political emancipation and economic distress have clearly exacerbated East-West trade issues within the alliance.

The lesson of this pipeline embargo, as with the previous one, is that it is virtually impossible to secure allied coordination when restrictions are imposed unilaterally by the U.S. Despite the sanctions, the construction of the pipeline went ahead, and the USSR devoted special press coverage to the fact that it could build this without U.S. components. The Europeans defied the sanctions and sold their equipment. The situation in Poland improved somewhat, but not because of the pipeline sanctions. The main beneficiaries of the sanctions were the Washington lawyers who handled the myriad of legal suits arising from the extraterritorial issue and perhaps the USSR, which benefited from U.S.-European tensions. The one potentially positive outcome of the sanctions was the allied agreement to study issues of East-West trade, and it is to this issue that we now turn.

The Allied Studies

Since the lifting of the pipeline sanctions, the U.S. and its allies have been engaged in four sets of studies on East-West economic issues. Although the initial studies themselves are more or less complete (they are also not in the public domain) the process of trying to reach a Western consensus continues. The four studies are a NATO study of the security implications of East-West trade, an OECD examination of trade and credits that involves several studies, an International Energy Agency (IEA) examination of energy and security, and a CoCom study on strategic technology. Of course, none of these institutions is ideal for coordinating Western policy. Japan is not a formal member of NATO, although it cooperates with NATO; the OECD has neutral members who have different interests; France is not a member of IEA; and CoCom is an informal forum where decisions tend to represent the lowest common denominator, because they are based on unanimity. Nevertheless, each of these institutions has contributed something toward a more explicit discussion of the problem.

The NATO study has so far been the most general and has come up with broad outlines. It has emphasized that East-West economic relations must take into consideration the security implications of exports to the USSR and CMEA. Officials involved in the study say that, although the

French publicly were reticent about their participation in this study and objected to the discussion of its contents with the Japanese—since France in principle is opposed to widening NATO's competence—in practice, the French were cooperative in the study. Indeed, their concern about the security implications of East-West trade appears to be greater than that of the Germans, who are publicly more supportive of the United States. NATO now is conducting a more detailed follow-up study on the relationship between security and military technology.

The NATO study has taken the first step toward a more detailed allied examination of security, but the problem is that the U.S. and Europeans have different approaches toward security. The United States would, for instance, like to upgrade the importance of the NATO Economic Secretariat as a consultative mechanism, thereby emphasizing the connection between economic and military security. The Europeans are concerned about widening NATO's powers in the area and consider that the United States overemphasizes military power in relations with the East.[60] And the French are particularly sensitive to the upgrading of NATO committees. As one spokesman said, "The Economic Committee of the alliance is charged with evaluating the strengths and weaknesses of the Soviet economy. It is not empowered to coordinate the Western countries' commercial strategies toward the East."[61] The real problem with NATO is that it is not charged with making policy recommendations, nor with coordinating policies of member countries, although its role in providing information on East-West trade has been enhanced.

The OECD studies, one on credits and one on the balance of advantages, had similar problems, although the very fact that they were done represents a change in members' attitudes. In July 1982, the OECD had agreed to raise the USSR to a Category One (Advanced Recipient) country in terms of the appropriate rates of interest to charge it, and the USSR would henceforth have to pay a minimum 12.15 percent interest rate on Western government credits with maturities of 2–5 years, an increase of 1.15 percent from the previous accord. However, further concrete action on credits was complicated by the fact that the United States and other members disagree over the meaning of "subsidies," and most governments and commercial banks will not discuss their detailed credit dealings.[62] The other OECD study did, however, discuss in more general detail the balance of economic advantages in East-West trade, and here the neutral countries—Switzerland, Austria and Finland—were more cooperative than might have been expected. However, they insisted that the political content of the study be kept at a minimum. The study examined both the overall impact of exports and imports on the industrialized economies and the USSR and the sectoral importance of these economic relations for certain industries. Nevertheless, OECD officials admit that one cannot really study the balance of economic advantages without examining the political dimension and this was largely absent from the study because of the sensitivities of the member nations.

The problem with the studies, as one official pointed out, was that the OECD is an organization for economic cooperation, not coordination. Apart from the repositioning of the USSR in a different credit category, neither the OECD credit study nor its overall trade study makes policy recommendations, nor does it attempt to achieve a policy consensus. The OECD studies of East-West economic relations will continue, and will provide useful statistics, but they will not be an appropriate means of coordinating allied policy.

The IEA study was perhaps the most successful, in that it not only presented clear information but came up with policy recommendations that represented a compromise between U.S. and European views. Although the French do not belong to the IEA, they did in fact cooperate with the study and appear to have accepted its recommendations. The IEA study on natural gas and security warned of the dangers of excessive dependence on Soviet gas supplies, but also implied that at current, i.e., post-Urengoi, levels, this threshold has not been reached. Moreover, the study discussed alternative natural gas sources and recommended the development of more Norwegian gas as well as other sources.

In some ways, the issues involved in the energy study seem less pressing now, because the gas market in Europe has softened up, and the Soviets have so far only been able to sell 25 billion cubic meters (bcm) of the total 40 bcm that can go through the pipeline. In the long run, however, it appears as if Soviet gas may well be cheaper than gas from the Norwegian Troll fields—which would be the most logical noncommunist source of new gas—and the question that the West may face, is whether it is willing to pay the price to develop Norwegian gas instead of importing more Soviet gas. The Norwegian gas would exact an economic price, but it may in the long run be politically worth the cost to ensure that Western Europe has access to more non-Soviet gas. There is also the related issue of where European and Japanese manufacturers would sell their pipeline-related steel products if no more Soviet natural gas export pipelines were built. As a result of the IEA study, and other allied consultations, the Europeans agreed for the time being not to become involved in the construction of a possible Soviet second export pipeline.

Of all these exercises, the CoCom studies are probably the most important in terms of concrete policy, but also the most complex, because they involve detailed discussions of the question of technology transfer. In view of the fact that CoCom is a voluntary, informal organization dealing with sensitive topics, it has functioned remarkably well over the years.[63] CoCom's deliberations are secret, its powers of enforcement limited, and the U.S. is the only member that officially publishes data on it. Yet CoCom has worked as well as it has because all the allies, even if they disagree with aspects of the U.S. East-West trade policy, are committed to preventing the transfer of technology to the USSR that could directly enhance its military might. Thus CoCom is the one forum where the chances of allied agreement are relatively good, provided the United States does not attempt to introduce too many changes. CoCom was designed as a limited technical, not political, organization. Its main tasks are to meet weekly and make decisions on exception requests for items on the CoCom embargo list and to review these lists periodically. These decisions are based on technical criteria, that is, whether the products in question would have possible military applications. CoCom has never been charged with making political decisions about East-West trade, and its member delegates are trained to focus on purely technical issues. It is therefore unproductive to try to turn it into a broader political organization, which some parts of the U.S. government would favor. Moreover, CoCom can exist only as an informal organization because of domestic opposition in many member countries to making it a formal treaty organization and concern that, if it were formal, it would turn into another cumbersome bureaucracy. Thus, the United States will undoubtedly have to drop its attempt to create a formal CoCom treaty.[64]

One area where the United States has made some constructive proposals is in enhancing the structure of CoCom. This organization which controls the flow of sensitive Western technology has operated until now on a shoestring budget of $500,000, with a secretariat of fifteen people, and until recently they used manual typewriters.[65] The United States has agreed to increase its contribution to CoCom's budget, as have its allies, and to install computerized office equipment and word processors to lighten the workload of the staff and expedite decisions. The premises will also be enlarged.[66] More important, the U.S. has proposed a permanent military subcommittee in CoCom, separate from the main committee, to give a more coherent and institutionalized military input into CoCom decisions.[67] However, all other CoCom members have resisted this idea since they fear this would create another bureaucracy and upset the delicate balance between strategic and trade interests.[68]

It is unlikely that the U.S. proposals for a military committee will be accepted, yet U.S. concern does highlight one structural problem within CoCom which complicates this decision-making process, namely, the heterogeneity of the backgrounds of CoCom delegates and of their relationships to their respective governments. For instance, some CoCom delegates have a technical background, but others are foreign service officers who have no technical background and find it difficult to absorb all the complicated issues involved in list reviews or in considering exception requests. Some delegates, such as the American and the Japanese, are under the direction of their country's foreign service. Others, like the German, report to an economics ministry. Furthermore, the ministries of defense in the various member countries have diverging inputs into the whole process. For instance, the U.S. Department of Defense has a considerable influence over CoCom decisions both nationally and with consultations in Paris. The British and French have also recently upgraded the role of their military in national and CoCom decisions partly as a result of U.S. pressure and partly out of concern for growing technology leaks. However, the German Ministry of Defense has no regularized input into export licensing decisions, and the Japanese Self-Defense Agency has even less. Some delegates have more autonomy than others, and some have far better communication with their home governments than others. In view of this wide variety of relationships between individual delegates and their various home ministries, it would make sense to try to have a uniform institutionalized military input from all member countries, even if it is impossible to create a separate military committee. Otherwise, the discrepancies in prior outlook of the delegates will be too great.

A constant complaint of both European and Japanese delegates to CoCom is that the U.S. does not come forward with unified suggestions, but that the different U.S. government agencies with an interest in CoCom—specifically the Departments of State and Defense—come up with different proposals and that the United States exports its domestic bureaucratic battles to Paris. This may to some extent to be true, but, since the lifting of the pipeline sanctions, the United States has indeed come up with various concrete proposals, all of which its CoCom allies have resisted in different degrees. Since the invasion of Afghanistan, a "no exceptions" policy for the USSR, and later on for Poland, has been in effect, and all members now accept this. This means that there are no discussions on exporting listed items to these countries. In 1982–84 CoCom was engaged in its triennial list review process, which was completed in July 1984. This list review, a part of CoCom's normal work, was particularly difficult because the United States sought to broaden the range of products on the list, while agreeing to take off items that were no longer state-of-the-art technology. The most difficult item was revising the computer list, which had remained the same for ten years because of lack of agreement. In the final compromise, most home computers were freed from licensing, except for "super" mini-computers; some software was put on the list; and a new agreement was made to stop sales of telecommunications equipment.[69] Describing the difficulties of making decisions on dual-use civilian technology, one French official observed "if CoCom had existed in 10,000 B.C., the wheel would still be on the list today."[70]

The United States submitted to its CoCom partners more than 100 proposals to put new technologies on the embargo list. Some were accepted by its partners, but others, particularly in the robotics and computer field, were more controversial. The United States also proposed controls on a range of oil and gas equipment, and an ad hoc CoCom group on the energy sector decided to study further controls on certain militarily sensitive items, such as offshore sonar equipment. Finally, CoCom has drafted a "watch list" of emerging technologies such as genetic engineering, which will be monitored for any future military applications and possibly embargoed at a later date.[71] Thus, apart from the regular list review, these CoCom discussions on computers, energy technology, and emerging technologies constitute in effect a separate CoCom study on strategic technologies. One problem in all of these debates is that the United States would still like to have its allies accept the Militarily Critical Technologies List (MCTL) concept, which would imply that disembodied as well as embodied technology would be controlled, including blueprints, computer software, etc. Although the Bucy concepts should also imply the shortening of lists controlling products— Commerce Secretary Baldrige has apparently suggested that CoCom lists should be cut by 40 percent—in practice very little technology appears to have been decontrolled. And the United States has somewhat weakened its case about tightening controls on exports to the USSR, Poland, and other CMEA nations by loosening technology controls for China even in the military field—a policy about which its other CoCom allies are more skeptical. They believe that the new China differential calls into question the rationale for controlling exports to Communist countries. Moreover, they are reluctant to incur Soviet displeasure by openly favoring exports to China.

The differences between the United States and its CoCom allies have led to strains over two key issues. One is the question of third countries. How can one ensure that, if a CoCom member exports a high technology item to a country like Austria—which has few export controls—that it will not be shipped from there to the USSR or another CMEA nation? The United States is insisting on tighter controls on exports to third, non-communist countries. Moreover, having itself introduced Operation Exodus—to stem the illegal transfer of technology to CMEA nations—the United States is trying to persuade its allies to do the same, and has met with some success.

The more sensitive issue is the proposed new Department of Commerce rule on distribution licenses, which are granted for two years to cover multiple shipments of a U.S. company to a foreign customer. The new rules would forbid the shipping of some technologies, such as some computers, to non-CoCom members under distribution license. Moreover, they would also require CoCom members buying U.S. goods shipped under distribution licenses to report four times a year on all their customers outside the CoCom area, including all of the third world. The reaction to these proposals has been negative.[72] Since the U.S. cannot achieve CoCom agreement on more restrictive rules, it has begun unilaterally to place new restrictions on its trade with its allies, to ensure that sensitive technology does not leak out. It is likely to continue and intensify this process in the future.

Thus, although there is more agreement in CoCom about the need for a unified strategy, as soon as it comes to specifics, the United States and its allies tend to disagree, and these differences reflect wider divergences over the economics and politics of East-West economic relations.

What Is To Be Done?

As the preceding analysis suggests, there is ample reason for pessimism about the ability of the Western alliance to reach a modus vivendi on East-West trade questions that is acceptable on both sides of the Atlantic. It is particularly difficult to decouple the purely East-West economic issues from the broader questions of East-West political relations and West-West economic relations. Yet there has been some movement on these issues in the past few years. At any rate, it would be worthwhile for the West to continue its attempts to improve its cooperation and coordination on East-West commercial ties, because the alternative is continued disarray and squabbling over issues that are disproportionately divisive politically.

The alliance has three basic choices in dealing with these issues. It could continue to muddle through, as it has for the past thirty-five years, occasionally having an overt clash over specific projects and otherwise maintaining a strained but minimally workable system, with the United States and its partners disagreeing over specific and general issues, but agreeing on enough to get by. Indeed, some have argued that muddling through is the most desirable option, because explicitly confronting controversial issues might damage the alliance beyond repair.[73] But muddling through is unsatisfactory. Even when the economic situation is good, dissension over East-West trade can spill over into other alliance issues. In bad economic times, when every CoCom member is concerned about employment, no country wants to jeopardize even the limited gains reaped from exports to the East. The pipeline sanctions definitely had a detrimental impact on European willingness to support the deployment of U.S. missiles in Europe. And these allied quarrels are a boon for the USSR.

A second option would be to discuss the issues explicitly, and then agree to disagree. While this might prevent future misunderstandings and the need for the United States to take unilateral action to force its allies to accept its policies, it would nevertheless involve constant tensions and growing isolationism on both sides of the Atlantic, and would make it very difficult for CoCom to operate. As long as there is a Western alliance, it would be unwise to designate the East-West commercial area as one on which there could be no agreement.

Thus the third option—to work out a compromise that might involve agreement to disagree on some issues, but a willingness to modify positions so as to reach agreement on other, more fundamental ones—appears to be the most promising, even though it would entail a loss of autonomy for all sides. Let us return to our four basic questions, and review what compromises are possible and what are impossible in these areas.

On the general question of how to deal with the USSR, all NATO members and Japan would presumably admit today that detente, as it was viewed in its mid-1970s heyday, is no longer viable because it was based on unrealistic expectations of Soviet behavior. But all the allies would agree that the relationship with the USSR must have some elements of cooperation as well as competition or even confrontation. Thus, it may be time to return to the two-track perspective, whereby the United States and its allies could agree to build up their defenses and continue arms control talks, and could designate the economic area one channel of cooperative communication. The U.S. will always have a different interest in relations with the USSR than either Western Europe or Japan, precisely because it is a global power, but there could be allied agreement to pursue negotiations based on mutual self-interest. Moreover, all alliance members should recognize that one element of Western security is a partnership that tries to contain its public quarrels, and that the commitment to formulate policies toward the USSR that do not overly irk one's allies is an important consideration.

If the allies were to accept that East-West commerce could be one area of cooperation with CMEA, then they would have to tackle the difficult issue of how to define security. The United States would probably have to narrow its current definition and concede that even if every East-West trade deal strengthens the Soviet economy, they do not *per se* constitute a security risk in a direct military sense. Europeans and Japanese may in turn have to broaden their definitions, and be more willing to accept the principle of the indirect security implications of major industrial transactions.

Since there is no definitive way of measuring the impact of Western agricultural and non-agricultural trade on the Soviet Union, the allies should consider a compromise. The Europeans and Japanese could consult more regularly with their own military experts and be more vigilant about illegal technology exports domestically. For their part, Americans could concede the truth of a long-standing European insight, namely, that economic well-being is an integral part of security. East-West trade benefits Western economies and contributes to their growth. A security framework must explicitly build on Japan's and the European countries' acute sense of economic vulnerability. In particular, Americans could desist from publicizing and politicizing particular industrial projects in such an overt way. Rather the United States should attempt to secure agreement from its allies that they will discuss large-scale East-West industrial and agricultural projects with the United States—and vice versa—before contracts are signed. Once contracts are completed, however, neither the United States nor the allies should try to prevent the other side from implementing them.

With respect to non-CoCom trade, Washington has two choices. One is to tolerate industrial and energy-related trade and concentrate instead on limiting European dependence through import substitution schemes, safety nets, market diversification, and the like. The other is for Washington to keep trying to persuade its allies that building up the manufacturing base and boosting the hard currency earnings of the Soviet Union runs counter to the long-term security interest of the alliance. This will be particularly difficult, since Europe and Japan export mainly industrial goods to the USSR, whereas the United States exports mainly agricultural products. Thus, the economic sacrifices demanded would be unequal. This is why prior consultation on the security implications—meaning military *and* economic—of certain key projects would be desirable.

Probably the potentially most useful forum for these discussions is CoCom. With respect to CoCom, tightening the lists and broadening security definitions begin to approach the American concepts. Indeed, since it is always the United States that provides the suggestions, it could benefit from European and Japanese passivity. All European statesmen claim they are in favor of tightening CoCom controls. They should now be willing to implement this. Americans should learn to live with the results of the discussions and not revoke their consent every time the White House changes hands.

If the United States is unwilling to trust its allies in the area of technology transfer, then it may continue the present trend of tightening up West-West technology flows to ensure that its allies do not obtain technologies that the United States considers dangerous to sell to the USSR. The Europeans and Japanese could do little in the economic realm to retaliate against these U.S. restrictions. However, even if this policy succeeded economically from the U.S. point of view, it would further disturb alliance relations and the detrimental political repercussions in the non-East-West trade areas could be significant.

It will be difficult for Washington to gain a viable agreement on credits. Most Europeans and Japanese believe that without subsidized credits their products might not be competitive with those of other countries on the Soviet market, and subsidized credits are a basic feature of their international economic relations. Trade and credit policies are not separated in Europe or Japan as they are here, and America's allies continue to deny that subsidized credits are a form of economic aid to the USSR. Probably the most that the United States can hope for is to continue this agreement on raising interest rates, reducing subsidies as opposed to guarantees and credit supports, and perhaps eliciting some promise that credit volumes could be restricted.

The question of economic/political linkage is the one on which it may be most difficult to reach agreement. The Europeans reject the use of sanctions and, short of a Soviet attack on Western Europe, would probably not be willing to implement them. Yet sanctions are part of the U.S. tradition, and one could make the argument that, from a unilateral U.S. point of view, it is legitimate to use them. After all, if one cannot react with economic levers to the Soviet actions which one deplores, what other levers are there? However, since its allies refuse to cooperate, the United States would have to be willing in the future to impose sanctions on its own, but not to try and force its allies to comply.

This policy, of course, would raise domestic problems. It would mean a loss of markets to U.S. exporters and a gain to its allies and competitors. More important, it would require revision of the current proposals for the EAA that embody the principle of extraterritoriality. Since America's allies reject the principle of interfering with trade for foreign policy purposes, as in the pipeline sanctions, if the U.S. Congress wants to retain foreign policy controls, it would have to restrict them to U.S. corporations. A continuation of the present policy whereby a U.S. President can embargo goods produced under American license abroad is an unnecessary burden on the alliance, and reduces the chances of securing consensus in other areas. Indeed Secretary of State Shultz has admitted that "disputes over extraterritoriality could become a bigger threat to our economic interests than the present concerns about tariffs, quotas, and exchange rates."[74]

Nevertheless, the Europeans, if not the Japanese, do accept the principle of positive linkage in certain circumstances. This might be an area where greater allied agreement is possible. For instance, even if the allies had decided that a certain project could go ahead because it did not represent a security threat, the credit terms for that project could be variable, and might be used as a potential form of positive leverage. There is some room for agreement on the question of trade incentives, whereas the issue of sanctions is a totally unproductive avenue for allied exploration.

A more difficult issue is the question of which institution should carry out these discussions. Clearly, CoCom is the appropriate forum for security questions, but not for political questions. NATO would be more appropriate for discussion of credit or general trade policy, provided there is consultation with the Japanese. Obviously, the IEA is still an appropriate place for energy discussions. But the OECD, because of its wide membership and non-policy functions, is not a promising forum for working out a consensus, except on the issue of interest rates. That statement implies, of course, that any Western consensus will probably be limited to CoCom members. However, at present this is the maximum possible scope for compromise.

For the United States, balancing the need to meet the Soviet challenge against the need to heed the interests of its allies is a delicate and complex task. The NATO alliance is democratic and pluralistic, and it is inevitable that differences of opinion över East-West economic relations will exist. If these disagreements cause needless tension within the alliance, as they did over the pipeline issue, then the allies must reflect on whether these disputes themselves jeopardize Western security by undermining the alliance, irrespective of what the USSR does.

The current outlook for a workable agreement is not promising. Although all the allies agree that the transatlantic and transpacific dispute over East-West economic relations must be defused, they have so far been reticent about coming to any concrete agreements. Yet some progress has been made, and an attempt to reach a consensus on security definitions and on consistency is worth the effort. The consensus would require compromises on the part of the United States, some of which would be problematic, given the nature of America's pluralistic democracy. Yet the compromise would be justified if it were to result in better allied coordination. If the United States can demonstrate consistent leadership, insisting on certain fundamental premises but remaining flexible enough to accommodate some European and Japanese concerns, then the alliance may be able to forge a new consensus and place East-West economic relations in their appropriate context—a significant but nevertheless limited element in the overall East-West competition.

NOTES

1. One might indeed question whether President Nixon and Secretary of State Henry Kissinger really expected the USSR to moderate its behavior in the Third World as a result of Soviet-U.S. agreements. Detente was, however, portrayed to the American public as a major change in U.S.-Soviet relations and an agreement to introduce a new code of conduct. When the Soviets were seen to violate that code in Angola, for instance, disillusionment with detente set in.

2. See the chapters by Millar and Bertsch.

3. For a critical assessment of the difficulties of coordinating policy just between State and Defense, see William A. Root, former Director, Office of East-West Trade, Department of State, "U.S.-European Economic Relations—

Problems and Prospects," Testimony to United States Senate Committee on Foreign Relations, Subcommittee on International Economic Policy (mimeograph), Washington, D.C., 26 October 1983.

4. For a recent restatement of this view, see Hans-Dietrich Genscher, "Toward an Overall Western Strategy for Peace, Freedom and Progress," *Foreign Affairs*, 61, no. 1 (Autumn 1982), pp. 42–66.

5. Cited in Angela Stent, *From Embargo to Ostpolitik: The Political Economy of West German-Soviet Relations, 1955–1980* (New York: Cambridge University Press, 1981), p. 94.

6. Joint Economic Committee, Congress of the United States, *East-West Commercial Policy: A Congressional Dialogue with the Reagan Administration,* 97th Congress, 2nd Session, 16 February 1982, p. 22.

7. Giovanni Agnelli, "East-West Trade: A European View," *Foreign Affairs*, 59, no. 3 (Summer 1980), p. 1027.

8. State Department Memorandum, 25 September 1963, cited in Stent, *From Embargo to Ostpolitik*, p. 122.

9. Ibid. p. 23.

10. *An Analysis of Export Control of U.S. Technology—A DOD Perspective. A Report of the Defense Science Board Task Force on the Export of U.S. Technology* (Washington, D.C., 1976), p. 24. This report is known as the Bucy Report.

11. R. M. Davis, "The Department of Defense Statement on Critical Technology for Export Controls," Statement before the Subcommittee on International Economic Policy and Trade, Committee on Foreign Affairs of the United States House of Representatives, 22 March 1979.

12. *New York Times*, 23 January 1984; United States Department of Commerce *News*, ITA-84-5.

13. Joint Economic Committee, *Dialogue*, p. 4.

14. See for instance the elegant defense of this idea by Samuel Huntington, "Trade, Technology, and Leverage: Economic Diplomacy," *Foreign Policy*, 32 (Autumn 1978), pp. 63–80.

15. For a representative sample of views on this subject, see Heinrich Vogel, *The Politics of East-West Economic Relations Reconsidered: A German View* (Cologne: Berichte des Bundesinstituts fuer ostwissenschaftliche und internationale Studien), no. 22, 1982; and his "Wirtschaftsbeziehungen mit dem Osten—Sicherheitsrisiko oder Chance zur Aussenpolitik?" *Europa Archiv*, no. 23 (1983), pp. 713–22; Karl-Herman Fink, "La République Fédérale D'Allemagne et la Cooperation Est-Ouest," *Politique Etrangère*, no. 3 (1982), pp. 1737–47.

16. Deutsches Institut fuer Wirtschaftsforschung (Berlin), *Wochenbericht*, no. 13 (1981).

17. *Der Spiegel*, 24 November 1984, pp. 26–27.

18. *Neue Zuercher Zeitung*, 4 January 1984.

19. Article by Graf Otto Lambsdorff, *Washington Post*, 23 July 1982; Joachim Jahnke, "The East Bloc and Western Credit," reprinted in *The German Tribune Political Affairs Review*, 19 September 1982.

20. Axel Lebahn, "Financing German Trade with the East," *Aussenpolitik* (English Edition), no. 2, 1982.

21. Jochen Bethkenhagen and Heinrich Machowski, Gutachten, "Entwicklung und Struktur des deutsch-sowjetischen Handels und seine Bedeutung fuer die Volkswirtschaft der Bundesrepublik und der Sowjetunion" (Berlin: May 1982), p. 60.

22. For a discussion of the impact of imports from CMEA on the German textile and clothing industry, see Claudia Woermann, *Der Osthandel der Bundes-*

republik Deutschland: Politische Rahmenbedingungen und oekonomische Bedeutung (Frankfurt: Campus Verlag, 1982), pp. 203–10.

23. Der Bundesminister fuer Wirtschaft, *Der Deutsche Osthandel 1982* (Bonn: 1982), p. 4.

24. For a detailed description of German laws covering East-West trade and technology transfer, see Angela E. Stent, *Technology Transfer to the Soviet Union: A Challenge for the Cohesiveness of the Western Alliance*, Arbeitspapiere zur Internationalen Politik, no. 24 (Bonn: Europa Union Verlag, 1983), pp. 44–64, 88–90.

25. See Stent, *From Embargo to Ostpolitik*, for details.

26. See the collection of essays in Freidemann Mueller (ed.), *Sanktionen in den Ost-West Beziehungen* (Ebenhausen: Stiftung Wissenschaft und Politik, August 1982).

27. Indeed, Schmidt, replying to questions about Germany's reactions to the Soviet invasion of Afghanistan, said, "Our economic relations with the Soviet Union have been built up through many years of cooperation, and primarily for political reasons." Quoted in Der Bundesminister fuer Wirtschaft, *Der Deutsche Osthandel 1980* (Bonn: 1980), p. 61.

28. See Michael J. Sodaro, "Moscow and Mitterrand," *Problems of Communism*, July–August 1982, pp. 20–36.

29. For a more extensive discussion of these issues, see Renate Fritsch-Bournazel, "Frankreichs Osthandel im Spannungsfeld von Ideologie und Wirtschaftlichem Sachzwang," in Hanns-Dieter Jacobsen and Reinhard Rode (eds.), *Wirtschaftskrieg oder Entspannung? Ein Bilanz Mitte der Achtziger Jahre* (Bonn: Die Neue Gesellschaft, 1984).

30. *Les Echos*, 23 July 1982.

31. Gerard Wild, "Les Dépendences de la France Dans Ses Relations Économiques avec L'Europe de L'Est," *Le Courrier des Pays de l'Est*, October 1981.

32. Suzanne Porter, *East-West Trade Financing: An Introductory Guide* (Washington: U.S. Department of Commerce, 1976), pp. 42–43.

33. For a discussion of this and of the general French secretiveness on these issues, see Françoise Haegel, "Les Restrictions Aux Exportateurs de Haute Technologie Vers Les Pays de l'Est," Ph.D. Thesis, University of Paris I—Pantheon Sorbonne, 1983, pp. 104–19. See also Stent, *Technology Transfer to the Soviet Union*, pp. 65–79, 91–93.

34. Cited in Fritsch-Bournazel, "Frankreichs Osthandel," p. 14.

35. The European Community imposed modest sanctions on "luxury" imports from the USSR after Polish martial law was declared.

36. For a fuller discussion of U.K.-Soviet Trade, see Stephen Woolcock, "British Policy on East-West Economic Relations," in Jacobsen and Rode, *Wirtschaftskrieg oder Entspannung?*

37. Woolcock, p. 8.

38. *Financial Times*, 18 January 1984.

39. *The Economist*, 17 July 1982, pp. 11–12, and 4 September 1982, p. 13.

40. *Financial Times*, 22 December 1983.

41. See for instance the *Financial Times* leader, 27 August 1982.

42. See Hiroshi Kimura, "Soviet Policy Toward Japan," *Working Paper #6*, August 1983 (Providence, R.I.: Brown University Center for Foreign Policy Development).

43. Yukio Satoh, *The Evolution of Japanese Security Policy*, Adelphi Papers, no. 178 (London: The International Institute for Strategic Studies, 1982), p. 33.

44. See Kimura, "Soviet Policy," pp. 20–23.

45. See Hiroshi Kimura, "The Soviet Threat and the Security of Japan," in Roger Kanet (ed.), *Soviet Foreign Policy in the 1980's* (New York: Praeger Publishers, 1982), pp. 231–46.

46. Satoh, *The Evolution*, p. 15.

47. See Stephen Sternheimer, *East-West Technology Transfer: Japan and the Communist Bloc*, The Washington Papers, no. 76 (Beverly Hills and London: Sage Publications, 1980), pp. 17–18.

48. For a discussion of the reasons for this position, see ibid., p. 62.

49. For more details, see Stent, *From Embargo to Ostpolitik*, ch. 5.

50. Senator Keating's subcommittee hearings, cited in ibid., p. 99.

51. Ibid., p. 107.

52. *New York Times*, 6 March 1984. For a fuller account of the issue involved in the pipeline, see Angela E. Stent, *Soviet Energy and Western Europe*, The Washington Papers, no. 90 (New York: Praeger Publishers, 1982).

53. *New York Times*, 13 November 1982.

54. *The Economist*, 20 November 1982, p. 11; *Der Spiegel*, 22 November 1982, pp. 149–50.

55. See Daniel Yergin, "Crisis and Adjustment," in Daniel Yergin and Martin Hillenbrand (eds.), *Global Insecurity* (Boston: Houghton Mifflin, 1982), pp. 1–28.

56. *New York Times*, 29 July 1982.

57. *The Economist*, 4 September 1982, p. 13.

58. For a detailed discussion of these mechanisms and a European defense of the pipeline, see Axel Lebahn, "The Yamal Gas Pipeline from the USSR to Western Europe in the East-West Conflict," *Aussenpolitik* (English-language edition), no. 3 (1983), pp. 3–27.

59. *Der Spiegel*, 26 July 1982, p. 17.

60. John P. Hardt and Donna Gold, "East-West Commercial Issues: The Western Alliance Studies" (Washington: Library of Congress, Congressional Research Service), Issue Brief no. IB 83086, 19 May 1983, p. 8.

61. Cited in *L'Express*, 22 April 1983, p. 58.

62. Hardt and Gold, "East-West Commercial Issues," pp. 13–14.

63. For a more detailed discussion of U.S. and allied attitudes toward it, see Stent, *Technology Transfer to the Soviet Union*, pp. 80–103.

64. *Financial Times*, 24 January 1984.

65. Richard N. Perle, "West-oestlicher Technologietransfer: Die Strategischen Konsequenzen," *Europa-Archiv*, 1 (1984) p. 17.

66. *Financial Times*, 13 December 1983.

67. Perle, "West-oestlicher Technologietransfer," p. 17.

68. *Financial Times*, 24 January 1983.

69. *Financial Times*, 25 July 1984.

70. *Business Week*, 4 April 1983, p. 95.

71. *Financial Times*, 24 January 1983.

72. *Financial Times*, 20 January 1984.

73. This section draws on Ellen L. Frost and Angela E. Stent, "NATO's Troubles with East-West Trade," *International Security*, 8, no. 1 (Summer 1983), pp. 179–200.

74. *New York Times*, 6 May 1984.

The Impact of Trade and Trade Denial on the U.S. Economy

James R. Millar

THE FIRST section of this essay provides a very broad typography of policy goals that have motivated U.S. trade sanctions and controls in the recent past. They are discussed with the aim of identifying the nature and defining the extent of potential counter impacts upon the U.S. economy. The second section provides a brief description of the mechanisms of trade sanctions and controls and shows how international market structure and other factors shape long- and short-term impacts of trade measures. It is followed by a brief discussion of three recent case studies. The fourth section looks at the broad issues that have been raised with regard to trade interruption or denial and seeks to draw some conclusions.

Policy Goals

A decision to embargo or restrict trade with a target country may be motivated by a number of objectives. Four broad objectives have predominated with respect to U.S.-Soviet trade. The first is purely strategic, without specific economic content: to deny access to commodities and/or technology that would have direct military applications. The Militarily Critical Technologies List (MCTL) that has been maintained under the 1979 Export Administration Act represents an attempt to screen commodities and technologies systematically in order to minimize leakage of strategically valuable items and know-how to the USSR.

There has been no serious disagreement among policy advisors about the need to identify and embargo both commodities and the transfer of technology, whether embodied or disembodied, where there are clear military applications. Determination of just what should be included in the MCTL has been more controversial. There are always

I would like to acknowledge the assistance of Thomas Richardson in the preparation of this chapter.

ambiguities, and there is great disagreement regarding how broadly to construe what is of "strategic value."

The maximalist position was stated clearly by Professor Herbert Stein:[1]

> U.S. trade with the Soviet bloc—whether we have it or do not have it, whether we interrupt it in whole or in part, or make it contingent on political events—is of trivial economic consequence to the United States. If there is anything we can do with this trade that is of even slight value to U.S. security or U.S. foreign policy, we should not be deterred by fear that it will damage the U.S. economy significantly. . . .
>
> I believe that the Soviet Union is our enemy and that trading with them is trading with the enemy.

This view constitutes a second strategy, one that treats Soviet economic power as a strategic objective. Adherents do not claim that there are no potential economic gains from trade for the United States; they deem them irrelevant. The goal of policy is not merely to deny strategic advantages to the Soviet military, but to deny the Soviet economy gains from trade as well. Thus, the Soviet economy would be denied the benefits of international division of labor. It would also be denied the use of U.S. credit facilities and thus the possibility of transferring real resources from the future to the present. Professor Stein argues that our allies should follow the same course of action.[2] The second possible policy option is, therefore, a policy of economic warfare against the Soviet Union. Restriction of otherwise legal non-trade transfers of technology, scientific findings, and so forth is a logical corollary of economic warfare. The aim of policy is to do everything possible to deny any benefit to the enemy.

Senator Rudy Boschwitz has stated a third and polar opposite policy, quoting the late Hubert Humphrey to the effect that "we should sell them [the Russians] anything they can't shoot back."[3] Underlying this third policy are two critical assumptions. One is that the Soviet Union will become more tractable the more it is enmeshed in international trade. The concept of "leverage" seems to have grown out of this idea. That is, that the Soviet Union would be willing to "pay" something to obtain, or to maintain, gains from trade. The aim of trade sanctions under this strategy would be limited to specific attempts to influence the political behavior of the target country, such as deterring military adventurism, provision of human rights to its citizens, and so forth.

The other assumption of the third trade strategy is that trade promotion rather than trade restriction should normally be the appropriate role for the U.S. government. This view also holds that the existing structure of international comparative advantage is rather fragile. The worry is, then, about the competitive position of U.S. industry. Senator Tsongas, for example, arguing against broad controls on high technology exports, criticized current U.S. export policy as having been "Made in Japan."[4] Controls and restraints on U.S. producers help make markets for their competitors.

Advocates of limited use of trade controls and sanctions are not as concerned about the loss of U.S. trade with the USSR and Eastern Europe as they are about the impact of restrictive policies upon the U.S. competitive position in West-West trade. The U.S. share in East-West trade is small, but West-West trade *is* significant for the U.S. economy and all the more important because East-West trade offers little potential offset under current policy.

The use of trade interruption or denial for foreign policy purposes against the Soviet Union may cause other customers, current and prospective, to shy away from U.S. producers, or, at a minimum, to hedge their bets by diversifying their purchases to the disadvantage of American producers. It was claimed, for example, that the Carter grain embargo cost U.S. producers their reputation for reliability, and many analysts believe that the Soviet Union will never again depend upon the United States for as large a percentage of its imports of grain as it did before the Carter embargo.

A fourth possible policy objective of trade sanctions was implied by President Carter's decision to boycott the Olympics, a decision which entailed an economic as well as an athletic boycott. The boycott was intended to symbolize U.S. displeasure over the invasion of Afghanistan. As in the case of warfare, the economic cost of morally driven sanctions is measurable but not relevant to the decision to restrict trade. In the case of trade sanctions that are imposed for moral ends, however, the actual impact upon the target country is also irrelevant to the decision to constrain trade. After all, one does not traffic with the Devil. The real "target" in this case may be wholly domestic, or it may be allies. That is, as Hufbauer and Schott put it: Sanctions may be imposed "because the cost of inaction—in lost confidence at home and abroad in the ability or willingness of the U.S. to act—is seen as greater than the cost of the sanction."[5]

Viewed historically, U.S. policy approximated economic warfare in the decade following World War II. Western exports to the East fell sharply after 1948, as did Eastern exports to the West. U.S. exports to the USSR fell essentially to zero and remained there until 1953. Although trade began to inch up afterward, a significant increase in trade did not begin until the 1970s. Official American policy gradually changed toward one of trade promotion, subject to specific restrictions on strategic commodities and technology. Growth of trade turnover formed, as Becker has noted, "the economic foundation of the theory of detente. . . . The aim (of which) was to create a network of interdependence with the USSR through the extension of trade and credit ties in order to tame Moscow's expansionist impulse."[6] The quest for "leverage" was an outgrowth of this strategy. Toward the end of the Carter administration, however, moral objectives increasingly dominated trade policy with the USSR.

The Reagan Administration has moved more toward a policy of economic warfare. Lifting the grain embargo was an exception resulting from an election promise. It is clear from the data in any case that trade had peaked during the Carter administration, before the invasion of Afghanistan (see figs. 1 and 2). It is too early to determine whether or not a downward trend has replaced the upward trend of the 1970s, but trade volume has clearly leveled off, and it is unlikely that the upward trend will reassert itself in the near future. The Reagan administration has deliberately subordinated trade and credit policy to security concerns, and potential military applications of science and technology have been defined quite broadly.

Apart from symbolic uses of trade sanctions, then, recent U.S. trade policy has reflected a tension between the desire to promote trade and the needs of national security. Trade has, it seems, followed rather than led changes in political tensions between the United States and the Soviet Union. Increasingly tense relations between the two superpowers at the present time portend reduced economic ties and increased specific restrictions on U.S.-Soviet trade.

The Economics of Trade Denial and Sanctions

Edward Hewett has proposed that we use the term "economic sanctions" to cover all the various ways in which the government may act to interrupt, deny, or otherwise restrict the flow of trade, credit, and other economic benefits to other countries.[7] Logically, sanctions should include the elimination or denial of access to "economic incentives" too, by which I refer to all those ways in which a government may offer or deny preferential access to its markets, to credit facilities and the like. Embargoes, quotas, tariffs, and quality requirements are examples of restrictions on access either to U.S. products or U.S. markets. Most-favored-nation (MFN) status, tax relief, and special quota assignments represent ways in which the government may encourage or facilitate access to U.S. markets and products.

Conceptually, all sanctions may be classified as ways by which the "sender" (of sanctions) may either (1) raise prices on its exports to the "target" country[8] or (2) raise the cost to the target country of exporting to the sender. All possible applications of economic sanctions can be reduced, therefore, to a form that is amenable to standard economic

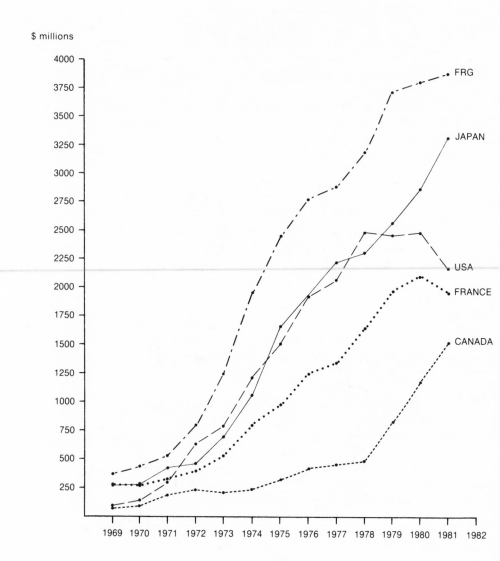

Figure 1

Total Exports to USSR - 3 Year Moving Averages

iillions

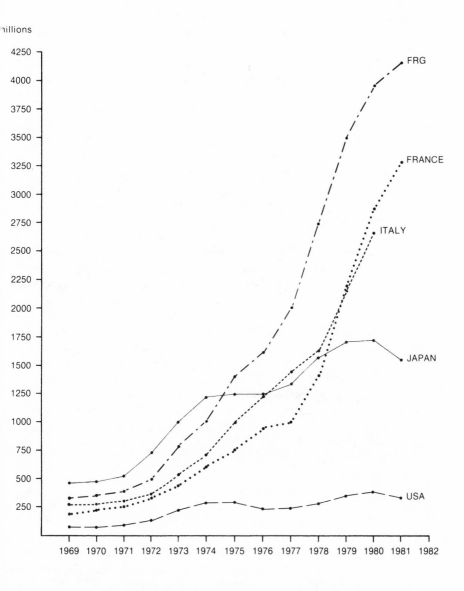

Figure 2

Total Imports from USSR - 3 Year Moving Averages

analysis of market structure and behavior. The cost to the sender nation depends upon the market structure it faces, that is, upon the income and substitution effects for the products and/or services it seeks to control or interrupt.

Some examples will illustrate this point. A total embargo on the export of a particular commodity or financial transaction implies the imposition of an infinite price or interest rate to the target country. The impact upon the sender economy is determined as the algebraic sum of the decrease in income occasioned by the embargo and of the net change in income brought about by sales of the probably lower-priced product or service to non-target countries. The cost to the target equals the increased cost of purchasing the commodity or obtaining the loan elsewhere. Which country suffers the greater economic loss is determined by the specific market structures each finds itself in for the goods or services involved.

The erection of any kind of barrier for sender products, such as time-consuming clearance procedures, licensing red tape, or even the threat of an embargo (which imposes a risk premium), represents a form of price increase to the target country. Each of these instances, just as in the case of an embargo, represents a form of price discrimination within the international market.

The effectiveness of the use of monopoly power by the sender depends upon the degree of competition in the markets in question and upon the ability of the sender to keep the markets in which different prices are charged separate. The greater the degree of competition in relevant markets, the more easily the target will find substitutes and the cheaper substitutes will be. Similarly, the more watertight the market in which higher prices are being charged, the more successful discrimination will be. A successful total embargo is merely a special case in which an infinite price makes the commodity in question unattainable to the target country.

The elimination of a preferred position, such as MFN status, has the effect of increasing the cost to the target of doing business with the sender. The cost imposed on either country depends upon the ease with which either may find alternative customers (suppliers). Economic and military aid represent instances in which goods or services are supplied at reduced, or zero, prices. Elimination of aid, then, represents an increase in price to the target country. In this instance, the cost to the sender is likely to be negative in economic terms. This may be why it is that the threat to withdraw aid has been one of the more effective sanctions historically.

The same analysis applies to the transfer of technology. Where technology is embodied in the goods that are traded, in the form, say, of machine tools, turnkey factories or advanced weapons systems, the price at which the transaction takes place should reflect the cost of the technology as well as the resources incorporated in the commodity, factory or system.

An example will clarify the point. Let us assume that country A has sole possession of the technology to produce commodity Y. It may sell the commodity to another country, or it may sell the technology, say in the form of a turnkey factory. To be profitable, the price set on the factory must equal at a minimum the discounted value of the stream of receipts that would otherwise have been received from sales of the final commodity Y over the period that the technology could have been monopolized (through patents, copyrights, or security classification) by country A.

Thus, the transfer of technology is not an issue separate from trade per se. The only issue in any case is one of price setting. A country that underprices its technology is obviously putting itself at a disadvantage in exchange with the rest of the world.

Publication of scientific findings and the open exchange of scientific methods and results pose an interesting dilemma. At present, the decision to patent or to copyright scientific findings or methods is a business decision in the West. The free exchange of scientific findings and methods is beneficial to all, apparently, up to a point. Otherwise, each researcher would have to develop all steps of any particular process, and science would break up into hundreds or thousands of tiny isolated operations. It is clear that there exists some optimum degree of openness with respect to the development of science.

The substitution of "national security" criteria for market criteria may yield a different rate of scientific progress. Those who argue for minimum government interference in the case of technology transfer do so, presumably, because they believe that the outcome is more likely to be non-optimal than where market considerations prevail.

Economic Sanctions

Economic sanctions and incentives may be applied to the demand or to the supply side of the economy, and the degree of market power that may be exercised ordinarily differs sharply for each side of the market. For example, the United States government has much greater control over access to the domestic market than it does over international markets. In principle, the government could exercise almost perfect monopsonistic power over the rest of the world's exports to U.S. domestic markets. As the U.S. market is very rich and large, the government has considerable bargaining power in dealing with countries or businesses that export or wish to export to the United States.

There are two serious general constraints, however, on the exercise of monopsonistic power. First, there is the possibility of retaliation by countries that import U.S. products and services, which would affect U.S. exports adversely. Second, this power is ordinarily used to protect U.S. producers or the health and safety of U.S. consumers. The effect is to raise the price of imports to the U.S. consumer. This side of the market is of minor current relevance, for U.S. imports from the USSR are negligible and likely to remain so for the indefinite future regardless of U.S. import policy.

For the Soviet Union, the issue is access to U.S. products, technology and/or credit. The U.S. government has very substantial power to restrict or deny exports of particular U.S. commodities or services and over access to credit institutions in, or controlled by, the United States, and it has made use of these powers more often than any other major power and with increasing frequency. According to Hufbauer and Schott, for example, the United States has exercised sanctions in 62 of the 99 cases they identified and documented for the period since WWI.[9]

Few of these applications of sanctions were successful because alternative suppliers normally provide sufficient competition both in price and quality in most international markets to prevent the exercise of decisive market power by the United States government or its agencies acting alone.

Control over trading in specific commodities is complicated by the existence of multinational firms and international licensing of technology. The attempt to prevent the sale of specific technology related to the Soviet gas pipeline project foundered on the refusal of West European governments to accept U.S. sanctions imposed upon foreign branches of U.S. firms or with respect to licenses previously granted by U.S. establishments. The principle of "extraterritoriality" and its retroactive application were firmly rejected by our European allies.

The gas pipeline case illustrates the fact that an effective policy of denial requires international cooperation. This normally means forming a cartel. A cartel offers a way to increase market power to the extent required to force and maintain a price rise (decrease) favorable to its members.

Cartels

Effective application of trade denial or other uses of market power for most U.S. commodities or services would require the formation of a cartel with a sufficient number of other countries to yield the degree of market power required for success. As is well known, however, cartels among nation states tend to be unstable. The incentive to cheat is very great, and enforcement can be both financially and politically costly.

A recent systematic evaluation of potential costs and benefits that might derive from a cartel led by the United States against CMEA countries taken as a whole illustrates the political problem.[10] The authors calculated the direct economic benefit-cost ratios derived from an assumed 10 percent export price increase to CMEA importers for thirteen SITC categories.[11]

All required a cartel among at least the four largest exporters to achieve a significant benefit-cost ratio (i.e., in excess of 4:1), where the benefit was the pecuniary damage imposed on the target countries, and the cost was the net economic cost to the members of the cartel. A cartel of the seven top exporters ensured a high ratio for all thirteen categories.

The list of countries required to form an effective cartel, however, is not the same for any two categories. Moreover, the list includes for the various commodities such diverse political systems as Yugoslavia, Finland, Argentina, Sweden, Brazil, New Zealand, Austria, Algeria, Greece, Turkey, and India, along with the major OECD countries. The political feasibility of forming cartels with such a heterogeneous variety of political and economic systems is nil.

In addition, economic costs were underestimated (admittedly) by the study, for the authors did not attempt to estimate costs of enforcement of cartel policy, and the commodities selected were selected on economic, not military-strategic, grounds. Moreover, the authors did not attempt to estimate the period over which the various cartels could be expected to endure. Here the problem is not enforcement among cartel members, but the development of domestic substitutes by its importers and the appearance of new suppliers outside the cartel. The study does argue persuasively that trade dependency of CMEA upon the noncommunist world is sufficient for certain commodities to offer a possible short-run economic payoff to cartelization. The study does not, however, suggest a basis for successfully embargoing strategic commodities, technology or materials.

Income, Employment, and Foreign Exchange

In the analysis of monopolistic/monopsonistic practices in the private sector, it is assumed that market power is exercised so as to maximize profits. The creation of cartels led by the United States, as conceived by Bayard, Pelzman, and Perez-Lopez, would also focus on profits. Apart from national security concerns, the federal government is ordinarily interested at the national level in maximizing or minimizing the impact of trade policy upon national income, employment, and/or the foreign exchange balance, not profits.

According to recent calculations using the Data Resources model, the export multiplier for Gross National Product over the ten-year period 1976–85 is approximately 3.9.[12] That is, a $1 billion permanent increase (decrease) in exports will cause increases (decreases) in GNP over the ten-year period that rise from $1.8 billion to $3.9 billion. The net favorable (unfavorable) effect upon the current-account foreign balance would range from $0.9 billion in the initial year to $0.4 billion in the tenth.

According to Lester A. Davis, of the Commerce Department's Trade Research Division, each $1 billion in U.S. exports generated an average of 25,200 jobs in 1982.[13] The employment effect of changes in exports differs by industry. In 1982, for example, the employment displacement of $1 billion in exports of products of agriculture, forestry, and fisheries was 27,200 (in full-time equivalents), of which somewhat more than 64.7 percent impacted directly upon this sector. That is, other sectors that either provide inputs or add value by transporting and marketing these products would absorb 35.3 percent of the impact of any unit reduction in exports.

For manufactures, the displacement would have been 25,000 jobs, of which only 47.1 percent impacted directly upon the sector.[14] Thus, the domestic economic and political impact of any given embargo is unique. Some are more highly focussed than others. It is obvious that the impact of the grain embargo was highly focussed and thus more noticeable than would have been the case with manufactures.

U.S. exports to the USSR averaged $2.5 billion in the late 1970s. Using the GNP and employment multipliers given above as approximate constants, we can estimate what the impact of a total trade embargo would have been beginning in 1980. If permanent, the $2.5 billion decrease in exports would have generated a $9.6 billion decrease in GNP by 1990. The unfavorable effect upon the U.S. current-account balance would have ranged from a −$3.6 billion in 1980 to a −$0.9 billion in 1990. And approximately 60,000 jobs would have been displaced from 1980 onward.

Trade with the USSR during the 1970s was "favorable" to the United States in at least two senses. First, exports increased from an annual average of less than $100 million in the late 1960s to $2.5 billion in the late 1970s (see figs. 1 and 2), with attendant favorable effects upon both GNP and employment. Second, the balance of trade with the USSR was highly favorable to the United States, increasing from an annual average of $32 million in the late 1960s to $2.1 billion in the late 1970s, which obviously helped to offset trade deficits elsewhere, and especially with Japan.

Reservations Concerning Trade Denial or Interruptions as Policies

Most Western economists are skeptical about the utility of trade interruption or denial as a policy instrument because they generally

Table 1

Exports to the U.S.S.R.: 3–Year Moving Average
($ Millions)

Country Year	CANADA	U.S.A.	JAPAN	FRANCE	FRG
1969	64	94	263	264	367
1970	78	129	271	265	430
1971	170	274	408	288	532
1972	234	632	455	387	785
1973	203	781	697	520	1,250
1974	242	1,211	1,070	790	1,954
1975	325	1,503	1,660	973	2,455
1976	428	1,921	1,937	1,254	2,766
1977	459	2,060	2,229	1,357	2,871
1978	496	2,492	2,299	1,653	3,183
1979	822	2,454	2,581	1,976	3,711
1980	1,175	2,490	2,833	2,108	3,795
1981	1,515	2,152	3,312	1,957	3,879

SOURCE: OECD Trade Series C from Data Resources Inc.

Table 2

Imports from the U.S.S.R.: 3–Year Moving Average
($ Millions)

Country Year	U.S.A.	JAPAN	FRANCE	FRG	ITALY
1969	61	469	197	323	272
1970	60	480	223	348	275
1971	75	524	252	377	301
1972	124	730	327	501	355
1973	222	1,028	437	785	524
1974	275	1,219	597	1,077	708
1975	275	1,251	758	1,406	1,013
1976	237	1,250	947	1,616	1,227
1977	243	1,330	1,098	2,014	1,446
1978	286	1,565	1,390	2,742	1,628
1979	347	1,697	2,194	3,469	2,142
1980	374	1,722	2,919	3,953	2,659
1981	338	1,537	3,272	4,149	N.A.

SOURCE: OECD Trade Series C from Data Resources Inc.

share Adam Smith's conception of the favorable effect of trade upon international specialization and the division of labor. The wider the market, the greater the opportunities for specialization and the division of labor and thus for productivity increases. Trade freely entered into under competitive conditions is viewed as mutually beneficial. In the absence of monopolistic or monopsonistic market conditions, no one can gain differentially. The market integrates the interests of all trading partners.

Apart from agricultural exports, the comparative advantage of U.S. exports is in high technology. High technology, of course, almost always has some military application, and much new high technology flows from prior research on problems set by the defense community. Both the current military and the long-run strategic economic strength of the economy depend, therefore, upon continued development of high technology. Unfortunately, there is a built-in conflict with respect to trade.

The United States economy holds an enormous comparative advantage in the production of a wide range of military technologies. It cannot exploit this advantage fully for purposes of international trade for obvious reasons. The best that can be done is to dominate the market for obsolescent military equipment. Similarly, and probably more significant in the long run, exports of the most advanced technologies that have actual or potential military applications are subject to control under the 1979 Export Administration Act. The act mandates maintenance of a Militarily Critical Technologies List (MCTL).

The current list is classified (except for the table of contents) and has been described as a "Modern Technologies List" by critics because of its inclusiveness.[15] Lionel Olmer of the Commerce Department argues that the MTCL could have been useful had it been restricted to well-defined military technologies and keystone equipment. Instead, "controls continue on *all* exports of technical data to proscribed countries, whether it be technical data to manufacture baby formula, Pampers, antibiotics, farm combines, or any other item."[16]

To a very significant extent, therefore, the United States cannot export what it produces uniquely and/or most efficiently. Strategic concerns have tended to constrict exploitation of our comparative advantages. Concern about Soviet access to new scientific developments and new technology with possible military applications has led to attempts to restrict or control even "exports" of such things as scientific publications, scholarly seminars, and scientific exchanges.[17]

U.S. trade policy faces a real dilemma because there are real economic costs associated with "holding back" the latest scientific and technological advances for reasons of national security. As was pointed out above, holding back developments tends to reduce the competitiveness of U.S. producers in foreign markets. Controls tend to reduce profits of

U.S. producers because they either raise costs of production or reduce the extent of the market.

Licensing procedures for all exporters, for example, cause delays. The Department of Commerce required an average of 32 days to clear a license to *non-communist* destinations in 1983, according to William Archey, Acting Assistant Secretary of Commerce for Export Administration.[18] The effect is equivalent to an increase in the price of the commodities being offered for export. Predictably, a 1980 study found that "queuing time" was a significant (and negative) determinant of world demand for U.S. exports.[19]

This is only one of the ways that restrictions imposed with an eye to U.S. participation in East-West trade impinge upon West-West trade. It is easy to show that multilateral trade yields better benefits for a community of trading nations than bilateral trade could produce. Under multilateral trade, any pair of trading partners may sustain unbalanced trade, that is, a trade deficit for either party, indefinitely if the deficit partner is able to generate a trade surplus with third parties.

The fact that the USSR covers only a tiny fraction of its imports from the United States by a counterflow of exports does not mean that the USSR is benefiting unilaterally or disproportionately from Soviet-U.S. trade. The benefits to the United States are being recovered in trade with other countries, which, in this instance, means in West-West trade. Interruption of trade with the USSR must, therefore, also interrupt West-West trade to the same degree. This is the essence of multilateralism.

The long-run comparative advantage of U.S. products is also affected by another cost that is even more difficult to measure. There seems to be a consensus among scientists that open and free exchange of research and findings is crucial to the advancement of science. There appears, in fact, to be wider agreement among scientists on this proposition than there is among economists on the benefits of unfettered free trade. If it is true that isolation tends to inhibit scientific development, then it follows that "holding back" research findings and new developments will ultimately have an adverse effect on the development of science in this country. This is another reason why lists of proscribed scientific findings, technologies, and the like ought to be kept as short as possible. A slow erosion of our edge in science and technology would have strategic as well as economic costs.

To Adam Smith's conception of the benefits of comparative advantage, modern economics adds the income and employment impacts of increases and decreases in exports. Growth of one country's economy in an open system induces growth in all systems, because exports generate income, which in turn generates domestic demand for imports from other countries.

Economists are wary of trade interruptions and trade denial on macroeconomic grounds because measures designed to disadvantage the rest of the world tend to generate retaliation, and the employment and GNP foreign trade multipliers work in reverse. In international trade, a "beggar thy neighbor" policy is likely to make everyone worse off. For many years U.S. economists tended to play down the importance of international trade for the domestic economy because it represented so small a fraction of total GNP. The growth of U.S. participation in trade and, in particular, the growth in the deficit on merchandise account in recent years have changed attitudes. The large trade deficits that have been incurred recently compete for savings and thus aggravate the problems caused by the large federal budget deficits of the last several years.

Many have pointed to the historical fact that technologically backward countries tend to gain relative to the advanced through technology transfer that occurs as a result of trade. Thorstein Veblen pointed out the "penalty of taking the lead" and the "advantages of borrowing" in his 1915 comparison of Imperial Germany and Great Britain, which allowed him to predict accurately the superiority of German technology in the war.[20] The relative "backwardness" of the Soviet economy with respect to the United States economy affords it potential gains from such borrowing.

As Thomas Wolf has noted, however, if gains and benefits are measured in economic terms, setting aside clear military applications of technology, the "advantage" the Soviet Union receives is available to all countries that are relatively backward, and "it should not be evaluated as a kind of 'loss' to the Western side in East-West trade."[21] The "advantage of backwardness" is more ironic metaphor than economic description because the greater the degree of backwardness, the greater the potential advantage to be reaped by borrowing technology. Also, the more rapidly the more advanced system develops technology, the "greater" is this potential advantage to backwardness. The less developed country avoids the cost of research and development. But the largest advantage of backwardness is not in borrowing per se but in not being encumbered by in-place obsolete technology. The real disadvantage of being backward, however, is the difficulty posed by the transfer of technology from an advanced to a more backward economic system.

Historically, no relatively advanced country has succeeded in preventing the transfer of its advanced technology to less advanced countries. History is replete with examples of import substitution based upon acquired technology. The United States is itself a stellar historical example. When it comes to technology transfer by a country as highly developed in science and technology as the USSR, even the knowledge that a particular product or process has been successfully attempted may be sufficient to induce success in the "lagging" system. This suggests that fostering the development of science and of critical technologies by the U.S. science and technology community may be a more promising policy than seeking to curtail the transfer of existing technology abroad on other than highly selective grounds.

A fair assessment of the position of most Western economists, to quote again from Wolf, is that "the overwhelming majority of economists concerned directly or indirectly with East-West trade issues seem to be very skeptical that manipulation of trade policies can achieve predictable economic impacts or that such impacts, whether they are policy-induced or not, will have predictable long-run systemic or political implications."[22]

Herbert Stein, whom I quoted above, is clearly an exception to this assessment. He is, of course, correct in pointing out that the direct economic cost of reducing U.S.-Soviet trade to zero would not be large. A total of 60,000 jobs is insignificant in an economy that employs over 100 million people. Nonetheless, the job loss would be concentrated on a small number of sectors, which means that it would still cause a noticeable impact and possible unpalatable political repercussions.

Given that, proportionally speaking, Japan, West Germany, Italy, and France have benefited economically from expansion of trade with the USSR since 1953 even more than has the United States, and that trade with Eastern Europe is greater for all of them even in absolute terms, it is unlikely that any U.S. administration will be able to muster the cooperation required to do much more than embargo a list of specific strategic commodities and technologies. The economic cost to Western Europe and Japan of re-creation of the parallel international orders of the Cold War era is much greater today than it was then, and Europe's dependency upon the United States is less than it was in the days of the Marshall Plan. The prospects for a successful cartel movement led by the United States against the Soviet Union are not good, nor, as the foregoing suggests, would it necessarily be in the long-run interests of the United States.

Case Studies

I would like to consider very briefly three cases in which a U.S. administration has sought to use sanctions, controls, or "leverage." As two of these cases are discussed elsewhere by other participants in this symposium, I can be very brief and focus upon a few key aspects that highlight the economic impact on the United States.

A Case of Leverage Lost

The first case is the use of "leverage" to encourage the Soviet Union to permit a substantial increase in the legal out-migration of Soviet Jews. As of mid-1984 more than 250,000 Jews have been permitted to emigrate to Israel and the United States. The out-migration began in the late 1960s and averaged initially about 1500 per year. The outflow reached approximately 30,000 during 1972–73, as the Trade Reform Act was negotiated by the Nixon Administration and then debated in the Congress. Passage of the Jackson-Vanik and Stevenson Amendments in October 1974 was followed by Soviet nullification of the trade agreement and a reduction in the out-migration by one-half. The emigration increased again in 1978–79 in anticipation of the conclusion of SALT II. The peak occurred in 1979, when over 50,000 people left the Soviet Union. Since 1979, the outflow has dwindled to little more than 1000 per year.[23]

There can be no question that the Soviet Union was influenced in its policy on out-migration of Jews by the prospect of increased and more favorable conditions for trade with the United States. MFN status and access to U.S. Export-Import Bank credit were deliberately used as "incentives" to encourage the Soviet Union to adopt and maintain a liberal policy toward Jewish out-migration. This included revocation of an "education tax" ranging from $5,000 to $25,000 per person that was designed to compensate the Soviet state for its investment in the educations of those who wished to emigrate.[24]

Other factors than trade were involved, of course, as incentives. Detente was a general background condition, and the large increase in out-migration in 1979 clearly had much to do with Soviet hopes for successful ratification of SALT II. Nonetheless, economic incentives were significant in influencing Soviet domestic policy for a period of time. It was a classic case of the use of "leverage" to influence Soviet behavior.

In the end, U.S. leverage broke down. The failure of SALT II and the subsequent embargoes on grain and the Olympics completed the dissipation of leverage, but it is instructive to examine why it failed initially.

The October 1972 trade agreement anticipated an expansion of trade between the United States and the Soviet Union. It also offered a settlement of the Soviet Lend-Lease debt in exchange for MFN status. The Jackson and Vanik amendments were introduced early in 1973, and debate over them continued for more than two years. Kissinger and Gromyko apparently reached accord regarding the Jewish emigration in meetings in the spring and summer of 1974.[25]

> Kissinger wrote a letter to Senator Jackson describing Soviet emigration policies as conveyed by Soviet leaders to the U.S. government. . . . The understanding stipulated that there would be no interference with applications for emigration, harassment of applicants, nor obstacles to emigra-

tion except for reasons of national security; and that the emigration tax which the Soviet Union suspended in 1973 would remain suspended. Kissinger noted that the Soviet leaders had made assurances, and not commitments, to the U.S. government and that these guidelines would be followed in the future.

The Trade Reform Act, as amended by Jackson-Vanik, passed 20 December 1974. Concurrently, the Congress also passed an amendment submitted by Senator Adlai Stevenson. William Korey has argued recently that it was not the Jackson-Vanik Amendment that caused the Soviet leadership to nullify the trade agreement.[26] That amendment had been negotiated so as to reinforce U.S. leverage. The Stevenson Amendment, however, severely restricted maximum borrowing by the USSR through the Export-Import Bank—to a maximum of only $300 million for a four-year period, and it restricted even more severely the total that could be used for energy exploration. The ceiling on loans was made subject to Congressional approval, taking it out of the hands of the President. The aim of the amendment seems to have been to constrain the Presidency, not U.S.-Soviet trade, but it nonetheless had the latter effect.

U.S. leverage appears to have broken down, therefore, because the economic advantages became too small and too uncertain to warrant continuation of concessions by the USSR on the Jewish out-migration. The Soviet Union was, of course, using exit visas to obtain "leverage" over U.S. policy makers.

It is worth noting that, while it lasted, "leverage" worked for two reasons. There was a clear quid pro quo, and the "deal" was treated with great public discretion. For a period of years, in fact, research among Soviet émigrés was discouraged by the U.S. State Department, and little was reported in the press about the magnitude of the outflow from the USSR or the size of the inflow into the United States.

That the out-migration has continued, albeit at a very low rate, makes it clear that the USSR does not oppose it *in principle*. Thus, it remains a possible bargaining chip for Soviet negotiators.

The economic impact of the out-migration on both the United States and the Soviet Union has been, and will continue to be, large. More than 125,000 individuals have emigrated to the United States from the Soviet Union since 1970. Most of these individuals are relatively well-educated and experienced workers, scientists, doctors, and the like. The capitalized value of their educations and work experience could be estimated and is bound to be substantial. It represents a substantial economic loss to the Soviet economy and a comparable gain to the United States economy. Hence the abortive Soviet attempt to collect an exit tax.

In the implicit deal with the United States government, the Soviet

Union agreed to surrender a capital asset of considerable magnitude in the expectation of a flow of benefits from MFN and Exim Bank credits. The interesting fact is that the USSR cannot recover the lost assets now that the counterflow of benefits did not materialize. Moreover, the "good will" the USSR expected was lost once emigration was again constrained.

This case illustrates the hazards that confront any attempt to predict the consequences of trade strategy or to calculate costs and benefits in advance. It also illustrates the fragility of "leverage" as a policy instrument.

The Grain Embargo

Controversy continues about the efficacy of the grain embargo. As a symbolic act, it certainly gained headlines. As an attempt to change Soviet behavior in Afghanistan, it clearly had no effect. Disagreement over its results stems primarily, as was indicated earlier, from a failure to specify how success should be measured.

It has been shown that the embargo did have a measurable impact upon Soviet livestock herds. Thus, if the purpose was to impose a non-negligible economic cost on the Soviet economy, that goal was accomplished. The direct economic impact per capita was not, however, very large. The privileged members of Soviet society were, of course, not affected at all, as they receive "special distributions" of meat and other luxury goods that are in short supply. The populace at large was affected only marginally, for the impact was shared by all except the privileged.

Thus, if the purpose of the grain embargo was to cause the Soviet population at large to become discontented, it certainly failed. In fact, by providing the leadership with an "excuse" for shortages, one that blamed the United States, the embargo may have offset to some degree discontentment over poor harvests in 1979 and the early 1980s.

The economic and political impact of the embargo in the United States was more clear-cut. The initial burden of the embargo fell upon a readily identifiable group: grain farmers. And it fell with particular severity upon an even smaller group of farmers who dominate foreign grain sales. A 1982 study assembled for the National Corn Growers Association concluded that the effects of the 1980 grain embargo were quite large. Approximately 17 million metric tons were lost in U.S. grain exports over the two years following the 4 January 1980 embargo.[27] This had significant indirect as well as direct effects, diminishing activity in grain transport and farm input industries. Based on the Commerce Department's input-output model of the U.S. economy, the study concludes that the reduction in grain exports caused a loss of $11.4 billion in output of goods and services, reduced employment equivalent to 310,000 jobs, and reduced personal income by $3.1 billion.[28]

The study concludes by noting that the embargo probably damaged long-run U.S. competitiveness in the East bloc market for agricultural goods, as potential importers will be less willing to trust the United States, and because other grain exporters, notably Argentina, Australia, and Canada, have expanded output and seek to replace U.S. farm exports to the Soviet Union.

The National Corn Growers Association's estimate of the loss from the grain embargo is the highest of many, and it is probably based on a worst-case scenario. A more modest estimate puts the loss of farm income between 2 and 2.25 billion dollars, the increase in the U.S. government deficit between 2 and 3 billion dollars and the increased cost of grain purchased and stored by the government at $0.6 billion, for a grand total and minimum estimate of 4.6 to 5.85 billion dollars. This lower number is still a significant cost, and especially because it was so highly focussed.

The economic impact was much more highly focussed in the United States than in the USSR. It also took place in what turned out to be a boom year for grain production, a boom that had been generated in large part by the prior growth of international grain sales stimulated by increasing Soviet purchases. Grain prices would have been depressed in any case by the record harvest, for Soviet purchases in 1980 could not under any circumstances have increased sufficiently to compensate. The domestic economic impact of the embargo was small by comparison with the impact of the record harvest.

Politically, that made little difference. The embargo was an act of man, and it was seen as an aggravating cause of the farmers' income decline. It was also seen as inequitable, for the farmer paid a disproportionate share of the cost of this particular foreign policy, despite attempts by the Carter Administration to cushion the blow. The Reagan campaign made good use of the farmers' discontent in the 1980 election, but it subsequently paid a price. The Reagan Administration, reinforced by Congressional action, has renounced the use of selective embargoes on farm commodities in the future. It voluntarily pledged not to use leverage in the future, and this is embodied explicitly in the language of the new grain agreement between the two countries.[29]

The cost of income maintenance for U.S. grain farmers has increased astronomically since 1980 for reasons that are partly a consequence of the grain embargo of that year. Whenever the government supports prices, there is always great pressure upon it from producers to set "favorable" prices. Normally this means that price supports are set too high, given market demand. The result is, in more years than not, unsold surpluses. These surpluses cannot be put on the market, domestic or international, without bringing prices down below the support level or generating protests of dumping in foreign markets. Getting rid of surpluses becomes a chronic problem.

When the Soviet Union entered world grain markets in the late 1960s it helped to solve the problem of grain surpluses. It was an unexpected bonanza for the farmer and the U.S. government. Grain farmers' incomes rose, and they increased acreage in response. With a good growing year, U.S. grain farmers swamped the market. The grain embargo put the problem of a surplus back on the political agenda. The result was the Payment in Kind (PIK) program, which contributed to an estimated record $18.9 billion in U.S. government farm income support.[30]

There are several lessons to be learned from the grain embargo. One is that even in a market dominated by U.S. production, assurance of a significant economic impact requires formation of a cartel. The Soviet Union found alternative grain suppliers without much difficulty. Now that the embargo has been ended, the USSR has followed a much more conservative policy in importing grain than it did before the embargo. Its policy today is to diversify its suppliers as broadly as possible, thereby avoiding heavy dependence upon a single supplier. Second, the domestic political impact of an embargo is likely to be substantial where it falls on a readily identifiable interest group—especially a vocal group like farmers. Third, it is difficult to compensate "innocent" parties appropriately for losses attributable to an embargo, in this case the farmers. The expensive PIK program of 1983 represented, in substantial part, overcompensation.

The Soviet-West European Gas Pipeline

The attempt by the Reagan administration to prevent completion of the Soviet gas pipeline, or to slow its construction, failed, and it is instructive to examine what went wrong. In many ways, it appears as a classic lesson in how not to conduct an embargo.

At issue was a U.S. license, under which a West European subsidiary was to supply a crucial component of the pumping stations being built in the USSR. When the Reagan Administration sought to suspend the licensing agreement retroactively, the governments of England and France took action to ensure that the suspension would not take effect. As a result, the pipeline continued to be built using U.S. know-how. The United States was publicly rebuffed by its allies. The one clear domestic economic impact resulted from a prohibition on sales by Caterpillar Tractor of gas pipelaying machinery.

The direct economic consequences were as follows. Caterpillar lost sales to a Japanese firm. The total dollar loss, measured as a percentage of total U.S. trade turnover, was not large. It was on the order of $300 to $600 million (in total lost sales, including spare parts, etc.),[31] but it was a direct effect of government action and it came at a time of general unemployment of Caterpillar workers resulting from the 1981–83 recession and the secondary impact of the PIK program. That is, reduced planting and tillage brought about by the PIK program lowered induced demand for farm equipment. The impact fell heavily upon a single community: Peoria, Illinois.

More significant perhaps than the immediate cost of lost sales was the deterioration of Caterpillar's market share. In 1978, before any controls had been imposed on oil and gas equipment, Caterpillar had 85 percent of the Soviet market for heavy pipelaying equipment. Caterpillar's lone international competitor, Komatsu of Japan, had the remaining 15 percent. Currently, Caterpillar has only 15 percent, and Komatsu now has 85 percent and may end up with the entire market according to some assessments.[32]

In subsequent bidding for a construction contract let by the USSR, bidders were requested not to include U.S. equipment or licenses that might be embargoed. It has been argued, therefore, that the attempt to embargo U.S. technology has created a "less reliable" image, and, taken together with other U.S. embargoes, has undermined the competitiveness of U.S. technology exports in general.

This particular incident illustrates the limits and potential costs of applying embargoes that involve other countries as third parties. U.S. technology was in this instance quite unique, and it would have been possible to slow construction of the pipeline substantially with an effective embargo. The aim of the embargo was twofold. The Reagan administration did not want Western Europe to increase its dependency upon Soviet energy exports, and it wanted to limit future Soviet foreign exchange earnings from sales of gas to Europe.

The Europeans evidently viewed the pipeline, however, as a way to diversify their risks, particularly their dependence upon Middle Eastern energy sources. The first aim of the Reagan policy ran, therefore, counter to the self-defined interests of the Europeans. Formation of a cartel is out of the question when the interests of the necessary parties diverge 180 degrees. Thus Reagan's policy was doomed to failure from the outset.

The direct economic cost to the United States was small, and the long-run costs will also probably be small. The long-run costs depend, however, upon the importance of "reliability" as a factor in demand for U.S. technology. This is obviously difficult to measure, but as the United States has initiated almost two-thirds of all economic sanctions identified and investigated for the period since World War II (62 of 99), some sort of risk premium would appear to be appropriate for United States exporters.[33] In any event, the most significant immediate costs were political, and relations between the United States and the European allies were strained badly by the policy.

It is clear that the gas pipeline sanctions were not considered carefully in advance by the Reagan administration. Had they been, it would have been obvious that the U.S. could not stop, or significantly slow, the Soviet gas pipeline unilaterally and that the conflicting interests of the United States and Western Europe precluded successful joint action as a cartel.

Conclusions

There are several lessons to be learned from examination of these three case studies and the preceding analysis of economic sanctions. First, because trade is always two-sided, "leverage" is also always two-sided. Trade denial or interruption always involves costs on both sides. As in the case of the Jewish emigration from the Soviet Union, it is not obvious who was using leverage on whom. Through the 1970s the United States seems to have utilized its leverage successfully to facilitate out-migration. The combination of the Jackson-Vanik and the Stevenson amendments reduced Soviet economic benefits from a more liberal policy toward Soviet Jewish emigration. When SALT II fell through also, emigration returned to the status quo ante. Without a quid pro quo, the Soviet Union backed out.

Second, evaluation of the "success" or "failure" of any given sanction or incentive cannot escape ambiguity because goals differ, or change, and because impacts occur in what Ed Hewett has described as "different currencies."[34] Costs and benefits are "subjective" as well as objective, and even the objective costs and benefits are difficult at times to measure.

Third, trade sanctions have specific impacts upon domestic interest groups and upon other countries and their citizens. The total cost of any given sanction may be insignificant when compared to total employment or to GNP, but it may not be politically sustainable because of the specific interests that are contravened. Advance agreement and/or compensation is required in these cases. The higher the cost to the sender nation, the greater the chance of failure.

Fourth, the interdependency of the world's economies, the transitory nature of comparative advantage, and the availability of near substitutes for most commodities and technologies make the formation of a cartel essential to any economically successful application of trade denial or interruption. This makes the problem political rather than economic. Cartels are difficult to form because of divergent interests even of one's own allies. Cartels are also difficult to maintain because they depend upon the willingness of members of the coalition to pass up economic benefits that they might otherwise exploit. Cost of production differences offer temptations to cheat, and cheating will ultimately lead to a complete breakdown of the cartel. Hufbauer and Schott's historical survey reveals, in corroboration, that the greater the need for cooperation in imposing a sanction, the smaller the outlook for success.[35]

Fifth, it is widely believed by members of the U.S. exporting community that there are certain intangible costs associated with the use of trade sanctions. These include the "image of reliability" as a supplier, the notion of predictability with respect to agreements that run into the future, and good will generally. The absence of these qualities causes customers to apply a risk premium to the quoted price of the exports of countries that are prone to use economic sanctions for non-economic purposes. Moreover, there are set-up costs for businesses that conduct foreign trade. George Shultz was quoted during his tenure at Bechtel as saying:[36]

> It takes a long time to go abroad, get positioned. . . . In the process the company develops what the government may regard as a bargaining chip. But if the government takes that bargaining chip and spends it, where does that leave the company?

There are, then, many costs, tangible as well as intangible, that tend to be underestimated when trade sanctions are contemplated.

Sixth, from a strictly economic standpoint Herbert Stein is quite correct in claiming that the aggregate economic cost to the United States of total avoidance of trade with the Soviet Union would be small. Foreign trade is not a very large share of total U.S. GNP, and trade with the USSR is a very small fraction of total U.S. trade turnover. A corollary is, however, that the damage the U.S. can cause the Soviet economy is correspondingly small.

As Hufbauer and Schott underline in their comprehensive evaluation of embargoes and sanctions since World War I, countries as large and wealthy as the United States and the Soviet Union, which also have global political and security responsibilities, do not alter decisions for such paltry sums.[37] Trade sanctions and incentives figure at the margin only, if they figure at all. It is unrealistic, and dangerous, to think one can train a bear with a carrot and a switch. Successful "bargaining" with the Soviet Union has ordinarily been "silent trading," where face and prestige do not enter.

Seventh, the use of economic sanctions always entails an economic cost of some magnitude upon the sender's economy. The only credible exception is in the curtailment of economic aid, and even that is not unambiguously cost-free. Where economic sanctions are imposed for non-economic purposes, as responses to international aggression such as Afghanistan or to internal Soviet political repression such as that of the physicist Sakharov, the payoff, if there is one, is also non-economic. There is still the economic cost to be paid. Insofar as it places U.S. producers in a disadvantageous position in international trade, it produces a "drag" on the U.S. economy and makes it less competitive in the long run.

Thomas Wolf characterized trade policy under the Carter Administration as one of "excess demand for leverage." Converting this terminology back into the language of mechanics, excess demand for leverage causes the lever to break over the fulcrum, which means no work gets done because the strength of the lever was overestimated. An historical review of U.S. policy with respect to sanctions and trade denial suggests that U.S. administrations in general have exhibited excess demand for leverage. U.S. policy makers have either overestimated the power and effectiveness of economic sanctions, or they have treated U.S. international economic interests cavalierly, as though an accumulation of small insults to the U.S. domestic economy could do no permanent harm.

The analysis provided in this essay and the results of the Hufbauer and Schott study of ninety-nine trade sanctions in the years since World War I suggest that costs may be more significant over time than has been supposed and that the effective use of economic sanctions for non-economic purposes needs to be better thought out and confined to instances where success is probable. Sanctions seem to be attractive to U.S. administrations not so much because they promise success as because they offer ready dramatic means for appearing to do something about pressing but intractable problems.

NOTES

1. "Statement of Herbert Stein, Senior Fellow, American Enterprise Institute, Washington, D.C." in U.S. Congress, Senate Committee on Foreign Relations, Subcommittee on International Economic Policy, *Economic Relations With the Soviet Union*, hearings, 97th Cong., 2d sess., 30 July, 12 and 13 August 1982 (Washington: USGPO, 1982), pp. 199–201.

2. Ibid., p. 211. "We need to find a way, or at least to explore very seriously the possibility of mobilizing the combined economic resources of the West for dealing with the Soviet bloc. . . . And really, I think that our European friends enormously exaggerate the significance to them economically of this kind of dealing."

3. "Statement of Rudy Boschwitz, U.S. Senator from Minnesota," in U.S. Congress, Senate Committee on Banking, Housing, and Urban Affairs, Subcommittee on International Finance and Monetary Policy, *Agricultural Embargoes and the Sanctity of Contracts*, hearing, 97th Cong., 2d sess., 29 July 1982 (Washington: USGPO, 1982), p. 14.

4. "Statement of Paul E. Tsongas, U.S. Senator from Massachusetts," in U.S. Congress, Senate Committee on Banking, Housing, and Urban Affairs, Subcommittee on International Finance and Monetary Policy, *Reauthorization of the Export Administration Act*, hearings, 98th Cong., 1st sess., 2 and 16 March, 14

April 1983 (Washington: USGPO, 1983), p. 207. ". . . a lot of things in this country are stamped 'Made in Japan.' So is our policy on export controls. The Japanese must be delighted by all of this."

5. Gary Clyde Hufbauer and Jeffrey J. Schott, *Economic Sanctions in Support of Foreign Policy Goals*, Institute for International Economics, Policy Analyses in International Economics 6, October 1983 (Washington, D.C.: Institute for International Economics, 1983), p. 10.

6. Abraham S. Becker, *East-West Economic Relations: Conflict and Concord in Western Policy Choices*, Rand Corp. Paper P-6936, December 1983, p. 16.

7. "Statement of Ed. A. Hewett, Senior Staff, The Brookings Institution, Washington, D.C." in U.S. Congress, Senate Committee on Foreign Relations and Congressional Research Service, Library of Congress, *The Premises of East-West Commercial Relations, A Workshop, December 1982* (Washington: USGPO, 1983), p. 77.

8. Hufbauer and Schott, *Economic Sanctions*, p. 1. The terms "target" and "sender" are borrowed from Hufbauer and Schott.

9. Ibid., p. 8.

10. Thomas O. Bayard, Joseph Pelzman, and Jorge F. Perez-Lopez, "An Economic Model of United States and Western Controls on Exports to the Soviet Union and Eastern Europe," in U.S. Congress, Joint Economic Committee, *The Soviet Economy in the 1980s: Problems and Prospects, Part 2*, Selected Papers, Dec. 31, 1982 (Washington: USGPO, 1983), p. 539.

11. Ibid., p. 539. The 13 SITC categories are: 0–Food and live animals; 1–Beverages and tobacco; 5–Chemicals; 6–Basic manufactures; 7–Machines, transport equipment; 01–Meat and preparations; 04–Cereals and preparations; 041–Wheat, etc., unmilled; 044–Maize, unmilled; 71–Machinery, nonelectric; 72–Electric machinery; 73–Transport equipment; 861–Instruments, apparatus.

12. Richard E. Caves and Ronald W. Jones, *World Trade and Payments: An Introduction* (Boston: Little, Brown and Co., 1977), p. 266.

13. Lester A. Davis, *Domestic Employment Generated by U.S. Exports*, U.S. Department of Commerce, International Trade Administration, Office of Trade and Investment Analysis, Staff Report, April 1983, p. 12.

14. Ibid., p. 6. Davis distinguishes between direct employment, generated by the exporting industry itself, and indirect employment, generated by industries that supply goods and services, including transport of finished product, to the exporting industry.

15. Office of Technology Assessment, *Technology and East-West Trade: An Update* (Washington: USGPO, May 1983), p. 82.

16. "Statement of Lionel Olmer, Department of Commerce," *Reauthorization of the Export Administration Act*, p. 159.

17. David Burnham, "New Lid on Technology Flow Called Restrictive," *New York Times*, 27 February 1984, p. 8, and Phillip Boffey, "Curbing Flow of Technology," *New York Times*, 28 February 1984, p. 44.

18. Eduardo Lachica, "U.S. Effort to Stiffen Export Licensing Is Costly and Confusing, Industry Says," *Wall Street Journal*, 20 March 1984, p. 10.

19. Roger J. Robinson, "An Analysis of the Export Licensing Mechanism and Its Effect Upon the Competitiveness of U.S. High Technology Exports," Unpublished Ph.D. Thesis, University of Georgia: Athens, Georgia, 1980, p. 96.

20. Thorstein Veblen, *Imperial Germany and the Industrial Revolution* (New York: Macmillan, 1915).

21. Thomas A. Wolf, "East-West Trade: Economic Interests, Systemic Interaction and Political Rivalry," *ACES Bulletin* 25, no. 2, Summer 1983, p. 45.

22. Ibid., p. 48.

23. Dan Caldwell, "The Jackson-Vanik Amendment," in John Spanier and Joseph Nogee (eds.), *Congress, the Presidency and American Foreign Policy* (New York: Pergamon Press, 1981), p. 17, and records for the Soviet Interview Project.

24. Dan Caldwell, "The Jackson-Vanik Amendment," p. 13.

25. Ibid., pp. 14–15.

26. William Korey, "Jackson-Vanik and Soviet Jewry," *The Washington Quarterly*, Winter 1984, pp. 116–28.

27. "Effects of the 1980 and 1981 Limitations of Grain Exports to the USSR on Business Activity, Jobs, Government Costs, and Farmers." Prepared by Schnittker Associates for the National Corn Growers Association, in U.S. Congress, Senate Committee on Agriculture, Nutrition, and Forestry, Subcommittee on Foreign Agricultural Policy, *Economic Impact of Agricultural Embargoes*, hearings, 97th Cong., 2d sess., 3 and 5 February 1982 (Washington: USGPO, 1982), p. 114.

28. "Effects of the 1980 and 1981 Limitations of Grain Exports to the USSR on Business Activity, Jobs, Government Costs, and Farmers," *Economic Impact of Agricultural Embargoes*, p. 118.

29. "U.S. to Sell Soviets Grain Even in Times of Shortage," *Wall Street Journal*, 2 August 1983, p. 45.

30. Thomas J. Knudson, "In the Nation's Farm Belt, It's a Case of Use It or Lose It," *New York Times*, 4 March 1984, p. E3.

31. U.S. Congress, Office of Technology Assessment, *Technology and East-West Trade: An Update*, p. 57.

32. Ibid., p. 58.

33. Hufbauer and Schott, *Economic Sanctions*, p. 8.

34. "Statement of Ed. A. Hewett," in *The Premises of East-West Commercial Relations*, p. 78.

35. Hufbauer and Schott, *Economic Sanctions*, p. 83.

36. "Prepared Statement of Howard Lewis III, Assistant Vice President, National Association of Manufacturers, Washington, D.C.," in *The Premises of East-West Commercial Relations*, p. 32.

37. Hufbauer and Schott, *Economic Sanctions*, p. 76.

Conclusion

Bruce Parrott

IN A period of heightened tensions between the superpowers, Western economic and technological relations with the USSR pose troubling issues for American policymakers. History shows that the flow of trade and technology, although it may sometimes mitigate international tensions, can also alter the comparative economic and military capabilities of rival states. Viewed in this light, the implications of the widening movement of Western goods and know-how to the USSR are, potentially, extremely important. How large a contribution are Western inputs making to the development of the Soviet economy, and what economic benefits do the Western democracies derive in return? Are Western trade and technology facilitating the USSR's growing military power, and if so, what can the U.S. do to prevent this from happening? Can skillful Western profferment or interruption of commerce be used to moderate Soviet political behavior and promote mutual accommodation between East and West? Depending on their answers to these questions, American policymakers are likely to concentrate on reducing all Soviet-Western commerce, strengthening the controls over the transfer of militarily useful technology, manipulating commercial ties for diplomatic ends, or promoting trade for its own sake.

In trying to chart a wise course of action, it is vital to recognize that official U.S. perceptions of East-West trade and technology transfers have been profoundly affected by wide swings in the American national mood. During the late 1950s a combination of genuine Soviet achievements, propaganda, and American anxiety led many U.S. observers to conclude that the Soviet Union was technologically more dynamic than the United States and would soon outstrip it economically. In the absence of detailed Western studies of the USSR's technological development, the public had little understanding of the role Western technology had played in the growth of Soviet industry in the early 1930s. During the 1960s and 1970s, the American fear of Soviet technological dynamism was gradually dispelled by declining Soviet growth rates and by new scholarly studies that highlighted the limitations of Soviet R&D and the significant contributions of Western know-how to

Stalin's prewar industrialization campaign. Indeed, by the 1980s, a number of observers had carried these ideas to the opposite extreme. In their view, the Soviet system was not merely suffering from sluggish innovation and a sharp reduction of growth, but was hopelessly inept at achieving technological progress. Only massive technology transfers from the West were enabling it to perpetuate itself and to challenge U.S. military power.[1]

Just as American fears during the Sputnik era exaggerated the economic strengths of the Soviet system, the widespread scorn of the 1980s exaggerates Soviet economic and technological weaknesses. The USSR does indeed continue to lag behind the West in many fields of technology, but this does not mean that Soviet technology is standing still. Moreover, the role of Western technology in Soviet development is more complex than is commonly understood. Why, for instance, did the Soviet economy grow so rapidly under Stalin, even though it was cut off from Western technology during much of his time in power? And why has its growth slowed markedly in the post-Stalin years, when trade with the West has risen steeply? American conceptions of the Soviet system plainly touch on our fundamental national hopes and fears, and we must beware of a persisting impulse to oversimplify the realities of Soviet-American relations, economic as well as political.

Soviet Policy and the Economic Benefits of Soviet-Western Commerce

During the past two decades the USSR, prompted both by a reduced sense of international vulnerability and a decline of domestic economic dynamism, has proclaimed a new interest in extensive economic and technological ties with the West. The regime has tried to make fuller use of the existing pattern of comparative advantage by increasing its reliance on the West for continuing supplies of imports such as grain. It has also sought new infusions of Western technology that might allow it over time to improve its comparative advantage in some branches of production and reduce the costs of relying on domestic output in those sectors. In order to acquire and assimilate this Western know-how, the regime has begun to employ more active forms of commercial cooperation such as turnkey plants and licensing agreements.

Measured against the baseline of previous Soviet practice, the change in policy has been striking. The USSR has abandoned the extreme economic isolation inherited from Stalin, and the percentage growth of its trade and technological interchanges with the industrial democracies has been rapid. Together with more than a decade of high-flown Soviet rhetoric about mutually profitable economic cooperation between East and West, this trend has created a widespread American impression that the USSR, for better or for worse, has embarked on a policy of full participation in the world economy.

As Josef Brada points out, however, the degree of Soviet involvement in world trade is actually rather modest by international standards and should not be overstated. The Soviet leaders still feel a marked apprehension about the political danger of accepting greater economic dependence on the West, and they are reluctant to relax their control over the economic and cultural contacts of Soviet society with the outside world. As a result the leaders have continued to sacrifice many potential economic gains from East-West commerce. They have kept the overall level of dependence on Western imports relatively low, and in the wake of the recent Western embargoes they have shown increasing concern about accepting long-term dependence on imports such as grain and large-diameter pipe. The Soviet economy still draws much of its technology from a comprehensive domestic R&D effort which is hampered by numerous impediments but which is not stagnant, especially in high-priority sectors. Turnkey plants and other large ventures provide a valuable flow of Western technology, but relatively few foreign licenses have been purchased, and no foreign direct investment has been allowed. Notwithstanding the increased scientific and technological exchanges of the 1970s, a persisting shortage of personal contacts with foreign scientists and engineers still makes it difficult for Soviet specialists to assimilate Western know-how that is "unpackaged" in equipment or commercial deals. Stepped-up espionage and illegal acquisitions undoubtedly bring some benefits to the Soviet economy. But as S. E. Goodman notes in his discussion of the computer industry, these channels are among the least effective mechanisms of technology transfer. Particularly in a complex and rapidly changing industry such as computing, they cannot compensate for the absence of fuller and more active interchanges with the Western originators of new technology.

Equally important, much of the Western technology obtained by the USSR has been poorly integrated with domestic research and production. In the computer industry, domestic R&D has focused almost entirely on copying and assimilating Western know-how. This orientation has raised the level of Soviet computer technology. But it also means that the industry, rather than closing the gap with the West by combining foreign technology with highly innovative indigenous research, has in effect accepted the permanent lag that is inherent in arms-length technology transfers. Although other industries have given greater weight to performing original R&D, they too have had difficulty integrating this work with foreign know-how. The absence of internal economic competition means that few domestic actors have an overriding material interest in being the first to upgrade a foreign technology or to diffuse it. The chapters by Philip Hanson and George Holliday show that chemical and

automotive factories have been forced to duplicate previous Soviet purchases of Western know-how rather than obtain the technology from an
earlier Soviet buyer. Moreover, in sectors such as machine tools, the
effects of the management system and the quality of the labor force have
prevented Western equipment from achieving its rated levels of productivity.[2]

As a consequence, the changes in Soviet policy have brought positive but limited economic results. Although the aggregate effect is
difficult to establish, Western imports have allowed the regime to expand livestock production and improve the diet of Soviet consumers,
who would otherwise be forced to subsist on a diet containing much less
meat. In addition, Hanson estimates that in the industrial sector Western
equipment imports have contributed about one-half percent per year to
the rate of growth of Soviet output.[3] Thanks to Western technology
transfers, Soviet technology has progressed more rapidly than it would
have otherwise, but it has not closed the gap separating it from Western
achievements in most sectors. The available evidence suggests that the
USSR's overall technological lag behind the U.S. and the other industrial
democracies has not substantially diminished since 1960.[4] Unlike Japan,
the USSR has been unable to make foreign know-how a springboard to
world technological leadership in a number of industrial fields.

This picture reinforces the view that the overall economic benefits
obtained by the USSR and the industrial democracies from their commercial relations are probably roughly commensurate. As James Millar
points out, economic theory indicates that in the absence of monopolistic
or monopsonistic conditions, all parties participating in international
trade should benefit. Although the Soviet government is sometimes said
to enjoy a monopsonistic position in international commerce by virtue of
the state's control of foreign trade, this assertion confuses the Soviet
domestic market, which the government does indeed control, with the
world market for technology and goods, in which the Soviet Union is
one of many buyers and must pay full price for its acquisitions. In the
world agricultural market, where Soviet purchases constitute a bigger
share of total transactions than in other product markets, the U.S. government has countered Soviet buying power by requiring that the
Soviets obtain advance approval for purchases of American agricultural
products above certain specified limits. The fact that these purchases
contribute to a large imbalance in the trade flows between the two countries is not evidence that the USSR is obtaining a disproportionate economic advantage, since the United States can use the hard-currency
earnings from these sales to finance trade with other nations. In Japan
and Western Europe, although commerce with the USSR remains a
relatively small part of total trade, it creates jobs and helps bolster some
slack industrial markets. While the Soviet Union and its Western trading

partners may not all realize the gains from trade in precisely the same forms—for example, in more investment, jobs, or consumption—there is no persuasive reason to believe that their aggregate economic gains are not approximately equal.

Military Power and Export Controls

Even if Western trade and technology have had a relatively modest effect on the Soviet economy as a whole, the effect of Western transfers on Soviet military capacities is potentially far more dramatic. In the USSR military technology has reached a higher level of sophistication than most civilian technologies, partly because military R&D programs are distinguished from civilian R&D undertakings by a number of quasi-market features. In addition to enjoying first call on high-quality equipment and technical manpower, Soviet weapons development programs are characterized by centrally organized technological competitions among designers and by the powerful bureaucratic position of the military "consumer," who is free to reject unsatisfactory products in a way nonmilitary organizations cannot. Because the Soviet system is much more innovative in the military than the civilian sphere, it is better prepared to assimilate and improve on Western technology in the defense sector than in other industries. As Julian Cooper notes, during the 1930s and 1940s the defense industry was able to make Western technology a valuable stepping-stone to the creation of domestically designed weapons on a par with Western military equipment.

Concerned about an apparent rise in such transfers during the detente years, recent American administrations have sought to expand the range of technologies and the forms of technology transfer subject to government control. The compilation of a voluminous Militarily Critical Technologies List (MCTL), begun in the late 1970s, typifies this concern, as do the Reagan Administration's efforts to expand the coverage of CoCom controls and regulate the transmission of unclassified technical data through professional contacts and other channels. By claiming that virtually all Western technology transfers contribute, sooner or later, to Soviet military capabilities, Administration spokesmen have come close to embracing a policy of economic warfare toward the USSR.

Although obstructing the transfer of know-how to the Soviet defense industry must be a central goal of the Western allies, the most nettlesome questions are how broadly to define the range of proscribed technologies and what to expect of such restrictions. Cooper rightly observes that the fragmentary evidence concerning recent Western contributions to Soviet weapons systems is often difficult to interpret and urgently requires further objective study. His chapter does show, however, that even in the 1930s, when the absence of Western export controls gave the USSR much fuller access to foreign military technology than it has today, the Soviet leadership strove to create a military R&D establishment capable of designing and producing sophisticated weapons independently of the West. The history of Soviet weapons development reveals that Soviet designers have utilized Western know-how when revolutionary advances in foreign weaponry have outpaced Soviet accomplishments. But the historical record also shows that the USSR has achieved an impressive measure of success in the independent development of a wide range of military technologies. The recent pronouncements of Soviet officers indicate that they remain wary of extensive dependence on Western technology, which they wish to avoid for strategic reasons. The evidence thus suggests that although the USSR has been making vigorous efforts to evade CoCom controls and obtain militarily useful technology from the West, the impact of such efforts on the overall military competition between the superpowers has frequently been overstated. Cooper's analysis demonstrates that some American observers have a pronounced tendency to underestimate the indigenous capacities of Soviet military R&D and to exaggerate Soviet reliance on the West for weapons technologies.

This finding suggests that American policymakers should be skeptical of the notion that they can have a major impact on Soviet military programs by further widening the range of prohibited technologies. It is probably a mistake to assume, as some American officials do, that further expansion of controls can contribute significantly to attempts to shift the military balance between the superpowers in America's favor.[5] The discrepancy between Soviet and American R&D capacities is smaller in the defense sector than in any other, and America's margin of superiority in creating new weapons may well be offset by the Soviet regime's demonstrated ability to mobilize scarce resources for military programs over an extended period. Similarly, the idea of slowing Soviet military expansion by cutting back all Western trade and technology transfers, including those with purely civilian applications, should be approached with caution. Apart from obvious problems of political feasibility, this prescription rests on a mechanistic assumption that the availability of resources is the sole determinant of the level of Soviet military effort. Resource constraints undoubtedly influence the size of Soviet military programs, but so do Soviet perceptions of external threats, which are formed in part by Western behavior and rhetoric. In a world shaped entirely by economic forces, a comprehensive trade embargo which reduced Soviet industrial growth by one-half percent per year might cause a slowdown in military spending. But the increased political tensions generated by American efforts to cut trade and build up U.S. military power might also cause the Soviets to give military spending higher priority, thereby counteracting the reduction in economic resources. Western analysts still do not understand the determinants of Soviet military spending well enough to predict reliably which outcome is more probable. Until they do, American decision makers should be cautious about adopting a policy that might backfire in this way.

If more extensive controls are likely to have little effect on the quality and an uncertain impact on the quantity of future Soviet weaponry, then the political and economic costs of such measures should receive careful attention in the formulation of American policy. To begin with, the U.S. should avoid inflicting serious political damage on its alliance relationships by trying to compel other Western countries to adopt inclusive controls on East-West technology transfers. It may be possible to strengthen the effectiveness of the CoCom controls already in place, and to expand those controls somewhat to cover a slightly larger number of the most sensitive dual-use technologies. The Reagan Administration has succeeded in persuading some other CoCom countries to step up their enforcement of prohibitions against espionage and illegal diversions of technology, and cooperative attempts to strengthen enforcement should be continued. So should American efforts to obtain a stronger voice in CoCom deliberations for the military officials of the other CoCom countries, whose views would probably help mitigate some of the disagreements within the organization. But American efforts to expand significantly the definition of strategic technology will arouse European and Japanese suspicions that the underlying American purpose is to block all trade in technology, rather than East-West interchanges with a direct impact on Soviet military capabilities. As Angela Stent shows, recent American policies toward commerce with the East have introduced large strains into America's relations with its allies. Over time, such strains could threaten the political cohesion of the NATO alliance, which is just as important to American military security as slowing the USSR's accumulation of military power. Indeed, American attempts to force through a wider definition of strategic technology might gradually undermine the credibility of the concept and make it more difficult to win allied agreement to restrict the narrower band of technologies that are truly critical to Western military security.

Overly zealous efforts at control may also threaten American interests in other ways. One, of course, is economic. As James Millar shows, restrictions on Soviet-American trade have only a slight negative influence on the American economy in the short run, but the long-term effect on America's competitive standing in world trade, which may be more significant, should also be weighed in the balance. So should the impact of controls on American R&D. Rising concern about the leakage of military know-how has led the Reagan Administration to try to increase the level of secrecy in American scientific research—not merely classified research, but research being conducted in universities and discussed in professional meetings. However, the most thorough analysis of this problem to date concludes that the loss of militarily valuable knowledge through open scientific communication constitutes a very small share of the leakage that does occur.[6] While a plausible case can perhaps be made for a highly circumscribed increase in secrecy in an exceptional field like cryptography, most of the Administration's efforts to date have been so ill-defined and wide-ranging that they threaten to reduce the effectiveness of American R&D, which is a key element of the U.S. ability to compete militarily with the USSR.[7] Apart from the vital issues of constitutional rights and academic freedom raised by this matter, pragmatic calculations of effectiveness should prompt American policymakers to be extremely circumspect in introducing further restrictions on American scientific and technical communication. Such restrictions are one of the weaknesses that hamper Soviet R&D in many sectors. It would be ironic indeed if a new determination to compete effectively against the USSR led the United States to adopt some of the defective institutional arrangements that inhibit Soviet technological progress.

For these reasons, a sharp distinction should be drawn between strengthening the effectiveness and broadening the range of Western controls over technology transfers to the USSR. In the past several years the prevailing American response to the risk of losing militarily relevant know-how has been to expand the number of technologies covered by controls and to step up efforts to intercept illegal shipments of technology. There has been far less effort to establish which technologies are of greatest military importance or to concentrate on preventing their loss. Although originally intended to identify a selected group of new technologies having the greatest military significance, the Militarily Critical Technologies List has gradually been expanded to encompass a large proportion of all modern technologies.[8] Moreover, the government appears to have made little attempt to staff its agencies and departments with the large number of highly-trained specialists needed to assess Soviet and Western technological levels and make intelligent decisions about the permissibility of exporting particular technologies.[9] Rather than a sharply defined policy, there has been a diffuse disposition to restrict technology transfers, which has then been given concrete content only through extended interdepartmental and political battles of the kind analyzed in the chapter by Gary Bertsch. Apart from its impact on U.S. economic and scientific interests, this administrative pattern overburdens the numerous agencies involved in the control effort. By requiring that they monitor a very wide range of technologies, some only remotely connected to military uses, it increases the likelihood that technologies of real military value may inadvertently leak through the system.

Although there is no neat answer to such problems, they might be better managed by upgrading the government's expertise in monitoring the progress and movement of technologies. Acquiring such a capacity would require time and a large amount of money to attract the required specialists. But it would facilitate a sharper focus on controlling the most important technologies, and would thereby reduce the conflicts between American security, economic, and scientific interests. In addition, close policy guidance from the White House level is necessary if departmental conflicts are to be reduced and if diverging policy goals are to be carefully reviewed and a reasonable balance struck. If technology transfers are really a matter of national importance, the government cannot allow its policy toward them to be determined either by simple slogans or as the residual of decisions taken in other policy realms. It must create a more salient forum for the analysis and discussion of policy toward technology transfers, and it must build up far more expertise on the subject.

Trade and Diplomacy: Carrots and Sticks

The United States has tried to control the flow of goods and know-how to the USSR not only to curb the growth of Soviet military power, but to shape Soviet political behavior. In the Nixon-Kissinger era the impact of American economic inducements on Soviet conduct was considerable. The tactic of positive linkage helped change Soviet policy toward Jewish emigration. It also helped soften the Soviet line in the Middle East and contributed to the 1973 Soviet decision to withhold new military supplies from North Vietnam—a decision the Kremlin reversed when the U.S. Congress imposed a low ceiling on the government credits that would be available to the USSR. Whether more rapid growth and generous financing of Soviet-American commerce would have damped the USSR's increasing international assertiveness after 1974 remains an open question. Nevertheless, positive linkage did have a palpable if temporary effect, and the attempt to apply it in the Nixon years should not be dismissed as a naive belief that economic instruments can be substituted for political and military ones. The policy was more subtle, and in the conditions of the early 1970s it gave signs of yielding significant diplomatic results.

The results, however, hinged on a specific set of political and economic circumstances. These included West European dependence on the U.S. for the resolution of the postwar diplomatic stalemate in Europe, the sizable room for American diplomatic maneuver afforded by the absence of large East-West trade flows, and a substantial measure of Presidential control over the political tradeoffs between American commerce and Soviet behavior. Not least important, the economic inducements fit into a larger American diplomatic strategy which helped convince Moscow that it was both possible and necessary to reach mutually acceptable compromises with the United States.

During the last decade all these conditions have changed. Since the early 1970s, Western Europe and Japan have acquired a diplomatic and economic stake in detente that did not previously exist. In America domestic struggles and foreign policy debate have undermined the President's control over external economic policy, the previous consensus over East-West trade has broken down, and the farm bloc has acquired a considerable material interest in enlarging trade with the USSR. The result, as Gary Bertsch has demonstrated, is that the domestic political foundations needed for a policy of positive linkage have been badly undermined. Meanwhile Moscow has become quite pessimistic about the chances for Soviet-American diplomatic accommodations and seems bent on demonstrating the firmness of its political will. A substantial warming of Soviet-American relations might conceivably create some marginal new opportunities for positive linkage, but the divergence of the Western powers' attitudes toward linkage would greatly impede such a policy. Moreover, in order to stand any chance of success, such a stratagem would probably require a large expansion of American trade credits to the USSR and would therefore necessitate a significant revision of U.S. trade legislation. In 1984 it is hard to believe that political and economic trends will again make a policy of positive linkage feasible.

The 1980s American policy of economic sanctions, or negative linkage, has proved even less successful politically than the Nixon-Kissinger policy. Sanctions have been impossible for the U.S. to sustain in the sector with the most immediate impact on the Soviet economy—agricultural imports. Denial of agricultural supplies has a quicker effect than the termination of technology transfers, and agriculture is the economic sector where the U.S. has usually supplied the largest share of Soviet imports from the West. Yet, as Bertsch has shown, the dynamics of American domestic politics led the Reagan Administration to abandon this element of the post-Afghanistan sanctions only fifteen months after the Carter Administration had adopted the sanctions.

The sanctions also had disappointing effects because America's allies were reluctant to go along with them. James Millar's analysis suggests that the structure of the international economy may make a successful embargo against the USSR economically impossible for the West to achieve. But whatever chance there is hinges on America's ability to persuade its allies that it is shouldering a burden equal to what it is asking of them. It is worth emphasizing that the bulk of the industrial technology shipped to the USSR comes from Western Europe and Japan, not the U.S. The case studies show that alternative supplies of most technologies are available in the chemical, automotive, and energy industries; only the computer industry is a partial exception. Yet the

Reagan Administration undercut its own campaign for allied sanctions against the USSR by shipping grain to the Soviet Union at the same time it was asking Europe and Japan to restrict the flow of technology to the Soviets. The Administration justified its position by contending that grain sales would siphon off Soviet hard currency from purchases of Western technology, but this was a defective argument. Agriculture is the economic sector in which the USSR is most inefficient in comparison with the rest of the world, and foreign grain saved the USSR from spending more domestic resources in the sector where they yielded the lowest economic return.[10] Without Western grain the Soviet economy would have been under added economic strain and the political leadership would probably have been forced to divert added domestic resources into agriculture that otherwise would have gone into the industrial or military sectors of the economy. The American distinction between agricultural and nonagricultural trade, which the allies regarded as self-serving, strengthened allied reluctance to take painful economic actions against the USSR.

A third reason for the failure of economic sanctions is to be found in the Soviet Union itself. In a time of acrimonious East-West relations, the Kremlin leadership is unwilling to be seen as giving in to Western demands, particularly when those demands affect the USSR's central national security priorities. The war in Afghanistan has put Soviet prestige on the line, and avoiding withdrawal and defeat has become a major aim of Soviet policy. In Poland the stakes for Soviet decision makers are, if anything, higher still. In such instances, the chances that the regime will accede to Western economic pressures are virtually nil, not only because it is determined to avoid the appearance of political weakness but because the Soviet economy is still less vulnerable than almost any other to disruption through cut-offs in foreign trade.[11] As Anton Malish and Robert Campbell have shown, the agricultural and pipeline embargoes caused some economic problems for the USSR, but the problems were far from adequate to override major foreign-policy commitments. In the case of agriculture, the party authorities used the embargo to mobilize patriotic sentiment and justify consumer hardships that might have posed more serious political problems if there had been no foreign enemy to blame. Rather than force changes in Soviet foreign-policy behavior, the economic sanctions of the 1980s have aroused Soviet anxieties about the security implications of East-West commerce, and may have slowed the expansion of Soviet reliance on Western goods and technology.

None of this means that the United States should completely renounce the use of economic sanctions as a tool of diplomacy. A case can still be made for economic sanctions as a signal of American displeasure over Soviet conduct—particularly when the economic measures are coupled with other signals such as diplomatic protests, a general hardening of American foreign-policy positions toward the USSR, changed military deployments, and the like. But in that case, American policy-makers should clearly understand that the economic costs so imposed are unlikely to be large enough to reverse Soviet behavior, and they should take steps to avoid the politically self-defeating process of dis-mantling the sanctions while the objectionable conduct continues. One way of doing this is to make the economic sanctions effective only for a certain period of time, specified at the outset, and to avoid declaring that they will be lifted only when Soviet behavior changes. In this way, some discomfort might be inflicted on the USSR without conveying an impres-sion that the United States lacks the political determination to imple-ment its proclaimed policies. Signals of this kind, however, would have to be used very sparingly, simply because they would be hard to justify to interested domestic groups, which would be even less likely to accept material deprivation in order to signal the USSR than to force a change of Soviet behavior.

NOTES

1. Carl Gershman, "Selling Them the Rope: Business and the Soviets," *Commentary*, April 1979, pp. 42–45. For a similar but more nuanced view, see Richard Pipes, "How to Cope with the Soviet Threat," ibid., August 1984, pp. 27–30.

2. Philip Hanson, *Trade and Technology in Soviet-Western Relations* (New York: Columbia University Press, 1981), chapter 11.

3. Ibid., p. 211.

4. See Josef Brada's contribution to this volume, and R. W. Davies, "The Technological Level of Soviet Industry: An Overview," in Ronald Amann, Julian Cooper, and R. W. Davies (eds.), *The Technological Level of Soviet Industry* (New Haven: Yale University Press, 1977), p. 66.

5. See, for instance, "Sensitive Sales: U.S. Tries to Cut Trade in Items that Russians Might Use for Military," *Wall Street Journal*, 11 February 1982, p. 1.

6. *Scientific Communication and National Security: A Report Prepared by the Panel on Scientific Communication and National Security* (Washington, D.C.: National Academy Press, 1982).

7. Mitchel B. Wallerstein and Lawrence C. McCray, *Scientific Communication and National Security: The Issues in 1984*, Staff Report to the Panel on Scientific Communication and National Security (Washington, D.C.: National Research Council, 1984) (mimeograph).

8. *Scientific Communication and National Security: A Report*, pp. 54–55; Wallerstein and McCray, pp. 21–22.

9. *Scientific Communication and National Security: A Report*, p. 56; Gordon Smith, "The Politics of East-West Trade," in *The Politics of East-West Trade*, ed. Gordon B. Smith (Boulder, Colo.: Westview Press, 1984), p. 9.

10. See Jan Vanous, "Comparative Advantage in Soviet Grain and Energy Trade," in *The Politics of East-West Trade*, pp. 95–108.

11. "C.I.A. Says Soviet Can Almost Do Without Imports," *New York Times*, 9 January 1983, p. 16.

Chronology of U.S.-USSR Trade: 1971–1983

1971	
NOV	The U.S. Department of Agriculture announced that a $125 million grain sale had been arranged for the Soviet Union (the first since 1964).
NOV 20	Secretary of Commerce Stans traveled to the USSR to explore improved commercial relations. A grain sales agreement, MFN, export credits, establishment of a Joint Chamber of Commerce, and other trade matters were discussed.

1972	
JAN 6–18	A Department of Commerce/Soviet Ministry of Foreign Trade Working Group met in Washington to discuss possibilities for increasing U.S.-Soviet trade.
APR	Negotiations began on a Lend-Lease Settlement.
MAY	Soviet Foreign Trade Minister Patolichev visited the United States.
MAY 22	President Nixon arrived in Moscow for a summit conference.
	—On May 24 an agreement was signed covering Cooperation in Science and Technology, including the encouragement of the establishment of "contracts and arrangements between United States firms and Soviet enterprises. . . ."
	—A Communique was issued on May 26 establishing a Joint U.S.-U.S.S.R. Commercial Commission to monitor commercial relations and negotiate a trade agreement.
	—A text of "Basic Principles of Relations" was signed May 29. The seventh principle held that "the USA and the USSR regard commercial and economic ties as an important and necessary element in the strengthening of their bilateral relations and thus will actively promote the growth of such ties. They will facilitate cooperation between the relevant organizations and enterprises of the two countries and the conclusion of appropriate agreements and contracts, including long-term ones."
JUL 8	The United States and the Soviet Union signed a 3-year grain agreement covering the sale of up to $750 million of grain. The United States undertook to make available credit through the Commodity Credit Corporation.
JUL 20–AUG 1	The first session of the Joint U.S.-USSR Commercial Commission was held in Moscow. The U.S. side was

headed by Commerce Secretary Peterson and the Soviet side by Minister of Foreign Trade Patolichev. At this session negotiations were begun on a Trade Agreement and Maritime Agreement and continued on a Lend-Lease Settlement.

AUG 29   Amendment to the Export Administration Act of 1969, P.L. 92-412, was enacted. It called for further relaxation of controls on exports freely available from sources outside the United States.

OCT 4   Senator Jackson introduced an amendment (later known as the Jackson-Vanik Amendment) to the trade bill linking American trade privileges to Soviet emigration policy.

OCT 12–18   The second session of the Joint U.S.-USSR Commercial Commission was held in Washington.

OCT 14   A Maritime Agreement was signed which opened 40 ports in each country to the vessels of the other and provided cargo moving between the two countries.

OCT 18   U.S. and Soviet representatives signed a comprehensive trade agreement establishing a general framework for commercial relations. The Nixon Administration agreed to ask Congress to grant MFN status to the Soviet Union. Other agreements were signed arranging for Soviet repayment of its Lend-Lease debt (tied to U.S. extension of MFN) and for the extension of U.S. Export-Import Bank credits to the USSR (an operating "Agreement on Financing Procedures"). President Nixon signed a statement certifying that it was in the U.S. national interest for the Export-Import Bank to participate in transactions involving the Soviet Union.

1973

APR 2   Occidental signed a 20-year, $20 billion Global Agreement with the USSR covering the purchase of ammonia, urea, and potash and sale of superphosphoric acid. In addition, the Soviets were to purchase technology and equipment for ammonia plants, a pipeline, and port handling and storage facilities.

JUN 18–25   Soviet Communist Party General Secretary Brezhnev visited the United States.
—An Agreement on Cooperation in Agriculture was signed on June 19.
—A tax convention designed to avoid double taxation was signed on June 20.
—A protocol was signed on June 22 on the question of establishing a U.S.-USSR Chamber of Commerce (see September 5, 1973).

JUN 29   American and Japanese firms signed preliminary agreements with the USSR calling for joint development of Yakutsk gas in return for liquefied gas (LNG) to be shipped to the United States over a 20-year period (never consummated).

SEP 5   The U.S.-USSR Trade and Economic Council was incorporated in New York City.

OCT 1–3   The third session of the Joint U.S.-USSR Commercial Commission was held in Moscow. The two sides agreed to negotiate a long-term agreement to facilitate economic and technical cooperation (see June 29, 1974).

1974

MAY 21–22   The fourth session of the Joint U.S.-USSR Commercial Commission was held in Washington.

JUN 22   President Nixon arrived in Moscow for summit talks.

—An Energy Cooperation Agreement was signed on June 28.

—A long-term (10-year) agreement to facilitate economic, industrial, and technical cooperation (EITCA) was concluded on June 29. This included a business facilitation clause and creation of a working group of experts to regularly exchange information which helps U.S. firms and Soviet foreign trade organizations to identify projects for economic cooperation. The agreement required no Congressional authorization.

JUN 25   Before the passage of a joint House-Senate resolution extending the expiration date of the Export-Import Bank Act of 1945, Export-Import Bank President Casey in a letter to Senator Byrd provided assurance that the Bank would not extend further financing to the Soviet Union until Congress had decided what policies the Bank should follow in this regard and enacted the legislation pending before the Banking, Housing, and Urban Affairs Committee.

OCT 19   Treasury Secretary Simon announced that arrangements had been worked out to sell the Soviets 2.2 million metric tons of grain in return for a Soviet promise not to buy any more American grain until the summer of 1975.

DEC 20   Congress passed the Export-Import Bank Amendments and the Trade Act of 1974, which made MFN for Communist countries conditional on emigration policy, made MFN a prerequisite for access to U.S. government credit facilities, set an overall ceiling of $300 million on additional Eximbank credits for the USSR, and limited use of Eximbank credits for Soviet energy projects.

1975

JAN 14   Secretary of State Kissinger announced that the USSR had rejected a trade relationship with the United States based on the Trade Act of 1974 and would not bring into force the 1972 Trade Agreement.

APR 10–11   The fifth session of the Joint U.S.-USSR Commercial Commission was held in Moscow. The U.S. side affirmed the determination of the Administration to work with

Congress in obtaining enactment of legislation that would
make possible normalization of trade (see December 20,
1974 and January 14, 1975).

JUN 27   President Ford addressed to chairmen of four Congressional committees concerned with trade legislation a letter
urging a revision of East-West trade legislation to make
possible improved trade ties with communist countries. In
July a Senate delegation conveyed the contents of the letter to Soviet officials in Moscow.

AUG 11   Agriculture Secretary Butz asked grain exporters to
voluntarily withhold future grain sales to the Soviet
Union until their effect could be better ascertained.

SEP 9   The Ford Administration announced that all future grain
sales to the Soviet Union would be halted until mid-October.

OCT 5   A Grain Agreement was signed, setting a minimum of 6
million metric tons of corn and wheat to be purchased
annually by the Soviets (maximum of 8 million mt) with
further purchases subject to bilateral consultation.

DEC 29   A new Maritime Agreement was signed.

1976

MAR 16   The United States and Soviet Union agreed to recess
negotiations on an oil agreement. Negotiations, which
had been taking place in Washington since January 27,
had reached an impasse over acceptable formulas for oil
prices and shipping rates.

SPRING   The United States declined to schedule the sixth session
of the Joint Commercial Commission and postponed
other bilateral meetings in response to Soviet/Cuban intervention in Angola.

1977

APR   President Carter announced that the CIA had predicted
that Soviet oil production would decline, forcing the
USSR to compete with the rest of the world for Middle
Eastern oil.

JUN 9–10   The sixth session of the Joint U.S.-USSR Commercial
Commission was held in Washington.

1978

JUL   The United States denied an export license for a Sperry
Univac computer ordered by TASS for use at the 1980
Olympics. This action (and the new licensing requirements for oil and gas equipment imposed August 1)
reflected a deterioration in U.S.-Soviet relations connected with harsh Soviet treatment of dissidents, the arrest of a U.S. businessman, and the trial of two American
reporters in Moscow.

AUG 1   The Department of Commerce placed foreign policy export controls on oil and gas equipment and technology.

	Export to the Soviet Union of equipment and technology for oil and gas exploration and production now required a validated license. (The Department followed a policy of issuing licenses for these items with the exception of the periods January–March 1980 and January–November 1982 and, for technology, after January 1980.)
AUG 31	President Carter called for a review of a license issued earlier to Dresser Industries for export of a drill bit plant to the USSR.
SEP 6	President Carter reaffirmed the issuance of the Dresser license.
NOV 3	Occidental Petroleum signed contracts worth approximately $250 million with Soyuzpromexport and Soyuzchimexport for sale of superphosphoric acid used in liquid fertilizer production and purchase of ammonia and urea. These were the first major chemical sales contracts implementing the 20-year fertilizer exchange agreement between Occidental and the Soviet Ministry of Foreign Trade signed in 1973.
DEC 4–5	The seventh session of the Joint U.S.-USSR Commercial Commission was held in Moscow.

1979

JUN 16	President Carter and Soviet President Brezhnev held a summit meeting in Vienna. In the Summit Communique both sides confirmed the importance of trade in the development of bilateral ties.
OCT 11	The United States International Trade Commission determined that anhydrous ammonia imports from the USSR were causing, or threatening to cause, market disruption.
DEC 11	President Carter announced that he had decided not to provide import relief in connection with imports of Soviet ammonia (see previous items).
DEC (last week of)	The Soviet Union invaded Afghanistan.

1980

JAN 4	President Carter announced the following sanctions against the Soviets in response to the invasion of Afghanistan:

—An embargo on future grain exports (and other livestock and feed-related products), involving cancellation of an offer of 17 million metric tons (mmt) of wheat and corn but the allowance of delivery of the 8 mmt covered under the 1975 Agreement;

—Suspension of licensing of all high technology and other products requiring validated export licenses as well as all outstanding licenses, pending a review of licensing by an interagency committee chaired by Secretary of Commerce Klutznick;

—Reduction of Soviet fishing privileges in U.S. waters;

—Limitation of Aeroflot service to the United States.

JAN 9   International Longshoremen's Association (I.L.A.) announced a boycott of all Soviet cargo and/or ships at ports from Maine to Texas. This led over the next year to sharp reduction of Soviet liner service to the U.S. East Coast and Gulf ports, and the shifting of bulk cargoes to third-flag vessels.

JAN 18   President Carter imposed a quota on imports of Soviet ammonia in 1980 and remanded the case to the International Trade Commission.

FEB 25   The United States embargoed exports and re-exports from other countries of U.S.-origin phosphate rock, phosphoric acid, and phosphate fertilizers to the USSR. This followed an effective suspension in early February when the Commerce Department required validated licenses and suspended issuance of such licenses (previously, phosphates could be exported under general license).

MAR 13   The Department of Commerce announced that the President was asking all U.S. companies to cooperate with his call for U.S. non-participation in the 1980 summer Olympics in Moscow by voluntarily withdrawing products relating to the Olympics from export to the Soviet Union.

MAR 18   The Department of Commerce announced that a review of export control policy had been completed and that the President had decided on more restrictive criteria to be used in controlling exports of high technology to the Soviet Union. The Administration began a case-by-case review of outstanding export licenses and pending applications.

MAR 20   The International Trade Commission reversed an earlier ruling and found that market disruption did not exist as a result of imports of Soviet ammonia. The quota imposed in January was lifted.

MAR 28   The Secretary of Commerce announced that, at the direction of the President, he was barring exports of U.S. goods and technology to be used at the 1980 summer Olympics in Moscow as well as other transactions and payments associated with Olympic-related exports.

MAY 31   The United States approved Soviet purchases of up to 8 mmt of corn and wheat during the fifth and final year of the U.S.-Soviet Grain Agreement.

JUL 3   Presidential candidate Ronald Reagan endorsed efforts by a group of Congressmen to lift the grain embargo.

JUL 10   Argentina signed an agreement to provide the Soviet Union with 22.5 mmt of soybeans, corn and sorghum during the five years beginning Jan. 1, 1981.

NOV 14   Secretary of Commerce Klutznick announced approval of a validated license for export by Caterpillar of 200 pipelayers (worth about $80 million) to the USSR for use on the Yamal pipeline.

NOV 28   The Department of Commerce revoked a license previously issued to Dresser Industries for export of technical data for a drill bit plant. The license had been among those suspended in January.

DEC 23   President-elect Reagan's nominee for Secretary of Ag-
                      riculture, John Block, announced that he would recom-
                      mend lifting the partial grain embargo at an appropriate
                      time.

1981

APR 24   President Reagan lifted the grains and phosphates embar-
                      goes. The International Longshoremen's Association
                      lifted its boycott of grain destined for the Soviet Union.
                      (The boycott of other cargoes remained until June.)
JUL 19–21   In response to an initiative by President Reagan, the par-
                      ticipants at the Ottawa Summit agreed to consult on im-
                      proving the system of controls on trade in strategic goods
                      and technology with the USSR. A high-level meeting was
                      planned in CoCom in the fall. President Reagan also
                      raised concerns about security implications of the pro-
                      posed Western Europe–USSR Yamal gas pipeline.
JUL 31   The Department of Commerce announced approval of a
                      validated license for Caterpillar for export of 100 pipelay-
                      ers (worth about $40 million) for use on pipelines other
                      than the Yamal line. Caterpillar had requested this
                      amendment to its November 1980 licenses.
AUG 3   The United States and the Soviet Union extended the
                      current Grains Agreement for one year from October 1,
                      1981 and agreed to plan for early negotiations in 1982 on
                      a new agreement.
DEC 13   Polish military government imposed martial law in Po-
                      land.
DEC 21   Assistant Secretary of State for European Affairs Ea-
                      gleburger began consultations with European allies on
                      Poland.
DEC 29   Citing Soviet complicity in the repression in Poland, Presi-
                      dent Reagan announced the following sanctions on eco-
                      nomic relations with the USSR:
                      —Suspension of all Aeroflot service;
                      —Closing of the Soviet Purchasing Commission (formerly
                        the Kama Purchasing Commission);
                      —Suspension of issuance or renewal of all validated ex-
                        port licenses for the USSR;
                      —Postponement of negotiations on a new long-term
                        Grain Agreement;
                      —Suspension of negotiations on a new U.S.-Soviet
                        Maritime Agreement;
                      —Expansion of the list of oil and gas equipment requiring
                        validated export licenses and suspension of the issuance
                        of such licenses;
                      —Non-renewal of exchange agreements for energy and
                        technology.
DEC 31   The Maritime Agreement expired.

1982

JAN 11	NATO condemned the Soviet Union for its active support of "the systematic suppression" in Poland and warned that Western Europe might join the United States in imposing economic sanctions. The allies said that they would remain in close touch and "not undermine the effect of each other's measures." They endorsed the three conditions on Poland set forth by President Reagan in December: that martial law must be lifted, the detainees released, and a dialogue restored between the government, the church, and Solidarity.
JAN 19	President Reagan stated that the situation in Poland was deteriorating and that he would not "wait forever" for an improvement. In response, the Reagan Administration was discussing additional steps or sanctions.
JAN 20	CoCom began a two-day high-level meeting on tightening of controls on strategic trade with the Soviet Union pursuant to an agreement at the Ottawa Summit.
MAR	Under Secretary of State Buckley began a series of meetings with European officials on credit and energy policy vis-à-vis the Soviet Union. The United States sought to increase the exchange of information on credit extensions and establish a mechanism for credit restriction.
APR 20	In a case connected with the 1980 International Longshoremen's Association boycott of Soviet cargo, the Supreme Court affirmed that a refusal by an American longshoremen's union to unload cargoes shipped from the Soviet Union was an illegal secondary boycott under the National Labor Relations Act, as amended.
JUN 5–6	At the Versailles Summit President Reagan proposed that the participants agree to limit and raise the cost of credits for the Soviet Union.
JUN 10	NATO heads of government and state agreed to "take steps necessary to restrict the transfer of military relevant technology to the Warsaw Pact" and to approach economic relations with the Soviet bloc in a "prudent and diversified manner."
JUN 18	President Reagan announced that as a further step to encourage reconciliation in Poland he was extending the December 29 controls covering oil and gas equipment and technology to U.S. subsidiaries and licensees abroad.
JUN 30	President Reagan signed a Congressional Joint Resolution extending for one year the U.S.-USSR Governing International Fishery Agreement.
JUL 14	The European Community lodged a formal protest to the United States over the Reagan Administration's decision to extend sanctions to companies in Western Europe.
AUG 2	The Soviet Union accepted President Reagan's offer of a one-year extension of the current grain agreement.
AUG 13	Senator Jake Garn (R-Utah) introduced legislation which would move export control and administration functions into a new office of strategic trade.

OCT 27	President Reagan signed a proclamation suspending MFN treatment for Poland.
NOV 13	President Reagan, citing "substantial agreement" among the allies on an economic strategy toward the Soviet Union, announced the lifting of foreign policy export controls imposed in December and June on the shipment of oil and gas transmission and refining equipment and technical data.

1983

FEB	Reagan Administration split over what to do about extending Export Administration Act.
APR 22	President Reagan announced intention to renegotiate long-term grain agreement with USSR. Soviet Union agreed to negotiate.
AUG 25	Agriculture Secretary John Block signed the new long-term grain agreement in Moscow. The five-year agreement imposes a minimum of nine million metric tons of wheat and corn yearly.
SEP 24	Citing "arrogance of the U.S. government," William Root, Director of the State Department's Office of East-West Trade, resigned in protest.
SEP 30	After months of debate, the Senate avoided a lapse in the Export Administration Act by agreeing to a 14-day extension of the old Act.
OCT 13	Lawrence Brady announced his resignation as Assistant Secretary of Commerce for Trade Administration.
OCT 14	Declaring a national economic emergency, President Reagan invoked the International Emergency Economic Powers Act to continue the authorities of the Export Administration Act. Congress still unable to agree on new Act.
NOV 18	Still deadlocked on the new Act, Congress passed legislation to extend the 1979 Export Administration Act through the end of February 1984.

Gary K. Bertsch prepared the Chronology. The information for 1971 through June 30, 1982 has been adapted from that compiled by Jack Brougher and Cynthia Giordano, USSR Affairs Division, International Trade Administration, U.S. Department of Commerce.

Statistical Appendix

Table 1

USSR Hard Currency Debt, 1970–1983
(*$ Millions*)

YEAR	DEBT[1] GROSS	NET	MATURITY[2] SHORT	LONG	TYPE COMMER-CIAL	OFFICIALLY BACKED	DEBT SERVICE[3]
70	1,400	NA	NA	NA	NA	NA	200
71	1,800	600	NA	NA	400	1,400	300
72	2,400	600	NA	NA	1,600	800	400
73	3,700	1,200	NA	NA	2,000	1,700	700
74	5,200	1,700	NA	NA	2,800	2,400	1,100
75	10,500	7,400	NA	NA	6,900	3,600	1,800
76	14,700	10,000	NA	NA	9,700	5,000	2,400
77	15,600	11,200	NA	NA	9,800	5,800	3,100
78	16,400	10,400	3,100	6,400	9,500	6,900	3,600
79	18,100	9,300	3,300	7,200	10,500	7,600	4,200
80	17,800	9,200	3,900	6,100	10,000	7,800	4,700
81	20,900	12,500	5,500	7,500	13,000	7,900	5,400
82	20,100	10,100	4,000	7,500	11,300	8,700	5,800
83	20,500	10,900	NA	NA	11,500	9,000	6,000

SOURCE: CIA, National Foreign Assessment Center, *Handbook of Economic Statistics*, selected years.

All quantities rounded to nearest 100 million.

NA = Not available.

[1]Gross-Net Debt = Soviet assets in Western banks as reported by the Bank for International Settlements.

[2]Short term maturity is less than one year.

[3]Debt Service includes interest and repayment of principal.

Table 2

OECD Countries' Exports to the USSR, 1960–1983
($ Millions)*

Year	U.S.	Canada	Australia	Japan	New Zealand	Austria	Belgium Luxembourg	Denmark
1960	40.0	8.1	29.8	60.0	7.0	39.1	19.0	16.3
1961	46.0	24.3	17.8	65.4	5.4	43.2	27.3	5.1
1962	20.0	3.4	29.5	149.4	2.5	53.9	25.6	20.7
1963	23.0	139.2	52.5	158.3	NA	61.7	13.2	29.0
1964	146.0	293.2	120.3	181.9	3.3	57.7	14.7	35.0
1965	45.0	183.0	90.8	168.3	4.7	57.1	22.6	30.7
1966	42.0	296.6	33.1	215.0	14.5	59.3	26.5	22.0
1967	60.0	119.1	20.4	157.7	5.4	59.5	40.3	17.9
1968	58.0	82.8	38.9	179.0	10.9	68.4	47.7	18.9
1969	106.0	9.1	46.0	268.3	14.5	68.6	51.1	17.9
1970	118.0	97.2	72.1	340.9	18.4	82.1	54.2	26.5
1971	166.0	125.4	68.1	377.7	27.4	69.7	62.5	25.4
1972	542.0	285.9	102.0	512.3	25.0	94.2	92.0	26.8
1973	1,202.1	291.9	247.1	487.5	48.8	92.2	212.5	35.0
1974	616.9	30.1	240.2	1,094.8	76.2	188.2	369.6	42.7
1975	1,848.7	400.3	352.3	1,625.9	37.8	216.8	353.5	64.8
1976	2,332.7	557.7	484.3	2,254.2	98.7	237.7	297.3	70.3
1977	1,658.2	337.5	332.5	1,951.0	135.6	279.3	272.7	77.9
1978	2,282.7	494.3	300.9	2,529.3	73.6	370.8	351.7	67.6
1979	3,615.5	645.8	563.0	2,442.7	196.3	515.4	467.4	103.1
1980	1,515.0	1,302.6	1,137.1	2,795.8	225.5	477.5	618.0	97.7
1981	2,431.6	1,491.8	711.7	3,253.0	237.8	484.4	594.9	94.7
1982	2,592.6	1,665.8	692.9	3,893.2	306.2	551.2	533.4	88.8
1983	2,002.9	1,430.7	483.0	2,821.7	232.8	598.5	666.1	76.6

374

Year	Finland	France	Germany (FRG)	Italy	Iceland	Ireland	Neth'lands	Norway
1960	139.8	115.6	185.0	78.6	10.0	NA	11.8	12.9
1961	127.8	110.0	204.0	89.5	5.2	NA	19.7	12.5
1962	196.3	138.1	207.0	102.3	10.9	0.1	32.0	10.4
1963	185.2	64.2	154.0	113.6	10.7	0.4	23.7	12.7
1964	155.7	64.1	194.0	90.7	10.1	0.1	14.9	17.0
1965	226.6	72.0	146.0	98.1	6.8	2.1	29.3	18.5
1966	213.5	75.6	135.0	90.1	9.9	0.0	25.2	14.5
1967	267.9	155.3	198.0	132.0	11.6	0.1	66.5	18.7
1968	251.4	256.5	273.0	179.0	8.9	0.8	46.8	19.0
1969	277.4	265.1	406.0	284.5	9.5	0.5	55.8	15.3
1970	282.5	273.1	422.0	307.9	10.0	0.1	45.5	24.8
1971	254.1	256.2	459.0	294.8	12.2	0.5	46.0	19.1
1972	365.0	341.5	720.0	268.4	14.0	0.6	54.8	19.7
1973	451.4	577.3	1,184.0	351.5	10.1	1.3	78.3	22.0
1974	767.0	660.7	1,854.0	620.6	23.6	19.2	170.9	39.9
1975	1,130.9	1,142.9	2,824.0	1,023.3	32.3	23.6	209.4	96.5
1976	1,287.0	1,119.2	2,686.0	984.4	22.2	3.3	174.0	76.7
1977	1,484.8	1,496.4	2,789.8	1,231.1	36.1	11.1	203.5	76.0
1978	1,525.6	1,462.3	3,140.5	1,133.9	25.3	10.6	210.9	89.1
1979	1,538.4	2,005.1	3,619.0	1,222.1	30.5	44.9	303.7	87.2
1980	2,491.2	2,465.3	4,373.4	1,267.1	50.3	49.5	508.6	112.2
1981	3,467.6	1,865.6	3,394.2	1,284.8	58.4	39.2	623.3	125.0
1982	3,469.2	1,559.2	3,870.3	1,499.2	56.6	41.9	425.3	96.5
1983	3,287.4	2,240.2	4,417.8	1,884.0	60.8	61.2	541.9	119.2

Year	Spain	Sweden	Switz.	U.K.	Portugal	Turkey	Greece	TOTAL OECD
1960	7.1	38.2	10.4	148.9	2.5	4.9	18.8	1,003.8
1961	3.0	43.8	8.9	194.4	0.0	4.5	18.8	1,076.6
1962	0.4	78.7	7.0	161.0	0.0	5.5	19.2	1,273.9
1963	0.7	54.4	11.7	179.7	0.0	7.1	22.4	1,317.4
1964	3.3	86.7	10.0	111.3	0.0	9.0	24.2	1,643.2
1965	2.0	50.3	15.4	128.6	0.0	18.5	26.9	1,443.3
1966	6.0	39.3	22.2	141.1	0.0	18.5	28.3	1,528.2
1967	9.4	57.9	22.9	178.8	0.0	28.4	30.5	1,658.3
1968	17.8	78.8	27.2	249.5	0.0	29.9	24.4	1,967.6
1969	4.6	111.2	35.9	233.2	0.0	30.0	30.0	2,340.6
1970	5.9	131.4	50.0	245.1	0.0	29.4	34.5	2,671.6
1971	10.1	87.3	47.2	216.6	0.0	34.3	20.4	2,679.9
1972	30.3	84.6	69.2	227.4	0.3	41.6	35.8	3,953.2
1973	17.0	116.3	96.0	238.9	0.6	50.4	44.6	5,856.8
1974	58.0	180.4	142.2	256.7	1.5	77.5	81.0	7,611.9
1975	74.6	292.3	181.4	463.5	18.1	73.6	87.3	12,573.8
1976	99.9	279.6	201.4	434.0	55.2	81.0	83.0	13,919.6
1977	101.4	256.5	238.4	605.5	41.8	80.4	103.0	13,800.2
1978	142.0	212.2	266.3	813.1	39.6	105.3	95.1	15,742.6
1979	266.8	338.9	267.4	891.0	53.5	126.7	55.0	19,399.2
1980	258.8	420.1	301.8	1,058.1	51.7	169.0	90.9	21,837.1
1981	365.1	422.9	209.2	832.4	52.3	193.8	74.6	22,308.4
1982	219.0	353.2	214.9	620.2	52.0	124.0	145.2	23,070.7
1983	334.5	290.6	223.4	676.1	50.6	NA	141.7	22,641.7

SOURCE: IMF, *Directions of Trade*, from Data Resources Inc.
*NA = Not Available

Table 3

OECD Countries' High Technology Exports to the USSR, 1961–1982
($ Thousands)*

Year	Canada	U.S.	Japan	Austria	Belgium Luxemb.	Denmark	Finland	France	Germany (FRG)
1961	0	2,654	0	6,557	3,686	1,131	0	31,782	49,018
1962	0	1,203	11,308	9,133	4,424	7,674	0	42,059	22,760
1963	29	830	23,969	10,322	200	8,334	0	16,181	36,030
1964	46	1,941	16,918	11,817	325	543	11,492	6,297	70,038
1965	2	915	15,441	10,716	1,120	476	20,463	12,539	37,956
1966	75	2,212	24,948	7,737	388	3,297	18,627	15,472	30,684
1967	45	2,547	25,561	6,433	2,441	2,497	18,860	42,557	37,216
1968	277	4,843	27,694	8,808	1,647	2,380	32,929	72,597	50,127
1969	181	14,068	35,869	8,085	7,366	2,269	38,072	67,517	73,919
1970	155	13,411	37,980	9,815	3,438	3,032	29,578	49,194	55,919
1971	355	31,035	45,260	8,564	2,914	6,277	12,112	55,622	74,354
1972	1,537	28,675	89,563	10,270	1,911	8,758	24,337	66,192	179,949
1973	324	120,266	76,089	6,149	3,941	4,785	51,454	100,678	280,416
1974	681	85,462	92,297	8,678	10,475	3,874	68,336	174,523	351,384
1975	13,532	165,610	182,266	24,175	18,980	11,206	82,107	331,703	593,584
1976	6,672	230,574	312,079	35,773	6,653	28,264	221,727	271,591	597,536
1977	6,474	176,093	388,670	41,958	11,305	9,535	345,316	385,747	697,073
1978	22,512	102,035	669,571	42,800	35,084	15,671	283,690	422,532	638,103
1979	35,608	180,505	367,168	42,326	19,088	11,615	154,446	584,042	615,541
1980	29,108	88,154	335,156	39,256	12,995	17,570	220,265	418,619	559,050
1981	1,733	73,012	319,354	35,604	7,340	21,444	334,619	186,942	414,165
1982	2,484	31,349	587,963	47,230	8,692	14,644	447,103	244,339	521,892

Year	Ireland	Italy	Neth'lds.	Norway	Spain	Sweden	Switz.	U.K.	TOTAL OECD
1961	0	14,097	2,073	80	0	8,922	1,531	30,108	151,589
1962	0	15,470	14,108	75	0	35,457	1,336	20,891	185,898
1963	0	22,820	5,537	95	0	14,633	1,695	26,071	166,746
1964	0	4,249	916	160	49	6,478	2,091	19,639	152,999
1965	0	12,156	1,979	175	0	3,966	2,860	30,064	150,828
1966	0	12,250	1,353	195	20	3,329	3,922	50,250	174,759
1967	2	24,217	19,797	395	0	14,295	4,871	52,346	254,080
1968	0	23,272	9,372	1,956	2	15,807	5,300	60,234	317,245
1969	0	71,680	4,502	357	4	11,689	5,624	51,369	392,571
1970	1	73,342	2,926	476	7	19,390	9,665	51,669	359,998
1971	322	77,848	4,971	906	36	14,121	14,496	52,036	401,229
1972	182	80,424	3,291	1,781	0	17,461	17,420	59,007	590,758
1973	1,002	97,128	5,424	2,384	0	20,158	21,589	61,357	853,144
1974	101	90,959	8,442	1,953	3	40,322	25,000	42,317	1,004,807
1975	317	202,303	20,578	10,739	1,960	71,982	37,848	84,952	1,853,842
1976	43	202,028	19,600	2,623	1,457	71,210	43,455	93,523	2,144,808
1977	1,993	338,251	13,869	2,776	885	41,730	52,850	79,622	2,594,147
1978	3,030	310,872	12,693	37,344	2,670	36,656	44,574	153,713	2,833,550
1979	2,055	274,792	13,240	10,769	7,670	40,966	50,825	218,960	2,629,616
1980	794	286,131	13,640	11,353	900	38,899	65,938	230,949	2,368,777
1981	97	211,050	16,289	9,009	988	45,479	46,076	123,083	1,846,284
1982	3,501	0	0	11,400	0	52,596	38,762	108,581	2,120,536

SOURCE: OECD Trade Series C from Data Resources, Inc. Washington, D.C.

*This is an approximation. These categories do not correspond precisely to customary definitions of high technology. The table includes SITC's 714 (office machines), 719 (machinery and appliances [other than electrical] and machine parts not elsewhere specified), 724 (telecommunications apparatus), and 86 (professional, scientific and controlling instruments, photographic and optical goods, watches and clocks.) Figures were not available for Australia, New Zealand, Greece, Iceland, Portugal, Turkey. Unavailable 1982 data are shown as 0.

Table 4

OECD Countries' Imports from the USSR, 1960–1983
($ Millions)*

Year	U.S.	Canada	Australia	Japan	New Zealand	Austria	Belgium Luxembourg	Denmark
1960	25.0	3.3	1.5	87.0	0.0	40.4	28.6	28.9
1961	25.0	2.6	2.6	145.4	0.1	45.8	35.3	27.8
1962	18.0	1.9	1.5	147.2	0.0	43.8	46.0	23.5
1963	23.0	2.3	2.0	162.0	0.0	51.8	51.0	24.8
1964	23.0	2.9	2.2	226.7	NA	52.1	49.5	26.1
1965	46.0	10.1	2.6	240.2	0.0	52.7	46.3	33.4
1966	54.0	11.9	1.6	300.4	0.0	48.8	60.6	38.8
1967	44.0	23.4	2.4	454.0	0.0	48.9	59.5	35.4
1968	62.0	22.1	2.4	463.5	NA	58.4	66.3	29.2
1969	55.0	12.5	3.1	461.6	1.1	66.2	58.8	35.8
1970	77.5	9.7	4.0	481.0	1.1	79.5	78.0	35.6
1971	61.7	13.8	2.4	497.0	1.8	106.7	103.3	31.4
1972	103.2	16.9	3.0	603.5	1.6	111.4	105.3	36.9
1973	233.4	25.2	5.6	1,077.6	2.2	136.3	178.4	95.6
1974	375.4	25.7	12.2	1,416.8	4.4	237.8	271.2	125.4
1975	280.3	30.6	6.3	1,168.8	3.7	318.4	300.0	171.5
1976	243.9	61.6	6.1	1,169.3	4.3	420.2	300.3	232.5
1977	472.1	57.7	7.4	1,433.2	4.4	509.5	405.5	282.4
1978	563.3	36.0	8.0	1,453.4	7.6	611.4	472.1	314.3
1979	906.5	58.9	71.6	1,894.9	7.4	774.1	595.4	439.0
1980	485.7	55.6	20.1	1,872.7	11.5	1,026.7	1,096.7	422.5
1981	376.8	67.8	10.7	2,019.5	6.6	1,300.8	974.0	283.1
1982	247.1	38.2	14.1	1,668.4	9.7	990.0	1,459.6	333.2
1983	374.5	31.5	11.4	1,457.6	5.6	825.6	1,168.6	270.5

Year	Finland	France	Germany (FRG)	Italy	Iceland	Ireland	Neth'lands	Norway
1960	150.8	94.7	160.0	125.8	12.5	2.2	44.4	19.4
1961	151.0	97.3	198.0	150.1	11.1	3.9	39.2	19.5
1962	168.1	110.7	215.0	166.3	10.4	6.0	36.4	18.3
1963	195.2	141.1	209.0	175.9	11.9	2.9	47.3	21.4
1964	247.4	141.2	234.0	147.2	11.0	2.3	35.7	25.8
1965	231.2	146.0	275.0	181.3	12.1	3.1	52.9	28.2
1966	262.6	171.6	288.0	190.0	11.0	3.9	48.4	31.5
1967	263.0	187.1	275.0	273.7	10.4	6.8	51.5	35.4
1968	262.8	182.8	294.0	284.5	11.4	6.6	54.0	27.0
1969	257.3	205.2	335.0	246.8	9.9	4.3	68.1	22.6
1970	331.3	203.4	342.0	281.5	11.1	3.8	58.1	30.8
1971	385.4	259.6	367.0	297.1	14.9	7.2	65.3	54.3
1972	385.1	295.9	435.0	325.0	13.5	6.3	79.2	28.1
1973	529.4	433.8	762.0	441.5	22.3	7.8	129.4	47.2
1974	1,255.7	588.0	1,269.0	803.6	49.1	35.0	237.3	69.3
1975	1,266.7	769.8	1,313.0	876.5	49.9	39.3	300.9	85.0
1976	1,370.9	915.4	1,735.0	1,356.8	54.9	39.4	386.4	85.9
1977	1,492.9	1,158.1	1,965.3	1,456.6	54.6	44.7	431.9	117.1
1978	1,467.4	1,227.0	2,724.0	1,670.5	57.1	47.7	539.5	101.4
1979	2,228.0	1,798.2	4,060.9	2,070.2	90.4	86.6	848.0	146.6
1980	3,290.8	3,556.4	4,075.5	3,062.7	99.1	48.6	1,258.1	92.6
1981	3,334.5	3,360.0	4,071.6	3,072.8	81.3	51.2	1,767.3	178.2
1982	3,254.0	2,883.6	4,690.4	3,529.4	84.2	53.1	2,571.3	224.6
1983	3,278.4	2,801.1	4,631.3	3,581.6	82.9	50.3	2,627.2	131.0

Year	Spain	Sweden	Switz.	U.K.	Portugal	Turkey	Greece	TOTAL OECD
1960	3.7	62.9	5.8	219.5	2.3	5.9	28.3	1,152.9
1961	1.4	63.9	6.9	252.9	1.6	8.4	19.9	1,309.8
1962	2.1	63.6	5.9	248.7	0.0	6.4	20.3	1,360.1
1963	15.0	75.7	6.3	271.2	0.0	8.9	28.4	1,527.1
1964	3.6	69.3	8.2	271.5	0.0	8.0	27.4	1,615.1
1965	21.1	72.3	12.1	333.0	0.0	16.7	36.5	1,852.8
1966	7.0	85.6	20.7	351.8	0.0	26.1	38.1	2,052.5
1967	17.7	87.1	11.3	337.0	0.5	27.7	37.5	2,289.3
1968	18.9	106.7	13.6	379.4	2.6	30.5	27.1	2,405.9
1969	21.1	125.9	19.9	473.2	0.8	33.5	30.3	2,547.8
1970	9.7	155.7	26.8	528.1	1.0	38.7	36.2	2,824.6
1971	13.0	162.6	27.6	512.3	0.5	64.0	31.2	3,080.0
1972	29.6	159.4	30.4	569.1	0.1	120.0	42.4	3,500.9
1973	51.1	208.4	64.4	813.6	0.0	125.9	44.7	5,435.8
1974	85.3	402.6	121.2	926.4	2.7	95.0	59.9	8,468.8
1975	142.6	531.1	121.2	899.7	55.4	73.7	102.8	8,907.0
1976	163.0	476.8	259.1	826.8	101.5	88.7	175.0	10,473.7
1977	122.4	487.1	362.9	950.9	124.1	82.0	115.0	12,137.9
1978	110.8	542.3	515.1	1,354.1	97.2	68.3	264.3	14,252.8
1979	217.8	1,057.9	786.6	1,044.0	148.5	108.2	205.3	19,645.3
1980	443.5	748.6	971.2	977.0	157.4	180.7	150.2	24,103.9
1981	465.3	524.2	887.8	845.9	231.0	163.5	329.5	24,403.3
1982	487.5	796.7	834.1	1,101.1	86.9	106.7	223.7	25,687.6
1983	494.1	953.8	677.1	1,100.9	84.2	NA	248.9	24,888.2

SOURCE: IMF, *Directions of Trade*, from Data Resources Inc.
*NA = Not Available

Table 5
OECD Countries' Trade Balances with the USSR, 1960–1983
($ Millions)*

Year	U.S.	Canada	Australia	Japan	New Zealand	Austria	Belgium Luxembourg	Denmark
1960	15.0	4.8	28.3	-27.0	7.0	-1.3	-9.6	-12.6
1961	21.0	21.7	15.2	-80.0	5.3	-2.6	-8.0	-22.7
1962	2.0	1.5	28.0	2.2	2.5	10.1	-20.4	-2.8
1963	0.0	136.9	50.5	-3.7	NA	9.9	-37.8	4.2
1964	123.0	290.3	118.1	-44.8	NA	5.6	-34.8	8.9
1965	-1.0	172.9	88.2	-71.9	4.7	4.4	-23.7	-2.7
1966	-12.0	284.7	31.4	-85.4	14.5	10.5	-34.1	-16.8
1967	16.0	95.7	18.0	-296.3	5.4	10.6	-19.2	-17.5
1968	-4.0	60.7	36.5	-284.5	NA	10.0	-18.6	-10.3
1969	51.0	-3.4	42.9	-193.3	13.4	2.5	-7.7	-17.9
1970	40.5	87.5	68.1	-140.1	17.3	2.5	-23.8	-9.1
1971	104.3	111.6	65.7	-119.3	25.7	-37.0	-40.8	-6.0
1972	438.8	269.0	98.9	-91.2	23.4	-17.2	-13.3	-10.2
1973	968.7	266.7	241.5	-590.1	46.6	-44.1	34.1	-60.7
1974	241.5	4.4	228.0	-322.0	71.9	-49.5	98.4	-82.7
1975	1,568.4	369.7	346.1	457.1	34.1	-101.6	53.5	-106.7
1976	2,088.8	496.1	478.1	1,084.9	94.4	-182.4	-3.0	-162.3
1977	1,186.1	279.8	325.0	517.8	131.2	-230.2	-132.8	-204.5
1978	1,719.4	458.3	292.8	1,075.9	66.0	-240.6	-120.4	-246.7
1979	2,709.0	586.9	491.4	547.8	188.8	-258.7	-128.0	-336.0
1980	1,029.3	1,247.0	1,117.0	923.1	214.0	-549.3	-478.7	-324.9
1981	2,054.8	1,424.0	701.1	1,233.5	231.3	-816.5	-379.1	-188.4
1982	2,345.5	1,627.6	678.8	2,224.8	296.6	-438.7	-926.2	-244.4
1983	1,628.4	1,399.2	471.6	1,364.1	227.2	-227.1	-502.5	-193.9

Year	Finland	France	Germany (FRG)	Italy	Iceland	Ireland	Neth'lands	Norway
1960	−11.0	20.9	25.0	−47.2	−2.5	NA	−32.6	−6.5
1961	−23.2	12.7	6.0	−60.6	−5.9	NA	−19.5	−7.0
1962	28.2	27.4	−8.0	−64.0	0.5	−5.9	−4.4	−7.9
1963	−10.0	−76.9	−55.0	−62.3	−1.2	−2.5	−23.6	−8.7
1964	−91.7	−77.1	−40.0	−56.5	−0.9	−2.2	−20.8	−8.8
1965	−4.6	−74.0	−129.0	−83.2	−5.3	−1.0	−23.6	−9.7
1966	−49.1	−96.0	−153.0	−99.9	−1.1	−3.9	−23.2	−17.0
1967	4.9	−31.8	−77.0	−141.7	1.2	−6.7	15.0	−16.7
1968	−11.4	73.7	−21.0	−105.5	−2.5	−5.8	−7.2	−8.0
1969	20.1	59.9	71.0	37.7	−0.3	−3.7	−12.3	−7.3
1970	−48.7	69.7	80.0	26.4	−1.1	−3.7	−12.6	−6.0
1971	−131.3	−3.4	92.0	−2.3	−2.7	−6.7	−19.3	−35.2
1972	−20.1	45.6	285.0	−56.6	0.5	−5.7	−24.4	−8.4
1973	−78.1	143.5	422.0	−90.0	−12.2	−6.4	−51.1	−25.2
1974	−488.7	72.7	585.0	−183.0	−25.5	−15.7	−66.4	−29.4
1975	−135.8	373.1	1,511.0	146.8	−17.6	−15.6	−91.5	11.5
1976	−83.9	203.8	951.0	−372.4	−32.7	−36.1	−212.4	−9.2
1977	−8.1	338.3	824.5	−225.5	−18.6	−33.6	−228.4	−41.2
1978	58.3	235.3	416.5	−536.6	−31.8	−37.1	−328.6	−12.3
1979	−689.6	206.9	−441.9	−848.1	−59.9	−41.7	−544.3	−59.5
1980	−799.6	−1,091.1	297.9	−1,795.6	−48.7	0.9	−749.5	19.6
1981	133.0	−1,494.4	−677.4	−1,788.0	−22.9	−12.0	−1,144.0	−53.1
1982	215.1	−1,324.4	−820.1	−2,030.2	−27.6	−11.2	−2,146.0	−128.1
1983	9.0	−560.9	−213.5	−1,697.6	−22.1	10.9	−2,085.3	−11.9

Year	Spain	Sweden	Switz.	U.K.	Portugal	Turkey	Greece	TOTAL OECD
1960	3.4	-24.7	4.6	-70.6	0.2	-1.0	-9.5	-149.1
1961	1.6	-20.1	2.0	-58.5	-1.6	-3.9	-1.1	-233.2
1962	-1.7	15.1	1.1	-87.7	0.0	-0.9	-1.1	-86.2
1963	-14.3	-21.3	5.4	-91.5	0.0	-1.8	-6.0	-209.7
1964	-0.3	17.4	1.8	-160.2	0.0	1.0	-3.2	28.1
1965	-19.1	-22.0	3.3	-204.4	0.0	1.8	-9.6	-409.5
1966	-1.0	-46.3	1.5	-210.7	0.0	-7.6	-9.8	-524.3
1967	-8.3	-29.2	11.6	-158.2	-0.5	0.7	-7.0	-631.0
1968	-1.1	-27.9	13.6	-129.9	-2.6	-0.6	-2.7	-438.3
1969	-16.5	-14.7	16.0	-240.0	-0.8	-3.6	-0.3	-207.2
1970	-3.8	-24.3	23.2	-283.0	-1.0	-9.3	-1.7	-153.0
1971	-2.9	-75.3	19.6	-295.7	-0.5	-29.7	-10.9	-400.1
1972	0.7	-74.8	38.8	-341.7	0.2	-78.4	-6.6	452.2
1973	-34.1	-92.1	31.6	-574.7	0.6	-75.5	-0.1	421.0
1974	-27.2	-222.2	21.0	-669.7	-1.2	-17.5	21.0	-856.9
1975	-68.0	-238.8	60.2	-436.2	-37.3	0.0	-15.6	3,666.8
1976	-63.1	-197.2	-57.7	-392.8	-46.3	-7.7	-92.0	3,445.9
1977	-21.0	-230.6	-124.5	-345.4	-82.4	-1.5	-12.0	1,662.4
1978	31.2	-330.1	-248.8	-541.0	-57.6	36.9	-169.1	1,489.7
1979	48.9	-719.0	-519.2	-153.0	-95.0	18.5	-150.4	-246.1
1980	-184.7	-328.5	-669.4	81.1	-105.7	-11.7	-59.3	-2,266.9
1981	-100.2	-101.3	-678.6	-13.5	-178.7	30.4	-254.9	-2,094.9
1982	-268.6	-443.5	-619.2	-480.9	-35.0	17.3	-78.5	-2,616.9
1983	-159.6	-663.2	-453.7	-424.8	-33.6	NA	-107.3	-2,246.5

SOURCE: IMF, *Directions of Trade*, from Data Resources Inc.
*NA = Not Available

Table 6

USSR Imports from East European CMEA Countries, 1961–1983
(Millions of Current Rubles)

YEAR	TOTAL	MACHINERY SHARE*
1961	2739.7	1197.9
1962	3231.3	1550.1
1963	3732.1	1805.9
1964	4005.4	1997.5
1965	4205.3	2112.7
1966	4015.9	1926.0
1967	4583.2	2166.1
1968	5079.2	2468.2
1969	5410.3	2634.3
1970	5970.3	2899.3
1971	6532.6	3048.2
1972	7686.9	3720.3
1973	8092.8	4214.2
1974	8600.1	4450.2
1975	11311.6	5616.1
1976	12226.1	6321.3
1977	13851.7	7330.6
1978	16775.9	10064.8
1979	17491.0	10195.7
1980	19095.1	10584.8
1981	21137.9	NA
1982	24368.9	NA
1983	27611.4	NA

SOURCE: Centrally Planned Economies Service, Wharton Econometrics Forecasting Associates, Washington, D.C., and CIA, *Handbook of Economic Indicators,* 1984.
*Note: Classified according to the 1962 version of CMEA Trade Nomenclature.

Table 7

USSR Exports to East European CMEA Countries, 1961–1983
(Millions of Current Rubles)

YEAR	TOTAL	MACHINERY SHARE*
1961	3059.7	779.5
1962	3574.0	974.4
1963	3747.0	1083.4
1964	4049.3	1280.1
1965	4097.3	1244.5
1966	4222.8	1325.6
1967	4534.8	1438.1
1968	5072.5	1671.9
1969	5578.4	1829.0
1970	6082.6	1944.4
1971	6517.2	2090.4
1972	6726.6	2300.8
1973	7380.8	2681.9
1974	8705.3	3184.9
1975	11866.2	3580.9
1976	13106.6	4216.4
1977	15266.1	4982.2
1978	16945.5	5604.6
1979	18548.5	5908.0
1980	20919.2	6219.4
1981	24283.5	NA
1982	26345.1	NA
1983	29240.1	NA

SOURCE: Centrally Planned Economies Service, Wharton Econometrics Forecasting Associates, Washington, D.C., and CIA, *Handbook of Economic Indicators*, 1984.
*Note: Classified according to the 1962 version of CMEA Trade Nomenclature.

Mark Ellyne prepared the Statistical Appendix.

Contributors

Gary K. Bertsch is Sandy Beaver Professor of Political Science at the University of Georgia, author of *East-West Strategic Trade* and *COCOM and the Atlantic Alliance,* and coeditor of *The Strategic Dimensions of East-West Trade.*

Josef C. Brada is Professor of Economics at Arizona State University. Among his publications are *Technology Transfer between the United States and the Countries of the Soviet Bloc* and *Romania: Crisis or Turning Point?*

Robert W. Campbell is Professor of Economics and Director of the Russian and East European Institute at Indiana University. Among his recent publications is *Soviet Energy Technologies: Planning, Policy, Research and Development.*

Julian M. Cooper is Lecturer at the Centre for Russian and East European Studies at the University of Birmingham, England, and coauthor of *The Technological Level of Soviet Industry* and *Industrial Innovation in the Soviet Union.*

Seymour E. Goodman is Professor of Management Information Systems, Management, and Policy at the University of Arizona. He is the author of numerous articles on the Soviet computer industry and the impact of technology transfer.

Philip Hanson, Reader in Soviet Economics at the University of Birmingham, England, is author of *Trade and Technology in Soviet-Western Relations* and coeditor of *Soviet-East European Dilemmas.*

George Holliday is a specialist in international trade and finance with the Congressional Research Service, Library of Congress. His recent publications include *Technology Transfer to the USSR, 1928–1937 and 1966–1975: The Role of Western Technology in Soviet Economic Development.*

Anton F. Malish is Chief of the Eastern Europe and USSR Branch of the United States Department of Agriculture's Economic Research Service.

James R. Millar, Professor of Economics at the University of Illinois at Urbana-Champaign, is author of *The ABCs of Soviet Socialism.*

Bruce Parrott is Director of Soviet Studies at the School of Advanced International Studies, Johns Hopkins University. His publications include *Politics and Technology in the Soviet Union* and *Information Transfer in Soviet Science and Engineering.*

Angela E. Stent is Associate Professor of Government and Director of the Russian Area Studies Program at Georgetown University. Her publications include *From Embargo to Ostpolitik: The Political Economy of West German-Soviet Relations, 1955–1980* and *East-West Technology Transfer: A Challenge for the Cohesiveness of the Atlantic Alliance.*

Index

Adenauer, Konrad, 288, 304
Afghanistan issue, 46–47, 255–256, 306
Agricultural trade, Soviet, 203–240: chemicals, 221–225; commodity trends, 209–211; distribution system, 207–208; exports, 233, 236; Food Program, 229–230; grain embargo, 211–217; grain trade and policy, 209–211; imports, 118–120, 217–218, 232, 235; imports of technology vs. of commodities, 204, 231; livestock, 225–227; machinery, 220–221; marketing system, 207–208; performance indicators, 205–206; Reagan administration stand on, 259–262; research exchange, 228–229; technology gap with U.S., 206–207; technology imports, 118–120
Agrochemicals, 221–225
Aircraft industry, Soviet, 172–176
Aleksandrov, A. P., 48
Alekseev, N. N., 177
American politics. *See* U.S. politics
American trade with USSR. *See* Soviet-Western trade
Andropov, Iurii, 50–53, 56
Archey, William, 337
Artamonov, G. T., 188
Artillery production, 174–175
Assimilation of Western technology, 63–81: case studies, 75–78; by chemical industry, 73–75; by computer industry, 120–121; definition of, 63–65; measures of success in, 69–73; Soviet procedures, 65–69; as training process, 192; *see also* Technology transfer
ASU (automated management systems), 129
Automotive industry, Soviet, 82–116: assimilation in, 69; attitudes to imports, 101–103; expansion, 83–88; import sources, 103–105; modernization, 83–88, 96–98, 101; passenger car production, 84–86, 102–111; production trends, 88–101; research and development in, 98–99; technology imports and domestic investment, 91–93; technology imports and domestic technology, 93–101; selection of trade partners, 103–107; trends in, 1976–1985, 88–101; truck production, 86–88; and U.S. trade policy, 105–107
Aver'ianov, A. A., 152
Aviation industry, Soviet, 172–176
Avtoeksport, 109
AZLK (Lenin Komsomol Passenger Car Plant), 86, 94–95, 97–100, 110

Baldridge, Malcolm, 268, 315
Barr, Joel, 124

Bartini, Roberto, 171
Becker, Abraham S., 326
Berg, A. I., 176
Berg, Joseph, 124
Bergson, Abram, 73
Bertsch, Gary, 358
Bilak, Vasil, 51
Bingham, Jonathan, 253, 254, 260
Blumenthal, Michael, 252
Bogomolov, O., 54–55
Bohr, Niels, 177
Bonker, Don, 271, 273
Boschwitz, Rudy, 325
Brada, Josef C., 27, 353
Brady, Lawrence, 183, 266, 268
Brezhnev, Leonid, 35–41, 47–52, 145–146, 181, 206, 250
Brooks, Karen, 207
Broomfield, William, 265
Brown, Harold, 252
Brzezinski, Zbigniew, 250–256, 261
Buckley, James, 264
Bucy Report, 186–187, 252, 289
Burmistrov, V., 227
Bush, Keith, 8
Buzhinskiy, A. I., 100
Byrd, Robert, 259

CAD (computer-aided design), 127, 135
CAM (computer-aided manufacturing), 127, 135
Campbell, Robert, 361
Cargill Grain Co., 261
Cars. *See* Automotive industry; Passenger cars
Cartels, 332–333, 346
Carter, Jimmy, and his administration: agricultural embargo, 203, 214; foreign trade policy, 243, 250–257, 276, 278; trade sanctions, 326–327, 348
Cast study methods, 75–78
Caterpillar Tractor Co., 153, 344–345
CCC (Commodity Credit Corporation), 216
Chemical industry, Soviet, 73–75
Chemicals, agricultural, 221–225
Chernenko, Konstantin, 50, 56
Chronology of U.S.-USSR trade, 363–371
CMEA (Council for Mutual Economic Assistance) countries: British trade with, 299; French trade with, 297; German economic ties with, 291–295; Soviet exports to, 386; Soviet imports from, 385; and technology transfer, 121, 122, 285; U.S. views of trade with, 289–290
Coal, and Soviet energy policy, 146–147, 158–159
COCOM: export controls, 189, 266–269, 357;

389